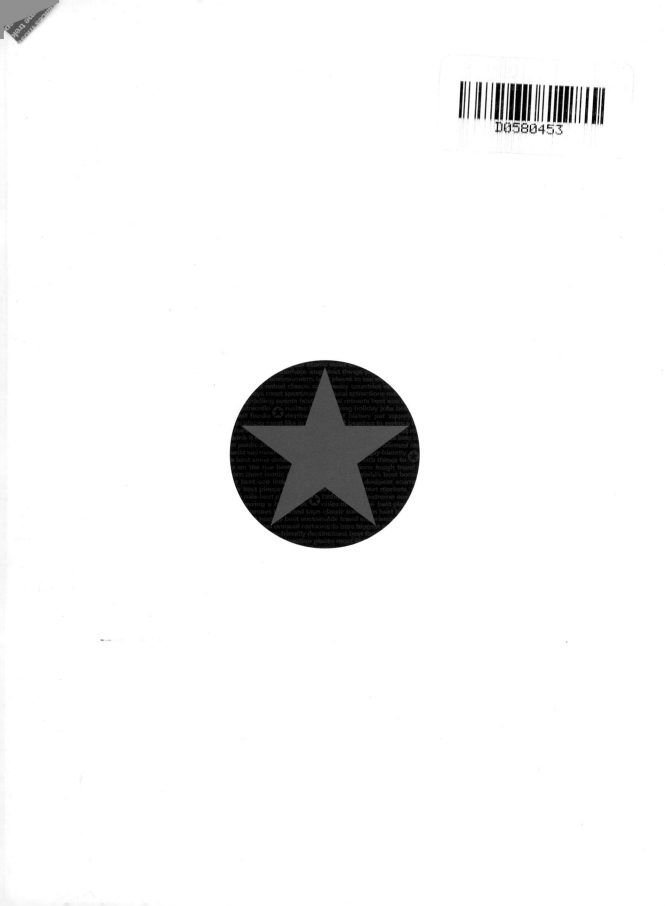

k cities on the rise best places to get naked classic city breaks countries on the rise best kid-friendly destinations tough travel destinations most awe
ic train trips best boat journeys most spectacular natural attractions most iconic man-made structures world's best booze and where to drink it most icon
vel experiences most gruelling events best spiritual retreats best eco lodges best travel gadgets dodgiest scams most unusual hotels best public art most
bars biggest adrenalin rushes best working holiday jobs best places to experience music greatest markets stupidest things you've heard a tourist say most
tions best foodie destinations most history per square mile best places for fashion most extreme environments best places to see wildlife best value des
laces most like in the film best beaches to swing a hammock cities on the rise best places to get naked classic city breaks countries on the rise best ki
most awesome treks greatest historical journeys best road trips classic train trips best boat journeys most spectacular natural attractions most iconic
here to drink it most iconic sporting events hippest hostels best sustainable travel experiences most gruelling events best spiritual retreats best ec
st unusual hotels best public art most extraordinary festivals most unusual restaurants & bars biggest adrenalin rushes best working holiday jobs best places
things you've heard a tourist say most remote places on earth best gay-friendly destinations best foodie destinations most history per square mile best pla
places to see wildlife best value destinations places to love with things to question places most like in the film best beaches to swing a hammock citie
y breaks countries on the rise best kid-friendly destinations tough travel destinations most awesome treks greatest historical journeys best road trips
acular natural attractions most iconic man-made structures world's best booze and where to drink it most iconic sporting events hippest hostels best s
s best spiritual retreats best eco lodges best travel gadgets dodgiest scams most unusual hotels best public art mo st extraordinary festivals most unusual resta
g holiday jobs best places to experience music greatest markets stupidest things you've heard a tourist say most remote places on earth best gay-frien
istory per square mile best places for fashion most extreme environments best places to see wildlife best value destinations places to love with things to qu
swing a hammock cities on the rise best places to get naked classic city breaks countries on the rise best kid-friendly destinations tough travel desti
journeys best road trips classic train trips best boat journeys most spectacular natural attractions most iconic man-made structures world's best
events hippest hostels best sustainable travel experiences most gruelling events best spiritual retreats best eco lodges best travel gadgets dodgiest sca
aordinary festivals most unusual restaurants bars biggest adrenalin rushes best working holiday jobs best places to experience music greatest markets stu
note places on earth best gay-friendly destinations best foodie destinations most history per square mile best places for fashion most extreme environments b
laces to love with things to question places most like in the film best beaches to swing a hammock cities on the rise best places to get naked classic city bre
ions tough travel destinations most awesome treks greatest historical journeys best road trips classic train trips best boat journeys most spectacular natural
rld's best booze and where to drink it most iconic sporting events hippest hostels best sustainable travel experiences most gruelling events best spiritual retrea
ams most unusual hotels best public art most extraordinary festivals most unusual restaurants bars biggest adrenalin rushes best working holiday jobs bes
upidest things you've heard a tourist say most remote places on earth best gay-friendly destinations best foodie destinations most history per square mile
nts best places to see wildlife best value destinations places to love with things to question places most like in the film best beaches to swing a
aked classic city breaks countries on the rise best kid-friendly destinations tough travel destinations most awesome treks greatest historical journeys
eys most spectacular natural attractions most iconic man-made structures world's best booze and where to drink it most iconic sporting events hippest h
ruelling events best spiritual retreats best eco lodges best travel gadgets dodgiest scams most unusual hotels best public art most extraordinary
biggest adrenalin rushes best working holiday jobs best places to experience music greatest markets stupidest things you've heard a tourist say
dly destinations best foodie destinations most history per square mile best places for fashion most extreme environments best places to see wildlife bes
uestion places most like in the film best beaches to swing a hammock cities on the rise best places to get naked classic city breaks countries on the rise
tions most awesome treks greatest historical journeys best road trips classic train trips best boat journeys most spectacular natural attractions most
nd where to drink it most iconic sporting events hippest hostels best sustainable travel experiences most gruelling events best spiritual retreats best ec
st unusual hotels best public art mo st extraordinary festivals most unusual restaurants bars biggest adrenalin rushes best working holiday jobs best places
things you've heard a tourist say most remote places on earth best gay-friendly destinations best foodie destinations most history per square mile
nts best places to see wildlife best value destinations places to love with things to question places most like in the film best beaches to swing a
aked classic city breaks countries on the rise best kid-friendly destinations tough travel destinations most awesome treks greatest historical journeys b
neys most spectacular natural attractions most iconic man-made structures world's best booze and where to drink it most iconic sporting events hip
most gruelling events best spiritual retreats best eco lodges best travel gadgets dodgiest scams most unusual hotels best public art most
bars biggest adrenalin rushes best working holiday jobs best places to experience music greatest markets stupidest things you've heard a tourist say
stinations best foodie destinations most history per square mile best places for fashion most extreme environments best places to see wildlife best valu
tion places most like in the film best beaches to swing a hammock cities on the rise best places to get naked classic city breaks countries on the rise best ki
most awesome treks greatest historical journeys best road trips classic train trips best boat journeys most spectacular natural attractions most iconic man-
drink it most iconic sporting events hippest hostels best sustainable travel experiences most gruelling events best spiritual retreats best eco lodges
hotels best public art most extraordinary festivals most unusual restaurants bars biggest adrenalin rushes best working holiday jobs best places to experi
've heard a tourist say most remote places on earth best gay-friendly destinations best foodie destinations most history per square mile best places for fashion
ildlife best value destinations places to love with things to question places most like in the film best beaches to swing a hammock cities on the rise best pla
the rise best kid-friendly destinations tough travel destinations most awesome treks greatest historical journeys best road trips classic train trips best bo
most iconic man-made structures world's best booze and where to drink it most iconic sporting events hippest hostels best sustainable travel
retreats best eco lodges best travel gadgets dodgiest scams most unusual hotels best public art most extraordinary festivals most
rushes best working holiday jobs best places to experience music greatest markets stupidest things you've heard a tourist say
friendly destinations best foodie destinations most history per square mile best places for fashion most extreme environ
estinations and places to love with things to question places most like in the film best beaches to swing a hamm
classic city breaks countries on the rise best kid-friendly destinations tough travel destinations most awesc
ourneys best road trips classic train trips best boat journeys most spectacular natural attractions most iconic
best booze and where to drink it most iconic sporting events hippest hostels best sustainable love to love
ruelling events best spiritual retreats best eco lodges best travel gadgets dodgiest scams most unusual hotels be
extraordinary festivals most unusual restaurants bars biggest adrenalin rushes best working holiday jobs best
music greatest markets stupidest things you've heard a tourist say most remote places on earth
-friendly destinations best foodie destinations most history per square mile best kid-friendly
hion most extreme environments places best places to see wildlife destinations tough
ns places to love with things to question places most like in the film best travel destinations
a hammock cities on the rise best places to get naked classic city most awesome treks
on the rise best kid-friendly destinations tough travel destinations greatest historical
eks greatest historical journeys best road trips classic train trips best journeys best
nost spectacular natural attractions most iconic man-made structures world's road
re to drink it most iconic sporting events hippest hostels best sustainable trips
e most gruelling events best spiritual retreats best eco classic
d gadgets dodgiest scams most unusual hotels best public train
ordinary festivals most unusual bars biggest adrenalin trips
working holiday jobs best places to music
stupidest things heard and a tourist most
places earth best most spec-
places to love history tacular
unusual hotels per natural
best beaches square attractions
holiday mile best most iconic
places for man-made
unusual most structures
extreme scams world's
best places to wildlife
best value places to love
treks with remote places and
things to question
places that most like
in the film best beaches to
swing a hammock cities on the rise best
places to get naked classic city breaks countries on
the rise best kid-friendly tough travel destinations most world's awesome
treks greatest historical journeys best road trips classic train trips boat journeys most
spectacular natural attractions most iconic man-made structures world's

LONELY PLANET
BLUE
LIST.

618 THINGS TO DO & PLACES TO GO.
06-07.

MELBOURNE ✪ OAKLAND ✪ LONDON

CONTENTS

INTRODUCTION

About the Bluelist, Roz Hopkins, Publisher   6
An Introduction, Tony Wheeler   8
Defining Moments in Travel, Don George   10

PART ONE – THINGS TO DO

Most History Per Square Mile   18
Best Places to See Wildlife   20
Best Foodie Destinations   22
Most Remote Places on Earth   24
Best Places to Get Naked   26
Best Value Destinations   28
Best Gay-Friendly Destinations   30
Tough Travel Destinations   32
Cities on the Rise   34
Best Kid-Friendly Destinations   36
Countries on the Rise   38
Places Most Like They Are in the Film   40
Most Extreme Environments   42
Places to Love With Things to Question   44
Classic City Breaks   46
Best Beaches to Swing a Hammock   48
Most Awesome Treks   50
Best Road Trips   52
Classic Train Trips   54
Greatest Historical Journeys   56

Most Iconic Man-Made Structures   58
World's Best Booze and Where to Drink It   60
Most Iconic Sporting Events   62
Most Spectacular Natural Attractions   64
Most Extraordinary Festivals   66
Best Sustainable Travel Experiences   68
Best Places to Experience Music   70
Best Boat Journeys   72
Most Gruelling Events   74
Best Spiritual Retreats   76
Best Travel Gadgets   78
Hippest Hostels   80
Greatest Markets   82
Best Public Art   84
Most Unusual Places to Stay   86
Best Eco Lodges   88
Best Working Holiday Jobs   90
Most Unusual Restaurants & Bars   92
Most Stupid Things You've Heard a Tourist Say   93
Biggest Adrenalin Rushes   94
Dodgiest Scams   96

PART TWO – PLACES TO GO

AMERICAS

Argentina   104
Belize   107
Brazil   110
Chile   113
Colombia   116
Ecuador & Galapagos   119
El Salvador   122
French Guiana   125
Mexico   128
Nicaragua   131
Peru   134
Uruguay   137
United States of America   140
Americas Country Snapshots   143

ASIA

Cambodia	152
China	155
Hong Kong	158
India	161
Japan	164
Laos	167
Nepal	169
South Korea	170
Sri Lanka	173
Tibet	179
Vietnam	182
Asia Country Snapshots	185

AUSTRALASIA & PACIFIC

Australia	192
East Timor	194
Guam & Northern Mariana Islands	198
Indonesia	201
New Zealand	204
Samoa	207
Australasia & Pacific Country Snapshots	210

EUROPE

Croatia	216
England	219
France	222
Greece	225
Greenland	228
Iceland	231
Italy	234
Serbia & Montenegro	237
Slovenia	240
Spain	243
Switzerland	246
Turkey	249
Ukraine	251
Europe Country Snapshots	255

MIDDLE EAST & NORTH AFRICA

Egypt	264
Iran	267
Israel	270
Jordon	273
Morocco	276
Oman	279
Syria	282
Tunisia	285
Yemen	288
Middle East & North Africa Country Snapshots	291

SUB-SAHARAN AFRICA

Botswana	296
Ethiopia	299
Kenya	302
Madagascar	305
Mali	308
Mozambique	311
South Africa	314
Tanzania and Zanzibar	317
Sub-Saharan Africa Country Snapshots	320

WORLD MAP	324
ACKNOWLEDGEMENTS	326
INDEX	326

BLUELIST[1] (blu₁list) *v.*
to recommend a travel experience.

That's right, this isn't just about a new book, but a new word: Bluelist.

We created this because there is no word to describe what we set out to do with this new book, which is to 'create an evolving selection of classic and current travel experiences and destinations selected by Lonely Planet staff, authors and travellers'.

Sounds impressive? We reckon it's all that and much more. Let's take a look.

EVOLVING...

We hope this is the start of something big, new and different. This is Volume One, and our first shot at putting together a list of what's hot and happening in the travel world at the moment. It's a stake in the ground, and its intended as the beginning and not the end of the debate. We want to update this list every year and publish an annual book, and we also plan to have an ongoing spot on our website where you can get involved in recommending and discussing new categories, experiences, destinations, events and anything else travel-related. Go here to check this out: www.lonelyplanet/bluelist.

CLASSIC AND CURRENT TRAVEL EXPERIENCES AND DESTINATIONS...

It's no easy task coming up with the debut list of things to do and places to go when you have the whole world to select from...

We all know that it's a special and unique combination of experiences that make our travels so memorable. It's not always about the coolest and the hippest, the most extreme or the weirdest; it's the things that we can't stop talking about when we get home, and we urge others to try too. We tried to select a combination of those elements – the classic, the iconic, the unusual, the unexpected, the gritty and the gorgeous; elements that add zing to great travel experiences.

In the first part of the book you'll find classic travel experiences, such as greatest train journeys and most spectacular natural attractions, which can never fail to capture any traveller's imagination, as well as things and places that are really taking off at the moment, like emerging city break destinations or hippest hostels. It was pretty hard to select just 40 categories and 400 entries. But we didn't just pull them from a

most spec-
tacular
natural
attractions
most iconic
man-made
structures
world's

places earth best
places to love
unusual hotels
best beaches
holiday

most
history
per
square
mile best
places for
unusual most
extreme scams
best places to wildlife
best value places to love
treks with remote places and
things to question
places that most like
in the film best beaches to
swing a hammock cities on the rise best
places to get naked classic city breaks countries on
the rise best kid-friendly tough travel destinations most world's
treks greatest historical journeys best road trips classic train trips boat journeys most

awesome

place where the sun doesn't shine, hell no. These category lists come from understanding what we like to do, see, visit, eat, drink, play, listen to, hang from, jump off, revel in, sleep in, walk over and experience when we travel. We are sure you'll let us know if you have a better idea.

In our 'world-view' (part two of the book), we have featured countries that are interesting to visit now, and provided an up-to-date view of news, views, tips and talking points for these countries. The book covers every single country in the world. It's broken down by continent, and within each continent we have selected the countries we most recommend visiting now. This was tough. It's not easy to drill 218 countries down to 60. How do you choose 13 out of a possible 49 European countries to visit? We want to go to all of them! But we've made this initial selection, based on information such as industry data, and (more importantly) our authors' opinions and direct feedback we get from travellers. Share your view on our world-view at www.lonelyplanet/bluelist.

SELECTED BY LONELY PLANET STAFF, AUTHORS AND TRAVELLERS...

This launch volume of the Lonely Planet Bluelist is written by Lonely Planet staff and authors, with input from travellers, who travel frequently and are passionate and opinionated about the places they write about. We know this because they tell us.

At Lonely Planet, we know travel, but we never want to stop learning about new experiences, destinations and journeys, so we look forward to the opportunity Bluelist provides to stimulate discussion about travel and the world, and help us all experience as much as we can of its myriad people and places.

Travel far, travel thoughtfully and keep us posted on what makes your Bluelist.

- Roz Hopkins
Publisher, Lonely Planet

SO WHAT'S NEXT?

That's my usual question when I start mapping out my personal bluelist, next year's travel wish list.

It's likely to be a mix of the familiar (there are places that are always great to go back to), the new and the overdue.

Last year one trip to Europe managed to fit all three categories. It was great to visit London again, great to explore an unfamiliar part (Sicily) of a familiar destination (Italy) and great to get back to a place which has recently re-established itself. Croatia was an old favourite in the Yugoslavia days, then a 'don't go' destination and now has returned with flavour of the month status. Surprisingly neighbouring Bosnia & Hercegovina also shows signs of acquiring that label. My European travels also took me to the Baltic states: Estonia, Latvia and Lithuania, three small countries which have become extraordinarily popular over the past decade. Next year I expect Europe to provide a similar blend of the familiar (with a trip back to Ireland) and the new (a circuit of the Scandinavian countries).

Sometimes, however, simply getting there is half the fun and some of the past year's trips have been as important for the travel as for the destination. Like a trip from Singapore to Shanghai with the basic rule that it would stick strictly to surface transport; no planes would be involved. It was hardly surprising that my travels on boats, trains, buses and, around the cities at least, a surprising number of motorcycles, were always interesting. Later in the year, with a group of friends and a couple of 4WDs, we tackled two of Australia's classic outback routes, the Tanami Track running northwest from Alice Springs and the Gibb River Road traversing the rugged Kimberley region. Asia or Australia, both trips underlined the magic that comes from simply being on the road. And next year I might finally get around to that greatest of rail trips, the Trans-Siberian Railway.

Of course travel needs challenges and since there were no tough treks or rugged regions for me in the past 12 months, something to push the boundaries is clearly overdue. Perhaps that could be Afghanistan, a place I visited in the hippy trail era of the 1970s and where, it would appear, intrepid visitors are beginning to trickle back. Or perhaps it could be a go at the Plymouth–Dakar Rally. A Lonely Planet author tackled this much less serious, far cheaper (and heaps more fun) piss-take on the Paris–Dakar Rally and my first thought when I heard about it was, 'Me too!' The rules for the Plymouth–Dakar are straightforward, the car should cost less than £100 and at the end you must give the vehicle away to charity. Sounds like my sort of rally. On the other hand, the 120-day Cairo to Cape Town bicycle race, the Tour d'Afrique, is probably way too challenging. I met the band of intrepid cyclists competing in the 2005 event while I was in Ethiopia.

TONY'S BLUELIST

PLACES TO GO...

✪ Afghanistan ✪ Bosnia and Hercegovina ✪ Croatia ✪ Estonia ✪ Iceland ✪ Ireland ✪ Latvia ✪ Lithuania ✪ London, England ✪ Scandinavia ✪ Sicily, Italy ✪ Tallin, Estonia ✪ Vietnam ✪ Warsaw, Poland

THINGS TO DO...

✪ Travel from Singapore to Shanghai using only surface transport ✪ Drive along the rugged Tanami track and the Gibb River Road, Australia ✪ Travel on the Trans-Siberian Railway ✪ Compete in the Plymouth–Dakar Rally ✪ Marvel at the supermen and -women who compete in the Everest Marathon ✪ Observe the Tour d'Afrique, the Cairo to Cape Town bicycle race ✪ Embrace the advances in technology to once remote areas such as ATMs in remote towns in Vietnam; text messaging in Cambodia and the new Internet cafés in China ✪ Use a GPS to navigate, purely for fun ✪ Follow polar explorer Alfred Shackleton's epic trek across South Georgia Island ✪ Try to find a way to make travel truly sustainable

places earth best
places to love
unusual hotels
best beaches
holiday

most
history
per
square
mile best
places for
unusual most
extreme scams
best places to wildlife
best value places to love
treks with remote places and
things to question
places that most like
in the film best beaches to
swing a hammock cities on the rise best
places to get naked classic city breaks countries on
the rise best kid-friendly tough travel destinations most world's
treks greatest historical journeys best road trips classic train trips boat journeys most

most
spec-
tacular
natural
attractions
most iconic
man-made
structures
world's

awesome

My Singapore to Shanghai trip also explored the changes that technology and progress are bringing to travel in general and to the East Asian region in particular. Repeatedly I was reminded how much easier travel had become and so often the change was because of technology. Money? The trusty ATM could always be counted on to spit out a walletful of local currency. Arriving in Bangkok by train from Malaysia, a bank of ATM machines loomed up in front of me before I'd even had time to think, 'Must get some baht'. Two weeks later I walked across the border from Vietnam to China. Chinese ATMs first appeared in Beijing, Shanghai and other major metropolises. Gradually they'd spread down the line, but had they reached a remote border town like Hekou? Of course they had, there was an ATM machine only a few steps from the border post.

A week earlier, riding a bus through the back blocks of Cambodia, the young monk sitting next to me suddenly started to scrabble beneath his orange robe. A text message had just popped up on his mobile phone. The changes in communication have been as far reaching as those in banking. The bad old days of queuing for hours outside a phone office to put through a static-laden call you could barely decipher are long gone. From Singapore to Shanghai and, a few months later, anywhere between Tallinn (in Estonia) and Warsaw (Poland), I never seemed to be out of mobile range . Similarly the old story of collecting poste restante letters has disappeared in favour of collecting emails from internet cafés, which fortunately can provide just as much interest, style and variety as post offices ever did. My 2005 favourites were the huge (but hidden) Chinese internet cafés, generally down some questionable back alley or up grubby flights of dark stairways. For me, Internet cafés, ATMs and mobile phones are all 'can't live without them' advances, but my GPS (where am I? where am I going? How long will it take to get there?) is pure fun.

Then there are the new travel experiences, like hotels at either extreme of the price spectrum. The old days when cheap equalled grotty (as in flea-bitten backstreet dive) or rule bound (as in 'lights out by 10 pm' youth hostels) are changing rapidly with bright new hotels offering low-cost but high-tech rooms and hostels which have clearly thrown the rule book out the nearest window. At the other end of the scale expensive doesn't have to mean big and stuffy; increasingly budget-bursting hotels can be small and (take your pick) eccentric, stylish, hip, luxurious, even mind-blowing.

I'm intrigued by the new experiences on offer as well. Once upon a time getting to the top of Mt Everest was strictly for national expeditions, but now it's open to anyone with enough cash and a wide enough streak of insanity. Soon a short jaunt into outer space will be in the same category. Not many of us are up to an Everest ascent, even if we had the money to spare, but travel is increasingly turning up opportunities which may not be as adventurous, but would still have seemed incredible not long ago. A couple of years ago I joined an intrepid group following polar explorer Alfred Shackleton's epic trek across the frozen island of South Georgia. Now who would have thought that sort of adventure was there for the asking 10 years ago?

If we're going to keep travelling, however, we're going to have to look harder at how we do it. How to make travel truly sustainable is definitely a question for my travel bluelist. Travel today is more important than it has ever been, both as an economic force and as a means of contact between the disparate parts of an often polarised world. If it's going to continue to be a force for good, we're going to have to work very hard to ensure it has a long-term future.

-Tony Wheeler
Cofounder of Lonely Planet

LOOKING BACK...
World Events and the Trends They've Stirred.

Disaster demarcated the travel timeline in the twenty months from the beginning of 2004 to September 2005, when these words are being written. On 11 March 2004, 200 people were killed and 1400 injured in Madrid when 10 bombs exploded aboard four commuter trains at the height of the city's morning rush hour. And on 7 July 2005, 60 people were killed and 700 injured in London when three bombs exploded on Underground trains and one on a bus during that city's morning rush hour. The two other most significant travel events during this period were disasters of another kind: the natural disasters of the tsunami that devastated Indian Ocean regions in Indonesia, Sri Lanka, the Maldives, Thailand, India and other neighbouring countries on 26 December 2004, and hurricane Katrina's deadly flooding in the southeast United States, which devastated New Orleans and other areas of Louisiana, Mississippi and Alabama in late August and early September of 2005. The death toll from the tsunamis reached 300,000, with 1.5 million more people displaced, and the economic toll was virtually incalculable as entire coastal communities were destroyed. Katrina's shattering effects were still being calculated as this book went to press; at the time of this writing, Katrina-related deaths were estimated to run as high as 10,000 and economic consequences to total as much as US$100 billion as hundreds of thousands of people were displaced, possessions were destroyed and businesses were swept away.

These disasters were shocking and horrifying, and their reverberations all continue to this day. But in the aftermath of their horror, some encouraging truths about the new travel world and the evolving attitudes of travellers can be discerned. Most striking of all was the global response to the tsunamis. Immediately after news of the destruction spread, an extraordinary amount of aid began to pour in from all around the world to a broad spectrum of recipients, from large international organizations such as Médecins Sans Frontières, the Red Cross and the Red Crescent to smaller-scale NGOs and other aid groups, to individual fishermen, store owners and guesthouse operators. (The southeast of the United States is experiencing a similar generous outpouring of aid in Katrina's wake.)

places earth best
places to love
unusual hotels
best beaches
holiday

most
history
per
square
mile best
places for
unusual most
extreme scams
best places to wildlife
best value places to love
treks with remote places and
things to question
places that most like
in the film best beaches to
swing a hammock cities on the rise best
places to get naked classic city breaks countries on
the rise best kid-friendly tough travel destinations most world's
treks greatest historical journeys best road trips classic train trips boat journeys most

most
spec-
tacular
natural
attractions
most iconic
man-made
structures
world's

awesome

»

In addition to this monetary help, many travellers also chose to give more directly – by travelling to affected areas and volunteering in a variety of ways, providing medical assistance, rebuilding homes and shops, distributing food and clothing, facilitating coordination and communication. The tsunami has elicited the greatest collective outpouring of human compassion in history, and while some people did indeed cancel their plans to visit affected areas, an inspiring number of other travellers either kept their plans or created new plans to journey to those areas, with the explicit goal of helping local communities recover.

The aftermath of the tsunami and hurricane Katrina have also demonstrated another way in which the travel world has changed: the rapidly expanding use of the Internet. At Lonely Planet, as elsewhere, our web team immediately went to work after both disasters, posting travel information as we received it and hosting messages on our global bulletin board, the Thorn Tree. As an instantaneous, person-to-person communication tool, the Thorn Tree became a vital link in the effort to locate missing persons and to connect people around the globe. In the minutes, hours and days following the disasters, lonelyplanet.com and other websites played – and still continue to play – roles of critical connection: disseminating updated travel information, facilitating communication, and detailing options for people who want to donate money or volunteer to help in person.

The aftermath of the Madrid and London terrorist disasters illuminated a second travel truth that the tsunami had also suggested: travellers have become more resilient. In the cases of both Madrid and London, perhaps buoyed by the calm commitment of locals to maintain their normal lives, relatively few travellers cancelled trips to those cities or nearby areas. This response indicated that in the years since the September 11, 2001 attacks in the US and the nightclub bombings in Bali on 12 October 2002, travellers seem to have made peace with the truth that life is uncertain and instable wherever they may be, and seem to have recommitted themselves to travelling no matter what may happen. In part this may have been in recognition of terrorism's geographic »

« unpredictability, the sense that no place is recognizably safer than another these days, but it was also clearly in part a gritty defiance of the terrorists' goals of disrupting global commerce and communication, and of propagating intercultural distrust and fear. This new resolve seems to affirm the importance of travel in peoples' lives and symbolize the understanding that travel – and the knowledge and sense of connection it bestows – is fundamentally important to the future of the planet.

A corollary truth that seems to be growing in acceptance and impact is the notion that travellers invariably affect the places they visit and that it is correspondingly imperative that we all travel mindfully, responsibly, sustainably. While still hazily defined and sometimes misused, 'ecotourism' – a broad conglomeration of tours, accommodations, activities and attractions based on ecologically responsible principles – has expanded its reach and appeal, and explicitly ecofriendly tour operators and hotels are on the rise. 'Volunteer vacations' such as assisting archaeological digs or jungle research

expeditions have been growing in popularity over the past decade, but in the past couple of years this category has stretched to include holiday programmes that actively and directly impact local communities, such as building houses, planting crops or teaching in schools. Another outgrowth of this movement has been efforts undertaken by individuals to directly aid overseas communities through personal fundraising activities and donation-oriented trips. Two examples of these are Marc Gold's 100 Friends (www.100friends.com) and Brad Newsham's Backpack Nation (www.backpacknation.org). Gold personally raises and distributes money on his own travels, while Newsham sponsors an online competition through which four individuals are selected to fulfil the donation journey of their dreams. This spirit of enlightened adventure informed travellers' choice of destinations in the past twenty months as well. Travellers continued to venture further and further off the beaten track, with South America emerging as the hottest 'new' destination on the planet, especially Argentina, Brazil, Chile and Peru. Asian destinations were hot, too, in particular

China, Cambodia and Laos. Other newly popular destinations included El Salvador, Guatemala and Panama, as well as the Baltic countries and Eastern Europe in general.

A third trend related to both this individual empowerment and the expanding use of the Internet is a precipitous surge in travel-related email dispatches, online journals and web logs, or blogs. The Internet has made it possible for one person to communicate instantaneously – and in a variety of media, if desired – with innumerable other people. Over the past 18 months, ever increasing numbers of travellers took advantage of this technology, updating family and friends through mass-emails or online journals that featured on-the-road accounts supplemented with photos and in some cases, audio and video snippets as well. Blogs took this innovation one step further. Bloggers created websites open to anyone with Internet access, where they posted ongoing collages of their thoughts and experiences at home and on the road, including interviews and book reviews, recipes and photo galleries. As technology has evolved, the world has truly grown smaller and smaller – or at least, people in far-flung places have been able to communicate directly and personally with one another in ways they never could before. Of course, the opposite has been true as well: as the world has grown smaller, our sense of just how mind-bogglingly big and diverse this planet is has grown.

Connection, compassion, courage – looking back, these are the qualities that have distinctively emerged in the travel world over the past 18 months. Given this, we might seem to be poised on an uncharted territory of spectacular possibility – a virtual new age of visionary interaction and understanding. But of course, the disasters that have partly inspired these qualities also remind us that the path of the world is more fraught with potential disaster now than ever before. Still, if we tread this path with the courage, compassion and connection we have evidenced so far, we walk with hope. And with the awareness that, more than ever, we are all responsible for this lovely, lonely planet we share.

- Don George
Global travel editor, Lonely Planet

TRAVEL PLANNER 06-07.

JANUARY

PLACES TO GO
- Colombia
- Laos
- Nicaragua
- Tanzania + Zanzibar
- Ethiopia
- Mexico

THINGS TO DO
- Leddet, Lalibela, Ethiopia
- Timkat, Gonder, Ethiopia
- Haerbin Ice & Snow Festival, China
- LoveParade, Santiago, Chile
- Human chess, Hanoi, Vietnam
- Festival au Désert Timbuktu, Timbuktu, Mali
- Camel Wrestling Championship,Selçuk, Turkey
- Wakakusa Yamayaki, Nara, Japan
- Super Bowl, various venues, USA
- End of polar night celebrations, Greenland

FEBRUARY

PLACES TO GO
- Brazil
- French Guiana
- New Zealand

THINGS TO DO
- Carnaval, Brazil & French Guiana
- Mardi Gras, New Orleans, USA
- New Zealand International Arts Festival, Wellington, New Zealand
- New Zealand Sevens, Wellington, New Zealand
- Hong Kong Arts Festival, Hong Kong
- XXth Winter Olympic Games, 2006, Turin, Italy
- Suchitoto Arts & Culture Festival, Suchitoto, El Salvador
- Venice Carnival, Italy
- Kilimanjaro Marathon, Tanzania
- Tango Festival, Buenos Aires, Argentina

MARCH

PLACES TO GO
- Chile
- Guam & Northern Mariana Islands
- Madagascar
- Syria
- Turkey
- Uruguay

THINGS TO DO
- Kanamara Matsuri, Kawasaki, Japan
- Semana Santa, Antigua, Guatemala
- Marathon des Sables, Morocco
- Gay & Lesbian Mardi Gras, Sydney, Australia
- Baron Bliss Day, Belize
- Pasifika Festival, Auckland, New Zealand
- St Patrick's Day, Ireland & USA
- Holi, India & Nepal
- Commonwealth Games 2006, Melbourne, Australia
- Nuuk Snow Festival, Greenland

JULY

PLACES TO GO
- England
- Greenland
- Nepal
- Samoan Islands
- Serbia and Montenegro
- Tunisia

THINGS TO DO
- Il Palio, Siena, Italy
- Arctic Team Challenge, Greenland
- Tour de France, France
- Running with the Bulls, Pamplona, Spain
- Victory Day, Yemen
- The Proms, London, England
- Inuit gathering & pop festival, Aasivik, Greenland
- Exit Festival, Novi Sad, Serbia & Montenegro
- International Festival of Carthage, Tunisia
- Independence Day, USA

AUGUST

PLACES TO GO
- Botswana
- Indonesia
- Morocco
- Sri Lanka
- Iceland

THINGS TO DO
- La Tomatina, Buñol, Spain
- Il Palio, Siena, Italy
- World Bog Snorkelling Championship, Wales
- Cultural Night, Reykjavík, Iceland
- Trung Nguyen, Vietnam
- Tel Aviv Love Parade, Israel
- Carling Weekend, Reading & Leeds, England
- Crab Soup Festival, Corn Islands, Nicaragua
- Beer Festival, Belgrade, Serbia & Montenegro
- National Hobo Convention, Britt, USA

SEPTEMBER

PLACES TO GO
- East Timor
- South Africa
- Spain

THINGS TO DO
- Burning Man, Black Rock City, USA
- Adventure Race, Greenland
- Raid World Championship
- Liberation Day, East Timor
- Arts Alive, Johannesburg, South Africa
- Teuila Festival, Apia, Samoan Islands
- Meskel, Addis Ababa, Ethiopia
- Kravji Bal, Bohinj, Slovenia
- Museums' long night, Zürich, Switzerland
- Reykjavík Jazz Festival, Iceland

places earth best
places to love
unusual hotels
best beaches
holiday

most
history
per
square
mile best
places for
unusual most
extreme
best places to wildlife

most
spec-
tacular
natural
attractions
most iconic
man-made
structures
world's

APRIL

PLACES TO GO
- France
- Jordan
- Slovenia
- South Korea
- Tibet
- USA

THINGS TO DO
- Cherry Blossom Festival, Jinhae, South Korea
- Buddha's Birthday, South Korea
- Dead Sea Ultra Marathon, Jordan
- Holy Week, Jerusalem, Israel
- Buddha Jayanti, Lumbini, Nepal
- Maitisong Festival, Gaborone, Botswana
- Chaul Chnam Chen, Cambodia
- Golden Week, Japan
- Water Splashing Festival, China
- Fête des Masques, Dogon Country, Mali

MAY

PLACES TO GO
- Argentina
- Israel
- Italy
- Japan
- Ukraine

THINGS TO DO
- Kyiv Days, Kyiv, Ukraine
- National Virtuoso, Lviv, Ukraine
- Cantine Aperte, Italy
- Fiesta de San Isidro, Madrid, Spain
- Malojloj Fiesta, Guam, Guam
- Eurovision Song Contest 2006, Athens, Greece
- Independence Day, East Timor
- Bun Bang Fai, Laos
- Reykjavík Arts Festival, Iceland
- Maulid Festival, Lamu, Kenya

JUNE

PLACES TO GO
- Croatia
- Ecuador & Galapagos
- Greece
- Mozambique
- Peru

THINGS TO DO
- Posidonia Cup offshore yacht race, Piraeus, Greece
- Independence Day, Mozambique
- World Cup Football 2006, Germany
- Shanghai International Film Festival, China
- Gnawa & World Music Festival, Essaouira, Morocco
- Kirkpinar Oil Wrestling, Turkey
- Inti Raymi, Peru
- Queen Elizabeth's 80th birthday celebrations, 2006, England
- Famidihana, Madagascar
- Summer Puppet Festival, Ljubljana, Slovenia

OCTOBER

PLACES TO GO
- China
- Hong Kong
- Kenya
- Oman

THINGS TO DO
- World Iron Man Triathlon, USA
- Eid al-Fitr, Oman
- Camel-racing season, Oman
- Festival Internacional Cervantino, Guanajuato, Mexico
- Chuseok, South Korea
- Círio De Nazaré, Belém, Brazil
- Columbus Day, Belize
- El Señor de los Milagros, Peru
- Diwali, India
- Dragon boat races, Mekong near Vientiane, Laos

NOVEMBER

PLACES TO GO
- Belize
- El Salvador
- Iran
- Mali
- Yemen
- India

THINGS TO DO
- Día de Muertos, Mexico
- Diwali, India
- Everest Marathon, Nepal
- Camel Fair, Pushkar, India
- Garifuna Settlement Day, Belize
- Independence Day, Yemen
- Festival del Barrio Brazil, Santiago, Chile
- Melbourne Cup, Australia
- Bom Om Tuk, Cambodia
- Mombassa Carnival, Kenya

DECEMBER

PLACES TO GO
- Australia
- Cambodia
- Egypt
- Switzerland
- Vietnam

THINGS TO DO
- Noche de los Rábanos, Oaxaca, Mexico
- Reconciliation Day, South Africa
- Hari Natal, Indonesia
- Eid al-Adha, Syria & Yemen
- Winterfest; Hong Kong
- Quema del Diablo, Guatemala
- Día de Nuestra Señora de Guadeloupe, Mexico
- Kulubi Gabriel, Dire Dawa, Ethiopia
- Christmas
- New Year's Eve

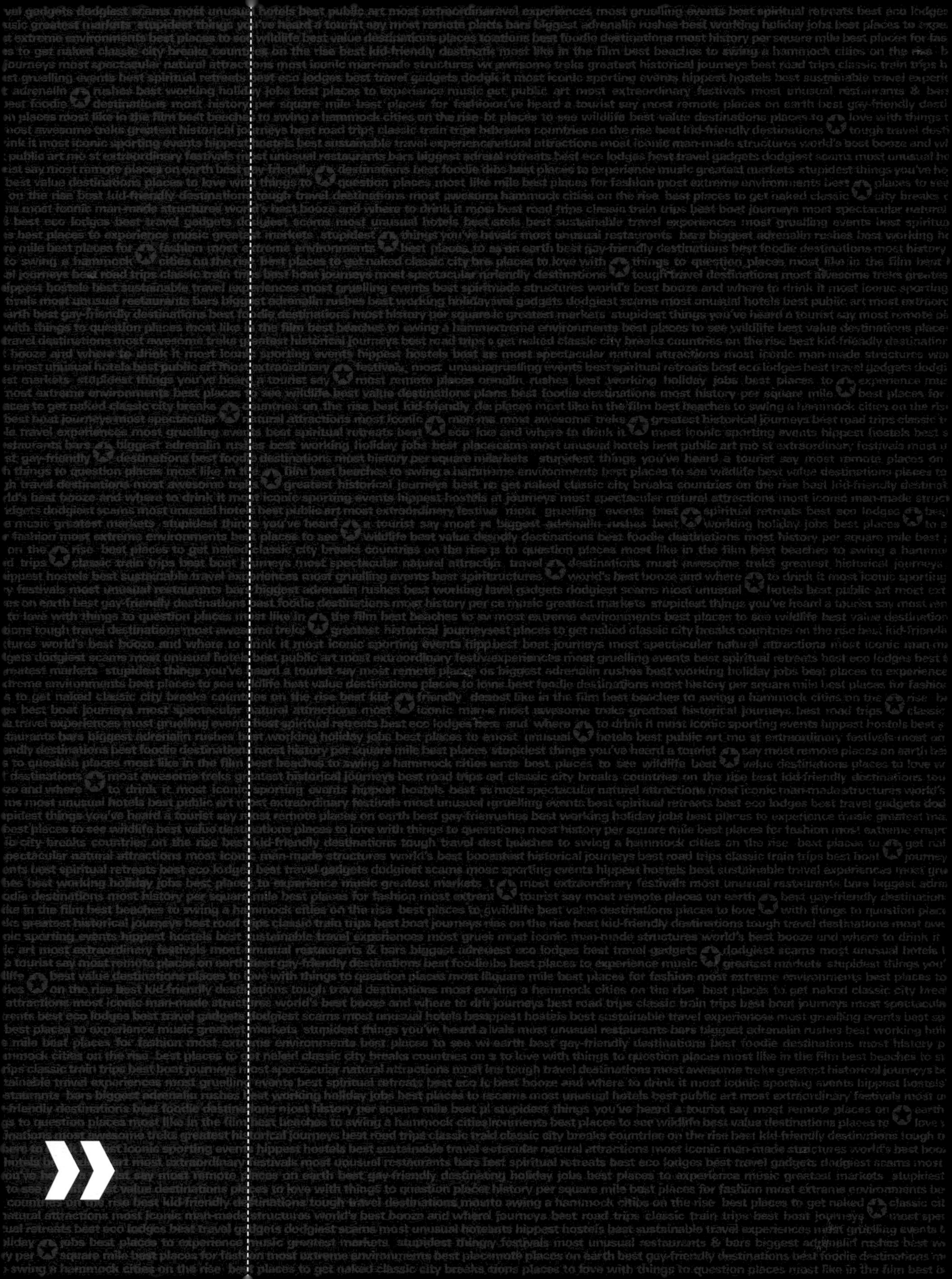

PART. #01.
» THINGS TO DO.

MOST HISTORY PER SQUARE
#01.MILE.

GLENN BEANLAND / LONELY PLANET IMAGES

TOWER BRIDGE, A LANDMARK ON THE RIVER THAMES SINCE 1894.

✪ BELGIUM

Belgium was born in 1830 – the result of an opera in Brussels that sparked a revolution. The opera, which tells of a 1647 Naples uprising against the Spanish, sparked an actual rebellion that resulted in Belgium's independence from Dutch rulers. Its long history of power struggles began with the first invasion by the Romans in 57 BC and included Napoleon who was defeated here at the Battle of Waterloo in 1815. Germany invaded in the 20th century, despite Belgium's declared neutrality.

✪ EGYPT

To cut a long history short, the Nile's fertile banks – the source of economic, social, political and religious life – gave birth to the world's first nation state and a powerful civilisation that invented writing and erected the first stone monuments. What began in 250,000 BC gave rise to the unification of independent river states around 5000 years ago, which was responsible for the rise of the first dynasty of pharaohs who built the famous pyramids.

✪ INDIA

India's history is one of the grand epics of the world. From the first signs of civilisation of nomadic tribes in the Indus Valley around 3500 BC, India has nurtured many great civilisations over thousands of years. It has weathered countless invasions and cataclysms, and hosted many religions, including Islam, Buddhism and Hinduism. Famously, Mahatma Gandhi launched an antiviolence campaign against British occupiers in 1942, eventually ending centuries of British rule.

✪ LONDON, ENGLAND

The Romans first developed the square mile now known as the City of London in AD 43. They built a bridge and an impressive city wall, and made Londinium an important port and the hub of their road system. The Romans left but the trade went on, such that London grew to be the kingdom's richest and largest city. The grand old city has seen a lot of stages from medieval through Tudor and Elizabethan; it's been plagued by plague and fire and come through it with the Restoration.

✪ PARIS, FRANCE

Founded at the end of the 3rd century by a tribe of Celtic Gauls, the city was originally called Parisii. Centuries of conflict with the Romans ended in 52 BC when Julius Caesar's legions took control of the territory. Paris' prosperous Middle Ages produced the cathedral Notre Dame, the Sorbonne and the Louvre – which began life as a riverside fortress. The following centuries were marked by the Hundred Years' War, the Renaissance, revolutions and the *belle époque* (beautiful age).

✪ TUNISIA

The smallest country in north Africa has a colourful past. The Phoenicians, Romans, Vandals, Byzantines, Arabs, Ottomans and French have all picked at the region at one point. The earliest humans to set foot here were probably a group of *Homo erectus* who stumbled onto the place a few hundred thousand years ago as they journeyed northwest across the Sahara from East Africa. The earliest hard evidence of human inhabitation was unearthed near the southern oasis town of Kebili and dates back about 200,000 years.

✪ VENICE, ITALY

The islands of the Venetian lagoon were first settled during the barbarian invasions of the 5th and 6th centuries AD, when the people of the Veneto mainland sought refuge in the marshy region. The refugees built watery villages on rafts of wooden posts driven into the subsoil, laying the foundations for the floating palaces of today. Settlement slowly evolved into the Repubblica Serenissima (Most Serene Republic), which was involved in the not-so-serene First and Fourth Crusades. The city's rapid expansion was subsequently curbed by the Turks, and more recently by water which continues to reclaim the land.

PLAINPICTURE | PHOTOLIBRARY

GUOHUA ZHONG | PHOTOLIBRARY

OLIVER STREWE | LONELY PLANET IMAGES

WITH THE COLOSSEUM IN SIGHT, SIGNS DIRECT VISITORS TO ROME'S HISTORIC LANDMARKS.

MONKS CONGREGATE IN ABA, SICHUAN, CHINA.

ORTHODOX JEWS PRAY AT THE WESTERN WALL (WAILING WALL) IN THE ANCIENT CITY OF JERUSALEM.

✪ ROME, ITALY

#o1. Kicking off in 753 BC, Rome's lasting buildings and institutions certainly flog that cliché about taking more than a day to build. Its ancient history is imbued with a healthy dose of mythology and packed with events that saw secular rule seesawing with the state. The original rulers, Etruscan kings, ushered in the emperors by 44 BC, who were responsible for Rome's magnificent skyline. Rome then became the centre for Christendom in the 4th century AD before striking a balance in the late 8th century to create the Holy Roman Empire.

✪ CHINA

#o2. Littered with sieges, cults, kidnappings, indolent emperors and grand gestures such as the Terracotta Warriors of the Qin dynasty and the communists' Long March, Chinese history twists its way through nearly 6000 intriguing years. China's timeline stretches from around 4000 BC with early settlements, and includes important figures such as Confucius, Genghis Khan and Mao. Often touted as the world's oldest living civilization, China has seen as many changes as the Great Wall has bricks.

✪ JERUSALEM, ISRAEL

#o3. Israel's capital city has a high-drama history of Biblical proportions. More than 3000 years ago Jews settled here with the conviction that the land had been divinely assigned to them. Ever since, and during 2000 years of exile, Jews have completely identified with Jerusalem as the capital of their homeland. Jerusalem subsequently acquired spiritual importance for Christians due to its association with the life and death of Jesus; for Muslims it became the third holiest city, and the place where Mohammed ascended to heaven.

⭐ KENYA

#o1.
There's such a dazzling array of animals in Kenya that you're likely to get a crook neck as you constantly crane it in search of animals and birds. Safaris are the most common mode of accessing the wildlife, whether it be by truck, camel or aeroplane, but it's also possible to do it on your own. Many choose to join a safari visiting a park with a high hit rate of seeing the 'big five': elephant, rhino, leopard, lion and buffalo, but these are also guaranteed to be crowded with other wildlife-watchers.

⭐ MALAYSIAN BORNEO

#o2.
If you've got a nose for seeking out monkeys, then Bako National Park is for you – the best place to see the rare proboscis, as well as common macaques. The best way to visit is to hike the 30km (19mi) of well-marked trails within the park. Also of note are the orang-utan sanctuaries: in Sarawak at the Semenggoh Wildlife Rehabilitation Centre, and at Sepilok Rehabilitation Centre in Sabah.

⭐ MADAGASCAR

#o3.
The national parks of Madagascar are rightly famous among wildlife aficionados worldwide. Lemurs are their best-known draw (from the red-bellied variety to the ring-tail), but there's also a bevy of weird and wonderful birds and reptiles – keep a keen eye out for chameleons. The country is diverse, often mountainous, and parks are most accessible to the entirely self-sufficient with hire vehicles. Organised tours are another option.

A CHEETAH ON THE LOOKOUT FOR PREY IN THE MASAI MARA NATIONAL REFUGE, KENYA

DRINK UP – AN ORPHANED ORANG UTAN GETS HIS DAILY FEED OF SUGARED MILK FROM A VOLUNTEER

A RING-TAILED LEMUR IS ONE OF THE MANY ODDBALL CHARACTERS OF MADAGASCAR'S NATIONAL PARKS.

BEST PLACES TO SEE
#02.WILDLIFE.

✪ BELIZE
Belize is brimming with accessible wilderness areas that include protected parks laden with wildlife and coastal cays with loads of marine life. To spy Belize's rarer species, such as Bairds tapirs or scarlet macaws, the services of a guide are required. But you're guaranteed to spot lots of creatures and critters on your own, too. Swim with sharks and stingrays or look for land animals such as pacas (giant guinea pigs), or jaguars at the Cockscomb Basin Wildlife Sanctuary.

✪ BOTSWANA
A safari (which means 'we go' in Swahili) is the best way to access the best of Botswana's wild and pristine parks. With about 35% of the country designated as protected areas, there are plenty of places to put yourself in the presence of lions, hippos, elephants, zebras, giraffes and antelope. There are also lots of opportunities to appreciate the little things in life, such as dung beetles or dancing sand lizards.

✪ COSTA RICA
The lush jungles here are home to playful monkeys, languid sloths, crocodiles, countless lizards, poison-dart frogs and a huge assortment of exotic birds, insects and butterflies. Endangered sea turtles nest on both coasts and cloud forests protect elusive birds and jungle cats. Costa Rica is enlightened to conservation, giving back more than 27% of the country to nature. The parks are readily accessible to independent travellers, though regulated in terms of numbers allowed in at any given time.

✪ EVERGLADES, USA
The largest subtropical wilderness in continental USA, the Everglades National Park is a wetland wonderland. It's a place where bird boffins unite to watch for large wading species such as spoonbills, egrets and wood storks. It's also the only place in the world where alligators and crocodiles co-exist. Paths within the park allow you to walk or cycle an alligator-strewn loop – and it's all within a 45-minute drive from midtown Miami.

✪ GREAT BARRIER REEF, AUSTRALIA
Mother Nature summoned all the colours of her vast palette and applied them in exquisite, liberal detail to the Great Barrier Reef. The Reef is one of the seven natural wonders of the world; it spans 200km (124mi) and is composed entirely of living organisms. The most extensive reef system in the world, it keeps a staggering array of marine species, including turtles, sharks, fish and corals. There's an armada of tour boats to shuttle divers and snorkellers out to the Reef from various points along the Queensland coast.

✪ BOLIVIA
Thanks to its varied geography, sparse human population and lack of extensive development, Bolivia's national parks offer some of the world's best places to observe wildlife. The Parque Nacional Madidi is one of South America's most intact ecosystems. This wild, little-trodden utopia is home to an eye-popping variety of Amazonian wildlife, including 44% of all New World mammal species, 38% of tropical amphibian species, more than 10% of all bird species known to science and more protected species than any park in the world.

A MARINE IGUANA BASKS IN THE SUN OF THE ISLA SANTA CRUZ, GALÁPAGOS ISLANDS.

✪ GALÁPAGOS ISLANDS, ECUADOR
This little string of islands offers the wildlife experience of a lifetime. You can witness the handful of animals which somehow made it out here, 1000km (621mi) from the Ecuador mainland, and were isolated for eons losing all fear of predators. Follow in the footsteps of Charles Darwin, whose theory of evolution was born out of his visit here in the 1830s aboard the HMS *Beagle*, and take a cruise among the volcanic islands. You'll see iguanas, sea lions and blue-footed boobies to name a few.

BEST FOODIE
#03. DESTINATIONS. »

CAREFUL WITH THAT BAGUETTE, MONSIEUR!

MEXICAN GRITS ARE WAY MORE THAN A SPOONFUL.

AN EARLY-MORNING FOCACCIA RUN IN ITALY.

JAPAN SERVES IT UP AS FRESH AS FRESH CAN BE.

✪ FRANCE

From cheese and champagne to snails and baguettes, the French are famous for their foodstuffs. French cuisine has long distinguished itself for dallying with a great variety of foods. Each region's distinct climate and geography have influenced the array of regional specialities. Many in France consider lunch as the day's main meal, though the two-hour marathon meal is increasingly rare. The crowning meal is a fully fledged home-cooked dinner comprising six distinct plats (courses).

✪ SPAIN

Best in Barcelona, Catalan cooking is racking up the accolades from gourmands around the globe. Like other regional Spanish cuisines, Catalan cooking favours spices such as saffron and cumin, as well as honeyed sweets (a historical hangover). A mixture of ingredients and traditions adds flair to Barcelona's fare: using seafood and meats in a rich array of sauces. Dinner is the main event, but never before 9pm.

✪ MEXICO

Would you like some magic-realism with that enchilada? The Mexican sensibility for enchanting influences is also brought to the table in its food, particularly during celebrations. Mexican cuisine has an overriding Spanish influence, with a twist of French and African thanks to its history. Corn- and bean-based dishes are prominent – prepared in a multitude of world-renowned ways including tacos, enchiladas and quesadillas. And who could forget the worm that waits at the bottom of a bottle of Mezcal?

✪ ITALY

Its food is arguably its most famous export, and it's with good reason that the world wants it. Despite all the variations that exist between regions, some common staples bind the country's culinary creations. Think thin-crust pizza and *al dente* pastas and risottos. And to drink? One word: coffee. The Italians do it best – from perfecting a distinguished roast to the gentle extraction of its essence into the cup. *Perfecto!*

✪ INDIA

India's protean gastronomy changes shape as you move between neighbourhoods, towns and states. The basis of all meals is rice in the south, and roti in the north. These are generally partnered with dhal, vegetables and chutney. Fish or meat may also be added. Whatever the ingredients: the dish usually contains a heady cast of exotic spices that make the taste buds stand up and take notice.

✪ JAPAN

If you can wrap your tongue around pronouncing the menu, Japan's cuisine is a most rewarding mouthful. Most Japanese restaurants concentrate on a specialty cuisine, such as *yakitori* (skewers of grilled chicken or veg), sushi and sashimi (raw fish), tempura (lightly battered and fried ingredients) and *ramen* noodle bars. The pinnacle of Japanese cooking, *kaiseki* (derived as an adjunct to the tea ceremony), combines ingredients, preparation, setting and ceremony over several small courses to distinguish the gentle art of eating.

✪ INDONESIA

Indonesian cuisine is one big food swap: Chinese, Portuguese, colonists and traders have all influenced its ingredients and culinary concepts. It's a nation well represented by its food. The abundance of rice is characteristic of the country's fertile terraced landscape, the spices are reminiscent of a time of trade and invasion (the Spice Islands), and fiery chilli echoes the people's passion. Indonesian cooking is not complex, and tastes here stay separate, simple and substantial.

BANGKOK'S MANY STREET STALLS SERVE FISH WITH A KICK.

HUNG OUT TO DRY IN GREECE.

CHINA'S NOODLE MAKERS EXTEND THE LIMITS OF FINE CUISINE.

⭐ THAILAND

#01. Standing at the crossroads of India, China and Oceania, Thai cuisine is like a best-of of all three's techniques and ingredients. Dishes generally go in hard with garlic and chillies (especially the *phrik khii nuu* variety, which literally translates as 'mouse-shit peppers'). Other signature ingredients include lime juice, coriander and lemon grass, which give the cuisine its characteristic tang. Legendary fish sauce or shrimp paste looks after the salt.

⭐ GREECE

#02. From olives to octopus, the true taste of Greece depends on fresh, unadulterated staples. Masking or complicating original flavours is not the done thing, especially when you're dealing with oven-fresh bread, rosy tomatoes and fish fresh from the Mediterranean. The midday meal is the main event with a procession of goodies brought to the table as they're ready. With Wednesday and Friday traditionally reserved as fast days (ie no-meat days), vegetarians are also looked after.

⭐ CHINA

#03. From back-alley dumpling shops to four-star banquet halls, China has one of the world's finest palates. Cultural precepts of Yin and Yang (balance and harmony) are evident in the bowl: with food for the day including cooling foods such as vegetables and fruit to counter warming spices and meat. The Chinese revere rice but also choose noodles, with either almost always accompanying a meal. A range of regional specialities exist, variously influenced by geography and history.

#04.EARTH. »

✲ DEATH VALLEY, USA

#01.

With such welcoming nomenclature, it's a wonder Death Valley isn't awash with fun seekers. One of the world's hottest places (with average summer temperatures around 38°C, or 100°F), the lonely arid desert of Death Valley embodies Old Testament severity with salient features such as Furnace Creek and Funeral Mountain. Located in California (though closer to Las Vegas), the Valley is littered with ghost towns, Jurassic fossil remains and sand dunes.

✲ ANTARCTICA

#02.

The southernmost land mass on earth is a place of extremes. The continent is the earth's largest (14.25 million sq km, 5.5 million sq mi) and has the smallest population (around 1200). The world's coldest climate – inhospitable winter temperatures around -80°C (-112°F) and almost 24-hour darkness – compound the isolation here. Ice and weather set the schedules, not clocks and calendars. In summer months flightseers launch from Australia and icebreaker ships begin pulling in after long, slow journeys.

✪ SIBERIA, RUSSIA

#03.

The frozen, vast and barren landscape conspires with history to isolate Siberia as a cold inhospitable place. Historically, Russian rulers banished any **persona non grata** to this region, which eventually became synonymous with Stalin's nefarious Gulag. Spanning a colossal 13.5 million sq km (5.2 million sq mi), Siberia is larger than Canada – the world's second largest country (second to Russia). The magnificent *Trans-Siberian* steams its way across southern Siberia through its major towns, including Omsk – about 2500km (1550mi) east of Moscow.

✪ BARROW, USA

The folks of Barrow, Alaska, live in the USA's northernmost community. There are no roads connecting it to the rest of the state, and to reach it you'll need to fly via a series of interconnecting flights that trace back to either Seattle, Los Angeles, Detroit or Vancouver. In the North Pole, Barrow is 1800km from Alaska's capital, Anchorage. Look to the skies for a perpetually encircling summer sun and sometime natural lightshow of an aurora.

✪ CLIFFS OF MOHER, IRELAND

The bitingly cold Atlantic Ocean claws at these 230m (754ft) cliffs, which stretch 8km (5mi) along Ireland's west coast. Despite being only 2.5km (1.5mi) from the nearest town of Liscannor, standing atop the rugged precipice peering out to an unending horizon lends a humbling sense of seclusion. From here you can sympathise with the flat-earth theory – this being where it falls away. The limestone ground fissured by centuries of erosion is known as Burren, and famous for the profusion of wildflowers that bloom there.

✪ JAN MAYEN, NORWAY

The volcanic island of Jan Mayen, 950km (590mi) west of mainland Norway, has a population somewhere between 18 and 20, plus one dog. The tiny team of meteorological observers have the stunning North Atlantic island to themselves. The landscape is dominated by lava flows courtesy of the Beerenberg volcano (2277m, 7470ft), which last erupted in 1985. To visit you'll either need to get yourself on the research team, or stow away in the Hercules that regularly drops off supplies.

✪ AMAZON BASIN, BOLIVIA

Located 1000km (620mi) upstream from the great Amazon River, Bolivia's section of the Amazon Basin is a deep mysterious Eden. In the northernmost reaches of the Santa Cruz department is the Parque Nacional Noel Kempff Mercado encompassing 1.5 million hectares (3.7 million acres) of dramatic scenery and verdant wildlife. It's a slow boat trip (12 hours) from the pleasant village of Piso Firme or a pricey charter flight from Santa Cruz to get here, but it's instant Indiana Jones when you do.

✪ NUNAVUT, CANADA

The simple purity of this stunning Arctic archetype is a long way from the pollution-clogged commotion of any city. Northern lights, icebergs and plunging fjords are residents here. It is harsh country: home to fewer humans than Monaco in a million times more space. The Inuit have thrived here for eons, attuned to the region's natural rhythms. To get here fork out a small fortune for a flight from Quebec or Montreal.

✪ EASTER ISLAND, CHILE

Enigmatic Easter Island (Rapa Nui), 3700km (2294m) west of the Chilean mainland, is the world's most remote inhabited island. More Polynesian than Chilean, the presence of Pacific Islanders in this isolated pocket of the world is as much a mystery as the origin of those famous stone heads. You can sail more than 1900km (1880mi) in any direction without sighting inhabited land; sail far enough south and you'll find yourself in the spectacular ice walls of the Patagonian Channels.

✪ PERTH, AUSTRALIA

Tucked away in the southwest corner of Australia, Perth is the capital of the country's largest and least populated state. Located 4400km (2750m) from Sydney by road, and surrounded on all sides by desert or sea, the city's assets are many: sunny weather, first-rate ocean beaches and hillside hideaways affording a comfortable pace of life. The vast mineral-rich lands of Western Australia saw the state contributing huge wealth to the country's economy; combined with its isolation, this caused rumbles of secession in the days of yore.

⭐ ONSEN, JAPAN

#o1. Soaking in *onsen* (natural, mineral-rich hot springs) is a centuries-old health-giving tradition in which most Japanese immerse themselves. *Onsen* etiquette prescribes that the soaker washes thoroughly before entering the male or female bathing area. When walking around, cover your private parts with tiny towels and, once in, don't make waves. Some facts worth checking: some *onsen* waters are also intended for drinking, check before you gulp. And some don't allow bathers with tattoos.

⭐ SPENCER TUNICK INSTALLATIONS

#o2. Novice nudies can bare all in the name of art by taking part in one of American photographer Spencer Tunick's mass nude gatherings (www.spencertunick. com). In 2001, over 4000 Melburnians put the city's murky Yarra River to shame by forming a pinkish sea of flesh on its banks. In 2003 Barcelona's Institut de Cultura was transformed by 7000 bodies who volunteered to strip off for the cause. Everybody receives a photographic print from their day of declothed glory.

⭐ 300 CLUB, ANTARCTICA

#o3. Initiation to the 300 Club involves the wannabe member enduring a 300°F (149°C) change in temperature. Mother Nature takes care of the cold factor, with Antarctic winters plummeting to -100°F (-73°C). To make up the difference, nudies crank up the sauna to 200°F (93°C), then dash – steaming and screaming – to the geographic pole. The tricky part is to not run too hard, as the freezing temperature outside can damage lungs – not to mention bite exposed bits.

ESCAPING THE COLD WITH JAPANESE MACAQUES IN THE HOT SPRINGS AT JIGOKUDANI ONSEN IN YUDANAKA.

NOT FOR THE SHRINKING VIOLETS.

BEST PLACES TO GET
#05.NAKED. »

✪ FORTY FOOT POOL, IRELAND

The historic Mortello tower, 8km (5mi) south of Dublin, is a James Joyce museum that keeps a number of treasures, including a precious edition of *Ulysses* illustrated by Henri Matisse. Below the tower is a seawater pool mentioned at the close of *Ulysess'* first chapter. In the tradition of Joyce celebrating 'heroic commonplace', many locals become everyday heroes by braving the skin-shrinking temperature of the sea sans swimming costume. But heed the sign: 'Togs must be worn after 9am'.

✪ SAUNA, FINLAND

First shower, then swelter in a 100°C (210°F) hot box before streaking starkers outside and rolling in the snow (preferably the soft powdery kind) or jumping into a small hole cut into the ice. Then repeat. In summer, gently flagellate yourself with wet birch branches (called a *vihta*), which stimulates circulation and smells nice. Traditionally wood heated, sauna-ing was born out of necessity, it being the only practical place to wash during long Finnish winters. Today, there are over two million saunas across the country, as well as a Finnish Sauna Society with 3100 members.

ATTENDANTS AT THE HISTORIC GALATASARAY TURKISH BATH.

✪ TURKISH BATHS, HUNGARY

Budapest's bountiful baths are fed by 123 hot springs. Locals have been taking in the combination of hygiene, health-giving properties and sociability since the 4th century BC. The health benefits of the mineral springs is instituted in the national health plan, which subsidises regular visits. Pad your way through labyrinthine chambers of various showers, pools (from tepid to hot to cold), saunas and steam rooms. And wallow in grand Art Nouveau surrounds: think cherub statues and sea-creature mosaics inlaid on the floor.

✪ BAY TO BREAKERS, USA

This historic foot race, traversing 12km (7.5mi) of San Francisco's peninsula, began in 1912 as a morale booster following a devastating earthquake. Many of the 75,000 participants run in costume (notables include Smurfs and a gang of Elvises), while

TAN LINE THERAPY ON EUROPE'S BEACHES.

others choose to run sans costume. Nude runners are advised to wear a sun hat and shoes only, plus the racing bib for those officially registered. Male runners are reminded that nature takes care of their floppy bits, as genitals naturally tighten during exercise. Ladies: unsecured breasts may cause discomfort; wear a flesh-coloured bra as required.

✪ MASLIN BEACH, AUSTRALIA

Best Bum, nude Frisbee Toss and Tug-o-War are not usual Olympic events, but at Maslin Beach's Nude Olympics in South Australia, they're the norm. Maslin Beach's coloured cliffs afford it some seclusion, as well as providing the perfect viewing platform (provided you're naked) for this event, held annually in January and in its 30th year in 2005. Australia's first nudist beach, Maslin Beach was officially declared 'unclad' in the late seventies.

A FULLY CLOTHED SPENCER TUNICK EXPLAINS TO HIS NUDE VOLUNTEERS HOW TO POSE.

✪ TIERGARTEN, GERMANY

A section of this stately park, smack bang in the centre of Berlin, is reserved for nude sunbathing. Once a hunting reserve for royalty, this section of the park is now something of a hunting ground for the mostly male sun worshippers looking for more than an all-over tan. Getting nude in the centre of the city is thrilling only in summer, otherwise just chilling.

LIFE-DRAWING CLASS, ENGLAND

Why not make a living out of being nude? Strike a pose and hold it for anywhere from a few minutes to quarter of an hour, while studious types scrutinise your form and try to render it in charcoal. London is the home of the Pre-Raphaelite artistic movement whose manifesto was to test and defy convention. In its heyday, the mid-19th century, being nude – let alone rendering it – was downright unconventional.

BEST VALUE
#06.DESTINATIONS. »

RAY LASKOWITZ | LONELY PLANET IMAGES

SPEED SHOPPING IN THAILAND.

✪ INDIA

Nothing in India is ever quite predictable; the only thing to expect is the unexpected, which comes in many forms and always wants to sit next to you. Your rupees get you in to an astonishing array of sacred sites, countless monuments and ancient ruins. Travelling around in the fabulous old trains, you'll get to sample India's many variations in religion, language, customs, art and cuisine that clamour together in one big sensory overload. You may even come home with a carpet that'll magically transport you back to India each time you look at it.

✪ MEXICO

Mexico's charm lies in its heady mix of modern and traditional, and the clichéd and the surreal. Whether you're throwing back margaritas or *cerveza* (beer), listening to howler monkeys, scrambling over ancient Mayan ruins or expanding your Day of the Dead collection of posable skeletons, Mexico is a traveller's paradise. Bus transport and even flights are inexpensive, and wherever you lay your sombrero there's a reasonably priced bed and meal.

✪ VIETNAM

In its cities, along its coast and in its countryside, Vietnam crams in a lot and generally costs a little. In Vietnam, you're guaranteed to get a great deal of bang for your dong. Vietnam's cuisine is a cracker, and a bowl of the country's staple dish *pho bo* (rice noodle soup with beef) usually costs loose change. Swimming in the emerald-green waters around karst islands in Halong Bay costs nothing. And it's free to weave through the magnificent city streets of Ho Chi Minh City and Hanoi.

✪ BULGARIA

Bulgaria is bulging with sights for travellers. It's a land of pine-clad mountains, fairy-tale villages and long stretches of Black Sea beaches. All food (heavily influenced by Greek and Turkish cooking), drink (coffee or beer) and transport (buses and taxis) are deliciously inexpensive compared with Western European countries. Accommodation is also a bargain and ranges from mountain huts to a room in a monastery, such as at Rila Monastery.

✪ THAILAND

Without battering the wallet, the visitor can claim a small piece of island paradise, gorge on the country's world-renowned cuisine or even become a devoted student of the Thai language. Thailand draws more visitors than any other country in Southeast Asia. Food and accommodation, especially outside bustling Bangkok, are ludicrously good value for money. Thai silk or hill tribe crafts can make for bargain souvenirs.

✪ CAMBODIA

Cambodia is kicking, and costs vary anywhere from almost free to extremely expensive. Penny pinchers can get by on as little as US$10 per day, while budget travellers with an eye on enjoyment can double the fun for US$20. Whatever your budget there's value in your dol-lar here. Long stretches of tropical beaches, a buzzy capital, the mighty Mekong and the magnificent temples of Angkor are all within fiscal reach. But bargain hard for that betel-nut box souvenir.

✪ CHINA

The world's most populous country is a colossal nation full of ferocious contrasts. Outside the thrumming hubs of über-cool Shanghai and bustling Beijing, budget travellers can stretch their dollar further – thanks to the abundance of economical accommodation and cheap eateries. Go west to the tropical rainforest and snow-capped peaks in Yunnan, or the stunning riverine karst upthrusts found in Guangxi. The best value is had by doing as the locals do: travel by bus or train and eat at street stalls – 1.3 billion people can't be wrong.

WAYNE WALTON | LONELY PLANET IMAGES

MICHAEL GEBICKI | LONELY PLANET IMAGES

EOIN CLARKE | LONELY PLANET IMAGES

BRIGHTEN UP YOUR DAY IN LA BOCA, ARGENTINA.

WHERE COURAGE IS THE MAIN CURRENCY: ADVENTURE TRAVEL IN NEW ZEALAND'S GLACIERS

TANGIERS' STREET PERFORMERS ADD MORE BANG FOR YOUR BUCK.

✪ BUENOS AIRES, ARGENTINA

#o1. In bargain-priced Buenos Aires you can chow down on a succulent steak, watch a tango show, grab a couple of beers and sleep in a clean hostel – all for under US$20. Kicking back in one of the city's elegant parks or walking the streets filled with grand European architecture costs you nothing. And you can shop around for a cheap leather jacket for yourself or that special someone back home.

✪ NEW ZEALAND

#o2. Unless you plan to throw yourself out of a plane or cling to a jet-boat every day of your trip, New Zealand's extraordinary outdoors makes for an economical experience. Self-catering travellers who camp or frequent hostels and tackle attractions independently can get among the scenery for as little as NZ$50 a day. New Zealand's award-winning fare is quality, fresh and affordable: with skies abuzz with honey bees and rich pastures feeding free-range cows, they don't call this the land of milk and honey for nothing.

✪ MOROCCO

#o3. With a few small tips here and there, taxi fares, plus entry charges to museums, you can get to see one of the greatest shows on earth – Morocco – for around US$35 a day. The intense density of life here throws up a colourful melange of experiences and infinite possibilities. In Morocco you can join the throng in a sweltering marketplace, ramble through Roman ruins and trek through a cool Atlas village in the space of a day.

⭐ SAN FRANCISCO, USA

#o1. Rainbow flags adorn apartment windows and bar entrances in many San Fran neighbourhoods, with nearly every bar and business in the Castro catering to gays and lesbians. Pride Week is capped by the often-outrageous 'Lesbian, Gay, Bisexual & Transgender Pride Parade' – where half a million people party in the street on the last Sunday in June. Also in June is the long-running queer film festival.

⭐ SYDNEY, AUSTRALIA

#o2. Hey, in Sydney gay is the new straight. Gay and lesbian culture forms a vocal, vital, well-organised and colourful part of Sydney's social fabric. Host of the 2002 Gay Games, Sydney also plays host to Australia's biggest annual tourist event – the Mardi Gras. The joy-filled hedonism-meets-political-protest parade is attended by more than half a million people. Beach life also reigns here, so boys should buff up before hitting the sand.

⭐ BRIGHTON, ENGLAND

#o3. Perhaps it's Brighton's long-time association with the theatre, but for more than 100 years the city has been a gay haven. The vibrant queer community is made-up of 40,000 residents – almost a quarter of the total population. Kemptown (aka Camptown) is where it's all at, with a rank of gay-owned bars, hotels, cafés, bookshops and saunas. There's even a 'Gay's the Word' walking tour.

FROM CLUBS AND PARADES TO ART AND FASHION – GREAT CITIES OF THE WORLD EMBRACE ONE AND ALL.

BEST GAY-FRIENDLY
#07. DESTINATIONS. »

GLOWSTICKS, LYCRA AND BOAS TAKE PRIDE OF PLACE AT THE SYDNEY GAY AND LESBIAN MARDI GRAS.

✪ AMSTERDAM, THE NETHERLANDS

Touted as the gay and lesbian capital of Europe, partisan estimates put the proportion of gay and lesbian people in Amsterdam at 20% to 30%. Though the figures are probably exaggerated, there's no underestimating the number of venues for gays and lesbians. There are more than 100 bars and nightclubs, gay hotels, bookshops, sport clubs, choirs and support services. Amsterdam hosts the only water-borne gay-pride parade in the world, held on the canals on the first Saturday in August. Even bigger is Koninginnedag (Queen's Day) on 30 April around the Homomonument – dedicated to those who were persecuted by the Nazis for their sexual preferences.

✪ BERLIN, GERMANY

Berlin's legendary liberalism has spawned one of the world's biggest gay and lesbian scenes. Openly gay mayor Klaus Wowereit outed himself with the now-popular words: 'I'm gay, and that's a good thing'. As befits Berlin's decentralised nature, the city has no dedicated gay ghetto although it contains a number of established scenes. Huge crowds turn out in early June for Schwul-Lesbisches Strassenfest (Gay-Lesbian Street Fair), which is basically a warm-up for Christopher Street Day later that month.

✪ PUERTO VALLARTA, MEXICO

Do as the *Love Boat* used to, and dock in the world-famous resort town of Puerto Vallarta. The gay scene here is pumping, with accommodations, tours, cruises and a variety of venues all catering to the gay market. Meet *amigos* in town (with cobblestone streets and red-roofed adobe-style buildings) at one of the many martini bars, strip clubs or drag shows. And strut or sloth on one of the glorious white-sand beaches.

✪ NEW YORK CITY, USA

New York's Chelsea and Greenwich Village are synonymous with gay life, possessing a thriving out-there scene. A number

SOMETHING FOR EVERYONE AT A TRANSVESTITE SHOW IN THAILAND.

of quieter clubs and bars continue to flourish further uptown in Chelsea as well. Every scene, from art to fashion, is hot in New York – and the gay scene is no exception, with great galleries, bars and clubs. June sees the obligatory Gay Pride parade attracting revellers from around the world.

✪ RIO DE JANEIRO, BRAZIL

During Carnaval (February or March), thousands of expatriate Brazilian and gringo gays fly in to take part in the fun, with transvestites stealing the show at most balls. Outside Carnaval the gay scene is active, though less visible than in cities such as San Francisco and Sydney. The gay capital of Latin America is a mostly integrated scene, with the Entertainment sections of local newspapers and magazines branding establishments 'GLS': Gays, Lesbians and Sympathisers.

THERE'S NO GIRL FROM IPANEMA HERE.

✪ PRAGUE, CZECH REPUBLIC

The beguiling bohemian city of Prague inspired Kafka to warn visitors: 'this little mother has claws'. Its maze of medieval lanes keeps a bevy of bars catering to all fancies: from leather through to rent boy. The cradle of Czech culture, Prague also stages a gay and lesbian film festival annually in November. Despite the city's wholesale acceptance of same-sex partnerships, there's a segregated gay scene, and public displays of affection are generally ill advised.

✪ BANGKOK, THAILAND

There's no 'gay movement' as such in Bangkok, as there's no antigay establishment to move against. Thai culture is generally accepting of male and female homosexuality; however, public displays of affection per se are mostly frowned upon. The fairly prominent scene centres on the proliferation of bars, often enlivened by high-camp cabaret.

✪ PAKISTAN

#o1. *Pakistan has a proud history, awe-inspiring landscapes and a variety of cultures, but...* Is there anywhere you can go? Karachi has recently been rocked by suicide bombs and sectarian unrest makes it doubly unsafe; Sindh province suffers from anti-Western sentiment that occasionally spills over into violence; visitors to upper Sindh are encouraged to notify authorities beforehand; and trekkers heading for Gilgit, Hunza, Chitral and the upper Swat Valley should hire reputable guides to guard against assault.

✪ COLOMBIA

#o2. *The natural landscapes are beautiful and the citizens are enchanting in this diverse country, but...* Let's get a few home truths out of the way: Colombia has a murder rate of 81 per 100,000 people; it's in the grip of superviolent drug wars and ultravicious street crime; the government is severely undermined by the cocaine cartels; and the place is popularly known as 'Locombia' (Mad Country). Still feel like visiting? At least you'll be free from other travellers.

✪ AFGHANISTAN

#o3. *Its people are friendly, its countryside is beautiful, it's blessed with an impressive history and rich and diverse culture, but...* Afghanistan, post-Taliban, is still a country to be avoided by the casual backpacker. Warlords still (attempt to) exert control over a large proportion of the country; Taliban cells still try to regain power; and anti-American protests have seen violence return to many towns and cities. The cherry on top: there are more active landmines here than just about anywhere else.

TOUGH TRAVEL
#08. DESTINATIONS. »

✪ ALGERIA
With its Sahara dunes, Atlas Mountains, Turkish palaces and Berber culture, it's one of North Africa's most diverse and fascinating countries, but... This is another land scarred by extremism – in the 1990s Islamic rebels went throat to throat with the government and neither side gave a hoot who got in the way. Random execution and wholesale slaughter of entire villages were the flavour of the day and large numbers of tourists were killed in the crossfire. They say the violence has died down, but random bombings still occur and tourists still stay away in droves.

✪ DAGESTAN
It's atmospheric and picturesque, but... Not only is this Russian republic lawless, it's also inaccessible at the best of times – some parts are so high they can only be reached by helicopter. But back to the lawlessness: mafia barons rule and they get their kicks from a high-fibre diet of kidnappings, executions and general gun-fuelled psychosis. Ethnic tensions also shred the republic raw; in 1999 Islamic militants not only declared independence from Dagestan but also announced a jihad against Russia. Today, bomb and missile attacks ensure that Dagestan remains as unstable as nitroglycerine.

✪ HAITI
The people are passionate and known for their humour and passion, and the musical tradition is luminous, but... Haiti suffers from overpopulation, disease (one in 20 Haitians has HIV/AIDS), a devastated environment, civil disorder, savage rebellion, lack of facilities (six out of 10 Haitians drink unsafe water and there's just one doctor for every 10,000 people), out-of-control drug warlords, and poverty (it's the poorest country in the western hemisphere). Installation of a UN stabilisation force was meant to strengthen Haiti's long-term security but the situation remains volatile; a list like the above won't be shortened in the foreseeable future.

✪ SYRIA
Syria is truly unique, full of hidden treasures and surprisingly easy to get around. It's a treasure-trove of amazing archaeological treats, but... Anti-US protests and the constant threat of violence make travel to Syria a no-no for Americans and quite possibly the rest of the world. Families of US embassy members and other US nationals have been advised to leave Syria, while Kurdish populations were recently reported to have been restive.

✪ NIGERIA
It's colourful and rich in history, but... Polio vaccination is sporadic so Nigeria has a shockingly high rate of infection. If polio doesn't claim you then religious tensions, border conflict with Cameroon and violent crime almost certainly will. Robberies and muggings in broad daylight are commonplace, as are carjackings, kidnappings, piracy and riots.

✪ SIERRA LEONE
It has some of west Africa's best beaches, abundant wildlife reserves and a vibrant capital, but... Sierra Leone still has to deal with the aftershocks of decades of political corruption and disorder. The civil war finally ended in 2002 after 10 long, ferocious years of terror and turmoil, but drug and gem smuggling remains a problem and the regions bordering Liberia are still insecure and unsafe for travel.

✪ YEMEN
It's a tantalising blend of Arabian exotica and rural charm, and you feel you might meet Aladdin or Sinbad or any of the characters of the Arabian Nights, but... Fighting between Yemen's government and rebels continues in the north and kidnapping foreigners is almost a national sport. Yemen also has a severe landmine problem: in 1994 between 75,000 and 100,000 mines were laid by inexperienced soldiers in random fashion in the Aden and Hadramawt areas, with scant marking or fencing to indicate location. Desperate attempts are still being made to clear them.

CITIES ON THE
#09.RISE.

WALTER BIBIKOW | PHOTOLIBRARY

FUN AND FRENCH, MONTREAL EMBODIES ITS STAR QUALITIES.

✪ LJUBLJANA, SLOVENIA

They say that Ljubljana is the 'new Prague', and the comparisons are immediately apparent. Both cities are long-standing crucibles of intellectual and artistic activity – enjoying an attendant, Bohemian café society – and both are blessed with remarkable, baroque architecture and elegant cobbled streets. But whereas Prague appears to be overrun by crowds, Ljubljana is relatively low key and just that bit more off the radar.

✪ SOFIA, BULGARIA

Bulgaria has changed swiftly over the last decade as the country has rushed to embrace capitalism – especially urban Bulgaria, and Sofia in particular. The Bulgarian capital's compact city centre is an eclectic mix of architectural styles, largely rebuilt after WWII bombings and complete with a yellow-brick boulevard. It's a place of real charm, especially since the EU's 'Beautiful Bulgaria Project' has spruced up historic buildings and energised old neighbourhoods.

✪ HANOI, VIETNAM

Beguiling Hanoi has shaken off its sleepy past to become one of Asia's most desirable destinations, boasting an appealing combination of lakes, shaded boulevards, verdant public parks and French-colonial architecture – and Eastern tradition and spirituality. Hollywood is discovering Hanoi's appeal, too, always a barometer of popular trends in some respect; recently *The Quiet American* was shot here, the first Hollywood film to be made in Vietnam, and more flicks are likely.

✪ CAPE TOWN, SOUTH AFRICA

Once you've been to Cape Town you can never forget her. This vibrant, gorgeous city is small in scale but supplies grandeur in spades, with its Mediterranean-style climate, stunning Table Mountain surrounds, wonderful beaches, delightful vineyards, rugged landscapes, and intriguing plants and animals. Accordingly, travellers are beginning to realise that Cape Town offers the lot, without the hassle of big-city life.

✪ MONTRÉAL, CANADA

This friendly, French-speaking city is Québec's economic and cultural centre, but it's also Europe and America wrapped into one – hip and cool, proud and multicultural, relaxed yet oozing star quality – and that's why people come here, for a potted Continental or North American experience. Montréal is a good-time town and visitors can expect bustling street fairs and festivals, and cafés inhabited by sociable and sophisticated locals.

✪ AUSTIN, USA

In the early '90s Austin, Texas, took over from Seattle as the hippest city in the States. It's vibrant and charming but doesn't really boast 'touristy' attractions; instead it's the self-proclaimed 'Live Music Capital of the World', hosting the annual South by Southwest music-industry extravaganza and numerous other music festivals. Austin has risen through the ranks to become the de facto cultural centre of Texas and perhaps of the USA's entire Southwest.

✪ MAPUTO, MOZAMBIQUE

Maputo has emerged from the shadows in recent times, having been eclipsed by colonialism and then by war. Today it features lively and colourful markets, stimulating architecture, great nightlife, opportunities for rest and relaxation galore, a Mediterranean atmosphere, white sandy beaches, friendly locals, tempting pavement cafés and a chilled atmosphere. Check out that setting: Maputo is on a small cliff overlooking Maputo Bay, and features wide avenues lined by jacaranda and flame trees.

SHANGHAI HAS EMBRACED ITS EMERGING STATUS WITH GUSTO.

POLAND'S HAZY AND PEACEFUL COBBLED STREETS... BEAT THE RUSH.

PHNOM PENH'S NATIONAL MUSEUM CAPTURES THE BEST OF TRADITIONAL ARCHITECTURE FOR VISITORS TO THE REGION.

✪ SHANGHAI, CHINA

#o1. Since market restrictions were lifted, sparkling Shanghai has positively bristled with hyper-driven cultural change, embracing the world of business and design and rewriting its own destiny: it's a sophisticated, inventive city with all eyes firmly fixed on the future. Shanghai still embodies full-tilt sensory overload, but whereas in the colonial era that meant visions of brothels and opium dens, today it's fine art, fine dining and contemporary urban living.

✪ KRAKÓW, POLAND

#o2. Here's another of communism's ugly daughters that has recently bloomed to become the Belle of the Ball. Kraków, Poland's Royal City, is capricious and attractive, with parklands and the river Vistula circling the Old Town, and a treasure-trove of historical architecture on show; the spires of its old churches catch the eye wherever you go. Kraków was anointed the European City of Culture in 1992 and 2000 – so, as they say, the word is most definitely out.

✪ PHNOM PENH, CAMBODIA

#o3. It's beautiful yet charmless, subtle yet anarchic, juggling the past and the present, embodying poverty and excess... Cambodia's capital is baffling and bewitching, and it's now attracting the big tourist dollars. Despite decades of war, genocide and isolation, Phnom Penh has retained its innate charm, with faded colonial architecture providing an atmospheric backdrop to chirpy streetside cafés and the redeveloped, bustling riverfront precinct.

✪ WILDLIFE SAFARI, AFRICA

#o1. Africa's animal kingdom is the benchmark of wildlife. Seeing an elephant, giraffe or big cat in its own environment is a wild experience for children (and adults). Kid-friendly safaris, which provide a separate vehicle for the family, bring the *Lion King* and *Jungle Book* to life. And the dung beetle's perpetual pursuit of pooh can provide hours of humorous musing. It's worth remembering that Africa's mozzies and heat can turn your angels into animals – of the grizzly variety.

✪ INDIA

#o2. Every day in this colossal country is a sensory overload, with cows wandering the tiny twisted streets and swirls of cartoon-coloured saris. Travelling children are lavished with attention – like or it or not. Families love the Taj Mahal: its shiny white marble floors make a great skidding surface for shoeless feet (a requirement upon entering). And the intricately carved buildings clinging to the edge of the Great Thar Desert look like giant sand castles from atop a camel.

✪ LEGOLAND, ENGLAND

#o3. Over 35 million little coloured bricks were painstakingly snapped together to build a little London Bridge, London Eye and other familiar sights at Miniland in Windsor's Legoland. Look out for traffic, which consists of Lego cars, boats and a balloon that kids can drive. My Town harbour and lighthouse is the domain of Johnny Thunder who fends off crocodiles, snakes and dragons – all in a day's work for a Lego action man. Legolands around the world can be found in Carlsbad (California, USA), Günzburg (Germany) and Billund (Denmark).

BEST KID-FRIENDLY
#10. DESTINATIONS. »

✪ DISNEY RESORT, JAPAN

This purpose-built Tokyo theme park has 'suburbs' such as Critter Country, Western Land, Toon Town and Tomorrow Land, with celebrity residents such as Goofy, Donald, Minnie and Mickey. Disbelief is easily suspended when you're hanging from a giant blowfish gondola or sitting in a swirling kelp cup surrounded by mermaids. And this self-contained land has loads of restaurants, shops and accommodation so you can make believe for days on end.

✪ SENTOSA ISLAND, SINGAPORE

Travelling to this theme-park island by cable car should curb any are-we-there-yets. Though the promise of seeing pink dolphins in the Underwater World Dolphin Lagoon makes the trip about more than just the journey. Also in the water park is an enormous see-through tunnel; enter it to be surrounded by giant gropers, brown stingrays and sharks. Visit the butterfly park with thousands of pairs of coloured blinking wings, or play in a giant sand pit on the island's imported-sand beach.

✪ UNIVERSAL STUDIOS, USA

Kids can cast themselves in a blockbuster at the world's largest movie studio and theme park in Hollywood. Metaphorically carpeted red, wandering characters like Spiderman, Shrek and Donkey happily pose for photos. Stunt shows and a special-effects stage take visitors behind the scenes, and there are movie-themed rides and games aimed squarely at starry-eyed kids.

✪ MADAME TUSSAUD'S, ENGLAND

Life-size likenesses of monsters, megastars, presidents and sporty sorts made from wax have a larger-than-life wow factor for children. Cosy up to Kylie without being slapped away by bodyguards or get the scoop on Spiderman first-hand. Kiddies can also mix it up with the adults by taking Air Guitar Star lessons, where they learn to scissor jump and wheel their arms with abandon. Nowhere near London? Tussaud's wax museums are also located in New York (USA), Las Vegas (Nevada, USA), Amsterdam (the Netherlands) and Hong Kong.

✪ MAYAN RUINS, MEXICO

The Maya's monumental ceremonial spaces make it easy to imagine gods of fire and water, as well as the dirt-eating goddess worshipped by this ancient civilisation. These hidden cities, often anatomically aligned, provide rare opportunities to clamber in the shadows of pyramids. It's also possible to stumble upon sacrificial altars and Days of the Dead celebrations – when the dead return from the Netherworld to reunite with their relations on earth. Mythical Mayan sites are also located in Guatemala and Belize.

✪ SAN DIEGO ZOO, USA

This famous zoo in San Diego has an enlightened management approach – re-creating an animal's natural habitat as much as possible. Meet Miss Houdini the spectacled bear, so named for escaping from her enclosure as a cub. And Chips the 100-year-old Galápagos tortoise who wears red nail polish on her 'chipped' shell (so the keepers can identify her easily) and loves to eat red fruit. Zoo programmes especially for kids include games and recipes, such as for Flamingo Fruit: watermelon, strawberries, pink grapefruit and sherbet – which must be eaten while standing on one leg.

✪ OAHU, HAWAII

The hula capital of the world, Oahu is a kid magnet, with a huge range of purpose-built attractions, as well as some natural wonders. If you can get them out of the grass skirts and into some pint-sized hibiscus-print boardshorts there are surfing lessons on offer, or horse rides for land lovers. You could lose them for hours in the colossal pineapple garden maze or water theme park, and teach them some Polynesian life lessons at the cultural centre, with child-friendly programmes.

COUNTRIES ON THE
#11.RISE.

SOOTHING THE SOUL IN ICELAND'S BLUE LAGOON.

PAUL HARDING | LONELY PLANET IMAGES

✪ ICELAND

Iceland is one of Europe's more unusual destinations, with its wonderful sense of escape and isolation. It's a country of wild open spaces and empty black-sand beaches, of sapphire-blue glaciers, ice breaking into the ocean and rainbows thrown up by waterfalls as they hammer through tortured lava flows. Then there's Reykjavík, small but coming on like a European metropolis, with theatres, opera houses, galleries and some of the best and busiest bars in Scandinavia.

✪ SERBIA & MONTENEGRO

Bent on rapid reform, Serbia & Montenegro has been consigning its associations with despots, socialism, death and war to history's dustbin. Travellers are reaping the rewards, as this region of forgotten beauty, culture and history begins to shine; the capital, Belgrade, in particular, is in danger of rapidly becoming one of Europe's hippest cities, with its pumping nightlife and obligatory bar and club scene. But it's not all onwards and forwards; there are plenty of textured, cultural reminders of the Austro-Hungarian empire, as well as of Islam, to whet your appetite for exotic good times.

✪ SLOVENIA

Slovenia is a peaceful country: affluent, affable, free of strife. It suffered just 10 days of fighting during the bitter independence wars in 1991, when it was left to quietly go about its business while Bosnia, Serbia and Croatia raised hell on earth. Slovenia boasts a grand heritage, rolling fields of green and the luscious capital, Ljubljana. It also shares the Alps with its geographical neighbours, hence the nickname 'Little Switzerland'. Surprisingly, Slovenia receives fewer visitors now than it did before the Balkans wars, although the number is slowly increasing.

✪ UKRAINE

Ukrainians really have suffered: at the hands of Stalin and his systematic genocide of millions and through the horror of Chornobyl. The 'Orange Revolution' turned things around, though, when hundreds of thousands of Ukrainians flooded the streets to protest the corrupt November 2004 elections. There's still a long way to go before things are back on track, but in the meantime travellers are gearing up to enjoy everything from treks through the Carpathian Mountains to Gothic and Byzantine architectural wonders, from strolls through the cosmopolitan port city of Odesa to trips along the coast of Crimea by the Black Sea.

✪ CHILE

Since the return of democracy in the late 1980s, Chile has steadily attracted more and more visitors with its extensive national-park system, well-developed infrastructure and accessible natural attractions. Visitation tends to revolve around soft adventure (cruising fjords, bird-watching, fishing, glacier-watching, wine tasting), but there's an increasing emphasis on harder-core activities (trekking, white-water rafting, skiing, snowboarding, surfing, bicycle touring, climbing volcanoes), particularly in the lightly developed southern reaches of Patagonia and the sparsely inhabited islands of Tierra del Fuego.

✪ CROATIA

Croatia has always been one of Europe's most stunning jewels, with its 1000km-long (620mi) Adriatic coast, inspiring (though rocky) beaches and more than 1000 idyllic islands. But its love affair with tourism suffered coitus interruptus in 1991 during the 'Homeland War', when Croatia declared independence from Yugoslavia while its Serbian enclave, Krajina, declared independence from Croatia. Now travellers are being lured back to that sublime coastline and the giddy thrill of hopping between olive grove– and lemon tree–encrusted islands, accompanied by the type of sun-ripened, old-world charm that's rapidly becoming scarce in Europe's overpopulated, overdeveloped west.

✪ EL SALVADOR

El Salvador's name still evokes images of the brutal civil war fought throughout the 1980s in its tangle of mountains and farmlands. But that war is over and now the most turbulent aspect of El Salvador is its volcanic landscape. Tourists are also beginning to discover that El Salvador is also hot for its surfing spots, especially El Sunzal, considered one of America's best point breaks, and La Libertad, with its hollow waves.

RICARDO GOMES | LONELY PLANET IMAGES

DAVID ELSE | LONELY PLANET IMAGES

RICHARD I'ANSON | LONELY PLANET IMAGES

AS CHINA'S STATUS CHANGES, SO TOO DO ITS TRANSPORT OFFERINGS.

A GROUP OF WELL-WISHERS CELEBRATE A BRIDE-TO-BE'S FORTHCOMING WEDDING IN A VILLAGE NEAR MOPTI.

CELEBRATIONS ARE BRAZIL'S HEART AND SOUL, BOTAFOGO.

✪ CHINA

#o1. Fast, brash, unpredictable – that's today's China, where Mao suits and bicycles have been replaced by Cadillacs and hot pants. Modern China bursts with creative energy, rampant construction, the old making way for the new. A cacophony of fresh voices has emerged, challenging the way the country presents itself in the 21st century, but even so, traditional China is never far away. The Great Wall and the Forbidden City retain all their awe and allure, while China's 200 ethnic minorities, each with their own distinct set of customs and traditions, ensure a host of diverse delights.

✪ MALI

#o2. Just because it's in Africa doesn't mean Mali is the place to go for safaris. Instead, tourists come here for a smorgasbord of surreal landscapes, sublime art and music, Timbuktu, castellated mosques made entirely of mud, pink-sandstone villages carved into cliff faces, and undulating desert scenes that evoke Lawrence of Arabia. There's more than a touch of surreality here: Mali is also home to the Dogon people, an animist race who have claimed extraterrestrial contact for thousands of years and who discovered certain celestial bodies a long, long time before Western astronomers.

✪ BRAZIL

#o3. Brazil is vivacious, sassy, sexy and awe-inspiring, yet it's home to staggering poverty, street violence and corruption. Brazil has become the destination of choice for those keen on exotic tropical holidays and romantic, sun-soaked vibes, but it's also at the coalface of a number of recent travel trends. The state of the Amazon and the plight of its native inhabitants has spawned a burgeoning ecotourism industry, while the country's dire poverty has given rise to 'volunteer tourism', where travellers teach English in schools or orphanages or contribute skills to community projects.

✪ PETRA, JORDAN

#o1.
They say that the forgotten city of Petra was concealed in the Jordanian mountains for thousands of years until its discovery in 1812 by Swiss explorer Johan Ludwig Burckhardt…and then again in 1989 by Steven Spielberg. Spielberg used Petra's dramatic red-sandstone temples and tombs as a key location for his blockbuster *Indian Jones and the Last Crusade*. Indy discovers the Holy Grail in Petra's 'treasury', so whatever else you might think about Spielberg's directing abilities, you can't deny he has a great eye for detail.

✪ PARIS, FRANCE

#o2.
It's possible that, aside from American locations, Paris has been the setting for more films than any other city. The City of Light played host to the groundbreaking gangster film *A Bout de Souffle* (1960); the tragic love triangle of *Jules et Jim* (1962); the futuristic thriller *Alphaville* (1965); and the saccharine shenanigans of *Amélie* (2001). This kind of genre-hopping makes sense: there's so much to see and do in Paris, with its glorious architecture, its sweeping avenues, and its wonderfully rich cultural life, that the city simply becomes all things to all people.

✪ TOKYO, JAPAN

#o3.
Those who have never been to Tokyo accuse Sophia Coppola of racism in her film *Lost In Translation*. But those who have spent time there know that Tokyo is exactly as she describes it: bamboozling yet obvious, archaic yet futuristic, mysterious yet crass. Plus there's all that neon and the wacky TV hosts and the food. Tokyo is a city that bludgeons the unwary, chewing them up and spitting them out before they know what's hit them, and *Lost In Translation* is a beautifully succinct summary of the traveller's experience.

✪ OUTBACK, AUSTRALIA

Think of *Mad Max 2: The Road Warrior* (1981) and what comes to mind: sandblasted rock? Road kill? Flat desert plains as far as the eye can see? Dry creek beds? No special effects were used to create that particular postapocalyptic environment because – minus the leather-clad berserk bikers and Mel Gibson – that's exactly what you can expect to find at Broken Hill in remote New South Wales, where much of *The Road Warrior* was filmed. This is real outback territory, where men are men and sheep run for cover.

✪ DUBLIN, IRELAND

Shot entirely on location in north Dublin, *The Commitments* (1991), about a ragtag group of youths bringing soul to the masses, evokes the melancholy of that city. Drugs, factories, housing estates and the healing power of music are as much a part of Dublin's fabric as are the standard romantic depictions of the city, and *The Commitments* doesn't flinch in this regard. Trawling through the suburbs, the camera brings home the single-minded optimism – and the unfulfilled ambitions – that define the Irish dream.

PLACES MOST LIKE
#12. IN THE FILM.

✪ MANHATTAN, USA

Woody Allen is perhaps Manhattan's most famous mythologiser, recording its streets and people in a huge body of work that includes *Annie Hall* (1977), *Manhattan* (1979) and *Hannah and Her Sisters* (1986). There are loads of walking tours that can take you in and out of the nooks and crannies of Woody's Manhattan: the delis; the bars; the Beekman Theatre; John's Pizzeria; Elaine's restaurant; the 59th St Bridge. Woody's direction lovingly lingers on each location – encountering them in real life is almost exactly like the movie.

✪ ANGKOR WAT, CAMBODIA

The 12th-century temples at Angkor Wat, or what remains of them, starred in the smash-hit actioner *Tomb Raider* (2001): their labyrinthine, decrepit mazes, shrines, platforms, alcoves and spires provided the perfect backdrop for Angelina Jolie's gyrations as curvaceous archaeologist Lara Croft. In real life the majesty of this mystical location is even more overwhelming than in the movie, and you might be moved to ponder the fact that a far greater intelligence than even Hollywood was behind it all, some 900 years ago.

✪ NEW ZEALAND

Peter Jackson's mega-successful *Lord of the Rings* trilogy (2001–03) really put New Zealand on the world stage. It's no accident that the land of the Kiwi was chosen to portray the land of the hobbit: Jackson, a Kiwi himself, knew that places like Twizel and the south of the South Island, with their mountainous, rolling fields of green, would provide the perfect setting for Middle Earth. Of course, the locations were digitally enhanced for the final product, but there will still be enough similarity to provide kinky thrills for any *LOTR* fan.

✪ VENICE, ITALY

Venice is undeniably beautiful but decidedly unsettling as well. Three very creepy films have used it as their setting: *Death In Venice* (1971), about a dying misanthrope driven mad by lust; *Don't Look Now* (1974), about a man driven mad by his ability to foresee death; and *The Comfort of Strangers* (1991), about a sexually sadistic couple who were already mad. As you get lost in one of Venice's mazelike alleyways or become gripped by the surreal sight of a city floating on water, then chances are you'll think of at least one of these films.

✪ WADI RUM, JORDAN

Not only is this where the epic *Lawrence of Arabia* (1962) was shot, but it's where the real-life Lawrence led the famous 'Arab Revolt' campaign in 1917. As you explore Wadi Rum's desert interior, marvelling at the moonlike landscapes, contemplating the ancient carved inscriptions and sipping tea with Bedouin locals, you might just give a whoop and a yell, Peter O'Toole style, and wish you had a fine Arab charger at your disposal rather than that boring old Jeep.

❂ SAHARA DESERT, MALI

#o1. With snowcapped peaks in the central region of the Sahara and winter temperatures that drop as low as 14°C (57°F), you'd be forgiven for asking whether this was any way for a self-respecting desert to behave. Luckily for popular imagination there's still enough sand, sun and space to go around. Today the Sahara stretches over 8370km (5200mi) and covers a whopping 9,000,000 sq km (3,500,000 sq mi) – about the size of the USA – and it's growing larger by the day.

❂ ATACAMA DESERT, CHILE

#o2. It's dry, it's barren and it's empty. The world's driest desert is Chile's Atacama Desert. There are parts of it that have never been touched by rain, and the precious little precipitation that does fall (1cm or 0.3in per year) comes from fog. Flanked on one side by Pacific coastal ranges and on the other by the snowcapped peaks of the Andes, the desert is a series of salt basins that supports virtually no vegetation.

❂ DANAKIL DEPRESSION, ETHIOPIA

#o3. The temperature in Ethiopia may be pleasant enough in the shade, but in the salt basin of the Danakil Depression, the only shade to be had is from cupping your hand over your eyes. And you'll need to do this in order to see across the shimmering white salt surface punctuated by steaming yellow sulphur fields. Reaching a depth of more than 100m (330ft) below sea level, the depression is the lowest point on earth not covered by water, and is purported to be the hottest place on earth.

EVEN DESERT SHIPS NEED A BREAK FROM THE EXTREME SAHARA ENVIRONMENT.

MINERS DIG FOR COPPER IN THE ATACAMA DESERT IN CHILE.

EVEN THE EARTH'S CENTRE TAKES A TURN IN ETHIOPIA'S EXTREME ENVIRONMENT.

#13. ENVIRONMENTS. »

✪ THE OUTBACK, AUSTRALIA

Apart from the sand in the Simpson Desert and the crimson earth of the MacDonnell Ranges, there's just spinifex, heat and vast skies in that *looooooonnngggg* stretch of land between the southern tip of Australia's mainland and Darwin at the Top End. Often the only sounds are the harsh and melancholy cries of crows, as though they were commenting on the land below. The emptiness of the landscape is the physical equivalent to mental meditation.

✪ BANFF NATIONAL PARK, CANADA

This 6641-sq-km (2564-sq-mi) park envelops some radically rugged sections of the Canadian Rockies. Incorporating 25 majestic mountains rising 3000m (9843ft) or higher, the skyline here is a stunner. Opalescent turquoise lakes and lush forests in the foothills imbue the whole region with intense beauty. These salient features conspire with rivers fed by snow melts and high alpine meadows to support a range of wildlife. Moose, bear, bison and wolves share the park with skiers, kayakers and climbers.

✪ LADAKH, INDIA

Set deep in a valley between the Himalayas and the Karakoram Range is the district capital of Ladakh. Its dramatic bare expanse is in India's highest-altitude plateau, and purportedly has the highest pass in the world at 5602m (18,380ft). The valley is sprinkled with Buddhist monasteries, which are the only blips on the bald contemplative surrounds. Devoid of trees, precarious swinging foot bridges clinging to the lower walls of giant canyons, and snow-covered peaks are often threaded by glaciers.

✪ MEXICO CITY, MEXICO

This seething cosmopolitan megalopolis is by turns exhilarating and overpowering. All of Mexico's ingredients collide, creating a confusion of elements; there's music and noise, brown air and green parks, colonial palaces and skyscrapers, as well as world-renowned museums and ever-sprawling slums. Severe pollution from traffic and industry associated with the city's 18 million residents is kept hovering above town by the mountains that ring around it.

FROM ITS CROWDED STREETS TO ITS HIGHEST PEAKS, INDIA IS FULL OF EXTREMES.

✪ THE ANDES, ECUADOR

The rugged Andes range cuts this relatively compact country in half. Few people penetrate the central highlands region with its heaving volcanic undulations. Dubbed the 'Avenue of the Volcanoes', a number are still active – breathing life into the surrounding rocky furrowed landscape. The northernmost volcano, Tungurahua (5016m, or 16,457ft), is covered in snow and responsible for sending tremors, steam, gas and ash across the land. Even more remote, Volcán Sangay (5230m, or 17,160ft) has been perpetually burping sulphur fumes and spewing rocks since the 1930s.

✪ DELHI, INDIA

This is a city of contrasts and extremes. A population of 13.8 million people occupy the relatively small area of 1483 sq km (573 sq mi). The city's two contrasting parts –
Old Delhi and New Delhi – play off the perceived chaos of the older town's tangle of narrow streets with the apparent calm of New Delhi's spacious tree-lined avenues. Delhi summers are serious, with 45°C (113°F) temperatures accompanied by furious dust storms and monsoonal rains.

✪ ALASKA RANGE, USA

This North American belt of mountains and its surrounds attracts severe, inhospitable Arctic weather. Winter temperatures can plummet to -50°C (-58°F) and storms are the norm, courtesy of the nearby sea. It's a restless environment, with gravity forcing glaciers to 'flow' like frozen rivers in the lowland sound. That the state pays residents annually to live in Alaska says something about its challenges. Another such challenge for locals is eating Spam as a staple during winter, when the snow is up past the windows and even the dogs won't go outside.

PLACES TO LOVE WITH THINGS TO
#14.QUESTION.

»

CAMELS MIX WITH ISRAELI MILITARY MANOEUVRES IN THE NEGEV DESERT.

✪ USA
It's hard to neatly sum up the appeal of the USA. There's glitzy Las Vegas; edgy New York; tropical Hawai'i; celebrity-ridden Los Angeles; rugged Yosemite National Park; frozen Alaska. Plus the people are friendly and welcoming and the culture is rich and varied. There's so much on offer for the traveller – if you're not put off by the country's image problem, firstly, and if you can get in. The US-led War on Terror has polarised world opinion and increased security measures for people entering the country, and that means tough, edgy times ahead for all.

✪ NEPAL
Ancient Nepal is blessed with the most spectacular scenery – the Himalayas, including the world's highest mountain, Everest.

Generations of travellers have trekked the hippy trail to here in search of action, adventure and spirituality, yet Nepal languishes among the world's poorest countries – industry is mainly agricultural and around 40% of the population live in poverty. Plus it's a bloody nation – the UN says that internal conflicts between Maoist rebels and the constitutional monarchy have killed 11,000 people in the last 10 years and displaced a further 100,000.

✪ ZIMBABWE
Reasons to be cheerful: Victoria Falls, a timeless natural marvel; bountiful wilderness with herds of antelope, buffalo, hippos and elephants; a life-affirming musical and artistic culture; the Great Zimbabwe stone enclosures, showcasing an ancient civilisation… Reasons to be horrified: Robert Mugabe; a shattered economy; widespread poverty and corruption; appalling human-rights violations, including the bulldozing of slums with people still living there; forced elections at gunpoint; unrelieved HIV/AIDS infection.

✪ NORTH KOREA
If visiting a country that remains almost completely unexploited by commercial tourism sounds attractive, North Korea beckons. The flip side of exploring this intriguing and unique culture is that you'll be travelling in a country cited by human rights organisations as having one of the worst records in the world; not that you're likely to see examples of it. From the artificial preserve of the capital, Pyongyang, to the necessity of travelling with minders of one kind or another, this country is keeping its secrets close to its chest, and frank conversation with locals is almost impossible.

✪ ISRAEL
Israel still retains a fascinating allure for many travellers; this is the storied Holy Land, after all, and Jerusalem is one of the planet's most sacred cities. Even if you think you don't know much about Israel the chances are that, subliminally, you know quite a bit: do the names Galilee, Dead Sea, Bethlehem and Jericho ring a bell? But Israel still has to sort out its blood-spattered relationship with Palestine before outsiders can feel completely safe, with bombings, shootings and protests still occurring with regularity.

✪ INDONESIA
Indonesia is another place that's hard to sum up: spread across thousands of islands, it has the world's largest Muslim population plus a diverse range of other ethnicities (including over 300 languages). It's overwhelmingly urban in parts, amazingly rural in others – seductive and compelling in short. On the reverse side Indonesia is in chaos, juggling vicious ethnic tensions, the aftermath of the Bali bombing and militant Islamic cells with alleged al-Qaeda ties, not to mention the horror of 2004's devastating tsunami and the bad PR arising from the decision to imprison Australian Schapelle Corby for importing marijuana into Bali.

✪ PAPUA NEW GUINEA
Tropical Papua New Guinea is a beautiful, rugged land that boasts rich natural resources – pristine coral reefs, spectacular volcanic regions – and a vibrant heritage and culture. Yet PNG is in dire straits after the nine-year secessionist conflict on Bougainville took 20,000 lives. Subsequent social collapse has seemingly infected the whole territory: Amnesty International reports from 2005 suggest yet more deterioration of law and order, with 'gun-related crime, inter-communal violence, provincial power struggles, reprisal killings, corruption and government mismanagement' continuing apace. This is one of the grimmest pictures around.

STARTING THEM OFF YOUNG IN MYANMAR (BURMA).

WORKERS CYCLE HOME AFTER A DAY'S WORK AT A STEEL MILL IN BAOTOU, CHINA.

TEHRAN'S SOLDIERS MARCH WITH PASSION.

✪ MYANMAR (BURMA)

#01. Myanmar is among Asia's most beautiful territories, with multitudes of Buddhist pagodas and ancient towns attracting enlightenment seekers from far and wide. But the country has been under continuous, oppressive military rule for 40 years. Savage crackdowns on the media and judicial and civil rights, along with forced labour and forced-repatriation policies, means the country is a bloody mess under the tourism veil.

✪ CHINA

#02. China these days is brash and unpredictable, bursting with creative energy and the world's fastest-growing economy. The Great Wall and the Forbidden City pack the tourists in, while the Taklamakan desert and Tibet's magnificent plateaus provide geographic thrills. But modern China's development has brought new problems – pollution, rising crime and unemployment. And China's claim to Tibet and Taiwan is a divisive, highly controversial topic, drawing bitter condemnation from human-rights groups.

✪ IRAN

#03. Breathtaking Iran is the cradle of the Persians, among history's greatest civilisations, and despite generations of turmoil, some cultural features remain remarkably intact, such as the ruins of Persepolis, the magnificent city founded by the Persian ruler Darius. On the negative side, Amnesty International reports that political prisoners and prisoners of conscience continue to languish in jail after unfair trials, human-rights defenders are constantly harassed, and the families of those under suspicion are threatened. In 2004 Iran carried out 159 executions (including one minor) and 36 floggings (with two people dying as a result); exact figures are reckoned to be much higher.

⭐ AMSTERDAM, THE NETHERLANDS

#o1. With its 17th-century housing, canals, galleries and museums (and notorious sleaze), Amsterdam is known as the 'Venice of the North'. This city features enough sensory delights to keep the shortest attention spans occupied, while the endless cafés provide havens from rampant crowds. Most attractions are within the canal belt: grand, historical neighbourhoods, the infamous Red Light District, too-kool-for-school bars, old-time pubs, graceful bridges, and eccentric churches – so do as the Dutch do and hop on a bike. With pedal power, you could see a lot in a day or two.

⭐ BARCELONA, SPAIN

#o2. Barcelona has grown to be one of the planet's most dynamic cities, perched on the bleeding edge of food, fashion, style, music and seriously good times; it's vibrant and happening all year long, although summer is peak party time with week-long fiestas and rabble-rousing till all hours. Barcelona is also the home of Gaudí and his eccentric architectural legacy, as well as significant works by Picasso and Miró; the exuberant locals will fascinate you, even if the art doesn't.

⭐ ISTANBUL, TURKEY

#o3. Straddling the Bosphorus, its skyline studded with domes and minarets, Istanbul is a continent-spanning city with all the multiplicity of experience that implies. Walk the streets where crusaders and janissaries once marched; admire sublime mosques steeped in Islamic lore; peer into the sultan's harem; or follow the bargain trails in the Grand Bazaar. Most sights are within easy walking distance of one another – perfect for the time-poor traveller on a short break in one of the world's most romantic cities.

WITH SO MANY TEMPTATIONS, BICYCLES ARE THE SAFEST WAY TO GET AROUND AMSTERDAM.

FROM FASHION TO FOOD, BARCELONA PUTS PEOPLE IN A SPIN YEAR ROUND.

A GREAT WAY TO GET AROUND ON YOUR CITY BREAK.

CLASSIC CITY
#15. BREAKS. »

✪ SINGAPORE

Singapore is overwhelmingly modern and glossy but undeniably Asian as well, boasting a grab bag of Chinese, Malay and Indian traditions. And while the city may have traded in its sleazy rickshaw-and-opium image for hi-tech and high finance, you can still immerse yourself in colonial atmospherics with a gin sling under the ceiling fans at Raffles Hotel. Coordinate your visit to coincide with Thaipusam, a Hindu purification festival held in January, featuring extreme examples of body modification; the Singapore Food Festival in April; or the Great Singapore Sale in June.

✪ BERLIN, GERMANY

Welcome to Berlin, Germany's pumping cultural heart, with its grand public buildings, glorious museums and theatres, urbane restaurants, bustling pubs and raucous nightclubs all serving as the throbbing arteries of the city. Lovers of art, architecture and artefacts will be in heaven, culture vultures will devour the city's fantastic museums, while music lovers can take their pick from opera, dance, theatre, cabaret, techno and jazz. In fact, if you can't find something to do here, without too much planning, then you might as well burn your passport now.

✪ EDINBURGH, SCOTLAND

Edinburgh is a classic city for the short-break specialist, blending ancient and modern influences into compact experiences. Pick any street, go for a stroll and what do you find? Ultramodern dance clubs in 15th-century buildings or fire breathers outside Georgian mansions. Walk a bit further and what's before you? Looming battlements, cold volcanic peaks and hills steeped in ancient lore. Edinburgh is also known as the Festival City for very good reason, but you'll need to book way ahead for the Edinburgh International Festival, held in August, one of the world's largest and most raucous arts events.

✪ PARIS, FRANCE

Ah, Paris! What is there left to say about her? Everyone knows the score: Paris, in all her glory, is full-tilt sensory overload, from romance along the Seine to Bohemian types in cafés spouting forth on film; from saucy boulevards, breathcatching monuments and staggering art to gourmet cheese, chocolate, wine and seafood; from the Bastille to the Eiffel Tower. Many of the city's most momentous sights are strung along its river, and its neighbourhoods each have their own distinct personalities, so you can pack in a lot without travelling too far.

✪ PRAGUE, CZECH REPUBLIC

Shrugging off the hangover of communism with ridiculous ease, Prague has morphed to become one of Europe's most popular tourist destinations, with a wave of gourmet restaurants, cocktail bars and trendy cafés continuing to sprout forth. There are still a number of atmospheric old pubs and eateries, though, where you can wash down a heart starter of pork and dumplings with a beer chaser. Prague's compact medieval centre hosts a maze of cobbled lanes, ancient courtyards, dark passages and a multitude of churches, all presided over by an 1100-year-old castle; seeing this array alone is enough to firmly grasp the culture of one of Europe's most beautiful cities.

✪ NEW YORK CITY, USA

If it's first-class international events and gallery openings you're after, then look no further: the Big Apple has got the flamin' lot, from world-class museums to big statues and big buildings; from hedonism and excess to class, style and a cocky vibe it's renowned for (New Yorkers are a special breed of cat and probably an attraction in themselves). Then there's the Empire State Building, Times Square, Greenwich Village, Soho; wander

IT'S ALMOST ROCK AND ROLL AND WE LIKE IT, TOKYO, JAPAN.

around them all before hopping on the Staten Island ferry to round off the ultimate Noo Yawk experience.

✪ TOKYO, JAPAN

It doesn't take long to be initiated into Tokyo's madness: the city's sheer level of energy – fuelled by consumer culture in hyper drive – rubs raw against ancient tradition. Sightseeing can either be a sensory assault that leaves you elated or an encounter with understatement that leaves you in awe; stand in the heart of Shinjuku, though, surrounded by all that neon, all those bizarre fashions, and you might think you've stepped onto an alien planet. Alternatively, jump aboard the subway and see how this seething metropolis is really a city within a city within a city within a city…

✪ KERALA COAST, INDIA

#o1.
Beachy types generally don't hop up and down with glee when India is mentioned, but those in the know are enraptured. Tucked in among India's 600km-long (373mi) Kerala coast is a string of coconut-palm-fringed beaches adjoining lulling surf and the bluest waters. There are the larger resorts, like Kovalam, but also many more unspoilt delights where your hammock will be overworked as you gaze at rub-your-eyes-raw semicircular bays or expanses of sand that are so long you'll think they're a mirage. Thrillingly, there'll be no-one else around to pinch you and tell you you're dreaming.

✪ ISLA MUJERES, MEXICO

#o2.
This tiny unpretentious island, just 7km (4.5mi) long and barely 1km (0.6mi) wide, is offshore from Cancún and light years away from that glitzy mainland scene; its tropical beaches make it a cult fave, with those on the south side a big hit for their calm turquoise waters (the island itself blocks out the stronger wind currents). If you fancy get-on-down Caribbean fun, try Playa Norte, a very popular beach featuring roving waiters who will bring drinks to your spot on the sand; otherwise, more secluded options include Playa Paraiso and Playa Indios.

✪ JAMBIANI, TANZANIA

#o3.
Here's the Beach that Time Forgot, where men in fishing dhows set sail at sunset for the reefs, women gather seaweed daily, and people like you constantly boil to a crisp under the baking sun. There's not much to do (certainly not swimming; tides are low) except loll about and crack open a few coconuts. Remember: you're in Zanzibar, Mythical Africa, so just kick back and drink it (or your coconut milk) in.

BEST BEACHES TO SWING A
#16. HAMMOCK.

✪ KAI ISLANDS, INDONESIA

A growing chorus says these remote white-sand beaches are the finest in the world. Development has been slow around the Kai archipelago, so they remain unspoilt and as nature intended. If you're not big on pristine powdery sands, azure seas, rare and varicoloured birds frolicking, arresting fish and wondrous coral reefs then stay away.

✪ CURONIAN SPIT, LITHUANIA

This 98km (60mi) lick of sand is a wondrous mixture of dunes (some as high as 200m, 655ft) and forest – the smell of pine will impart an otherworldly quality to your hammock time. Wilhelm von Humboldt believed that a trip to the Curonian Spit was essential nourishment for the soul, and Thomas Mann was also drawn to this timeless wonderland; it's said that around 14 villages are buried under the endless, shifting dunes, making the Spit a kind of Baltic Sahara. You won't believe your eyes.

✪ DAHAB, EGYPT

'Dahab' means 'gold' in Arabic – a name given to the area because of its golden sands – and with a unique location on the edge of the Sinai desert, Dahab certainly remains an untapped treasure; budget accommodation almost on the beach means you can virtually roll out of your sleeping bag and into the water. Backed by mountain ranges, Dahab's Bedouin settlement, Assalah, is a favoured beach-bum haunt, with unspoilt charm and chilled beachside cafés, while up the coast are favoured and famous diving spots.

✪ PULAU PERHENTIAN, MALAYSIA

The palm-fringed beaches of the Perhentian Islands, covered in tropical rainforest, are about as naturalistic as they come: calm, hassle free and with virtually no signs of commercialism. Except for snorkelling, diving, frolicking, swimming, sunning your body or pretending you're either Brooke Shields or Christopher Atkins in the *Blue Lagoon,* there's nothing to do.

✪ PUNALU'U, USA

Hawai'i's black-sand wonderland has won a few 'best beach' awards in recent times, and it's truly an astonishing sight: Punalu'u's startling blue waters lap up against the jet-black beach, backed by rows of deep-green coconut palms. This is one place where your hammock will really come in handy – it's scenery that demands your constant, supine contemplation – and you might even spot a hawksbill turtle wandering onto the sand to lay its eggs. Don't touch them, though – they're an endangered species, vulnerable to bacteria, and who knows where your filthy hands have been.

✪ NORTH STRADBROKE ISLAND, AUSTRALIA

Straddie is among the world's largest sand islands – and 'sand' equals 'beach', right? So far, so good. The Queensland island's 30km (19mi) white-sand Main Beach is backed by an expanse of dunes, which makes it popular with four-wheel drives, but there are a number of more secluded spots around Point Lookout that are free of machinery. Here, the only thing to do is surf and sun yourself, perhaps paddling in the rock pools infested with marine life, or watching a mob of whales or some unique Aussie animals bounding away into the bushland.

✪ KO PHA-NGAN, THAILAND

A lovely island, with mostly deserted beaches that are perfect for solitude lovers and lovesick couples... except for Hat Rin, which holds its famous full-moon parties every month, perfect for hedonists and pleasure seekers. The twin beaches of Thong Nai Pan are a favourite of the Thai royals, which probably explains why development has been kept at bay; they're surrounded by coconut trees and mountains and the bliss is so overwhelming as to be almost *(almost)* unbearable.

DIZZYING HEIGHTS AND DIZZYING SIGHTS ALONG THE KHUMBU ICEFALL, APPROACHING MT EVEREST.

✪ EVEREST BASE CAMP, NEPAL

#o1. Reaching a height of 5545m (18,193ft) at Kala Pattar, this three-week trek is extremely popular with those who want to be able to say, 'I've been to the base of the world's highest mountain'. The difficult trek passes undeniably spectacular scenery and is trafficked by Sherpa people of the Solu Khumbu. The heights reached during this trek are literally dizzying until you acclimatise to the altitude, and the continuous cutting across valleys certainly has its ups and downs.

✪ INCA TRAIL, PERU

#o2. This 33km (20mi) ancient trail was laid by the Incas and is currently traversed by thousands each year. The trail leads from the Sacred Valley to Machu Picchu winding its way up and down and around the mountains, taking three high passes en route. Views of white-tipped mountains and high cloud forest combine with the magic of walking from one cliff-hugging ruin to the next – understandably making this South America's most famous trail.

✪ GR20, FRANCE

#o3. This demanding 15-day (168km, 104mi) slog through Corsica is legendary for the diversity of landscapes it traverses. There are forests, granite moonscapes, windswept craters, glacial lakes, torrents, peat bogs, maquis, snow-capped peaks, plains and névés (stretches of ice formed from snow). But it doesn't come easy: the path is rocky and sometimes steep, and includes rickety bridges and slippery rock faces – all part of the fun. Created in 1972, the GR20 links Calenzana, in the Balagne, with Conca, north of Porto Vecchio.

MOST AWESOME
#17.TREKS.

✪ PAYS DOGON, MALI

'The land of the Dogon people' is one of Africa's most breathtaking regions. A trek here can last anywhere between two and 10 days, and takes in the soaring cliffs of the Bandiagara escarpment inlaid with old abandoned cliff dwellings. Dogon villages dot the cliffs and are an extraordinary highlight of the journey. The Dogon are known for their masked stilt dancers, intricately carved doors and pueblo-like dwellings built into the side of the escarpment.

✪ INDIAN HIMALAYAS, INDIA

Fewer folk trek on the Indian side of the world's greatest mountain range. So, if isolation's your thing try trekking in Himachal Pradesh. Hardcore hikers can try teetering along the mountain tops for 24 days from Spiti to Ladakh. This extremely remote and challenging walk follows ancient trade routes. The bleak high-altitude desert terrain inspired Rudyard Kipling to exclaim, 'Surely the gods live here; this is no place for men'.

✪ OVERLAND TRACK, AUSTRALIA

Tasmania's prehistoric-looking wilderness is most accessible on the 80km (50mi, five- to six-day) Overland Track. Snaking its way between Cradle Mountain and Lake St Clair (Australia's deepest natural freshwater lake), the well-defined path (boardwalked in parts) passes craggy mountains, beautiful lakes and tarns, extensive forests and moorlands. Those who want more can take numerous side walks leading to waterfalls, valleys and still more summits including Mt Ossa (1617m, 5305ft) – Tassie's highest.

✪ ROUTEBURN TRACK, NEW ZEALAND

See the stunning subalpine scenery of New Zealand's South Island surrounding this medium three-day (32km, 20mi) track. At the base of New Zealand's Southern Alps, the track passes through two national parks: Fiordland and Mt Aspiring. Highlights include the views from Harris Saddle and atop Conical Hill – from where you can see waves breaking on the distant beach. The main challenge for this popular hike is actually securing a place among the limited numbers who are allowed on the track at any time.

✪ THE NARROWS, USA

A 26km (16mi) journey through dramatic canyons carved over centuries by the Virgin River, the Narrows in Zion National Park is a hike like no other. The route is the river, with over half of the hike spent wading and sometimes swimming. The hike can be traversed in a day, though some choose to take the hanging gardens and natural springs at a more leisurely pace – spending a night at one of the park's 12 camp grounds.

✪ THE HAUTE ROUTE, FRANCE– SWITZERLAND

Leading from Chamonix in France through the southern Valais to Zermatt in Switzerland, the Haute Route traverses some of the highest and most scenic country accessible to walkers anywhere in the Alps. The summer Haute Route walk (which takes a different course than the more famous winter ski-touring route) takes around two weeks to complete. It mainly involves 'pass hopping' and demands a high level of fitness, with every section containing a high huff factor.

PORTERS CARRY THE LOAD OVER THE BALTORO GLACIER IN KARAKORAM, PAKISTAN.

✪ BALTORO GLACIER & K2, PAKISTAN

This corridor of ice leads to the colossal peak of K2 (8611m, 28,251ft), the world's second-highest peak. This incomparable trek traverses some of the most humbling scenery on the planet. What begins following icy rivers boldly goes to the guts of the glacier before leading to the granite pyramidal mountains including Paiju (6610m, 21,686ft), Uli Biaho (6417m, 21,053ft), Great Trango Tower (6286m, 20,623ft) and ultimately K2. If the 15 days doesn't floor you, take side trips to more moraine-covered glaciers.

BEST ROAD
#18.TRIPS.

SOME THINGS DON'T CHANGE, YOU CAN STILL GET YOUR KICKS...

✪ ROUTE 66, USA

You can still get your kicks by driving on Route 66. Best travelled in an old Pontiac or Chevrolet, the 4000km (2500mi) cruise from Chicago to California, via Kansas, Texas and Arizona, will take you back in time. Of course you'll be subsisting on burgers, fries and pieces of pie (pronounced 'pahr'), and sippin' soda from a paper cup. Affectionately known as Main Street, USA, or the Mother Road, the ol' matriarch is gradually being superseded. Though muscled out by newer interstate highways, her legend will never be replaced.

✪ CABOT TRAIL, CAPE BRETON ISLAND, CANADA

In Nova Scotia, on Canada's east coast, the Cabot Trail (298km/185mi) loops around the northern tip of Cape Breton Island. There are plenty of opportunities to stretch your legs along the way. The Cape Breton Highlands National Park runs alongside the trail, with loads of walks. Whale-watching is a popular pastime in these parts, so pack your binoculars. The Cabot Trail is easily traversable and dotted with villages in which to regroup.

✪ SOUTH ISLAND'S WEST COAST, NEW ZEALAND

From the artful environs of Nelson, head south to the country's southern tip. Along the way you'll pass memorable Westport, which accesses the fabulous caverns of Oparara Basin. Other highlights include the dulcet attractions of Milford and Doubtful Sounds. Milford is a calm 22km-long (14mi) fiord dominated by sheer, weather-scuffed peaks attracting more than 14,000 visitors annually. By contrast, Doubtful Sound sees less traffic and sports an equally magnificent wilderness area of rugged peaks, dense forest and thundering post-rain waterfalls.

✪ AMSTERDAM, THE NETHERLANDS, TO ISTANBUL, TURKEY

As the crow flies it's around 2200km (1350mi), but 'as the car drives' the kilometres are innumerable. It depends how many of the dozen or so counties that cluster on either side of the route you choose to visit. You'll almost certainly pass through Germany, Czech Republic, Slovakia, Hungary, Romania and Bulgaria to get to Turkey. That's a lot of different road rules, road conditions and 'I Spy' games.

✪ DELHI TO AGRA, INDIA

If you're game enough to tackle the manic Indian roads, then this is the trip for you. (PS: you can also hire a driver so you can sit back and enjoy the ride.) The trip leaves the capital, which is a confusing tangle of 12.8 million people and the gateway to the rest of the country. Head southeast for 240km (150mi) and you'll be rewarded by reaching Agra – synonymous with the stunning Taj Mahal.

✪ COASTAL HIGHLANDS, SCOTLAND

Single-track roads hem Scotland's astonishingly beautiful west coast. From the long sea lochs and glacier-gouged valleys flooded by sea in the south, through the central coastal plain shouldered by magnanimous mountains, to the serried edges of the wild north, traversing the Scottish coast is a bonny journey. Castles are part of the scenery and plenty of pretty villages make perfect pit stops. This is whisky country too – making a most rewarding swill at the end of a day's driving.

✪ CAPE TOWN TO HERMANUS, SOUTH AFRICA

This southern coastal strip hugs charming seaside villages and envelops some inimitable South African natural wonders. Once you've taken in colourful Cape Town – skirted by vineyards and beaches – head east along False Bay. The 122km (75mi) stretch to Hermanus is within day-tripping distance, but worthy of a slow drive. A number of nature reserves include wetland areas (hippo territory), as well as sweeping beaches. Once in Hermanus, you can stop watching the road and start watching the whales that can be seen mucking around offshore between June and November.

POINT STRAIGHT AHEAD AND
SEE YOU IN A YEAR.

KEEP YOUR EYES ON THE
AMALFI COAST.

THE LONG, WINDING AND LONELY
ROAD TO SIWA, EGYPT.

⭐ EAST COAST, AUSTRALIA

#o1. Lined with stunning beaches and dotted with superb national parks, this classic route covers three diverse states. Victoria features the cosmopolitan city of Melbourne, as well the farming areas and out-of-the-way wilderness of the state's southeast. Stunning Sydney oozes capital consumerism before giving way to the hippy havens further north. And Las Vegas comes Down Under once you hit Queensland – although its real beauty lies with its tropical coast. Excellent roads make the kilometres easy companions.

⭐ AMALFI COAST, ITALY

#o2. Stretching 50km (30mi) east from Sorrento to Salerno, the stunning views along the Amalfi Coast (Costiera Amalfitana) demand your attention – making it difficult to keep your eyes on the road. The narrow ribbon of asphalt winds along cliffs that drop to crystal-clear blue waters and passes the beautiful towns of Positano and Amalfi. To drive the coast can be a nail-biting exercise, as bus drivers nonchalantly edge their way around hairpin bends. In summer it becomes one long traffic jam – allowing plenty of time to take in those views.

⭐ CAPE TOWN, SOUTH AFRICA, TO CAIRO, EGYPT

#o3. The ultimate adventure, you should allow at least 10 weeks for this African odyssey. Starting in cosmopolitan Cape Town, the journey heads through 11 countries and includes some stunning road stops. As if Victoria Falls, Mt Kilimanjaro and the Nubian Desert with the world's biggest sand dunes weren't enough, this mammoth stretch is also home to many species of African wildlife. Road conditions are dire, and an independent overland road trip bursts off the 'difficult' radar.

⊛ TRANS-SIBERIAN, RUSSIA TO CHINA

#o1. The classic Trans-Siberian service runs from Moscow's Yaroslavl Station across a third of the globe to the crumbling charm of Vladivostock. It memorably skirts Lake Baikal that seemingly appears out of nowhere in the middle of the Siberian taiga. Veering off the main line, the Trans-Mongolian continues past Russian gingerbread houses and stands of forest before giving way to the endless steppe and sky of Mongolia. The train trundles ever onward to Beijing, passing the spectacular Great Wall. Whether you take one week or 10, this is an epic trip.

⊛ COPPER CANYON RAILWAY, MEXICO

#o2. The Ferrocarril Chihuahua al Pacifico (Copper Canyon Railway) features 36 bridges and 87 tunnels along its 655km (407mi) length. Connecting the mountainous arid interior of northern Mexico with the Pacific coast, the railway line passes through landscapes that include sheer canyon walls, waterfalls and high desert plains. Two trains operate on this route between Los Mochis and Chihuahua: the *primera express* (first class) has a restaurant, bar and reclining seats and makes fewer stops than the *clase economica* (economy class).

⊛ ROCKY MOUNTAINEER, CANADA

#o3. This two-day tour through the magnificent Canadian Rockies is done in daylight, so you can see every dazzling canyon, each inspiring river and all its verdant valleys and glittering glacial lakes. Departing from coastal Vancouver, press your face up to the glass to view the spectacular mountains of British Columbia. Then the essence of the Rockies takes shape out the window as you pass Jasper or Banff and Calgary before pulling in to Alberta.

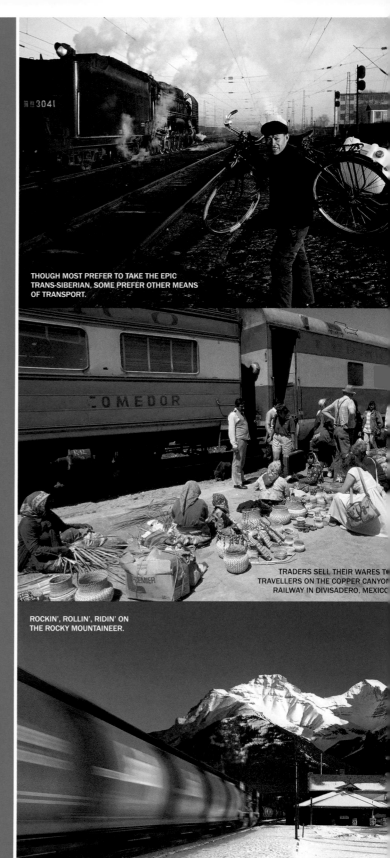

THOUGH MOST PREFER TO TAKE THE EPIC TRANS-SIBERIAN, SOME PREFER OTHER MEANS OF TRANSPORT.

TRADERS SELL THEIR WARES TO TRAVELLERS ON THE COPPER CANYON RAILWAY IN DIVISADERO, MEXICO

ROCKIN', ROLLIN', RIDIN' ON THE ROCKY MOUNTAINEER.

CLASSIC TRAIN
#19.TRIPS.

✪ VENICE SIMPLON-ORIENT EXPRESS, ITALY

Glamour pusses, this train trip is guaranteed to keep you purring all the way from Venice to London. Luxury abounds, from the sumptuously fitted dining car (with French silverware, linen-dressed tables and crystal glassware) to the piano-bar car – you'll need to pack your gowns and tuxedos. Ladies, Manolo Blahnik heels are perfect for teetering around Europe's most romantic cities: Vienna, Paris, Prague and Istanbul – all of which the *Orient* graces with its presence.

✪ OLD PATAGONIA EX-PRESS, ARGENTINA

It averages 35km/h, so calling it *'Express'* is something of a misnomer. Better known as *La Trochita,* this historic rattler steams its way 402km (250mi) from Esquel to Ingeniero Jacobacci, with half a dozen stations and another nine *apeaderos* (whistle-stops). From the little windows in your wooden cabin (c 1920), you can see the Chilean Andes, which parallel the southern leg of the journey, alleviating great expanses of nothingness. The narrow-gauge section of the track is 1m (3.3ft) wide and dates from 1922.

✪ OUTENIQUA CHOO-TJOE, SOUTH AFRICA

In operation since 1928, this quaintly named steam train chugs at a leisurely pace. From Knysna it huffs along the Indian Ocean coast, past the town of Wilderness with its vast sweeping beaches, crosses Kaimans Bridge and then choofs up the steep gorge to George. The return trip takes about 7½ hours, with stunning scenery that makes a cliché out of that old saying about enjoying the journey.

✪ CUSCO TO PUNO, PERU

Billed as a bit of a bone shaker, this 10-hour ride travels between the capital Cusco and Puno on the banks of Lake Titicaca. The high altitude around the lake makes for exceptionally clear air, and the luminescent quality of the sunlight suffuses the highland Altiplano and sparkles on the deep waters of the lake. At the other end of the journey, Cusco is a unique combination of colonial and religious splendour built on the hefty stone foundations of the Incas.

✪ COAST STARLIGHT, USA

Traversing America's west coast, the *Starlight* pulls in to some of the States' great cities: Seattle, Portland and Los Angeles.

A SPECTACULAR SLICE BETWEEN GEORGE AND KNYSNA, SOUTH AFRICA.

The trip takes a mere 35 hours to negotiate three states: Washington, Oregon and California. Modern conveniences make the hours pass even more quickly, including various comfort levels of accommodation, a dining car and lounge with on-board entertainment. But the window is likely to provide the most exhilarating entertainment as the train passes humbling mountains and vast oceanscapes.

EL NARIZ DEL DIABLO, ECUADOR

Heading south from Riobamba, the death-defying section of track known as El Nariz del Diablo (Devil's Nose) runs from Alausí to Sibambe. Construction began in 1908; at Sibambe a series of switchbacks were carved into the steep Andean rock to allow the train to ascend nearly 1000m (3280ft) to Alausí which sits at 2607m (6554ft). Some daredevils descend the 'Devil's Nose' standing on the train's flat roof, with nary a gap between their sombreros and the top of the tunnel.

✪ GHAN, AUSTRALIA

The saga that is the *Ghan* started in 1877 when the original railway line from Adelaide via Alice Springs to Darwin was laid – in the wrong place. This initial century-old stretch of line ran straight through a flood plain, resulting in frequent outback strandings after rain. In 1980 a new service on a different line made the run – replacing the old *Ghan*, which made its last journey in '82. The great *Ghan* cuts through Australia's remote Red Centre, its tropical north and gentle south.

✪ JULES VERNE: *AROUND THE WORLD IN EIGHTY DAYS*

#o1. Follow in the fictional footsteps of Phileas Fogg who travelled around the late-Victorian world in less than three months. Published in 1872, *Around the World in Eighty Days* was Jules Verne's ode to the technological advancements of the 19th century. So, limiting the journey to rail, steamer and...er...elephant, your itinerary follows, and your time starts...now: London to Suez to Bombay to Calcutta to Hong Kong to Yokohama to San Francisco to New York and London.

✪ GENGHIS KHAN

#o2. Born in the 13th century, Genghis Khan's superior military intelligence was responsible for uniting the tribes of Central Asia to form the formidable Mongol Empire (1266–1368). He made his conquering way from Mongolia to Beijing, eastern China, western China and finally Russia. If you are going to try to follow this ruthless historical leader, try to restrain from slaughtering 30 million people along the way – the estimated number of people to have died during the Empire's reign.

✪ IBN BATTUTAH

#o3. Born in Morocco in 1304, Battutah was a scholar and jurisprudent. At the age of 20 he set off on a pilgrimage to Mecca, and kept on travelling for almost 30 years. His published account of his travels, called the *Rihla,* tells of travels covering 120,700km (75,000mi) taking in the entire Muslim world and beyond, including 44 modern-day countries. Lost to the world for centuries, the *Rihla* was rediscovered in the 1800s and translated into several European languages. So, grab yourself a copy, set aside the next 30 years and bon voyage.

GREAT HISTORICAL
#20. JOURNEYS.

⭐ INCA TRAIL

Originally laid during the Inca Empire (1438–1533), this ancient trail in Peru is a clearly defined trek spanning 33km (20mi) leading up to the 'Lost City of the Incas' – better known as Machu Picchu. The trail passes through high cloud forest and hugs the mountainside before spilling into the ancient secret city, believed to be used as a weekend retreat for Inca royalty. It's breathtaking stuff – and not just due to the altitude (2350m or 7710ft).

⭐ CHARLES DARWIN: *VOYAGE OF THE BEAGLE*

The British naturalist set sail on a five-year odyssey aboard the HMS *Beagle* to observe and document the natural environment. His *Journal and Remarks* was published in 1839 and popularly known as the *Voyage of Beagle*. He travelled to South America, the Galápagos Islands, Tahiti and Australia before heading home again via the Keeling Islands. His notes on biology, geology and anthropology are, in hindsight, the precursors to his ideas of evolution.

⭐ EVELYN WAUGH: *LABELS*

Between marriages, the English satirical novelist Evelyn Waugh travelled restlessly. His cruise through the Mediterranean resulted in the book *Labels* (1930) – republished as part of a compendium called *When the Going Was Good* (1945). Stops in Malta, Cairo, Naples and Constantinople (Istanbul) are less of a feature as are his wry observations, including middle-aged widows excited by advertising copy and ambiguous praise for Gaudí's architecture in Barcelona. The real destination here is cutting satire, so remember to pack your wit.

⭐ ALEXANDER THE GREAT

Deemed 'Great' by some and 'Grotesque' by others, Alexander III was probably the most successful military commander of the an cient world. His conquests took him and his armies from Greece to India across 16 countries. Alexander's period of conquests spanned almost a decade and included the defeat of the Persian Empire and invasion of India. And he did so on a magic horse, between untangling mythical puzzles, losing friends and lovers, and variously being declared a god and a destroyer.

⭐ LEWIS & CLARK

To follow these two intrepid Americans across the West you'll need to assemble a party of about 30 men, steel yourself to cut off some of their frostbitten toes and get ready to encounter bears and buffaloes – just some of the fun that Meriwether Lewis and William Clark encountered on their three-year trip (1803–06) to explore the vast lands west of the Mississippi. The real point of the journey was to 'introduce' themselves to the Native American population, who were less than impressed with their offerings of beads, thimbles and brass curtain rings.

⭐ MARCO POLO

Travel was in the blood for Marco Polo (1254–1324), whose father was also a well-known explorer. Born in Venice, Marco sailed along the west coast of Greece to Turkey, and followed the Silk Road through the Middle East and Central Asia to China. There is some speculation as to the extent of Marco's travels (which he put at over 39,000km or 24,000mi), with sceptics accusing him to be something of a fibber. Were they just jealous?

⭐ BURKE & WILLS

This ill-fated journey to cross the then unexplored Australian continent eventually led Robert Burke and William Wills to their deaths. The well-equipped expedition departed Melbourne in August 1860 and hurried north in an attempt to claim the financial reward offered by the Victorian government to the first team to cross the continent. The expedition reached its destination – Normanton in the Gulf of Carpentaria; however, the team perished (malnutrition) in Cooper's Creek on the return journey in June 1861. The 'dig tree' inscribed with a message from one of the expedition's members is still visible at Inniminka.

⊛ TAJ MAHAL, INDIA

#01. This beauty was 23 years in the making (1630–53) and is remarkable for its perfect symmetry. The Taj was commissioned by Emperor Shah Jahan as a mausoleum for his wife, Arjumand Banu Begum (also known as Mumtaz Mahal). Made from white marble, this majestic mausoleum features intricate details that were inlaid with precious lapis lazuli – pilfered in the 19th century. Its exterior reflects the changing colours of the day, and its beauty on a full-moon night is legendary.

⊛ GREAT PYRAMID OF GIZA, EGYPT

#02. For the Egyptian pharaoh Khufu, back in 2560 BC, the notion of digging your own grave transposed elaborately into constructing the Great Pyramid. Around two million stone blocks, each weighing 2 tonnes, were brought together to serve as his tomb. The Great Pyramid is the planet's original tourist attraction – counting Antony (Cleopatra's beau) and Napoleon among its many early visitors – and keeps company with three other pyramids and that other illustrious attraction, the Sphinx.

⊛ GREAT WALL, CHINA

#03. Hordes hit the Wall, as they have for centuries. Built from the end of the 15th century to the start of the 16th (using an existing wall dating back 2000 years), it stretches an incredible 6350km (3946m). Though not really visible from space, its jagged, snaking presence across the mountains between China and Mongolia always impresses, and is a tribute to the manic energy we apply to systems of war and defence. The touristed parts of Badaling are not recommended; try instead a walk from Simatai to Jinshanling.

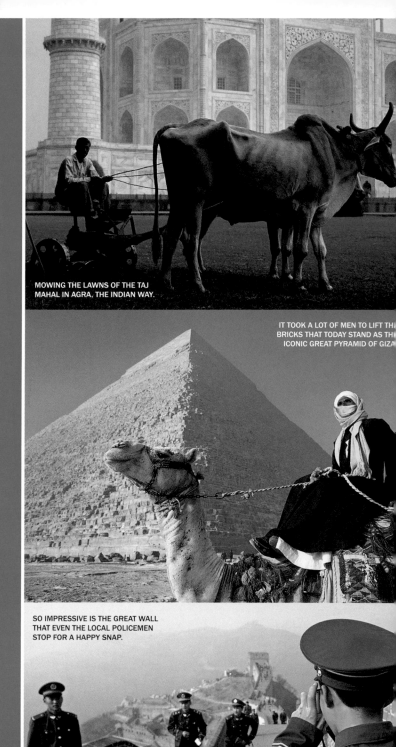

MOWING THE LAWNS OF THE TAJ MAHAL IN AGRA, THE INDIAN WAY.

IT TOOK A LOT OF MEN TO LIFT THE BRICKS THAT TODAY STAND AS THE ICONIC GREAT PYRAMID OF GIZA

SO IMPRESSIVE IS THE GREAT WALL THAT EVEN THE LOCAL POLICEMEN STOP FOR A HAPPY SNAP.

MOST ICONIC MAN-MADE
#21. STRUCTURES. »

✪ EIFFEL TOWER, FRANCE

How many electricians does it take to change a light bulb on the Eiffel Tower? A whole team is required to maintain the 10,000-odd light bulbs that illuminate the 324m (1060ft) tower. Built in 1889 for the Universal Exhibition and to celebrate the French Revolution, Paris' tower was designed by Stephen Sauvestre and was named after Gustave Eiffel – who specialised in iron construction including the Statue of Liberty and portable bridges sold around the world in kits.

✪ CHRYSLER BUILDING, USA

Architect William van Alen planned the dramatic unveiling of New York City's Chrysler Building's ornate tower by assembling it inside the building. Made of stainless steel and modelled on the hubcaps used on Chrysler cars of the late 1920s, the completed spire was hoisted into position in 1½ hours. Completed in 1930, the Art Deco building's 77 floors and ornamental top made it the world's highest structure – not just scraping the sky but piercing it at 319m (1046ft).

✪ BIG BEN, ENGLAND

'Big Ben' is the common name for the Palace of Westminster's clock and bell tower in London, and speculation reigns as to just which Benjamin was big enough to give his name to it. Perhaps it was Ben Hall, the Chief Commissioner of Works when it was built in 1888. Or maybe Ben Caunt, a heavyweight prizefighter – in reference to the heavyweight bell within: 13.76 tonnes. The tower has a slight lean – approx 22cm (8.7in) northwest – due to ground conditions.

✪ MACHU PICCHU, PERU

The 'Lost City of the Incas', Machu Picchu (literally 'old peak') sits at a lofty elevation of 2350m (7710ft) and is invisible from below. The secret city contains the ruins of palaces, baths and temples, and is believed to have served as a country retreat for Inca royalty. Rediscovered in 1911, construction of this ancient city is thought to have started in around 1440. Partly constructed without mortar, the precise joins won't allow even a credit card between them.

✪ MOUNT RUSHMORE, USA

In the Black Hills of South Dakota, this massive monument marks the first 150 years of American history. Carved into a mountain face are the 18m (60ft) faces of four former presidents: Washington, Jefferson, Lincoln and Roosevelt. The brainchild of Doane Robinson, the original concept was to immortalise figures of American folklore. Sculptor Gutzon Borglum (a student of a Rodin) thought devoting his life's work to folklore too trivial – hence the resulting busts, built between 1927 and 1941.

✪ STONEHENGE, ENGLAND

No-one knows exactly why these 50-tonne stones were dragged from South Wales 5000 years ago. What we do know is that it would have taken about 600 people to move one more than half an inch, and that the complex was constructed between 2500 BC and 2000 BC. Consisting of a ring of stones topped by lintels, an inner horseshoe, an outer circle and a ditch, Stonehenge likely had dual astrological and religious purposes.

ANGKOR WAT, CAMBODIA'S ANSWER TO THE HEAVENS ON EARTH.

✪ ANGKOR WAT, CAMBODIA

This temple complex, built early in the 12th century by a succession of Khmer kings, formed part of a larger administrative and religious centre. Built to honour the Hindu god Vishnu and abandoned in the 15th century, many of the stone structures have since been grasped by giant banyan tree roots or covered by the surrounding forest. Apparently the layout of the temples architecturally mirrors the constellation Draco in 10,500 BC to harmonise the earth and the stars.

THE WORLD'S BEST BOOZE AND WHERE
#22.TO DRINK IT. »

ABSINTHE IS SAID TO HAVE OPIUM-LIKE EFFECTS – TRY IT IF YOU'RE GAME.

✪ ABSINTHE, CZECH REPUBLIC

For instant bohemian, just add water. But ensure you add it a drop at a time through a sugar cube on a spoon placed over the glass of absinthe. This turns the emerald green 140-proof liquor a cloudy opalescent colour. Bohemians also burn sugar into their absinth to mellow its bitter anise flavour. Made from wormwood, fennel and anise, the 'Green Fairy' has opium-like effects – the inspiration for many artists such as Van Gogh, Ernest Hemingway and Oscar Wilde. Banned in European countries during the early 19th century, governments now limit the level of *thujone* (an ingredient in absinthe likened to cannabis' THC).

✪ BURGUNDY WINE, FRANCE

The sought-after wines of Burgundy (Bourgogne) possess particular qualities attributable to the region's 400 soil types. White Burgundy is essentially a chardonnay, with an added depth and delicacy courtesy of the limestone soil in which it's grown, while red Burgundy is a gutsy pinot noir. To be classified 'Burgundy', the wine must be produced within the recognised region of the AOC (Appellation d'Origine Contrôlée) in the Côte d'Or. The region's vineyards were originally entirely owned by the Church, then divided up among workers according to Napoleonic Inheritance Laws.

✪ CAIPIROSKA, BRAZIL

This simple three-step cocktail is composed of vodka, limes and sugar. In a short glass, muddle fresh limes with two teaspoons of sugar, add loads of crushed ice and then pour a good-quality vodka over the lot. This is of course the vodka version of the popularly known *caipirinha*, made with rum. Though native to Brazil, you should be able to walk into many bars around the world and ask for one by name.

✪ BECHEROVKA, CZECH REPUBLIC

Only two people know the secret recipe to produce this all-natural liquor (36% alcohol volume). The 'chosen few' are the only ones allowed into the 'Drogikamr' where many herbs and spices are combined, placed in a sack, then steeped in alcohol for a week. The mixture is then combined with water and sugar and placed in oak barrels for two months. No-one can agree on a definitive flavour, but it's traditionally served chilled, as a digestive. In 2007, Becherovka turns 200. Cheers.

✪ GEORGE DICKEL TENNESSEE WHISKY, USA

Back in 1870, ole George Dickel reckoned his whiskey resembles a scotch whisky, and so adopted that spelling (dropping the 'e') for his special brand. He also discovered that whiskey made in winter was smoother, so added a lengthy cooling step to the production process to distinguish his drop. He also refined a special combination of mashed corn, barley and rye to use as base ingredients. Double-distilled and aged in charred white-oak barrels for up to 12 years, Dickel Tennessee Whisky (40% to 45% alcohol volume) is a very fine drop.

✪ TEQUILA, MEXICO

Made from the hearts of blue agave plants grown in Mexico's Tequila region, tequila measures between 70 and 110 proof. This classic spirit is hit-the-wall stuff. Usually clear and transparent, other varieties include those that are aged or rested in oak casks. It's best served at room temperature and sipped slowly. Only gringos do the salt-and-lemon slammer, although some folk add lemon to their glass. All tequilas are mescals (made from agave plants), but only true tequila is 100% blue agave.

✪ VODKA, POLAND

As one of the countries that saw the genesis of vodka, Poland produces dozens of varieties. Made from starch (usually rye or potato) and alcohol, pure vodka is clear, filtered and refined. This versatile spirit, in its purest form, is considered neutral, and has little or no hangover effects – dependent on your consumption levels of course. Large-scale production of vodka began in Poland in the 16th century, becoming a major export from the 17th century. Probably Poland's best-known vodka, Zubrovka (40% alcohol volume), is infused with bison grass.

SAKE IS BEST SERVED WITH FRIENDS – HOT TUB OPTIONAL.

GUINNESS IS AS IRISH AS CLOVERS, LEPRECHAUNS AND YER MAN PADDY HIMSELF.

THE TRAPPIST MONKS HAVE BOUGHT BEER JOY TO PEOPLE FOR CENTURIES.

✪ SAKE, JAPAN

#o1. Called *nihonshu* in Japan, sake is a rice wine with an alcohol content of 15% to 17%. Prior to the first sake brewery being established at Kyoto's Imperial Palace in the 7th century, sake was consumed in a form that resembled porridge, with the rice primed for production by the chew-in-the-mouth method. There are more than 1600 brewers of this almost transparent alcohol, with varieties ranging from sweet to crisp and fragrantly fruity. Serving sake slightly chilled generally brings out its best qualities.

✪ GUINNESS, IRELAND

#o2. It takes 119.5 seconds to pour the perfect pint. The famous 'surge and settle' should be executed in a two-part pour, served at 6°C (43°F). But the malt-and-caramel-flavoured dark body (actually ruby coloured, rather than black) with a creamy head is worth getting right. Based in Dublin, the Guinness brew is a malt-heavy porter (dark, sweet ale brewed from black malt) – so called because it was the favourite beverage of porters.

✪ BEER, BELGIUM

#o3. Someone once said: 'beauty is in the eye of the beer holder'; if that's the case, then Belgium is exquisite. It produces around 450 varieties of beer, with a specifically shaped glass for each, and some world-renowned brews. The Trappist dark ales were first brewed by monks who fled France after the Napoleonic period. The best-known of them is Chimay – served in a gobletlike glass. Hoegaarden is a fine example of Belgian Witbier (white), distinguished by its pale golden colour, extra fizz, sediment and hint of herbs, such as coriander.

WITHIN AN INCH OF HIS...LIFE. A CLOSE CALL FOR THIS MATADOR KEEPING THE 'ART' OF BULLFIGHTING ALIVE.

SOUTH AMERICAN GUSTO FOR FOOTBALL IS CLOSER TO MANIA THAN PASSION

THERE'S NO WAY OUT OF HERE BUT DOWN.

⭐ BULLFIGHTING, SPAIN

#01. It's been going on since the middle of the 18th century, which guarantees it a place on the 'culturally significant' shelf, but there are increasingly vociferous calls for the 'art' of bullfighting to be left on the shelf permanently. Aficionados see past the lack of competition in each bull being physically impaired before a performance and being pitted against a team of spear-wielding humans, preferring to focus on the skill and bravery presented by a matador's fancy footwork. There are 400 bullrings throughout Spain – testament to this enduring tradition.

⭐ FOOTBALL, SOUTH AMERICA

#02. The national passion in every South American country, nothing unites South Americans more than football. Brazil carries the record for the winning the most World Cup finals, and Brazilian fans are not shy of showing their support – beating drums, singing and dancing in the stalls. One of football's legends is Brazilian-born Edson Arantes Nascimento (Pelé). The annual championship is the Copa Libertadores: a continent-wide competition played in odd-numbered years.

⭐ BIG-WAVE SURFING, HAWAI'I

#03. Hawai'i lies smack in the path of all major swells that surge across the Pacific. Even in ancient times, when the waves were up, everyone in Hawai'i was out in the water. Today, winter swells can bring in immense 10m (30ft) waves and create conditions in which legends are made. Oahu especially is notorious for its powerful waves. Mother Nature's colossal surf commands respect, and tackling these waves demands a fair share of skill and gumption.

MOST ICONIC SPORTING
#23. EVENTS.

✪ AUSTRALIAN FOOTBALL LEAGUE (AFL) GRAND FINAL, AUSTRALIA

Melbourne turns to mayhem for that one day in September when the two top sides slug it out for the Australian Rules premiership. The nation's most-watched sport was given the go-ahead in 1958 by the then dominant cricket faculty. Football was to keep cricketers fit in the off-season. The final is fought on the hallowed turf of the Melbourne Cricket Ground (MCG) from where every seemingly curious move, play and umpiring decision is televised around the globe.

✪ FORMULA ONE GRAND PRIX, MONACO

The excitement level of the world's most important professional motor race is heightened in picturesque Monte Carlo where spectators stand extremely close to the action. The 263km (163mi), 78-lap circuit holds many twists and turns and is deemed the world's most challenging course. Spectators line the streets to watch the machines whiz by, hear the screaming engines and smell burnt rubber. They first started their engines for the Monaco Formula One Grand Prix in 1929 reaching speeds of 80km/h (50mph); recent speeds clock 142km/h (88mph).

✪ THAI BOXING, THAILAND

High kicks and high jinks are all part of the Thai boxing (muay thai) spectacle, with wild musical accompaniment to the ceremonial beginning of each match and frenzied betting throughout the stadium. Bouts are limited to five three-minute rounds separated with two-minute breaks. Common blows include high kicks to the neck, elbow thrusts to the face and head, knee hooks to the ribs and low crescent kicks to the calf. Early accounts of Thai boxing date to the 15th century where it was used in warfare between Myanmar (Burma) and Thailand.

✪ TOUR DE FRANCE, FRANCE

In July the world's most prestigious bicycle race brings together 189 of the world's top male cyclists (21 teams of nine) and 15 million spectators for a spectacular 3000-plus-kilometre (1860-plus-mile) cycle around the country. The three-week route changes each year, but always labours through the Alps and Pyrenees and finishes on the Champs-Élysées in Paris. French journalist and cyclist Henri Desgranges came up with the Tour de France in 1903 as a means of promoting his sports newspaper *L'Auto* (today's *L'Équipe*). With the exception of two world war–induced intervals, it has been held every year since.

THAI BOXING WAS ONCE WARFARE AND NOW, ER, SPORT.

✪ BEACH VOLLEYBALL, BRAZIL

Buff men in bathing suits and babes in bikinis playing volleyball became a regular sight on the beaches of Ipanema and Copacabana in the heady '80s. It's little wonder the sport enjoyed a meteoric rise in popularity after debuting as an official Olympic sport at the 1996 Atlanta Games – where the Brazilian women won gold and silver. The first international beach volleyball exhibition was held in Rio de Janeiro in 1986, with 5000 spectators privy to the sport's signature dinks, digs and dives.

✪ SUPER BOWL, USA

America's National Football League (NFL) championship, the Super Bowl, is the pinnacle of American football. It's played at a different stadium each year, with no NFL team ever having played on its home turf. Held on the last Sunday in January or the first Sunday in February, it's estimated that 60% of America's televisions tune in to the event. As such, the telecast is also known for extravagantly expensive high-concept advertising, with a 30-second spot costing US$2.4 million in 2005.

✪ ASCOT RACES, ENGLAND

The first incarnation of the Royal Ascot races emerged with a four-day horse race in 1768. This grew into the internationally renowned five-day event we know today: a flurry of jockeys in silk, elegant horses, hats, frocks and suits. The Royal Procession tradition began in 1825 when the king and four other coaches carrying royalty drove up the centre of the racecourse. The iconic Ascot Racecourse, with a capacity of 80,000, closed between 2004 and 2006 for an extensive facelift.

✪ ATACAMA DESERT & EL TATIO GEYSERS, CHILE

It's believed that parts of Chile's Atacama Desert have never been touched by rain. The barren landscape is made up of a series of salt basins supporting virtually no vegetation. This dramatic landscape is also where you'll find extinct volcanoes standing over an Incan village, a stunning flurry of flamingos in Laguna Chaxa and the highest geyser field in the world. At 4267m (14,000ft) above sea level, the El Tatio geysers are continually blowing off steam.

✪ LAKE DISTRICT, ENGLAND

It's no surprise that the northwest corner of England, called the Lake District, comprises multitudinous lakes. Add luxuriant green dales and bald modest mountains and you have some pleasant countryside indeed. The inspiration for Wordsworth's worthy words in the 17th century, the region's middle name is 'romance'. Be prepared to hike into the hills and head closer to the clouds for some quiet time away from the visiting hordes.

✪ MILFORD SOUND, NEW ZEALAND

Echoes of Maori legend ricochet around the steep cliffs that rise sharply out of the seas of New Zealand's South Island. According to legend, the sheer valleys were cut by Tute Rakiwhanoa who used a magical adze. In fact carved by rivers of ice, the Sound is indisputably enchanting and forms part of the Unesco World Heritage list. Located at the end of the famed 53.5km (33mi) Milford Track, the fiord makes a fitting end for hikers who are met by the towering Mitre Peak (1695m, 5560ft).

✪ PLITVICE LAKES, CROATIA

Croatia's precious network of 16 lakes interlinked with waterfalls is acknowledged on the Unesco World Heritage list. The Plitvice Lakes are also known as the Devil's Garden, which refers to the associated tale of the area being flooded by the Black Queen after a long drought and countless prayers. Limestone and travertine caves pock the surrounding landscape, with dense forests crowding around the rims of the upper lakes.

✪ ANGEL FALLS (SALTO ANGEL), VENEZUELA

The world's highest waterfall crashes into a nameless tributary of the Río Caroni in Venezuela's Parque Nacional Canaima. Falling from a great height of 978m (3212ft) the fickle falls are best seen on a cloudless day (as a flight is involved) and in summer when the water is most voluminous. Known locally as Kerepakupai-meru, Angel Falls were named after Jimmy Angel – a gold-hunting aviator who spotted them in the 1930s.

✪ SOSSUSVLEI, NAMIBIA

In the heart of Namibia's Namib Desert, soaring sandscapes are continuously rearranged by the wind. The world's highest sand hills, up to 300m (984ft), are stacked here within the vast boundaries of the Namib-Naukluft Park – stretching 480km (300mi) along the coast and deep inland. Presenting every shade of orange and umber, older dunes are saturated orange through years of iron oxidisation. A sea mist moistens the marshland to sustain the resident lizards and beetles.

✪ GRAND CANYON, USA

The Colorado River has been conscientiously carving this impressive canyon for around six million years now. In the USA's arid state of Arizona, the grand old dame stretches 446km (277mi) long, cutting over 1500m (5000ft) deep into ancient layers of rock and gaping up to 29km (18mi) wide in parts. Hike among humbling red-rock spires, perch at a majestic lookout and look out for endangered California condors, or roar along the Colorado River rapids that keep the Canyon company.

✪ CANADIAN ROCKIES, CANADA

#o1. Straddling the British Colombia and Alberta state borders in the country's west, the humungous Rockies region (about the size of England) comprises a string of four national parks: Banff, Jasper, Kooteney and Yoho. Mother Nature started moulding the mountains, rivers, lakes, waterfalls and glaciers a mere 75 million years ago, but boy did she let it rip. Outdoorsy types can hike, bike, paddle, ride and climb among the stunning Unesco World Heritage–listed scenery, which is home to a glut of great wildlife: from moose and marmots to bears and birds.

✪ SALAR DE UYUNI, BOLIVIA

#o2. The startling white salt plain of Salar de Uyuni in southwest Bolivia is the world's largest – containing an estimated 10 billion tonnes of salt and covering an area of 12,000sq km (4600 sq mi). Near the crest of the Andes, the surrounding Altiplano burbles away with thermal activity and Ojos del Salar ('salt eyes') leak upward-flowing tears from underground pools. This is mirage territory – where squinting into the shimmering distance merges the illusory soft edges.

✪ GREAT BARRIER REEF, AUSTRALIA

#o3. The world's largest marine park stretches more than 2300km (1430mi) along the clear, shallow waters off the northeast coast of Australia. An extraordinary variety of species thrive in its tropical waters, including 400 types of coral, 1500 species of fish and 400 types of mollusc. An armada of tour boats shuttles snorkellers and divers to and from shore, providing myriad services and tours. Witness whales on their annual migration, car-sized cod fish and eerie shipwrecks at this Unesco World Heritage site.

MOST **EXTRAORDINARY**
#25.**FESTIVALS.**

DIA DE MUERTOS (DAY OF THE DEAD) COMES ALIVE IN MEXICO.

✪ SEMANA SANTA, GUATEMALA

Antigua; Easter
Semana Santa commemorates the Passion, the Crucifixion and the Resurrection in a week of feverish worship. Statues of Jesus are paraded through streets layered with flowers, pines and fruits in various designs – some up to a kilometre (0.6mi) long. Then the sentencing and crucifixion of Christ is re-enacted, complete with Roman centurions and Pilate, while, seemingly, the entire city is draped in black crepe and smelling of incense. Even an atheist's jaw would drop in awe at the sheer scale and passion of the proceedings.

✪ DIWALI, INDIA

October or November
This five-day festival (also known as Deepavaali or Festival of Lights), which unites all creeds and religions, sees homes all over India lit with lamps and candles to ward off the darkness of evil. The homes are then thoroughly spring-cleaned while the people take the opportunity to buy new clothes and set off an armada of firecrackers, which sees noise-pollution levels rise dramatically (actually, it's enough to perforate eardrums on the other side of the planet). On top of that, sweets are exchanged as hatchets are buried and grudges are forgotten…at least for now.

✪ KANAMARA MATSURI, JAPAN

Kawasaki; 31 March & 1 April
Japan is a study in contradictions. Here's a society that bans pubic hair from being shown in films, yet holds this absolutely bonkers fertility extravaganza. The 'Festival of the Steel Phallus' features transvestites carrying a whopping great pink penis through town while onlookers of all ages suck on phallus-shaped lollipops, kids straddle penile swings, and adults carve radishes into penises. The festival was originally held to ward against a syphilis surge in the 17th century and now raises money for AIDS research.

✪ NOCHE DE LOS RÁBANOS, MEXICO

Oaxaca; 23 December
The 'Night of the Radishes' began as a marketing gimmick: when the Spanish first brought radishes to Mexico in the 16th century, they carved them into fanciful shapes to attract buyers (although they didn't go quite as far as the Japanese; see 'Kanamara Matsuri'). Today the tradition takes the form of a contest, as local artisans carve tableaux from massive radishes for a cash prize and the respect of lovers of crisp, pungent roots worldwide.

✪ LA TOMATINA, SPAIN

Buñol; last Wednesday in August
Tomato buffs rejoice! For this is your festival. Each year around 10,000 people descend on Buñol for La Tomatina, the culmination of a week-long celebration of Buñol's patron saint. An estimated 125,000kg (275,625lb) of tomatoes are used, driven into the town square by a convoy of trucks. Drunken participants dive in, hurtling the fruit at each other until the streets run red like the sickest splatter film, and then it's all over – within an hour.

✪ MARDI GRAS, USA

New Orleans; early January
This famous two-week festival features parades headed by 'Kings' and 'Queens' leading a flotilla of garish floats manned by 'krewes' who throw trinkets to the crowds (who usually beg for it; if they don't, female krewe members bare their breasts in encouragement). The culmination is the wicked mayhem of Mardi Gras Day (also known as Fat Tuesday), when all inhibitions are let loose. The next day, Ash Wednesday, is the first day of Lent, when abstinence prevails, making Fat Tuesday the ultimate excuse for a piss up, a knees up and a throw up. Check New Orleans' recovery from hurricane Katrina (September 2005) before going.

✪ DÍA DE MUERTOS, MEXICO

1 & 2 November
Mexico's 'Day of the Dead' does not pay homage to filmmaker George Romero – rather, it's a two-day festival celebrating the reunion of relatives with their dear departed. Expect colourful costumes, loads of food and drink, skeletons on stilts, parties in cemeteries, skull-shaped lollies and mariachi bands performing next to graves. This beautiful, moving spectacle will demystify your fear of crossing over, because – unlike Halloween's witches and all-round terror – the Day of the Dead smashes the taboos surrounding death, celebrating the continuation of life beyond and the value of interdimensional communion.

A SAMBA DANCER TAKES IT OFF AND TURNS IT ON FOR THE RIO CARNAVAL.

THE RACE IS ONLY 90 SECONDS BUT THE CELEBRATIONS LAST ALL DAY..

FLAMES SHOOT FROM AN 'ART CAR', THRILLING AND DELIGHTING AUDIENCES AT THE 15TH ANNUAL BURNING MAN FESTIVAL IN THE BLACK ROCK DESERT, NEVADA.

✪ CARNAVAL, BRAZIL
Rio de Janeiro; early February

#01. This is sex and samba on a stick, drawing around a million people each year for its throbbing, four-day-long festivities. The centrepiece is the Sambódromo parade, when neighbourhood groups compete against each other for the title of best 'samba school'; flashy floats and nearly nude women feature prominently. The Masquerade Ball is almost as breathtaking, rammed to the gills with celebrities and mere mortals alike, all bemasked, bewigged and becostumed. Wear a G-string (thong) for best results.

✪ IL PALIO, ITALY
Siena; 2 July & 16 August

#02. This heart-stopping event revolves around a bone-crunching, bareback horse race run around the Piazza del Campo; it lasts 90 seconds although the rest of the day is taken up with major-league carousing. The frequently violent race features jockeys from Siena's 17 neighbourhoods, all traditional rivals (intermarriage is often forbidden). Expect to see riders thudding to the ground with alarming regularity (this truly is a no-holds-barred event) and don't be surprised to be offered a baby bottle of wine when it's all over – for the neighbourhoods, a win means rebirth.

✪ BURNING MAN, USA
Black Rock City, Nevada; August or September

#03. This week-long spectacle draws 30,000 people, making it Nevada's third-biggest 'city' for that brief period. What exactly is Burning Man? It's hard to say. The founder reckons it's a City of Art; the motto is 'No Spectators' and you have to contribute something, anything, to that year's theme. No money is allowed inside so you have to give it away – whatever 'it' may be (nudge nudge, wink wink). The entire shebang culminates in thousands of nude and nearly nude spectators witnessing a giant, burning effigy, possibly inspired by the pagan horror film *Wicker Man*.

RECENT GUIDELINES ENSURE THE BEAUTY OF
ANTARCTICA CAN BE ENJOYED WITH MINIMAL IMPACT.

SKIMMING ACROSS THE PACIFIC DOES MINIMAL
DAMAGE TO FIJI'S UNDERWATER ENVIRONMENT.

✪ SHADOW THE BUSHMEN OF THE KALAHARI, NAMIBIA

#o1. As a visitor at Tsumkwe Lodge, you'll tag along with the daily activities of the San (bushmen of the Kalahari). The San have survived in the Kalahari Desert for at least 40,000 years, so can teach a city-slicker a thing or two about living in the wilderness. A morning's outing may include sampling the 'fruits' of he desert (berries and tubers) or witnessing a finely honed hunt for antelope. Sunvil Africa (www.sunvil .co.uk/africa) in the UK works closely with the lodge, and can advise on its suitability for individual travellers.

✪ CRUISING, ANTARCTICA

#o2. You can't help but see the world differently while cruising the white wilderness of Antarctica. Where else would you regularly see whales flip-flopping among icebergs, hundreds of thousands of penguins, albatrosses wheeling overhead, and sea elephants nonchalantly belching? Around 30 cruise ships work in Antarctica; all are required to abide by strict minimum – environmental – impact guidelines set out by the Independent Association of Antarctic Tour Operators (www.iaato.org).

✪ SEA-KAYAKING, FIJI

#o3. Paddle past postcard beaches through aquamarine shallows mottled with reefs that are home to schools of teeny fish and turtles who break the surface to catch a breath. Sea-kayaking in the waters that lap the Pacific Islands and camping in traditional villages makes a negligible impact on this stunning environment. You'll need to pack some stamina for Southern Sea Ventures' nine-day kayaking trip (www .southernseaventures.com), and develop a taste for kava – a beverage whose flavour has been likened to that of a dirty puddle.

BEST SUSTAINABLE TRAVEL
#26.EXPERIENCES. »

✪ NATIONAL PARKS VOLUNTEER, USA

Fall asleep to a chorus of wolf calls and count bears as your neighbours by volunteering at one of the USA's national parks. Volunteering positions range from tourguiding to scientific research, and provide plenty of opportunities to gain a unique perspective on nature. Opportunities also exist for artist-in-residence programmes – where you can render the great outdoors. Every volunteer hour spent nourishes the chronically underfunded national parks system. For further info, check out www.nps.gov/volunteer.

✪ CARPATHIAN LARGE CARNIVORE PROJECT, ROMANIA

Europe's largest concentration of large carnivores roam Romania's alpine meadows. It can be akin to watching grass grow if nature doesn't lead a bear, lynx or wolf your way, but a portion of the price of these CLCP ecotours (www.clcp.ro) goes towards protecting habitat and community development. Low-impact tours benefit the local economy (by staying in local guesthouses) and demonstrate that large carnivores and humans can co-exist.

✪ MT BORRADAILE'S ABORIGINAL ROCK-ART SITE, AUSTRALIA

Mt Borradaile's honeycombed escarpments and outcrops keep an unknown number of rock paintings; some of which date back 50,000 years. By being one of the few visitors allowed here at any given time, you're not only participating in a momentous art-appreciation class, but also providing income to the traditional owners – the Ulba Bunidj people, who receive a share in the profits. Tours are strictly managed by Davidsons Arnhemland Safaris (www.arnhemland-safaris.com) and include interpretive time-out: exploring the magnificent Northern Territory outback.

✪ HIKING, BHUTAN

The world's last Buddhist kingdom, Bhutan measures its success in terms of Gross National Happiness. Such an ethos ensures a preserved environment both culturally and environmentally. A tour with a government-approved operator (see www.tourism.gov.bt) is a prerequisite, and will likely include a hike through yak meadows high in the Himalayas. Geographically cut off from the rest of the world, 70% of Bhutan remains covered in forest.

✪ ALBERGE ECOLOGICO CHALALAN, BOLIVIA

Deep in Amazonian Bolivia, a cluster of cabins is set in a fertile area that commands 11% of the world's species of flora and fauna. Chalalan lodge is entirely managed by the Quechua-Tacano indigenous community, and a share of profits funds community health and education facilities. Encircled by 14 well-marked nature trails, most guests swing through the jungle in the morning before swinging in one of the lodge's hammocks in the afternoon.

✪ MOUNTAIN GORILLA SAFARI, RWANDA & UGANDA

Sharing an hour with gorillas in the wild is utterly unforgettable, but requires some effort. It can take you and your machete-wielding guide most of a morning to track a family to its 'playground', and associated costs can be prohibitive. Tourism is confined to Rwanda and Uganda and is strictly limited. Discovery Initiatives (www.discoveryinitiatives.co.uk) has a 14-day itinerary developed in conjunction with nongovernmental organizations working for gorilla conservation.

A LONELY WHALE OFF THE KAIKOURA COAST, NEW ZEALAND.

✪ WHALE-WATCHING, NEW ZEALAND

The Maori-owned and -operated Whale Watch company (www.whalewatch.co.nz) supports the indigenous Ngai Tahu community, located in Kaikoura on New Zealand's South Island. Boats operate year-round and gentle-giant sightings are guaranteed, including sperm whales, humpbacks, blue whales and orcas. Boats keep a respectful distance from these celebrity creatures, and in-tour commentary focuses on conservation and cultural information.

BEST PLACES TO EXPERIENCE
#27. MUSIC.

LEELU | GETTY IMAGES

DJ ERICK MORILLO SPINS THE STEEL WHEELS AT PACHA, IBIZA.

✪ GRAND OLE OPRY, USA

This country-music phenomenon is actually a Saturday night, live radio broadcast that goes out on Nashville's WSM station. It's been around since 1925, making it the USA's longest continuous radio show, and takes place at the 4400-seat Grand Ole Opry House. Each year thousands of good-ole boys and girls from around the globe git on down to Tennessee to git a load of the legendary show that has played host to numerous country-music legends – Waylon Jennings, Hank Williams, Patsy Cline, Johnny Cash – and others, like Keith Urban.

✪ BERLIN CABARET, GERMANY

For many people the words 'decadent', 'cabaret' and 'Berlin' go together like 'oil', 'terror' and 'Bush'. German cabaret began in the 1920s and was a lot darker than its sultry French equivalent: more satirical, more political, a reflection of the horrors of war. Today,

although the scene just isn't what it used to be, Berliner cabaret still offers something of that edge (along with leggy, high-kicking girls, of course), as well as the giddy thrill of being transported back to a time when art actually *mattered*.

✪ CARLING WEEKEND: READING, ENGLAND

With a few decades of music history under its belt, the Reading festival is a worthy pilgrimage for fans of alternative pop, rock, rap and hip-hop. The three-day open-air event can feel like a home away from home (if your home has 10-million-watt speakers). Once your campsite is set up, head to a stage (there are six) and lose your mind with 60,000 other people. If an act doesn't measure up, contribute to a barrage of empty plastic bottles, a festival tradition. If you love the act, follow it to Leeds the next day, where a sister festival is held concurrently.

✪ VIENNA, AUSTRIA

Strauss, Schubert, Haydn, Mozart, Beethoven, Brahms, Schönberg and Mahler… These giants of classical music all at some stage lived or made music in Vienna, and their legacy is celebrated in the city with an annual performance season lasting from September to June plus an additional nine festivals per year, special events and one-off performances. For lovers of classical music, what could be finer than experiencing a world-class recital by the Vienna Philharmonic in the stately Wiener Konzerthaus – in the city where it all began?

✪ LONDON, ENGLAND

Many come to London for the music, whether they want to party hard in a Super Club like Ministry or Fabric; chill to an adventurous, possibly stoned DJ in some too-kool-for-skool bar; or get bladdered at one of London's unbeatable live-music venues (anyone who's anyone plays the capital at some stage). Think of the scenes that London has incubated, such as punk, rave and drum 'n' bass, and the many ultrafamous London musos such as Bowie, the Stones, the Clash, the Pistols and that annoying little git with the high-pitched whiny voice…you know, old what's-his-name. Irritating little muppet.

✪ AUSTIN, USA

Austin, Texas dubs itself the 'Live Music Capital of the World', which is a bit cheeky considering the claims of somewhere like London. How many famous Austin bands can you name off the top of your head? Now how many from London? Alright, calm down – let's not get into a fight. Let's just agree that live music is terribly important to Austin, which has more live-music venues per capita than Nashville, Las Vegas, New York City, Memphis or Los Angeles.

✪ DAKAR, SENEGAL

They say Dakar is the Paris of French West Africa, a cultural hub with intellectuals and artists aplenty. Fittingly, it has a throbbing live-music scene, powered by *mbalax*, a cross-hatching of Latin and Caribbean music with African drumming. Beloved Senegalese musician Youssou N'Dour is the most famous exponent of *mbalax*, but there are others who have followed his lead, including Baaba Maal and Cheikh Lo. *Mbalax* performances are addictive: the sight of a 10-piece band completely absorbed in the music while delirious punters stuff cash into the musicians' mouths and pockets is one not easily forgotten.

A GROUP OF MUSICIANS BLOW THEIR HORNS DURING THE TRADITIONAL PARRANDAS CELEBRATION IN REMEDIOS, CUBA.

DESPITE RECENT SETBACKS, JAZZ IS ESSENTIAL TO THE SPIRIT AND HERITAGE OF NEW ORLEANS.

✪ HAVANA, CUBA

#01. The absorbing documentary *Buena Vista Social Club* (1999) implanted Cuban music (specifically, the prerevolutionary *son* style) into the global consciousness, and today many pilgrims travel to Havana to experience *son*'s evocation of a time before Castro, before collectivisation, before poverty and isolation. They say *son* is connected to the hips (it's a prototype of salsa), but that's not all you can hear in Havana's bars and streets: rumba, salsa (of course) and Latin jazz will also shake your hips silly.

✪ IBIZA, SPAIN

#02. This small island off Spain's eastern coast is pretty much where it all began. In the late '80s British DJs would play at Ibiza's ecstasy-fuelled clubs before importing the hedonistic vibe back to England, where house music and techno was taking off; the rest is history. Ibizan clubs are a lot more commercial now, and there are a hell of a lot more lager louts to contend with, but the atmosphere is still undeniably riotous, self-indulgent and pleasure seeking.

✪ NEW ORLEANS JAZZ FESTIVAL, USA

#03. Also known as 'Jazz Fest', this 10-day gala event spread across 12 stages attracts 650,000 people per year (in April) and pretty much defines the spirit and heritage of New Orleans. It's eclectic, featuring gospel, funk, zydeco, rock and Caribbean in addition to jazz, but the best endorsement is the stellar roster of acts it has staged, including Fats Domino, Aretha Franklin, Dr John, Allen Toussaint, Miles Davis, Bob Dylan, Ella Fitzgerald, Dizzy Gillespie, Santana, BB King, James Brown, LL Cool J, Gladys Knight and Youssou N'Dour. Check New Orleans' recovery from hurricane Katrina (September 2005) before going.

✪ FRANKLIN RIVER, AUSTRALIA

Not for the faint-hearted, rubber-rafting down the wild Franklin River is a challenging and, at times, treacherous undertaking. The isolated wilderness of Tasmania's World Heritage area protects ancient plants and endemic creatures. Accessing it by boat can only be done between December and March, and requires eight to 14 days – only experienced rafters are eligible. Rafters usually access the unpredictable river – given to fits of flooding – at Collingwood River (49km or 31mi west of Derwent Bridge) and finish at Gordon River, having pre-arranged a pick-up.

✪ QUETICO PROVINCIAL PARK, CANADA

Paddling along the glassy surface of Northern Ontario's pristine lakes puts you smack in the middle of the country's signature wilderness. Combine canoeing and camping to spot moose mooching at the water's edge or drop a line for a spot of sport fishing. The 4800-sq-km (1853-sq-mi)

mote canoe routes (1500km, or 932mi, of them), and there are opportunities for guided and self-guided forays in and around the park.

✪ KERALA'S BACKWATERS, INDIA

The network of lagoons, lakes, rivers and canals that fringe the coast of Kerala make for some fascinating explorations. The basic little wooden boats cross shallow, palm-fringed lakes studded with cantilevered fishing nets, and travel along shady canals. A popular eight-hour cruise runs between Alappuzha and Kollam (also called Alleppey and Quilon), which includes a landing at the Matha Amrithanandamayi Mission – the residence of one of India's very few female gurus.

✪ MILFORD SOUND, NEW ZEALAND

You don't have to go far to see why Milford Sound is the South Island's most visited fiord. Sheer, weathered walls dominate the serenity here that's often doused with rains. Cruises run for an hour or two, and depart from a huge wharf – a five-minute walk from the car park. Choose

to sail or motor among the spectacular valleys looking for glimpses of the area's endemic wildlife, such as hoiho or yellow-eyed penguin. Overnight cruises are also worth considering, with boats sailing the full 22km (14mi) length of the Sound and offering kayaking trips to shore.

✪ ISLAND-HOPPING, GREECE

With more than 1400 islands, Greece has more coastline than any other country in Europe. So it makes sense to hop between at least a few, as the scenery varies dramatically: from the semitropical lushness of the Ionian and Northeastern Aegean Islands to the bare, sunbaked rocks of the Cyclades. Every island has a ferry service of some sort ranging from the giant 'super ferries' that work the major routes, to the small, ageing open ferries that chug around the backwaters.

✪ DISKO BAY, GREENLAND

The town of Ilulissat perches at the edge of a 40km (25mi) ice fjord that produces 20

million tonnes of ice per day. To cruise among the bergs is truly amazing. The blue-streaked giants bob about the bay, with their true bulk concealed beneath the surface of the water – seven-eighths of larger bergs typically lie out of view. A number of tour operators offer boat cruises around the ice fjords and the Bay in well-equipped vessels.

✪ GALÁPAGOS ISLANDS, ECUADOR

Get on board the wilderness experience of a lifetime by cruising the haunting beauty of the Galápagos Islands – 1000km (620mi) from mainland Ecuador. Here you can swim with sea lions, float nose-to-beak with a penguin and stand next to a blue-footed booby. Live-aboard boats range from small yachts to large cruise ships, with the most common variety being the motor sailer (a medium-sized motor boat), which carries up to 20 people and cruises for anywhere from three days to three weeks. You'll need to bury the bothers of hopping around on a fixed itinerary with a group of fellow travellers

✪ FJORDS, NORWAY

#o1.
For more than a century, Norway's legendary Hurtigruten ferry route has linked the numerous coastal villages and towns. Year-round, 11 modern ferries head north from Bergen, reaching Kirkenes before returning. Take the 11-day round-trip that pulls in to 34 ports and offers various opportunities for side-trips, or just cruise a stretch (or two) of this trip. Features on the full itinerary include fabulous fjords and islands that see the midnight sun, medieval monasteries and Art Nouveau towns.

✪ HALONG BAY, VIETNAM

#o2.
Bobbing on the emerald waters of Halong Bay and moving through its 3000-odd limestone islands is simply sublime. The tiny islands are dotted with beaches and grottoes created by wind and waves, and have sparsely forested slopes ringing with bird tunes. There are more than 300 boats based at Bai Chay Tourist Wharf waiting to sweep you away to the World Heritage waters. Day tours last from four to eight hours, though a few (recommended) overnighters are also available.

✪ AMAZON RIVER, SOUTH AMERICA

#o3.
From its inconspicuous source in the Peruvian highlands to its mouth near Belém in Brazil, the Amazon River measures more than 6200km (3853mi). Its flow is 12 times that of the Mississippi, and it carries one-fifth of the world's fresh water. String up a hammock on a slow boat (of varying quality) between Manaus and Belém in Brazil or Trinidad and Guayaramerín in Bolivia. Its edges are crowded with jungle or settlements, and your slow boat can take anywhere from four to six days.

⭐ TOUR DE FRANCE, FRANCE

#o1.
So you think iron men are mad? Get a load of the cyclists who compete in the Tour de France: they must cover about 3500km (2170mi), some of it flat, some of it hilly, and some of it on high-mountain climbs at high altitude through the Pyrenees and the Alps. Many reckon Le Tour is the toughest sporting event of them all: it has been likened to running 20 marathons in a row, with as much a premium placed on mental strength as physical. Iron-men events take around eight hours; the Tour last for three weeks. Now who's the toughest?

AXEL MERCKX WITH THE DEVIL IN HOT PURSUIT IN THE 2003 TOUR DE FRANCE.

A COMPETITOR STRIDES OUT IN THE 20TH MARATHON DES SABLES.

⭐ MARATHON DES SABLES, MOROCCO

#o2.
Marathons are always gruelling, but especially when they're run across the Sahara over six days, like this one. Surrounded by dunes hundreds of metres high, runners are often sand blind, unable to see their hand in front of their face; they wear goggles to keep the constant sand at bay, but it ends up streaming out of every orifice anyway. The fact that they must cart around necessities like sleeping bags and anti-snake-venom pumps in hotter-than-hell temperatures piles on the misery. Surprisingly, just one person has died in the competition's history, a Frenchman who had a heart attack.

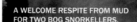

A WELCOME RESPITE FROM MUD FOR TWO BOG SNORKELLERS.

⭐ WORLD BOG SNORKELLING CHAMPIONSHIP, WALES

#o3.
Here's one for your true nut job – direct from the land that invented Man-vs-Horse racing. Competitors in the World Bog Snorkelling Championship make their way up and down two lengths of a 55m (60yd) trench carved into freezing, disgusting, noxious-smelling peat bog. They are allowed to wear snorkels and flippers but not allowed to use standard swimming strokes; only the legs must be used to propel the body. They say it's like swimming through treacle. Pass the leeks.

MOST GRUELLING
#29. EVENTS. »

✪ ARCTIC TEAM CHALLENGE, GREENLAND

Teams in this event mountain bike, canoe, trek and climb over mountains and glaciers across 250km (155mi) of the wilderness wonderland that is Ammassalik. The polar elements give the Arctic Challenge its legendary status as a test for the toughest of the tough: just you try paddling your canoe when your fingers are snap frozen or your hair hangs rock solid like stalactites.

✪ ECO CHALLENGE

This event has four-person, mixed-gender teams compete 24 hours a day to complete a 500km (310mi) course using trekking, canoeing, horse-riding, sea-kayaking, scuba-diving, mountaineering and mountain-biking skills. The biggest challenge competitors face is disease, especially when entering jungle terrain touched by infected animals. During the 2002 event in Fiji competitors came down with leptospirosis, giardiasis, foot rot, staph infections and filariasis, resulting in high fever, extreme migraines, constant vomiting and massive boils and pustules upon their person. Perhaps unsurprisingly, the event hasn't been held since Fiji, although there's talk of a return.

✪ EVEREST MARATHON, NEPAL

Like we said, marathons are *always* gruelling…especially when held 5184m (17,000ft) above sea level, like this one. This 42km (26mi) course traverses some very rough mountain terrain (starting near Everest Basecamp) and is pretty much downhill save for two sheer uphill components. But if you think that's soft, then remember: the air at 17,000ft is as thin as Elton John's hair and exposure from snow and ice is a constant worry. As a precondition of entry, all competitors must undergo a 26-day acclimatisation 'holiday' beforehand.

✪ ADVENTURE RACE, GREENLAND

You'd expect anything held in arctic Greenland to be gruelling and the Adventure Race is no exception. Here's what you have to do: run across a glacier for 20km (12mi); cross the glacier's melt-water river; cover 50 mountainous kilometres (31mi) on a bicycle; traverse a further 55km (34mi) over several mountain passes at around 1000m above sea level; strap on a kayak (paddle it across fjords and carry it across land); then run up and down yet more hills for 32km (20mi). Just to remind you, it's *bloody cold* in Greenland.

✪ RAID WORLD CHAMPIONSHIP

The Raid (formerly known as Raid Gauloises) is considered the granddaddy of Adventure Races (first held in 1989); it's also considered the world's toughest race. Mixed-gender teams consist of five people and there's no set course, so teams must try and work out the best way, in the space of 10 days, to get to the end of the 1000km (621mi) course. If one team member gets sick or dies, then the entire team is disqualified. One year, when the Raid was held in Madagascar, teams got lost in the jungle for four days; but every year competitors routinely battle severe dehydration, monsoons, leeches and the sudden realisation that they are cracking up.

✪ RUNNING WITH THE BULLS, SPAIN

Thousands of lunatics charging ahead of a pack of snorting, rampaging bulls through the narrow streets of Pamplona; men impaled on the end of bullhorns; men who compete year after year, forever walking wobbly due to their plastic hip replacements; men who can't piss straight because they got gored somewhere extremely nasty. What does it all add up to? An event that just isn't for the fainthearted…or the sound of brain.

PURE PHYSICAL TORTURE DOESN'T DETER HOARDS OF COMPETITORS TO THE IRONMAN EACH YEAR.

✪ WORLD IRON MAN TRIATHLON, USA

Four kilometres (2.5mi) of swimming in rough water; 180km (112mi) of bicycle racing in 95km/h (59mph) crosswinds; and a 42km (26mi) marathon in 90% humidity… Around 50,000 people from more than 50 countries attempt qualification for the right to torture themselves in the World Iron Man Triathlon in Hawai'i, with 1500 making it through to the actual event. Actually, all the numbers surrounding this event are big: 5000 volunteers work on it; athletes spend around 24 hours per week training for it; five million television spectators watch it; and the winner gets US$100,000 for it.

BEST SPIRITUAL
#30.RETREATS.

JACOB HALASKA | PHOTOLIBRARY

DIP INTO INDIA'S SPIRITUALITY.

✪ GREEN GULCH FARM ZEN CENTER, USA

Also known as the Green Dragon Temple, this Buddhist centre combines Zen meditation – daily classes and weekend workshops – with the discipline of work. The centre incorporates the Green Gulch Farm, where all the farmhands are practising Buddhists, so all together now: the crew that meditates together farms together! All of this is part of the San Francisco Zen Center, among the largest Buddhist Sanghas outside Asia.

✪ OSHO COMMUNE INTERNATIONAL, INDIA

This commune in Puna, India, is a phenomenon, receiving thousands of visitors daily and ranking among India's top tourist attractions. Founded by controversial guru Osho, the commune takes a somewhat unconventional, punning approach to spiritualism, with its 'zennis' matches (in which players who lose a point work through their anger with the umpire), the Club Meditation complex and the Osho Multiversity. Visitors must return negative AIDS tests to enter, a reflection of the commune's focus on tantric sex.

✪ RISHIKESH, INDIA

Rishikesh, in the Himalayas, attracts thousands of enlightenment seekers per year with its numerous spiritual retreats, holy shrines, temples and organisations to guide you on your quest. It was here that Lord Vishnu was supposed to have defeated the demon Madhu and it's also where the Beatles infamously gained an audience with the Maharishi Mahesh Yogi. What's more, Rishikesh is acknowledged as the birthplace of yoga, and if that's not enough endorsement for you then you must be Buddha himself.

✪ KOYA-SAN, JAPAN

This raised tableland, covered in thick forest and surrounded by eight peaks, is one of Japan's most beloved spiritual retreats, visited by around one million citizens per year; the founder of the Shingon school of Esoteric Buddhism, Kobo Daishi, established a religious community here in 816. Today Koya-san remains a thriving centre for Japanese Buddhism – there are more than 100 temples for the population of 7000 – while Kobo Daishi remains one of Japan's most treasured religious figures, revered as a Bodhisattva.

✪ LADAKH, INDIA

A developing travel trend is ecospiritualism, and Ladakh – in the Himalayas, next to Tibet – is right in the thick of it. This is a self-sufficient, agrarian region, but it's also part of a very fragile ecosystem – as well as being a Buddhist heartland. Ecospiritualists here therefore divide their time between volunteer work (managing alternative energy sources and waste-disposal systems, identifying endangered species) and spiritual pursuits (meditating, visiting monasteries, communing with monks, attending harvest festivals, making mandalas).

✪ FINDHORN FOUNDATION, SCOTLAND

From small beginnings in 1962 when three people were led by God to create an organic garden (now famous for its beauty and oversized vegetables), this community on Scotland's northern coast now welcomes thousands of visitors to share its philosophy of affinity with nature and attunement to the divinity within all beings. The many programmes on offer include Healing through Art, Creating Joyful Families, Biodanza – learning to be at ease with your body through dance – and Coming Back to Earth – celebrating the indigenous Celtic seasonal festivals of Samhain, Imbolc, Beltane and Lammas.

✪ MAYA SPA WELLNESS CENTRE, MEXICO

It might be the lucid dreaming that gets you walking on water, but it'll be this spa in Tulum that gets you dreaming in the first place. Local shamans work their magic on you with indigenous plants and treatments to help you on your way to blissed out harmony. And if it isn't the *temezcal* sweat lodge that provides a little corporeal purity, or the bendy exaltations of the yoga instructor, then it'll be the Caribbean gently calling you from your massage bench; one way or the other, you'll be leaving your old body behind.

JOHN BANAGAN | LONELY PLANET IMAGES

CLASSIC SUNSET AT
ULURU, AUSTRALIA

⭐ ULURU, AUSTRALIA

#01. Uluru (also known as Ayers Rock) is the largest monolith in the world, attracting half a million people yearly, many of whom climb the thing without a thought for its spiritual significance. But to Uluru's traditional owners, the Anangu Aboriginal people, virtually every one of the rock's caves, marks, gutters and incisions has spiritual significance. The Anangu say they can read Uluru like the bible, so it's no surprise that they consider climbing it as akin to going to church and stomping on the altar.

⭐ VARANASI, INDIA

#02. Varanasi, perhaps the world's oldest continuously inhabited city, has been called the 'Jerusalem of Hinduism' – the holiest of holy places. Its spiritual heritage is indeed staggering: Varanasi has more than 2000 mosques and temples, and around 100 ghats (steps descending to the water) along the Ganges, where, daily, thousands of pilgrims perform sacred rites, meditations and cremations. Multicoloured religious processions dominate the streets and you'll also find a preponderance of dogs – they're considered sacred creatures. Sick and infirm folk are another feature; apparently, if you die in Varanasi you'll achieve final enlightenment.

⭐ KALANI OCEANSIDE RETREAT, USA

#03. This tropical retreat near thermal springs in Hawai'i embodies various packages such as yoga escapes, volcano adventures and 'eruption parties', along with workshops that teach about Hawai'ian nature and culture, the 'body erotic', Thai massage, 'Hot Nude Yoga Training', water shiatsu and a whole lot more. It's a varied, eclectic programme that conforms to that very relaxed Hawai'ian way of getting things done. If you need more structure in your retreat experience, then this one might not be for you.

☆ THE INTERNET

#o1. These days, every man, woman and dog can travel at the drop of a hat. The Internet is a global wet nurse for any tourist worth their backpack, sorting everything from rent-a-car bookings to bargain airfares, while a plethora of online restaurant and hotel reviews mean you're an expert before you arrive. Some say the net takes the magic and the mystery out of travelling, but from the perspective of all those 'time-poor' professionals too weary to pick up a phone, you should be lynched for such blasphemy.

☆ GPS

#o2. Getting lost on holiday can really bring a person down, especially when you're in the middle of nowhere. Picture it: your paper map gets eaten by a dingo and here's you, unable to tell your compass from your boarding pass. But satellite-linked Global Positioning System devices turn even the most cartographically challenged traveller into Mr or Ms Adventure Discovery. Recent American legislation stipulated that all new cell phones must be fitted with GPS technology, which means you can be tracked – a blessing in times of strife, evil when you don't want to be found.

☆ IPOD/MP3 PLAYER

#o3. Every so often an invention comes along that really alters the cultural landscape. The iPod/mp3 player is one such device, entering the collective consciousness quicker than a Paris Hilton 'bedroom' video and spawning a multitude of clones. Not only can you take your entire music collection away with you, without burning a stack of CDs, but you can immerse yourself in your own 'private soundtrack' to your travels, totally drowning out the annoying passenger next to you on the bus.

TAKE THE REST OF THE WORLD WITH YOU TO THE PEAKS OF YOSEMITE USING A LAPTOP COMPUTER.

BEST TRAVEL
#31.GADGETS.

»

✪ MOBILE/CELL PHONES

Remember the bad old days? Arriving in a strange land three hours late after your plane's been delayed; panicking as you realise your hostel closes for the night in 20 minutes. Wanting to call them, to tell them you'll be late. Rifling through your pockets for change…only to realise you don't have the right currency. Traditionally you'd be stuffed, but not in the 21st century – and not after the rise of affordable mobile phones. The built-in camera means you can perpetually bore your friends with bang-up-to-date holiday snaps, too.

✪ DIGITAL CAMERA

There's no question that digital cameras have revolutionised travel – these little beauties just keep getting smaller and smaller, which means you can fake it like a pro without lugging tonnes of expensive equipment wherever you go. Operations are fairly basic, too: even your old mum, who thinks daguerreotypes are the latest thing, is now able to capture the Taj Mahal with the respect it deserves – although they still haven't figured out how to eliminate the tragic thumb over the lens.

✪ ELECTRONIC BANKING

Here's a litany of woe: losing traveller's checks, wiring money, getting robbed of your cash, strapping on a money belt. Who needs the hassle? The ease and efficiency of plastic cash means the only thing you have to worry about is data theft, and the only thing that can stop that is invisible barcodes tattooed onto your forehead. Best to stick with the card for now.

✪ SELF CHECK-IN

You get to the airport and the adrenalin's pumping – you're about to fly far from the rat race you've left behind. But there's a massive queue ahead and it's going nowhere fast. That whiny kid needs special treatment; that guy has a huge suitcase he wants to take into the cabin and he won't be told it won't fit; a woman wants to take her poodle with her… There has to be an easier way, and capitalism, naturally, has the answer: self check-in. Swipe your ticket, dump your luggage at the bag drop, and away you go.

✪ EVAPORATING HAND WASH

Hallelujah. Evaporating hand wash, which doesn't need soap or water, is just the ticket for travellers always on the go and too busy to find a lavatory, or the Arctic adventurers who can't take the risk of freeze-drying their hands by exposing them to water, or the germaphobes who just can't bear the thought of exposing themselves to dodgy overseas H_2O.

✪ IN-SEAT FLIGHT-ENTERTAINMENT SYSTEMS

Time was when, on a long-haul flight, you had to submit over and over to the same boring film as everyone else – Burt Reynolds' latest failure, say, or yet another interminable Woody Allen psychodrama-by-numbers. Now you can have the choice of several Woodies, right in your face, and you can flick between them and Steven Seagal to your heart's content. The future suggests that email and Internet will be the norm, which means that – as long as the infuriating passenger in front keeps their seat upright for longer than two minutes – you can totally forget about your mounting deep-vein thrombosis.

HAVE GPS, WILL ROAM.

✪ QUICK-DRY FABRICS

Another boon for the on-the-go traveller, the hygiene freak and the polar explorer (see 'Evaporating Hand Wash'). Also handy for travellers who don't have access to a laundry, or for those who are just bone idle. The future in travel time-savers? A portable toilet made from buckwheat that can be consumed after use, thereby eliminating waste from the environment.

✪ CELICA YOUTH HOSTEL, SLOVENIA

#o1.
This former military prison is located in the main street of Ljubljana, Slovenia. Celica (meaning 'cell') has had a radical make-over courtesy of more than 80 Slovenian artists who refurbished each cell individually. The result is 20 unique rooms: unique from any other accommodation and distinct from each other. Finding a favourite is hard work. What each has in common are the bars – we're talkin' straight lengths of metal for a door, not a tavern-type bar.

✪ HÔME DELUXE, SPAIN

#o2.
The fair city of Valencia is home to Hôme – a budget hotel with individually themed rooms. Valencia's famous nightlife carries over into the Insomnio room – painted pitch black, with in-room neons. Perhaps the Sexy Love room is more your shtick – the hot-pink walls and faux-leopard-skin bedspread is spankin' good. Or try the Safari room – where the leopard-skin changes its spots from the previous sexy theme to an African one – complete with mozzy nets.

✪ CIRCUS HOSTEL WEINBERGSWEG, GERMANY

#o3.
This self-contained Berlin hostel has six levels of stylish amenities: from the very cosy European café on the ground floor, through the industrial polished chic of the midlevel dorms (all beds, no bunks), right up to the lush penthouse apartments. The basement bar is characteristically cool and may keep you from experiencing the rest of Berlin's fab nightlife – within easy access from the hostel. All rooms are cheerfully painted; the showers are excellent and the staff competent and helpful.

#32. HOSTELS. »

✪ BASE BACKPACK-ERS, AUSTRALIA & NEW ZEALAND

Base has a total of eight complexes located in Australia and New Zealand. Something of a revolution in the backpacker market, Base provides resort-style accommodation for budget travellers. Many are purpose-built and Melbourne's St Kilda hostel is a schmick state-of-the-art affair. Bars are a feature at most Bases, and some have a 'Sanctuary' floor – for the ladies. The best Base for beach bunnies is Magnetic Island, with A-frame accommodations that sprawl along the seafront and a superb beachfront bar.

✪ HOSTAL FORESTAL, CHILE

This laid-back little number is superbly located in the Bohemian buzz of Chile's capital, Santiago. Hostal Forestal is a swagger away from the metro, a leafy park and some of the city's swanky suburbs graced with neoclassical architecture and classic streetside cafés. It's been described as akin to crashing at your brother's place thanks to the casual care imparted by the staff and the endearingly scruffy communal areas. All rooms have their own bathroom and breakfast is included.

✪ CLAY HOSTEL, USA

This muted pink hotel in Clay St, Miami has a colourful history, as it was a gambling den for mafia don Al Capone and a rumba dancing venue. The 100-year-old building was refurbished in the '80s and has a dated charm. In the heart of the beach action, it featured in *Miami Vice* and counts Don Johnson among its celebrity guests. So kids: put on yer roller skates and roll on in. The hostel section of the hotel offers everything from single-sex dorms to spacious suites with balconies.

✪ CROCODYLUS, AUSTRALIA

The permanent tent accommodation at Crocodylus plays hide and seek – surrounded as they are by the lush rainforest canopy that's a feature of the neighbouring Daintree National Park. Located in far north Queensland's famous Cape Tribulation, Crocodylus is nestled near a quiet and picture-prefect bay – Cow Bay. The accommodation offers the opportunity to commune with nature, which is just on the other side of the canvas. The complex has a restaurant and swimming pool, and runs sea-kayaking tours along the shore which is curtained by rainforest.

✪ CUCKOOS NEST, SOUTH AFRICA

This hostel is the main reason to stop in the tiny South African town of KwaMbonambi. The slightly eccentric Cuckoo offers you the chance to stay in a treehouse, expand the left side of your brain in the 'craft corner' or join the sing-along around the braai. Although off the beaten track, it makes a vibrant base from which backpackers can visit the neighbours – hippos and crocodiles – at the nearby Greater St Lucia Wetland Park.

✪ ORBIT, USA

Retro and colourful, the only old timer in this refurbished former retirement home is the style of furniture. The groovy movie lounge has sexy suedette chairs to rub up against, and there's a prevailing primary red and green theme throughout the '70s-style Café Delux, which serves breakfast and dinner. Six-bed dorms have private bathrooms and some have balconies. So get some big sunnies and bop along to Orbit, located near the hep epicentre of Los Angeles.

✪ STRANGER, POLAND

The couch is the thing here: it's super-sized and located in a den of entertainment. Called the 'Ju Ju Lounge', it features fast and free Internet access, plus DVDs and X-Box projected onto a 3m (10ft) screen. It's also something of a party place, where socialising with strangers over a big bottle of beer is fashionable. The Stranger is located within a five-minute walk of Kraków's majestic medieval Rynek (Market Square).

⭐ TSUKIJI FISH MARKET, JAPAN

#o1. Tokyo's frenzied fish fantasia is one of the largest, busiest markets in the world. Even those who aren't too keen on seafood are addicted to it, for the hustle and bustle of its three whole blocks single-mindedly devoted to the consumption of marine life, and for the codes and modes of behaviour. Auctioneers have a lingo all their own, buyers wear wetsuits, and the market handles around 3000 tonnes of fish each day and almost 800,000 tonnes per year. You can imagine the smell.

⭐ KHAN AL-KHALILI, EGYPT

#o2. The Khan dates back as far as 1382 and some of the delights on offer in its 900 shops include glassware, brassware, perfume and jewellery; a number of artisans practise their craft before eager shoppers, too. Go to the Street of the Tentmakers for something completely different: it's a market within the market, Cairo's last remaining medieval covered market, where tentmakers craft beautifully ornate tents.

⭐ CHIANG MAI, THAILAND

#o3. The Chiang Mai market opens after sundown and it's 'Bargain City'. Fancy a fake Rolex? Get it here. Pirate DVDs? You got it. Fabrics, silks, sunglasses, gems…mmm, it's all here, as are swords and chicken feet…The centrepiece is the Night Bazaar Building, three floors of all this and more. Bargain for all you're worth for a rollicking good time.

BUYERS WEAVE THEIR WAY THROUGH HUNDREDS OF TUNA AT THE TSUKIJI CENTRAL FISH MARKET.

EVEN THE GREATEST LEADERS OF THE WORLD TURN UP TO THE KHAN.

FROM FAKE DIESELS TO ELEPHANT ART, THE CHIANG MAI NIGHT BAZAAR DOESN'T SKIP A BEAT.

GREATEST
#33.MARKETS.

✪ CHATUCHAK, THAILAND

This Bangkok weekend market – actually a 'minicity' – has to be seen to be believed: over its 14 hectares (35 acres), Chatuchak contains between 9000 and 15,000 stalls (depending on what's on and who's doing the counting) and it attracts 200,000 visitors per day. Come here for Thai handicraft and antiques among many other delights, but don't come here on hot, humid days – pressed against all that flesh, you might faint or fade away.

✪ KASHGAR, CHINA

Crikey, this one's massive, too – like Chatuchak, it gets 200,000 souls each day it's on. At Kashgar you can buy and sell everything from a horse to furniture to a bicycle to possibly your grandmother. As you can imagine, the people-watching is unsurpassed in such an environment, so keep an ear to the ground, keep an eye on the crowds, keep out of sight and just sit back and enjoy the show.

✪ TEMPLE ST, HONG KONG

This famous night market in Yau Ma Tei sees a lot of action! Here you can try to beat the local chess geniuses or buy some ubiquitous jade, believed by the Chinese to ward off evil. Also choose from a huge selection of open-air restaurants and fortune-telling parrots. Temple St is also known as 'Men's Street' because of the huge amount of men's clothing for sale, because of the number of gangster films that are set here, and because of the variety of…um…gulp…'men's pleasures' to be found.

✪ GRAND BAZAAR, TURKEY

Istanbul's Grand Bazaar is Turkey's (and possibly the world's) largest covered market, with around 4000 shops selling jewellery, carpets, brassware, leather goods, hookahs, ceramics, pottery – all under ornate, grandiose passageways spread across 60-odd streets. It gets a reputed 400,000 people per day, which equates to distilled madness. That's not all: the Bazaar, which dates from 1520, is also home to a mosque, 21 inns, two vaulted bazaars, seven fountains and 18 gates.

✪ ALEPPO, SYRIA

A considered body of opinion says that Aleppo's covered *souqs* are the finest, the most beautiful and the most unique markets in the world. They extend for around 10km (4mi), a vast, stone-vaulted labyrinth of alleyways, and are named for traditional artisans – Souq of Gold, Souq of Cotton and so on. The *souqs* date back to the 15th century, and anything is for sale: flower tea, animal carcasses, tapestries, silverware etc. Do be careful down those narrow alleyways – those donkeys transporting goods to and fro may look placid but they take crap from no-one.

✪ PIKE PLACE MARKET, USA

Some say this Seattle market is a tourist trap, others that it's a national treasure; it's the USA's oldest surviving market, spanning 4 hectares (9 acres) and attracting 40,000 people per day. Books and antiques are sold here, along with the usual assortment found in the great markets worldwide…and a lot of fish. Watch out, though: you might get a cold-blooded aquatic vertebrate thrown at you when you place an order, playing

THINGS TO LOOK AT AND THINGS TO BUY, CAMDEN HAS IT ALL.

your part in a fishy shtick that's become famous among screwballs.

✪ CAMDEN, ENGLAND

This used to be a weekend London market; now it's a phenomenon held every day (ramping up to overdrive on the weekends), spilling over into the streets and attracting possibly the greatest concentration of freaks per square metre in the world today: punks, goths, hippies, ferals, ravers, rappers, chavs, gimps, celebs, grannies, pollies. There are a few components to it: Camden Lock Market, for craft-type thingies; Camden Stables, for alternative fashion; and an indoor fashion market at the Electric Ballroom.

BEST PUBLIC
#34.ART.

FORM FOLLOWS MISFUNCTION AT GAUDÍ'S PARC GÜELL.

SUNRISE OVER ROOSEVELT AND LINCOLN, MT RUSHMORE.

✪ CITYLIGHTS PROJECT, MELBOURNE

Melbourne, Australia, is in the grip of an obsession with public art right now, particularly nu-skool evocations of graffiti and stencil art. Citylights is among the more innovative (and legal) examples, using light boxes to display public art in lanes and alleyways in the central business district. The work is mainly classic stencil art infused with edgy political and pop-cult references.

✪ MANNEKEN PIS, BRUSSELS

This bronze statue of a little kid pissing water seems like it was commissioned by Benny Hill, but the Belgians also like that sort of thing. The original was created in 1388 but later destroyed and the people of Brussels were so outraged they demanded a replacement, which was granted to them in 1616. For national holidays and special occasions, the pissing boy gets to dress up: he's been Elvis, a samurai warrior and Mozart. He's been known to piss beer and wine, too.

✪ HENRY MOORE SCULPTURES, LONDON

Henry Moore's iconic, abstract sculptures are dotted around the parks of London, England. Among the more well-known examples are Hyde Park's *Nuclear Energy*, Moore's bronze commemoration of the first sustained nuclear reaction, and *Three Standing Figures* in Battersea Park. Moore's work tends towards the human body, generally female, and is characterised by hollow cavities. Some have interpreted his undulating forms as a reference to the Yorkshire hills of his childhood, although Moore himself said that all his sculptures were odes to his mum's hip, which he had to rub often to relieve her sciatica.

✪ MOUNT RUSHMORE, SOUTH DAKOTA

These gigantic carvings of four presidential noggins (Washington, Jefferson, Lincoln, Roosevelt), embedded into Mt Rushmore's side, have infiltrated all aspects of US pop culture, from heavy metal to *The Simpsons*. But their power hasn't diminished – if the heads were attached to bodies, these dudes would be nearly 150m (500ft) tall. Some see the carvings as a monument to racism: Mt Rushmore is in the middle of Sioux country; these early Presidents had a lot to with a decline in Native American populations; and the sculptor had ties with the Ku Klux Klan.

✪ ANGEL OF THE NORTH, TEAM VALLEY

This bizarre steel sculpture presides over Tyneside in England from its hilltop perch. It's huge – as tall as four double-decker buses and about as wide as a 747 aeroplane – and can be seen from miles around. The angel stands with its wings outstretched, although those peculiar, boxy things make it look more like a cyborg than an angel. It's bloody impressive, though.

✪ MISSION DISTRICT MURALS, SAN FRANCISCO

The world-famous murals of the Latino Mission district in San Franciso, USA, adorn the walls of dozens of buildings. These poignant pieces of public art build upon the Mexican mural movement from the 1920s, as well as a good dollop of hungover-from-the-60s hippy idealism. Common themes include Hispanic, Aztec and Mayan motifs, human rights, football, Carnival and Mexican cinema. The overarching theme, though, is 'community' and it's so thick in the air here you could carve it.

✪ STATUE OF LIBERTY, NEW YORK

Talk about 'public' art – it seems the public can do whatever the hell they like with the Statue of Liberty! As perhaps the most visible symbol of the USA (at least now the World Trade Center is no more), Liberty has suffered numerous indignities upon her person. She was almost blown up after a German attack in 1916; half-buried in radioactive sand in *Planet of the Apes* (1968); made to disappear by magician David Copperfield in 1983; brought to life in *Ghostbusters II* (1989); destroyed in *Independence Day* (1996); and submerged in snow in *The Day After Tomorrow* (2004).

JOST FUSTE RAGA | PHOTOLIBRARY

CAROL POLICH | LONELY PLANET IMAGES

AXEL DOHLER | PHOTOLIBRARY

JERRY GALEA | LONELY PLANET IMAGES

DOUG SCOTT | PHOTOLIBRARY

✪ EAST SIDE GALLERY, BERLIN

#o1. Germany's Berlin Wall, torn down by the people in September 1989, was a target for Berliners' rage against the communist machine; the so-called East Side Gallery, the longest extant stretch of the wall, has been covered with more than 100 murals and graffiti. Although vandalism and the elements have destroyed much of the gallery's power, it's still a powerful reminder of the former regime of iron, with artworks ranging from Dalíesque freak shows to Pink Floydian bricks. Happily, a restoration project is under way.

✪ PARC GÜELL, BARCELONA

#o2. Spain's beloved architect, Antoni Gaudí, is the visionary behind Parc Güell, built between 1900 and 1914; the park was originally designed as a housing estate, although that idea was quickly abandoned. Gaudí's strange, organic style conjures up below-level passages built like the giant ribcage of some alien creature; wavy columns resembling stalactites and composed of broken, multicoloured ceramic; a long bench shaped like a serpent; and grottoes, nooks and crannies galore. It remains unsurpassed today.

✪ RODINA MAT, VOLGOGRAD

#o3. Behold! The stainless-steel *Rodina Mat* ('Motherland') is one of the largest statues in the world: sitting atop the Mamayev Kurgan (a shrine to the fallen), she weighs in at a lazy 8000 tonnes and is 108m (354ft) high. There's good reason for the gigantic scale – Russia lost 30 million souls during WWII. Compared to the calm beauty of the Statue of Liberty, *Rodina* is every inch power and fury: brandishing a 22m-long (72ft-long) sword, her mouth is twisted with rage, a truly terrifying and awe-inspiring sight.

⭐ ICE HOTEL, SWEDEN

#01. This hotel is rebuilt to a different architectural theme every year. Why? Because it's made from ice, dummy – and ice melts in spring. Ten thousand tonnes of ice and 30,000 tonnes of snow go into the Jukkasjärvi hotel's construction, which includes an ice sauna, ice bar, ice cinema and ice chapel. Indoor temperatures plummet to -5°C (23°F).

⭐ GÖREME, TURKEY

#02. The Göreme region is surrounded by fairy chimneys – conical sandstone structures, coloured pink and yellow, that look way off the planet. A number of pensions are carved into the chimneys, a tradition deriving from persecuted Christians, who used to carve dwellings into the rocks to hide from their oppressors ('Göreme' means 'invisible'). Feel the weight of history on your shoulders even as the thrill of gazing upon an alien landscape lifts you into the stratosphere.

⭐ WIGWAM MOTEL, USA

#03. Along Route 66 in Arizona, these roadside concrete tepees are tacky and creaky, but odd and intriguing all the same. For many they're an endearing slice of Americana, warts and all (they date from the '40s), so get stuck in. Get a load of the way-out-west ambience. Dig those vintage cars permanently moored in front of each tepee and get jiggy with the hulking freight trains passing every hour (your tepee will shake to their beat).

'ON THE ROCKS' IN THE ABSOLUT ICE BAR AT THE ICE HOTEL IN SWEDEN.

CARVED FROM VOLCANIC ROCK FORMATIONS, THESE ROOMS ARE UNUSUAL NO MATTER WHICH WAY YOU LOOK AT THEM.

UP CLOSE AND PERSONAL AT THE WIGWAM MOTEL.

MOST UNUSUAL PLACES TO
#35.STAY.

»

✪ EXPLORANTER OVERLAND HOTEL, BRAZIL

This is a – wait for it – mobile hotel with a kitchen, showers, 30 leather seats and 28 beds. Trips range from three weeks to three months, taking in routes across Brazil, Chile and Argentina with themes including off-road rallies, trekking, historical routes, gastronomy, archaeology, fishing and rodeos. The kitchen is stowed below, while the sleeping area and bathrooms are towed behind in a trailer.

✪ UTTER INN, SWEDEN

This inn at Lake Mälaren, Västerås, has only one room – and that's 3m (10ft) underwater. Although the room is tiny (you'd be lucky to fit in a few kippers laid end to end), the view makes up for it: the walls are glass. Talk about sleeping with the fishes! Now marine life can observe you trapped in your own little aquarium, a humbling reversal of fortunes to be sure and not for the claustrophobic.

✪ WOODLYN PARK, NEW ZEALAND

Waitomo's Woodlyn Park claims to have the world's only subterranean self-contained motel units for hobbits. Whatever. You can't blame them for cashing in on the New Zealand/*Lord of the Rings* connection, but what's their excuse for the other accommodation on offer? Choose from digs in a 1950s railway carriage or a Bristol freight plane that's been converted into two units – in the cockpit and tail.

✪ LOVE HOTELS, JAPAN

In Japan young people often live with their parents until well into their thirties, not budging until marriage or death occurs. So it's easy to see why love hotels appeal: couples can hire a room for a night or just for a 'rest' (a euphemism for making whoopee), which equates to an hour or so. So that's that. However, this doesn't explain the absolute wackiness of some of these places: take your pick from Moorish themes, *Barbarella*-style spaceship designs or disco infernos. What about an *Anne of Green Gables* theme – now how in hell is that erotic?

✪ TREEHOUSE, INDIA

This ecofriendly accommodation (part of Green Magic Nature Resort in Kerala), 27m (90ft) above the earth, is guaranteed to bring out the inner kid in every adult (save the ones with acrophobia). Access is by a bamboo lift, counterbalanced by water, and the rooms are airy and light. They're quiet, too; there are only two levels, one couple to each, so keep your pillow talk down.

✪ HOSTEL CELICA, SLOVENIA

This former prison in Ljubljana has had each of its cells renovated by a different artist and turned into accommodation of a very different kind. The barbed wire on the walls and the bars on the windows have been retained, and despite the hip makeover, it's still quite eerie – some say all prisons are haunted, so if you want to take your chances, then check in. Just don't drop your soap in the shower block.

SCULPTURES ARE ABOUT THE ONLY THING THAT CAN SURVIVE THE HEAT ABOVE GROUND IN COOBER PEDY.

✪ DESERT CAVE HOTEL, AUSTRALIA

In Coober Pedy, an outback town where 80% of the population lives underground due to the scorching heat, it's fitting there should be an underground church and an underground hotel. The Desert Cave's subterranean rooms are cool and dark, conditions that are naturally conducive to a good sleep (as is being buried alive) – yea verily, the Desert Cave is undeniably mysterious and therefore alluring (unlike being buried alive…unless you're a taphephil).

⭐ ALANDALUZ HOSTERIA, ECUADOR

#01. If this place were any more self-sufficient it would be a base station on Mars. Alandaluz, on the beach, is a model for green building practices, mainly constructed using replenishable materials such as tagua palm leaves and featuring a host of organic gardens that supply much of the guests' food needs. Compost bogs and treated waste mean that Andaluz recovers a staggering 90% of all water used; treated water goes on to be used for irrigation.

⭐ BASATA, EGYPT

#02. 'Basata' means 'simplicity' and Basata is simplicity itself. Located on the Red Sea, near Nuweiba, Basata is also clean, green and beautiful, surrounded by the Sinai mountains. Littering is strictly forbidden, everything is recycled, and public displays of affection are frowned upon in favour of a community-based family atmosphere. And the accommodation? Bamboo huts and villas on the beach hold a maximum of 250 guests and face perfect coral reefs and blue waters.

⭐ NIKITA'S, RUSSIA

#03. Smack bang in the middle of Lake Baikal is Olkhon, the world's second-largest freshwater island. And smack bang in the middle (or thereabouts) of Olkhon is Nikita's, a homestead consisting of wooden houses heated by wood fire and accompanied by lovely old *banya* (steam baths). Nikita's hosts will tell you all about Olkhon's fragile environment and how it's important to not cut wild flowers, kill butterflies or drive cars all over the shop; they'll also guide you on ecotours around the island.

✪ DAINTREE ECO LODGE, AUSTRALIA

This place has won awards mainly for its location, surrounded by tropical rainforest more than a million years old. It also has 15 rustic villas, interesting culinary offerings (bush tucker blended with upmarket modern Australian stylings), and a vigorous range of activities (such as snorkelling and diving around the Great Barrier Reef). The sounds of the waterfalls provide a pleasing soundtrack.

✪ BLUMAU HOT SPRINGS VILLAGE, AUSTRIA

The late 'organic architect' and environmentalist Friedensreich Hundertwasser designed this hot-springs village in Styria, Austria, with ecological imperatives firmly at the forefront: the village's composting toilets feed waste to its roof gardens, a process illuminated by Hundertwasser himself. 'Shit turns into earth,' he wrote, 'which is put on the roof / it becomes lawn, forest, garden / shit becomes gold. The circle is closed, there is no more waste. Shit is our soul'. In the end no one pooh-poohed Hundertwasser's idea, allowing the Blumau Hot Springs Village to open to an enthusiastic reception.

✪ CHALALÁN LODGE, BOLIVIA

This ecolodge in Madidi National Park is fully operated and owned by the Quechua people, who lead tours of discovery, teaching tourists the rich heritage of indigenous culture as well as the secrets of the surrounding rainforest and its multitude of inhabitants. As for the lodge itself, it was constructed using traditional methods; waste water is treated and solar power is a feature.

✪ TREEHOUSE, INDIA

Part of the Green Magic Nature Resort in Kerala, this eco-friendly accommodation is not for acrophobes: it's 27m (90ft) above the earth and access is by a bamboo lift counterbalanced by water. The rooms are open plan, of course, and airy and light, naturally. There are two levels, hosting one couple to each, so it's a fairly low-key scene. The views are awesome each way you turn.

✪ CHUMBE ISLAND CORAL PARK, TANZANIA

This spectacular ecolodge on Chumbe, a coral-island ecosystem about 12km (7.5mi) south of Zanzibar Town, features seven bungalows that overhang the sea. The Coral Park is pretty damn close to paradise with its 3km (1.9mi) sand bar, pristine ocean swells, baobab trees and giant coconut crabs. The bungalows are solar-powered, the toilets are composting and the cuisine is a mix of African, Indian and Middle Eastern. Solitude is guaranteed, given that the island is privately managed and only 14 guests are allowed on at a time.

✪ COSTA RICA ARENAL HOTEL, COSTA RICA

Costa Rica is becoming synonymous with the concept of ecotourism and the Arenal Hotel upholds the standard. Its location is a doozy: in the Northern Pacific mountains, with a much-vaunted view across to Volcán Arenal, Lago Coter and Laguna de Arenal. The hotel touts its 'policy of interaction' with the local Maleku Indians as an attraction, and certainly the chance to learn and understand an indigenous culture from the people who actually live it is a special bonus.

✪ TURTLE ISLAND, FIJI

This ecolodge is consistently ranked among the world's best, not least for its pampered service: there are around 150 staff members for 14 couples maximum. Some say this equates to 'ecohedonism' but many more don't care, as long as the environment gets some tender loving care. The island itself is just 500 acres, with natural springs that provide water for the lodge's organic garden, and you can trek among black volcanic cliffs or frolic among the picture-perfect coral reefs. The latter may look familiar; Brooke Shields herself (or rather, her body double) frolicked naked here in *Blue Lagoon*.

BEST ECO
#36. LODGES.

✪ WORKING IN SKI RESORTS

#o1.
Working in a ski resort is less of a job, more of a lifestyle. You'll likely end up skiing all day and partying all night. Though competition is stiff, there are loads of opportunities to work in resorts: from instructing on the slopes to behind the scenes in a chalet. You'll need international instructor qualifications to work as an instructor – where the pay is modest but the cool factor's high. Chalet staff cook and clean and though this work carries less kudos and cash, there is usually a great camaraderie among workers.

✪ CREWING A YACHT

#o2.
Working for your passage can certainly put the wind in your sails. Getting on board a yacht will likely get you into nooks and crannies that most of us only dream about, particularly around the islands of the Aegean Sea, the Pacific Ocean, Indian Ocean and the Caribbean. Apart from some nifty knot-tying, you'll need to work well in a team and under pressure. Tasks vary according to the vessel, but generally involve rigging, cleaning and maintenance. It's common for crew to contribute a small amount of cash to cover food and sundry expenses.

✪ FARMING WORK

#o3.
If you don't mind getting your hands dirty there is loads of labour that allows you to work outdoors – improving your tan while you work. You might pick up work fruit picking or planting crops but in all cases long hours and physical exertion are involved. Farm wages are generally low, but accommodation is thrown in and you'll have few opportunities to fritter away your earnings. You don't need any particular skills, just endurance and determination.

TEACHING ASPIRING OLYMPIC HOPEFULS ON THE SLOPES?

SEEING THE WORLD ON WATER IS ONE WAY TO EARN SOME CASH FOR YOUR ADVENTURES.

GRAPE PICKING IN GALICIA, SPAIN – MOR FOR THE EXPERIENCE THAN THE MONEY

BEST WORKING HOLIDAY
#37. JOBS.

✪ TEACHING ENGLISH

If you're reading this, then you already possess the prime qualification required for rewarding work overseas. The phenomenal popularity of the English language has created a huge demand for teachers. Those with formal teaching qualifications and experience can make a veritable career out of teaching: feted by foreign schools who pay air fares and look after work permits and paperwork. English teaching can also pay well: it's possible to come home with savings after a year of work in Japan or South Korea for example.

✪ AU PAIRING

There are few better ways to get cosy with a foreign culture than to live and work with a local family. Au pairing may not pay well, but most use it as an opportunity to master a language – fluency is priceless. Essentially, you have to love children, but most employers also prefer to employ single people with no dependents, who're aged between 17 and 27. You'll need to prove that you've spent time caring for children – a job that's not short on responsibility.

✪ COOKING/ WORKING AS A KITCHEN HAND

If you're a maestro on the burners (and you're qualified), you could secure work as a chef in a restaurant or hotel. Those without qualifications can still get in the kitchen: prepping food, flipping burgers or doing the washing up (affectionately known as 'dish pigging'). Working in restaurants and hotels often puts you in touch with other travellers, and offers a casual environment to earn a bit of cash. And while washing up may not make you wealthy, it will give you hands as soft as your face.

✪ LEADING TOURS

The best thing about leading tour groups is being paid to sightsee in a foreign country. Working day-to-day with locals also allows you to get under a country's skin. As a tour leader you're responsible for the smooth running of the trip and the satisfaction of your group. Most operators require their leaders to speak a foreign language and to sign up for two or more seasons. You won't be doing this job for the pay, but whatever you do make will be on top of free accommodation, return air fare and often free meals.

✪ WRITING

Apart from heading to some exotic destination for inspiration to write that best-selling novel, journalism is probably the best known of the 'proper jobs' in which you can ensure some money dribbles into your account. If you've got a nose for a story and can write, pitch it to the editor responsible for the relevant section of an appropriate newspaper or magazine. You basically need to be contactable and have the capacity to deliver on your pitch.

✪ VOLUNTEERING

Get that warm and fuzzy feeling from doing something positive for someone or something you care about while gaining an insight into a foreign place and chalking up experience. Volunteering opportunities are many and varied, including professional placements to gain experience, joining an expedition and administration for a nongovernmental organisation. Costs to the volunteer also vary according to the activity and length of stay, but bank on contributing to food and sundry expenses.

NOT JUST FOR WANNABE ACTORS – CAFÉ AND BAR WORK IS A TOP WAY TO EARN SOME EXTRA TRAVEL COIN.

✪ WAITING/WORKING IN A BAR

Whether you're working the floor taking food orders in a bustling café or pulling pints in a village pub, this is people-focused work: it's not known as the hospitality industry for nothin'. Though the hours can be long and the pay a pittance, you'll likely come across a lot of locals, and tips can plump out an average earning. Most establishments require that you have some experience, particularly working a bar (changing kegs and mixing cocktails).

⭐ GIGER BAR, CHUR & CHÂTEAU ST GERMAIN

#o1. The Swiss graphic artist HR Giger is perhaps most famous for creating the eponymous creature in the sci-fi/horror flick *Alien,* along with the film's overall ambience of nightmare and dread. Giger invented the concept of 'biomechanoids', a hellish fusion of machine and utterly alien intelligence, and that precisely describes the décor of these bars in Switzerland. Interiors are dark and oppressive – it feels like you're in the tomb where *Alien*'s doomed spacemen first encountered their demonic nemesis; the seats impart a horrible sensation like you're sitting in the slimy monster's lap.

⭐ RED SEA STAR, EILAT

#o2. The Red Sea Star is a bit like Stromberg's underwater lair in the James Bond flick, *The Spy Who Loved Me* – unsurprising considering it's 5m (16ft) below the Red Sea in Israel. The interior of this bar/restaurant resembles a mermaid's lounge room, with fishy fantasy motifs – including jellyfish-shaped stools and starfish lights – and huge windows through which curious (or vengeful) fish and other marine creatures eyeball the customers eyeballing their seafood platter. If you crane your neck, you might see a ship overhead from time to time.

⭐ MARTON, TAIPEI

#o3. Marton in Taiwan ain't for the squeamish, given that it's themed after commodes, potties, the john, loo, dunny, throne, porcelain bus, can, bog… Plates are toilet-bowl shaped (Asian squat or Western sit) and if you reckon you could eat a runny curry out of one, then go right ahead! Good luck with the chocolate ice cream, too. Can you drink lemon squash from a toilet bowl? A cheers of 'bottoms up' would be appropriate. Naturally, chairs are shaped like toilets, and there's urinal art (although no Duchamp). The only thing missing is 'toilet lollies'.

THE OTHERWORLDLY MUSEUM HR GIGER BAR IN GRUYÈRES, SWITZERLAND.

MOST UNUSUAL RESTAURANTS AND
#38. BARS.

✪ REGATTA HOTEL, BRISBANE

The male toilets in this Australian joint are billed as the 'loo with a view'. The back wall of the urinal is a huge one-way mirror and many a chap (and his 'old chap') has been caught out entering here for the first time, drunk and unaware, getting down to business then looking up in horror to find a passer-by seemingly fixated on you know what. Relax: you can see them, but they can't see you (they're probably just adjusting their hair…you hope). How soon before a bar reverses the opticals?

✪ DEPECHE MODE BAAR, TALLINN

The most bizarre aspect of this tribute bar is its subject matter: '80s hair/synth band Depeche Mode. This dark corner of Estonia is filled with black-clad, rake-thin DM fans sipping on Master & Servant or Personal Jesus cocktails while listening to the band's cod melancholia. Autographed photos, DM artwork and tour memorabilia line the walls, while video screens play continuous Mode videos. A vision of bleakest hell for some; sweet heaven for others.

✪ LE REFUGE DES FONDUES, PARIS

Don't despair if you can't get into that posh Parisian restaurant – this place takes anyone (space permitting). It's tiny and the walls are covered with graffiti (add your own), only fondues are served, and there are only two tables, which are very long – diners sit cheek by jowl and those on the inner seats have to scramble over the table to leave. A bonus: you'll meet lots of people; it's hard not to as you plant your boot in someone's dinner in your rush to make the toilet after one baby bottle too many (that's what their wine comes in).

✪ ALBATROSS, TOKYO

Tokyo, Japan's tiny Albatross is in the bar-filled Shomben Yokocho (or 'Piss Alley'; all the bars share the same toilets). You'd be hard pressed to cram more than 10 bodies in here. There are three levels, including an art gallery, and the place is so skinny there's a hole in the upper floors through which the bar staff pass your drinks. If you don't breathe out, don't scratch your head and make sure you watch your step (people have been known to fall through the drinks hole) then you'll have a fine old time.

✪ NASA, BANGALORE

Bar staff resplendent in spacesuits; space-shuttle-style décor; spacey tags: 'Fuel Tank' for the bar, 'Humanoid Disposal' for the toilets; laser-light shows; tables attached to rocket fins; images of the earth seen from orbit through portholes on the walls… The only thing missing from this ode to the Infinite Vacuum in India is a dodgy heat-protection shield, although the cocktails can supply the blinding flash (and the stars before your eyes).

✪ RED ROOM, SAN FRANCISCO

It's all red, every bit of it: floors, walls, ceiling, drinks bottles and glasses, chairs, couches, curtains…your face after a few drinks. After a few more drinks, you might think you're trapped in a David Lynch nightmare dream sequence, where everyone talks backwards, your arms are on back to front, and funny little men do strange contortionist dances that defy time, space and gravity.

✪ HOBBIT HOUSE, MANILA

This Tolkien-themed bar and restaurant in the Philippines bills itself as 'the world's only bar owned and staffed by hobbits' – actually a team of dwarves and midgets. The décor is charming and rustic, with wood panelling and folksy flourishes, and tall people will need to bend over double to fit through the doorways. The Hobbit House is renowned for the quality of its live music.

MOST STUPID THING YOU HEARD A TOURIST SAY!

#01.
(In Zurich, Switzerland) 'Sorry, I don't speak Swiss.'

#02.
(In Edinburgh, Scotland) 'Why did they build the castle next to the railway?'

#03.
(In Paris, France) 'Honey, why are all the streets called Rue?'

#04.
(A guy in a nightclub in Prague, Czech Republic) 'Are you ready to rock, Berlin?'

#05.
(An American in Canada) 'It's almost like another country here.'

⊛ RUNNING WITH THE BULLS, SPAIN

#o1.
Is there any more potent sign of madness than the sight of thousands of lunatics charging ahead of a pack of snorting, rampaging bulls through the narrow streets of Pamplona? Actually, there is: the sight of a man impaled on the end of a bullhorn. Ever since Ernest Hemingway popularised it, running with the bulls has come to symbolise some kind of macho pinnacle. You can tell the ones who come back year after year: they walk wobbly due to their plastic hip, or they can't piss straight because they got gored and lost their manhood.

⊛ SWIMMING WITH SHARKS, SOUTH AFRICA

#o2.
So, tough guy – dolphins not edgy enough for you? Try swimming with a great white off Dyer Island. All you have to do is jump in a cage and be lowered into a school of hungry sharks. As they peer in helplessly at you with those dead black eyes, you might think 'this is soft!' Think again. Smaller sharks have been known to butt their way through the bars – there's your adrenalin rush, right there. Some operators bait sharks before sending tourists down, so a debate rages about subsequent harmful effects. Make an informed decision before descending.

⊛ ZAMBEZI RIVER RAFTING, ZAMBIA & ZIMBABWE

#o3.
The British Canoe Union classes this white-water run as an extreme Grade 5: violent rapids, steep gradients, massive drops. One of the rapids is called 'Oblivion' and is said to flip more canoes than any other on the planet; you might be able to flip it the bird once you've conquered it, but then you must contend with the 'Devil's Toilet Bowl', the 'Gnashing Jaws of Death' and 'Commercial Suicide'. It takes a special breed of cat to lick the Zambezi, as you'll discover as you're speared, sucked and jettisoned in and out of these rapids like a pinball.

IT'S THE THRILL OF THE CHASE AT THE ANNUAL RUNNING OF THE BULLS FESTIVAL IN PAMPLONA, SPAIN.

THE ONLY THING SEPARATING YOU FROM A SHARK ARE METAL BARS. OR ARE THEY?

HOLD ON TO YOUR HELMETS, AND YOUR LUNCH.

BIGGEST ADRENALIN
#39. RUSHES. »

✪ PARASAILING, MEXICO

Parasailing was invented in Acapulco and that's no surprise: it's an absolutely prime location for floating upon the air, with a spectacular, panoramic view of the city, the hills and the islands beyond Acapulco Bay. You take off from the beach and you land on the beach, and while it feels dangerous and edgy, it really is as safe as houses, except for the yapping jaws of the dogs that chase you on your descent.

✪ ROCK CLIMBING, USA

They say Yosemite Valley is climbing mecca, with climbs coveted by 'rock heads' far and wide and a degree of difficulty that has necessitated many technical innovations. Even today, as the most demanding ascents have crumbled, aficionados still point to El Capitan, Yosemite's 915m (3000ft) granite wall, as the planet's greatest rock climb. Just because it's been mastered doesn't mean it's now a pushover – recently, several experienced climbers died when the weather turned unexpectedly foul – so if you make it, you deserve to puff up your chest, because you're simply the best! Better than all the rest!

✪ SWIMMING WITH DOLPHINS, NEW ZEALAND

These graceful and playful creatures are guaranteed to quicken the pulse of anyone lucky enough to get near them, with their undeniable intelligence and transcendent personalities. They get frisky and acrobatic only if they feel like it (which is fair enough), so a new trend has taken root: swimmers sing not only to attract dolphins, but also to get them in the mood. Apparently Elvis tunes do the trick nicely.

✪ 'EDGE OF SPACE' FLIGHTS, RUSSIA

This must be the ultimate high for mainline adrenalin junkies: strapping yourself into a MiG-25 fighter jet and submitting to speeds of Mach 3.2 at a height of 25km (82,000ft) – the edge of space – where the sky is black and earth spreads out beneath you. The pilot might even let you take the controls but make sure you're not too jittery and bank too far, otherwise you might be forced to draw upon that ejector-seat training they put you through.

✪ BIG SHOT RIDE, USA

This ride – atop the 280m (921ft), 110-storey Stratosphere observation tower in Las Vegas – has incredible views but you'll be too busy vomiting up your intestines to notice. The Big Shot runs on compressed air, which,

HANGING OUT IN YOSEMITE, CALIFORNIA.

GREG EPPERSON | PHOTOLIBRARY

with incredible force, rockets you in your harness from the ride's base to the top of the Big Shot's 49m (160ft) tower in just over two seconds. As you shake about in your seat like a rag doll, at a combined total of over 300m (1000ft) above ground, you'll be thanking your lucky stars you didn't wear white underwear.

✪ SYDNEY HARBOUR BRIDGE CLIMB, AUSTRALIA

Follow in Aussie comedian Paul Hogan's footsteps: prefame, he worked as a rigger on the 'coat hanger' (the world's largest steel-arch bridge; its summit is 134m (440ft) above sea level). The climb takes more than three hours and it's a hairy thrill to be sure, with cars and people below like ants and the lovely Sydney Harbour before you, but old grannies do it, as do young kids (accompanied by adults). Apparently even Kylie Minogue has done it, and for some folk following in the Singing Budgie's footsteps is all the adrenalin shot they need.

✪ MOTORCYCLE-TAXI RIDE, THAILAND

This is one of the most dangerous rides of them all: three people die every hour in Bangkok traffic. Motorcycle-taxi riders bob in and out of endless lines of cars at alarming speeds, often mounting pavements, and wipe-outs occur with shocking regularity; often the injured rider or passenger is carted off to hospital in a passing *túk-túk* (motorised pedicab), not the most comforting way to get treatment. Just hang on tight, squeeze your legs in even tighter to avoid getting kneecapped by a passing car, say your Hail Marys and hope for the best.

⭐ THE ITALIAN FAKE-BABY SCAM

#o1. Oh please, not the old 'fake baby on a fake arm' trick! A woman holding a 'baby' trips; you lunge to catch the infant; your pockets are thoroughly picked by an accomplice as the 'mother' vanishes into thin air; and you realise you've been had when you stare into the baby's lifeless, artificial eyes. An innovative variation sees the ersatz child attached to an artificial arm, leaving the scammer's real arms free to wreak havoc. By all means help mums in distress, but just keep your peepers peeled: it can't be that hard to spot a fake kid.

⭐ THE CHINESE ART-STUDENT SCAM

#o2. This scam involves young Chinese people offering to take you to see a 'special' exhibition of their art; they might tug on the heartstrings, saying they need you to buy their work so they can visit their sick auntie overseas. They might claim they have been exhibited in the National Museum of China, although the paintings they will actually take you to see will be very clever reproductions of famous works, or of less-than-famous works (in which case you'll be paying more than the originals). So go easy, Tiger – visit a gallery instead.

⭐ THE SPANISH FLOWER SCAM

#o3. Flower Power rules, so know the rules of the game. A friendly lady offers you flowers – you might take one and offer some coins in return. It seems innocent enough but as you fumble for change, many fingers are making light work of the contents of your pockets. For shame! Another variation: the flower child might push your wallet away, apparently refusing payment. Wouldn't you know it? When you open your purse later, your cash has gone. Also beware the lady who drops your proffered coinage; while you're picking it up, someone's picking you.

⭐ THE INDIAN EXPORT-JEWELLERY SCAM

Because Indian jewellery dealers pay exorbitant export taxes, scammers approach tourists to send a parcel of diamonds home, throwing in a free flight there and back for you to ensure its safe delivery to 'a friend'. Before that can happen, though, you'll be asked for assurance, like divulging your bank details, to guarantee that you won't run off with the goods… Travellers have allegedly been kidnapped for refusing to do this, so tread carefully, OK? The jewels will be fake, by the way.

⭐ THE INDIAN FREE-TOUR-GUIDE SCAM

Steer clear of the friendly tour guide offering services for free. You'll be frogmarched to a series of shops where the only way to escape is to buy something – naturally, the guide takes a juicy commission. Never let a tour guide direct you to a luggage locker; chances are they'll have a duplicate key that they'll use to lighten your load while you're seeking enlightenment elsewhere.

⭐ THE AMERICAN BAD-JOKE SCAM

This one's so bad it's *almost* funny. A hulking dude walks up to you in the street. 'Hey buddy,' he says, 'for twenty bucks, I bet I can tell you where you got those shoes'. 'Yeah, right,' you think, figuring you can have this chump. 'Where?' you reply. The guy laughs, as he cracks his knuckles, 'You got those shoes on your feet!' If you fall for this one, you deserve everything you get.

✪ THE AMERICAN THREE-CARD TRICK

This classic scam, played out on New York street corners, continues to fleece greenhorns from far and wide, so read these words very carefully: *you cannot win*. Sure, the odds may look appealing – one in three – but it's a con, pure and simple. The Queen of Spades is mixed with two other cards. The scammer moves the cards around on a flat surface; your task is to pick where the Queen ends up. But these dudes are magicians; you won't see the sleight of hand, just as you won't see your money ever again.

✪ THE THAI GEM SCAM

The Thai Gem Scam is perhaps even more common than the Thai Taxi Scam. Beware the friendly Thai, or crooked *túk-túk* (motorised pedicab) driver, who escorts you to an 'official' jeweller, filling your head with stories of how much cash you can make back home by reselling gems such as sapphires and so on. The rocks you'll end up with will have very little value, so if you're so keen on making money, pick up some dirt off the ground and sell that back home – you'll probably make a bigger profit.

DODGIEST #40. SCAMS.

✪ THE THAI TAXI SCAM

This one's rife: scammers driving unregistered cabs will often claim their meter doesn't work, leaving them free to charge you through the nose. Or they'll claim your destination doesn't exist anymore, or is closed, instead taking you somewhere else where you'll be compelled to buy something. Always ask about the price before starting off, and if the deal smells fishy, stand firm and find another taxi – official Thai cabs carry the sign 'Taxi-Meter'. If you're staying at a hotel, get the staff to order your ride.

✪ THE EGYPTIAN BOTH-WAYS SCAM

Taxi scams work pretty much the same wherever they're found in the world (see 'The Thai Taxi Scam') – always make sure the driver understands what you want to pay and if it's too expensive, find another one. The 'Egyptian Both Ways' set-up is pretty cute, though. The cabbie takes you to your destination; you book him to pick you up a few hours' later. When he takes you back to the hotel, you find the price has been jacked up 100% (or more). Why? You've been charged for 'waiting' in between trips.

PART. #02.

» PLACES TO GO.

» **THE AMERICAS.**

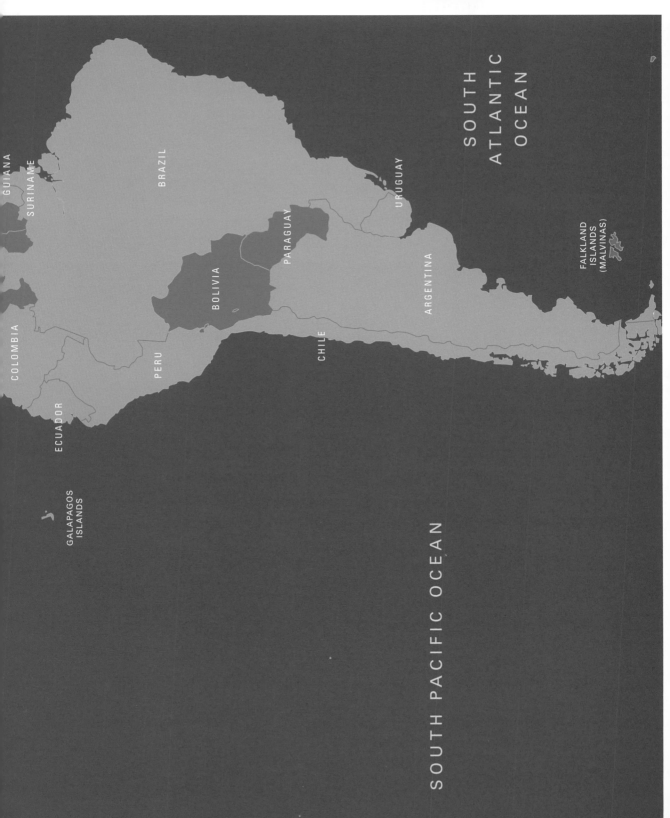

GUIANA

SURINAME

COLOMBIA

BRAZIL

PARAGUAY

BOLIVIA

URUGUAY

ARGENTINA

PERU

CHILE

ECUADOR

SOUTH
ATLANTIC
OCEAN

FALKLAND
ISLANDS
(MALVINAS)

GALAPAGOS
ISLANDS

SOUTH PACIFIC OCEAN

■ = BLUELIST. HOTSPOTS

ARGENTINA.

VITAL STATISTICS

◎ **POPULATION**
39.5 MILLION

◎ **VISITORS PER YEAR**
3.5 MILLION

◎ **UNIT OF CURRENCY**
PESO

◎ **STEAK DINNER WITH A DECENT BOTTLE OF WINE**
30 PESOS = US$10

◎ **CAPITAL**
BUENOS AIRES

◎ **LANGUAGES**
SPANISH, QUECHUA, ARAUCANIAN, GUARANI

COLOURFUL HOUSES FRINGE CAMINITO STREET IN BUENOS AIRES.

★ WORLD-CLASS BARGAIN HUNTING. In the aftermath of its recent economic and political crises, Argentina has attracted hordes of bargain hunters with rock-bottom deals on top-quality goods, top-notch outdoor activities and world-class cultural experiences.

Since many city dwellers are now out exploring their hinterlands for the first time, a highlight of visiting is meeting vivacious locals who are eager to share their enthusiasm for their inviting homeland.

Quiz urbane residents about why they adore and romanticize the wide-open southern expanses of Patagonia and Tierra del Fuego and most mention the skies: sunrise and sunset cast endless streaks of amber and red, and night skies drip with stars.

ON THE REBOUND

The trauma that has unfolded has left a huge scar on the overanalyzed Argentine psyche. Many observers have commented that the inflated national ego was long overdue for a healthy adjustment. The darkest days appear to be over, but a brutal hangover lingers in the form of a national credit rating six fathoms below investment grade. Many middle-class families, who had their

life savings deposited in pesos during the currency devaluation, are seeking restitution from the government via ongoing litigation.

Despite these setbacks, there's an upbeat momentum about the resilient nation, especially in Buenos Aires. *Porteños* (residents of the capital) are famously brash and cocky, but it's precisely this assertiveness that makes them so endearing. Argentina remains the most European of South American countries, with a proud heritage of immigration and a multicultural melting-pot vibe akin to London or New York City. Thanks to the ridiculously low cost of living compared with other major metropolises, Buenos Aires is now a magnet for international artists.

For many young Argentines, economic opportunity awaits overseas, which is why they are migrating (mostly illegally) to Spain in search of employment. In an ironic twist, TV production, computer programming, and call-centre jobs are increasingly being

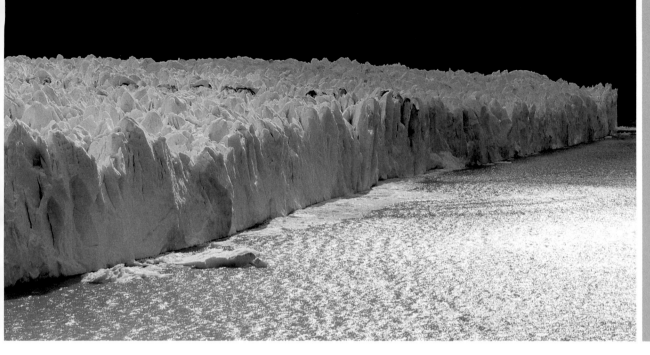

THE MONUMENTAL MORENO GLACIER SLOWLY EDGES ITS WAY ALONG LOS GLACIARES NATIONAL PARK.

outsourced to Buenos Aires. Meanwhile, underemployed *piqueteros* (picketers) assemble in the streets on a regular basis, wreaking havoc and clogging traffic with roadblocks while demanding raises in meagre monthly government-welfare payments.

Relations with the UK over the contested Islas Malvinas/Falkland Islands have mellowed considerably since London and Buenos Aires restored diplomatic relations in 1990. Other rivalries that help keep the troops motivated include national sovereignty concerns raised by recent foreign purchases of vast Patagonian *estancias* (ranches), and a long-running territorial dispute with Chile over the ill-defined border (and abundant frozen water resources) in the vast Southern Continental Ice Field.

With such a wealth and range of cultural, culinary and scenic attractions on offer at bargain-basement rates, there's never been a better time to tango in Argentina.

DEFINING EXPERIENCE

⊙ Witness the kaboom of the Perito Moreno Glacier, an advancing ice field the size of Gran Buenos Aires, situated at the foot of the soaring Andes. Then jet a couple of hours to tango the wee hours away (as well as those extra pounds gained from all that prime steak and red wine) in the Euro-style capital that never sleeps. The morning after, chill with a *mate* (tea) and replay memories of fresh-butchered lamb chops grilled over a split-wood fire at an *estancia* in Patagonia, the world's most stunning slice of the middle of nowhere.

RECENT FAD

⊙ Unruly coifs. Blame the comeback of stylistically suspect haircuts such as the mullet and medio-mohawk (spiked up, but minus the shaved sides) on Mexican *punk roqueros* (punk rockers) like Molotov and sassy soccer stars like the irrepressible Argentine national hero, Diego Maradona. »

MOST BIZARRE SIGHT! ✪

Gaiman's Parque El Desafío. The world's largest 'recycled park' is a whimsical tour de force of folksy junk, curated by an eccentric octogenarian dubbed the 'Dalí of Recycling'.

OH, MY GOD – AY, DIOS MIO!

If trying to get something repaired, say a digital camera, you're likely to hear the axiom: 'God lives everywhere…but his office is in Buenos Aires'. Translation: good luck getting anything fixed outside of the capital.

ARGENTINA.

FROM THE ROAD

> *We were winding up our exploration of Argentina, and we had been on the same bus for 20 hours. The bus drivers were also bored and they settled on the two gringas as their entertainment. They allowed us to perch on the dashboard, backs to the windshield as the bus sped down the highway at a speed I was afraid to acknowledge. Cigarettes were passed along, and* mate *(traditional tea) was prepared on an open-air propane flame. Lack of sleep, cigarette smoke and conversations in Spanish about love combined to give this little adventure a very dream-like quality.*

- Kate VanEmrik, USA

» FESTIVALS & EVENTS

- Tango Festival; Buenos Aires; late February. This festival promises to sweep the capital off its feet with impassioned dance exhibitions, visual art and cinema showcases and free classes at venues across town.

- Livestock competitions; La Rural International Exhibition complex, Buenos Aires; July. Beef is boss in Argentina.

- Spring sheep shearing; at a Patagonian *estancia;* November. The best way to experience quintessential rural gaucho (cowboy) life.

- Campeonato Abierto de Pato; San Isidro Jockey Club, Buenos Aires; mid-November. This traditional sport is akin to rugby on horseback (and a rather less civilized precursor of polo).

DO MENTION

- Argentine beef and wine are far superior to anything you have ever tasted.

DON'T MENTION

- Money. Argentines struggle to swallow their pride; don't make light of the increasing number of Brazilians, Chileans and Uruguayan tourists, and don't ask locals why they aren't vacationing in Miami or Paris this year.

RANDOM FACTS

- In 2002, the number of Argentines vacationing abroad dropped by 37%.

- Per capita, Buenos Aires is home to more psychoanalysts than even New York City.

- Patagonia's population density is less than one person per square kilometre – one of the world's lowest ratios.

- The 2500 permanent nonmilitary residents of the contested Falkland Islands/Islas Malvinas look after a population of 700,000 sheep.

THINGS TO TAKE

- A corkscrew for picnicking with bottles of world-class wine

- Tampons – it's a challenge to find them outside of big cities

- Peanut butter – the calorie-packed spread doesn't exist in Argentina

- Cash and/or means of extracting some, such as an ATM card with international PIN; cash advances are hit-or-miss and credit cards are not widely accepted

HOT TIPS FOR TRAVELLERS

- No contemporary electronica act blends accordion riffs and chill-out beats better than the Buenos Aires–based Gotan Project trio, who hit a groovy nerve with their *Revancha Del Tango* album.

- Subletting a Buenos Aires flat while studying tango and Spanish (or earning a certificate in teaching English as a foreign language) is all the rage. The City of Buenos Aires' Tango Portal (www.tangodata.com.ar) details everything aspiring bilingual dirty dancers need to know.

- The southern migration to the proverbial End of the World in Tierra del Fuego is as popular as ever. Don't attempt the long haul on a tight schedule during the January/February run-up to Carnival in Brazil, when flights and buses tend to get booked early.

THREE WORDS TO DESCRIBE THIS COUNTRY

- Beef, vino, tango

- Andrew Nystrom

LEAVE YOUR LOW-CARB, LOW-FAT HANG-UPS AT HOME. BELIZE IS HOME TO GOOD TIMES AND GREAT FOOD.

VITAL STATISTICS

BELIZE.

○ **POPULATION**
280,000

○ **VISITORS PER YEAR**
230,000

○ **UNIT OF CURRENCY**
BELIZEAN DOLLAR ($)

○ **COST OF A CUP OF COFFEE**
B$1 = US$0.50

○ **CAPITAL**
BELMOPAN

○ **LANGUAGE**
ENGLISH

★ WHATEVER THE OPPOSITE OF PANDORA'S BOX IS. What a funny little country Belize is. Although it's geographically and politically part of Central America, it absolutely refuses to go along with its neighbours.

Leave your Spanish phrasebooks back in Guatemala: everyone speaks English here. Looking for tacos, *chiles rellenos* (stuffed peppers) or steaks? Forget about it: the cuisine is pure Caribbean, with spicy meat delights and coconut juice the mainstays. And you know how Americans never go to Central America? Well, there's another stereotype shattered: these days, every other person you meet is likely to be a Yankee tourist.

Just a few years ago, Belize was a secret. No-one figured it to be one of the best diving destinations in the world (until Jacques Cousteau blabbed about it). No-one realised how easy it was to get to, how affordable it was to travel in, how easygoing Belizeans were and how diverse the country actually was.

That has all changed in the last couple of years. This year, Belize promises to be the hottest Central American destination – even more sizzling than Costa Rica. More and more folk are waking up to the fact that

this tiny nation provides all the excitement of a Caribbean island vacation without the expenditure and mass tourism of a cruise or the inconvenience of island-hopping. It's as though someone mashed together a variety of islands and glued the result onto the Central American isthmus. For swimmers, divers, wildlife-watchers, hikers, spelunkers and beach bums, it's a dream come true.

THE CLOUD BEHIND THE SILVER LINING

Although Belize looks to be sitting pretty on the travel front, it can't quite escape some of the problems bedevilling its mainland and island neighbours. As tourism becomes a key national industry, the livelihoods of people accustomed to a purely agrarian economy are deeply affected. Belizeans have recently found themselves stuck in a period of transition, with increased urban migration and sharply rising poverty in the cities. This in turn has brought about an upsurge in crime. Belize »

★ MOST BIZARRE SIGHT!

The Great Blue Hole of Belize is a circular cenote, the Mayan term for a limestone cavern. However, unlike most cenotes, which are inland and are used as freshwater wells, the Great Blue Hole is in the middle of the water. It's a deeper blue within the turquoise of the sea, and it contains strange and captivating limestone formations that add to its all-around surreality.

»

GARIFUNA BAND THE TURTLE SHELL PERFORMS A CHILLED SOUND TO A HOT SET

BELIZE.

» City in particular is noted by travellers as one of the more dangerous, unattractive Central American towns (and it's a shame that it's the point of entry for most visitors).

BELMOPAN TAKES ACTION!

The good news is that Belizeans are increasingly aware of how intricately tied their well-being is to the way visitors are treated. The government has begun cracking down on crimes against foreigners, and most touristed areas are likely to be safer and far easier to explore than the larger industrial towns. On the other end of the spectrum, Belize is full of relatively unexplored and sparsely inhabited areas (such as the south), where crime is almost zero and the lack of tourist infrastructure is compensated for by the opportunity to travel across virtually virgin lands.

The truth is that right now is probably the best time in history to visit Belize. At no other time has it boasted such a combination of easy tourist opportunities and chances to engage in more challenging ecotourism or exploration activities. One day, everyone will know about Belize, and it may well become a land of five-star resorts, cruise ships and World Poker Tour championships on the beach. But for now, only just enough people know about it to make it a really fun destination. Be one of them.

DEFINING EXPERIENCE

✪ Chowing down on some hard-earned jerk chicken on the beach after a rough day of exploring Mayan ruins and scuba diving for treasure

FESTIVALS & EVENTS

✪ Baron Bliss Day; March. This wonderfully named holiday is uniquely Belizean – see 'Random Facts'.

✪ The major time of celebration in Belize is the week and a half starting at Belize National Day and running through Independence Day (both in September). Expect the usual Caribbean festivities: dancing, drinking, parading and staying up all night.

✪ Columbus Day; October. This holiday is even bigger in Belize than in the USA. Belize City is the place to be on this day; it features sailboat racing and lots of picnicking.

✪ Garifuna Settlement Day; November. Commemorating the arrival of Garifunas

RECENT FAD! ★

Gambling, especially at slot machines, is on the upswing in Belize – much to the delight of casino owners and employees, and much to the dismay of property managers (as more and more people are failing to come up with the rent on time).

"

Placencia, Belize, drunk. My leg had swollen to twice its size, so I went to lie by the ocean. A local started poking my leg, mumbling something about an ancient salve. He took me to his house. 'It's probably a sand bug; if you were going to die it would have happened already', he said reassuringly. He applied his salve and my leg went numb. I was close to panicking so…I played board games. I laughed and listened to his stories while wondering about my leg. Two hours and more salve later, my leg was back to normal.

"

- Elizabeth Smith, USA

(also known as 'Black Caribs') from Honduras. This holiday is celebrated most enthusiastically in Dangriga and other southern areas of the country.

WHAT'S HOT…
☼ Governmental corruption is a current hot topic, especially on the heels of the financial mismanagement crises of 2004 and 2005. However, you won't see these matters being discussed on the street or in bars and restaurants; they fall solely within the purview of newspapers, TV programmes and conversations among close friends.

WHAT'S NOT…
☼ Low-fat and low-carb diets are definitely *not* on the menu. If you wanted to eat only raw vegetables, why did you come to the Caribbean?

RANDOM FACTS
☼ One of Belize's major holidays, Baron Bliss Day (9 March), is named after a paraplegic British benefactor who never set foot in the country. Upon his death, on a sailing yacht anchored just offshore, he willed almost his entire fortune to the

people of Belize. Nationwide celebrations on the anniversary of his death always include a harbour regatta.
☼ There is an exception to Belize's strict regulations prohibiting importing food: at Christmas time, you are allowed to bring one Christmas ham *or* turkey into the country – but you have to have a permit.
☼ Ambergris Caye, Belize's largest cay, was named after a smelly substance produced in sperm whales' intestines.
☼ Belize boasts the world's second-largest coastal reef, doffing its cap only to Australia's Great Barrier Reef.
☼ There are no baboons in Belize's Community Baboon Sanctuary. Lots of howler monkeys, no baboons.

DO MENTION
☼ Talking up Belize's chances (minuscule though they may be) for qualifying for the 2006 FIFA World Cup won't harden any hearts against you. In fact, mentioning soccer at all isn't a bad idea.

DON'T MENTION
☼ Avoid talking politics in casual settings – it's just not done. And even if you've crossed the border from Mexico or Guatemala, resist the temptation to speak Spanish. Most Belizeans have a degree of Spanish proficiency, but the national language is English…and don't you forget it.

THINGS TO TAKE
☼ Plenty of cash or travellers cheques; ATMs are uncommon and not incredibly reliable
☼ Basic scuba or snorkelling gear, unless you want your wealth to be slowly bled away by rental fees
☼ A completely relaxed attitude to life (including, most importantly, towards the passage of time)

HOT TOPIC OF THE DAY
☼ High oil prices are dominating the news. In a show of Caribbean solidarity, Venezuela is making overtures to Belize, promising to share oil resources with its little (and somewhat distant) neighbour.

THREE WORDS TO DESCRIBE THIS COUNTRY
☼ Mainland Caribbean island

- Vivek Wagle

BELIZE.

BRAZIL.

VITAL STATISTICS

- **POPULATION**
  186 MILLION
- **VISITORS PER YEAR**
  4 MILLION
- **UNIT OF CURRENCY**
  REAL (R$)
- **COST OF A FRESHLY
  SQUEEZED JUICE**
  R$2.45 = US$1
- **CAPITAL**
  BRASÍLIA
- **LANGUAGE**
  PORTUGUESE

THREE YOUNG YANOMAMI WOMEN
SMILE SWEETLY IN TIDY SHORT BOBS.

TALL & TANNED & YOUNG & LOVELY. The mention of Brazil evokes a plethora of vibrant imagery – the throngs of vivacious revellers in Rio's Carnaval, awe-inspiring beaches, a round-the-clock feast of samba, *cachaça* (sugarcane rum) and great coffee.

It is all these things and much more, and is also the source of some huge contradictions. Despite being home to some of the richest people in Latin America and being the world's 11th biggest economy, more than 40 million of its citizens live below the poverty line. Also for a nation noted for its passions for individuality, sport and carnivals, many a visitor has been surprised by how blasé some locals are about street violence, the omnipresent poverty and the archaic laws regarding freedom of the press.

For Westerners, Brazil is seen as the kingpin for exotic tropical holidays and this romantic, sun-soaked vibe is alive and kicking, available to anyone with the cash and enough energy to keep up in the conga line. Though Brazil may seem cliché to outsiders it's not easily discredited; for all the camp and grandeur of Carnaval and the gusto of most Brazilians, there is underlying sincerity that cannot be ignored.

AFTER THE CARNAVAL

Beyond the easily accessible Brazilian experience is a complicated and diverse nation, both socially and geographically. Since the mid-1500s when the Portuguese initially divided the nation into 15 captaincies, each region has developed its own unique culture and customs.

The state of the Amazon and the plight of its native inhabitants has brought international attention providing the groundwork for a burgeoning industry of ecotourism. In recent years this has instigated opportunities for unforgettable experiences of Brazil's natural wonders. There is a broad range of ecotours to suit most budgets and interests, including packages that use 'low-impact' lodge accommodation with toucan- and alligator-spotting safaris.

Social realist films such as *Pixot* (1981) and *City of Go* (2002) have opened the world's eyes to the dire poverty of many Brazilians.

SAMBA PERFORMERS REEL IN THE PARTY CROWDS ON COPACABANA BEACH, RIO DE JANEIRO.

This in turn has spurred the rise of more socially aware tourism, in the form of volunteers. Working in schools or orphanages, teaching English or even contributing specific skills to a community project can be an immensely satisfying, valuable and even life-changing experience. Most volunteer placements are made from your country of origin – www.amizade.org/Countries/Brazil .htm or http://www.volunteering.org.au /brazil_p.html are good places to start.

IS THAT A CONQUISTADOR IN YOUR POCKET?

Modern Brazil is the product of more than 500 years of tumultuous fusion of a range of wonderful and disparate cultures – most predominantly Portuguese, African and indigenous, although the Dutch, English and Japanese have also made significant contributions to the culture at different times. Trying to find a definitive Brazilian face would be a frivolous undertaking. Ever since the Portuguese arrived in 1500 (properly setting up shop in 1531) there has been a mixing of these varied cultures. The Portuguese were quite single-mindedly interested in trade and what wealth they could extract from their new-found

outposts and not in setting up towns or infrastructure. After an early foray into Brazil-wood harvesting (used in Europe as a reddish dye), for which they exploited mostly native labour, they realised that sugarcane flourished in this part of the world. Europe's fervent demand for sugar sparked a surge of trade in slaves from Africa. By the time slavery was abolished in 1888 it is estimated that 3.7 million Africans were torn from tribes in Angola, Mozambique, Guinea, Sudan and the Congo and shipped to Brazil.

FESTIVALS & EVENTS

✪ Football; year-round; www.futebol thebrazilianwayoflife.com. Aside from a few brief holidays (eg Christmas and Carnaval), the *futebol* season goes all year. There are also always games played by young hopefuls on pretty much any patch of spare ground.

✪ Carnaval; countrywide; February/March. This iconic festival may officially run for only five days but in Rio de Janeiro the build-up begins two weeks before the event and partying often spills over into March.

✪ Círio De Nazaré; Belém; October. The main port leading out of the Amazon hosts the »

BRAZIL.

> " *I was on a month-long bus trip around Brazil. One night, the bus came to a stop on a muddy road, because the road had washed out. No worries though, the bus coming from Maranhão was stuck on the other side. We simply had to walk through two miles of mud to resume our journey, while the passengers of the other bus did the same. People had already set up makeshift shops, selling candy and water and other things. Soon enough I was on the other bus and we were moving once again. Just a little speed bump!* "
>
> - Daniel Rowan, USA

» largest annual festival of this immense river.

◉ Onbongo Pro Surfing; Praia Mole, Florianópolis; November. This event is part of the men's World Championship Tour. It's the last event before the finals in Hawai'i and the world's top surfers will be in peak form, chasing valuable championship points and the hefty US$270,000 prize money.

◉ MiX Brasil; São Paulo; November. This festival of sexual diversity begins in São Paulo, then goes on a Latin American tour. It's the biggest celebration of queer culture in Latin America.

RANDOM FACTS

◉ Brazil has the largest Japanese community outside Japan.

◉ Brazil is the fifth most-populous country in the world.

◉ Though the military dictatorship is long gone, being a journalist who criticises the powers that be can be very dangerous.

◉ Like the capitals of the USA, Australia and Pakistan – Brazil's capital (Brasília) is a planned city built in 1960. But unlike these other countries Brasília is quite remote from most of the country's population; over 800km (497mi) from Rio de Janeiro and São Paulo. It's symbolically placed in the centre of the nation.

RECENT FAD

◉ Narghile, the Arabic 'table pipe' is a hit with young urbanities across the country.

WHAT'S HOT...

◉ 'Amazon Life' is a hip local label with a range of fashion and homewares made mostly from sustainable vegetal leather by Indians and rural workers from the Amazon region.

DO MENTION

◉ Soccer, any time, any place, but be prepared – Brazilians don't take their national pastime lightly.

DON'T MENTION

◉ The blatantly obvious inequities between the rich and poor.

THINGS TO TAKE

◉ Condoms – though great efforts have been made to prevent the spread of AIDS and treat sufferers (more than 600 000), it is still a big problem in urban areas.

◉ Earplugs for the Carnaval – there's no exaggeration in its reputation as a nonstop party.

HOT TIPS FOR TRAVELLERS

◉ Use common sense in larger cities, avoid obvious displays of wealth as street crime and muggings are still common.

◉ When planning your trip beyond the capital cities try www.southamerican experience.co.uk or the conscientious www.responsibletravel.com, which are both full of useful info.

◉ Though Rio hosts by far the largest Carnaval it by no means has a monopoly on the event. For those interested in a quieter, more traditional and less-expensive experience (Rio's accommodation skyrockets for the Carnaval weekend), try one of the many other towns in Brazil.

THREE WORDS TO DESCRIBE THIS COUNTRY

◉ Outrageous, contradictory, pulsating.
- *Robert Harding*

HOT TOPIC OF THE DAY! ★

The outcome of the presidential elections in October 2006: will Luiz Inacio Lula da Silva and his Workers Party prevail?

THE TORRES DEL PAINE LOOM STILL OVER A GOBSMACKINGLY BEAUTIFUL SUNRISE IN PATAGONIA.

VITAL STATISTICS

CHILE.

- ❂ **POPULATION**
  16.2 MILLION
- ❂ **VISITORS PER YEAR**
  1.8 MILLION
- ❂ **UNIT OF CURRENCY**
  CHILEAN PESO
- ❂ **COST OF A CUP OF COFFEE**
  600 PESOS = US$1
- ❂ **CAPITAL**
  SANTIAGO DE CHILE (COLLOQUIALLY ABBREVIATED TO 'SANTIAGO')
- ❂ **LANGUAGES**
  SPANISH, AYMARA, MAPUDUNGUN, RAPANUI

✪ RIPE FOR EXPLORATION. Slender Chile is noted for its orderly social life and relatively stable democracy in a notoriously unstable and dictator-ruled region. Thanks to its incredible range of latitudes, it has got plenty to offer year-round.

Since the return of democracy in the late 1980s, this string bean of a nation has steadily attracted an increasing number of visitors with its extensive national-park system, well-developed infrastructure and accessible natural attractions. As one of South America's most costly destinations, however, it's been having a hard time of late competing with Argentina for visitors' hard-earned cash.

Visitation tends to revolve around soft adventure (cruising fjords, bird-watching, fishing, glacier-watching and wine tasting), but there's an increasing emphasis on more hard-core activities (trekking, white-water rafting, skiing/snowboarding, surfing, cycle touring and climbing volcanoes), particularly in the lightly developed southern reaches of Patagonia and the sparsely inhabited islands of Tierra del Fuego.

The ambitious final push to complete the Carretera Austral (Southern Hwy) is opening up new road-tripping frontiers in the primeval temperate rainforests of the fjord-riddled Aisén region. Explora's (www.explora.com) new upmarket adventure lodge on enigmatic Easter Island (Rapa Nui) ushers in a new era of sophisticated contemplation of *moai* (large anthropomorphic statues) on the world's most remote inhabited island, 3800km (2400mi) west of Chile's central coast.

Despite extensive wildfires sparked by an overturned camping stove in a remote corner of the park in early 2005, Chilean Patagonia's crown jewel, Parque Nacional Torres del Paine, continues to lure visitors in record numbers. New campsites, expansion of the popular on-trail refuge network and the inauguration of a new southern entrance should help keep pace with skyrocketing demands. Several upstart airlines have initiated direct services from Santiago to Punta Arenas in anticipation of increased »

RECENT FAD! ❂

Legal divorce: despite fierce opposition from the powerful Roman Catholic church, Chilean President Ricardo Lagos signed a law giving Chileans the right to divorce, meaning they no longer have to travel to Argentina to amicably separate.

HUASOS SPECTATORS CATCH THE ACTION IN THE MEDIA LUNA DURING THE NATIONAL RODEO CHAMPIONSHIPS.

CHILE.

» Patagonian demand. Additionally, a new no-frills Spanish airline, Air Madrid, and new direct flights from Canada and Japan all signal rising international interest in Chile.

The future is looking increasingly bright and liberated for Chile's fairer sex, with men recently legally obliged to undergo DNA tests in paternity lawsuits. The medical doctor and former defence minister Michelle Bachelet, a left-leaning socialist candidate and political exile during the Pinochet regime, is projected as the front-runner in the December 2005 presidential elections.

DEFINING EXPERIENCE

✪ Traversing the varied geographic trickle, from surfable Pacific Coast beaches through sky-high Andean passes, in an action-packed weekend, stopping for a spot of wine tasting in the Valle Central; a dip in natural hot springs in the foothills; and to schuss the slopes near the Argentine frontier. Extreme thrill-seekers should top off their journey with a flight over Antarctica or Cabo de Hornos (Cape Horn), the continent's fabled southernmost tip.

FESTIVALS & EVENTS

✪ LoveParade; Santiago; January; www. loveparade.cl. Fresh off smash hits in Berlin, San Francisco and Tel Aviv, the world's most extravagant serialised electronic dance-music festival promises to rivet Santiago for the second year in a row with banging sound systems and a parade of 100 boffo DJs.

✪ Festival Internacional de la Canción; Viña del Mar; mid-February. Chile's premier beach resort hosts the week-long,

OUT OF THIS WORLD

Taking advantage of the clearest skies in the southern hemisphere, the Chilean government recently opened the powerful Cerro Mamalluca observatory (www.mamalluca.org), in the Andean foothills north of Santiago between La Serena and Copiapó, to public viewing.

CHILE.

> "
> *In the Lakes District of Southern Chile, the weather can, at times, be quite unpredictable. In the pouring rain we rented a little one bedroom cabin (directions: walk for half a mile and turn left at the yellow bush) with a kitchen, bathroom and a powerful heater. We awoke the next day to incredible views across the lake looking at the southern Chilean Andes and the snow-capped volcanoes.*
> "
>
> *- Martha Huettl, USA*

RANDOM FACTS

- In a 2005 quality-of-life survey, the *Economist* ranked Chile highest in Latin America and 31st out of 111 countries worldwide.

- Chile's 4329km (2690mi) longitudinal span is roughly equal to the distance between Moscow and Madrid.

- The Atacama Desert is one of the world's driest regions, averaging only 1mm (0.04in) of rainfall per year.

- According to a rarely enforced Chilean law, citizens can be imprisoned for not voting.

THINGS TO TAKE

- Altitude-sickness medication (available locally)

- Umbrella/poncho – rain is always a possibility south of Santiago

- Exact change for the entry fee if arriving by air from the USA, Canada or Australia – double check the current charges before arrival

HOT TIPS FOR TRAVELLERS

- Cheek-to-cheek kisses are customary greetings between men and women and between women (not between fellas) – always use your right cheek, and avoid lip puckering…unless you want to send a stronger signal.

- Pay in US dollars, either via cash or credit card, at nonbudget hotels to avoid the 18% value-added tax.

THREE WORDS TO DESCRIBE THIS COUNTRY

- Tall, slim, civilised

- Andrew Nystrom

ridiculously popular Latin American version of the Eurovision Song Contest.

- Festival del Barrio Brazil; Santiago; early November. Santiago's funkiest neighbourhood flaunts its non-Chileaness with a week of rampant self-expressions of artiness and free speech.

DO MENTION

- High-quality exports (fruit, wine, beef, seafood, organic produce), a widespread source of national pride

DON'T MENTION

- The stereotype that Chileans are more boring and less vivacious than their irrepressibly spunky neighbours, the Argentines

MOST BIZARRE SIGHT

- Puerto Williams: despite Argentina's vociferous claims, the most populous outpost in sleepy Chilean Tierra del Fuego is the Southern Cone's true southernmost settlement. Grab a crab sandwich and throw back a pisco sour with naval officers and sailors celebrating rounding Cabo de Hornos at the Club de Yates Micalvi.

HOT TOPIC OF THE DAY!

At 89 years old, and more than six years after his arrest in London on murder charges, former dictator Augusto Pinochet was stripped of his immunity from prosecution by Chilean courts and will stand trial, but probably only for tax evasion charges and not for alleged human rights abuses.

COLOMBIA.

VITAL STATISTICS

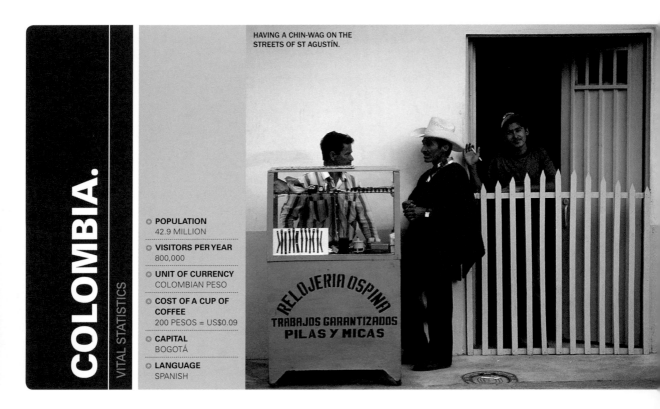

HAVING A CHIN-WAG ON THE STREETS OF ST AGUSTÍN.

- **POPULATION**
  42.9 MILLION
- **VISITORS PER YEAR**
  800,000
- **UNIT OF CURRENCY**
  COLOMBIAN PESO
- **COST OF A CUP OF COFFEE**
  200 PESOS = US$0.09
- **CAPITAL**
  BOGOTÁ
- **LANGUAGE**
  SPANISH

NOTHING VENTURED, NOTHING GAINED. Colombia is back, baby, and it wants a piece of the action. This wild, sprawling nation has long been an unknown quantity for outsiders – and until just recently, 'the unknown' was regarded with suspicion and fear.

To many foreigners, Colombia (or *Locombia*, the 'crazy land') was – and still is – the land of drug cartels and armed insurgents: a place where you would disappear as soon as you set foot outside the airport. Like most stereotypes, these perceptions have some roots in truth. Yes, Colombia endured a long civil war in the late 20th century and is still feeling the hangover. There are still some drug lords, and ladies, living opulent lives free from governmental retribution. The leftist guerrillas of FARC (Fuerzas Armadas Revolucionarias de Colombia) still make incessant trouble for the government.

But to dwell on these fading shortcomings is akin to giving up on love because you once got turned down at the school dance. Colombia is no longer merely the sum of its problems (as if it ever was!). Hardened and strengthened by a long conflict, that as far as anyone can tell, nobody ever wanted, Colombians have learned to approach everyday life practically, amiably and with good cheer. A marked decline in violence and a sharp drop-off in crimes against foreigners in the early 2000s have not gone unnoticed by visitors. International travellers are streaming back to the country, elevating tourism to pre-1990s levels. Colombia is capitalising on a renewed interest in Latin America by throwing open its gates and welcoming guests.

For visitors, a little bit of courage pays off handsomely. You'll wonder how you managed to get so far off the tourist track while having such a good time exploring the Amazon, climbing the Andean foothills or kicking back in such sparkling cities as Cartagena and Barranquilla. Of course, it's not a paradise on earth just yet; you won't want to venture too far from travelled areas or traverse remote areas at night, for example. But a bit of common sense, a good

deal of gumption and a few additional street smarts thrown in for good measure should do you just fine. As they say in Colombia, *Quien no arriesga nada, ni pierde ni gana* ('Whoever risks nothing will lose and gain nothing'). And what have you got to lose?

DEFINING EXPERIENCE

- Being crammed into an intercity 'tourist bus' full of Colombian families and heading down a highway lined with soldiers almost the whole way

FESTIVALS & EVENTS

- Carnaval de Barranquilla; Barranquilla; February/March. Everyone wants a ticket to the largest national festival. The city goes absolutely nuts before the solemn period of Lent. To get an idea of how intense the nonstop partying is, consider this: locals tell you to keep celebrating *hasta que el cuerpo aguante* ('until your body can't take it anymore'). Serious stuff.

- FIFA World Cup; 9 June–9 July 2006. OK, the football (soccer) World Cup won't be played in Colombia, but it'll be a great time to be there. Thousands of fans will be thronging the streets of every major city,

doing everything they can to boost their team from abroad.

- Carnaval de Blancos y Negros (Festival of Whites and Blacks); Pasto; July. Expect several days of parades, cultural activities and acts that celebrate Colombia's diverse ethnic make-up.

RECENT FAD

- *Chi kung*, the Colombian spelling of the Chinese art often written in English as qi gong, is sweeping the nation. It's the newest health craze, propelling urbanite Colombians to unleash their potential energy and live a healthier life. Of course, in a nation known for its love of the good life, it's no surprise that the most popular form of *chi kung* is the Shaolin school, which unlike other types does not prohibit eating meat or ingesting alcohol.

HOT TIP FOR TRAVELLERS

- Colombians are fashionable and pizzazzy, and you'll make friends much more easily if you try to blend in. Leave those crappy white sneakers at home, and at least put on a clean pair of blue jeans. However you dress, avoid wearing khakis or fatigues »

COLOMBIA.

> "
> *A Colombian friend and his brother were driving in a remote place in the Andes when they came upon a police checkpoint. The army men stopped them and asked them the usual questions: who they were, where were they going etc. After a while, they let them go. Further down the same road was another checkpoint. Again, the same questions. My friend asked one of the men: 'I don't understand, we were checked just 500m back', to which the soldier replied: 'Ah! That must be the guerrilla. Don't worry! Just carry on with your drive'.*
> "
>
> - Manuel Corral Valero, Spain

» purchased from military surplus stores – the military might mistake you for a guerrilla…or the guerrillas might mistake you for military. It's bad either way.

MOST BIZARRE SIGHT
- Going to a movie theatre and watching the patrons around you chowing down on roasted ants instead of popcorn

RANDOM FACTS
- Colombia was originally part of an enormous nation called 'Gran Colombia' and founded by Símon Bolívar; it included modern-day Venezuela and Ecuador. (Panama broke away later, in 1903.)

- Although Colombia was named after Columbus, he never set foot in the present-day country.

- Colombia is second only to Brazil when it comes to producing coffee, but first in the world when it comes to producing emeralds: 95% of the world's supply comes from Colombia.

- Candidates for Miss Colombia (the extraordinarily popular national beauty pageant) generally subsist on a diet of pineapple and tuna.

- Nobel Prize–winning author Gabriel García Márquez is Colombian.

THREE WORDS TO DESCRIBE THIS COUNTRY
- Mysterious, frightening, exhilarating
  - *Vivek Wagle*

THINGS TO TAKE! ★

Taking out hostage insurance isn't a terrible idea. It's not as though foreigners are particularly targeted, but it's nice to know that a big corporation will pay your ransom if you get spirited away.

»»

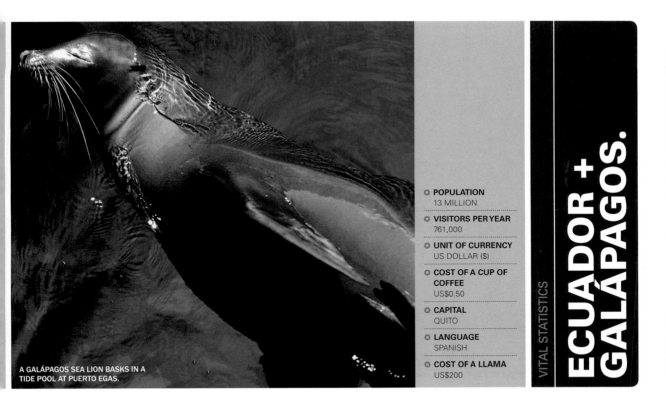

A GALÁPAGOS SEA LION BASKS IN A TIDE POOL AT PUERTO EGAS.

POPULATION
13 MILLION

VISITORS PER YEAR
761,000

UNIT OF CURRENCY
US DOLLAR ($)

COST OF A CUP OF COFFEE
US$0.50

CAPITAL
QUITO

LANGUAGE
SPANISH

COST OF A LLAMA
US$200

FIRE & ICE. Just how did mother nature pack so much natural variety into such a tiny country? Ecuador takes up just 0.2% of the planet's surface, yet it hosts 15% of the world's birds. Nearly 1650 species have been recorded; that's over 300 more than in China and nearly 600 more than in the USA.

Similarly astounding sums for plants and other animals make this Lilliputian nation one of the world's most species-rich areas.

While Ecuador doesn't spread far and wide, it climbs very high, which accounts for some of the megadiversity. A backbone of snowcapped Andean peaks features eternal springlike weather, gorgeous scenery and some of the world's most active volcanoes. Soak in their hot springs by day and watch them erupt at night. Volcán Cayambe, where 0° latitude and 0°C (32°F) converge, is the only place where permanent snow blankets the equator. Straddling this Avenue of the Volcanoes are palm-fringed Pacific beaches and deep Amazonian jungle. The theme of ample wildlife and impressive geology continues on the Galápagos Islands. Here, you can get eye-to-eye with blue-footed boobies and snorkel with sea lions.

TODO ES POSIBLE

Locals like to tell visitors that everything is possible in Ecuador, and you'll soon realise this is no empty boast. It's especially true about outdoor activities: trekking, mountain climbing, scuba diving, river running, whale-watching, jungle exploring, and of course, bird-watching are all world class. And it doesn't hurt that this is one of the world's cheapest destinations so you can go wild and still go home with some cash. The Galápagos are a costly exception, but few visitors don't consider a visit to these islands worth every penny.

It's really what you can see and do between adrenalin fixes that makes Ecuador so special. Many towns are graced with gorgeous colonial architecture. Quito's city centre is the best-preserved in all of Latin America and Cuenca's is nearly as »

MOST BIZARRE SIGHT!

Tourists in the Galápagos Islands and Isla de la Plata using wide-angle lenses to photograph birds.

A HUSBAND AND WIFE AMBLE PAST
THE MASONRY WORK OF THE NEW
CATHEDRAL IN CUENCA.

» spectacular. Both are Unesco World Heritage sites. At least a quarter of the country's population is indigenous and most have clung tightly to their traditions and lively dress; you can learn more about their cultures bargaining in weekly markets or joining in colourful festivals. Down at the coast you can laze on the beach, sip cocktails and buy a seafood dinner right of the boat. Add to all this good museums, fine food and friendly people and you have one amazing travel destination in Ecuador.

SETTLING DOWN

Famous as much for its political instability as its scenery, Ecuador has had nine presidents in the last 10 years. Corruption and incompetence inhibit development and strikes and street protests are common. While this unpredictability keeps Ecuador from becoming the new go-to destination for well-heeled tourists, it rarely affects those on the ground. And in the last few years people have begun to see beyond the country's political instability; as a result tourism has grown steadily. You still won't be tripping over tour groups but services are improving and the use of English is increasing, even in small towns. There's

never been a better – or easier – time to visit Ecuador and the Galápagos Islands.

DEFINING EXPERIENCE

☼ Waking up in a hammock on a palm-fringed Pacific beach to a breakfast of eggs and tamales, then boarding a standing-room-only bus and white-knuckling it up 2743m (9000ft) before going to sleep in a converted colonial home after a dinner of guinea pig

FESTIVALS & EVENTS

☼ International Sailing Federation Nations Cup Regional Finals; Salinas; January.

☼ All Souls' Day (Day of the Dead); November. Families gather in graveyards to lay flowers and eat, sharing some of the food with the deceased on this day.

RECENT FAD

☼ Many indigenous communities across the country now invite travellers to come and share their lives and learn about their traditional ways. Most programmes also incorporate ecotourism and so when you're not lending a hand with the cooking and other daily activities you'll be

ECUADOR + GALÁPAGOS.

> *I was travelling in Ecuador with some fellow students. We caught a bus out of town to a lovely little riverside spot, spent the day, had a great time. We went to catch the bus back only to find we had missed the last. We had to get back so we hitched – 25 of us on the back of a flat-bed semi trailer for a two-hour ride…*

- Warwick Ellis, Australia

hold their wings out at a 45-degree angle to let air pass over the less-feathered parts of their bodies.

- The world's first organic shrimp farm lies just outside the self-declared 'ecocity' of Bahía de Caráquez. The innovative process protects the increasingly rare coastal mangrove forests.

DO MENTION

- The Ecuadorian national football team. At press time, Ecuador was well on its way to a second consecutive (and second ever) World Cup appearance and the country is ecstatic over the prospect.

DON'T MENTION

- Ecuador's club football teams. Passions run just as high for fans' local squads and the rivalries are intense – fights at the stadiums are common. And if the national team does suffer a meltdown during its final three qualifying matches, you might want to stay away from that topic too.

WHAT'S HOT...

- Reventador and Tungurahua volcanoes

WHAT'S NOT...

- Cotopaxi and Pichincha volcanoes

HOT TIPS FOR TRAVELLERS

- The South American Explorer's Club (www.saexplorers.org) is the best source of up-to-date information on Ecuador. Make the clubhouse in Quito one of your first stops in the country. Membership is not required, but it has its benefits and is highly recommended.

- The Ministry of Information & Tourism's website (www.vivecuador.com) is an excellent source of planning and background information.

THREE WORDS TO DESCRIBE THIS COUNTRY

- Bountiful, unpredictable, divergent
  - *Tim Brewer*

out exploring the countryside with local guides. Community-based projects not only give travellers an inside view of a culture but all the money is invested back into the village. When done well, these are valuable, win-win projects. Currently most such programmes run in the Amazon but others have sprung up around the rest of the country.

THINGS TO TAKE

- A warm jacket – sure, you're in the tropics, but nights in the mountains can get very cold

- An extra wristwatch – many vendors in the indigenous village markets like to barter

RANDOM FACTS

- Panama hats are made only in Ecuador. They got their name because in the 19th century they were shipped to Panama for export overseas and later many workers digging the Panama Canal wore them.

- The Galápagos penguin is the only penguin residing in the northern hemisphere. The chilly Humboldt Current flowing up from Antarctica helps keep them cool in the water, and on land they

HOT TOPIC OF THE DAY!

The economy is on everyone's minds. It's been in shambles for years: inflation is high, oil production has not met predicted levels, and the middle class is vanishing. Over the past several years nearly a quarter of the country's population has fled to Europe and the USA; this has left some towns almost devoid of young men. Things do appear to be improving – as President Palacio has said, the situation can't really get any worse – but most Ecuadorians still fear an uncertain future.

EL SALVADOR.

VITAL STATISTICS

AN AQUAMARINE-HUED AGUARDIENTE BOOZE SHOP IN PUERTO LA LIBERTAD.

- **POPULATION**
  6.9 MILLION
- **VISITORS PER YEAR**
  966,000
- **UNIT OF CURRENCY**
  US DOLLAR ($)
- **COST OF A CUP OF COFFEE**
  $0.50
- **CAPITAL**
  SAN SALVADOR
- **LANGUAGE**
  SPANISH

WORTH A VISIT. The smallest and most densely populated country in Central America, El Salvador is also one of its least touristed – all the more reason to go there now.

Among Salvador's rewards: a dynamic, dramatic landscape pockmarked by 25 volcanoes (three active); a well-preserved wealth of national parks and regional preserves harbouring ample trekking and hiking trails; timeless native crafting villages such as Ilobasco (ceramics), La Palma (painted boxes), Panchimalco (weaving) and Nahuizalco (wicker and bamboo); migratory butterflies, birds and sea turtles and indigenous orchids, balsam and giant ferns; a 300km-long (185mi) Pacific coastline of untrammelled black-sand beaches fronting the best-kept-secret waves in all of Central America; and a proud, friendly people who've worked hard to rebuild their nation and economy after decades of corruption and war.

Like nearby Nicaragua, El Salvador is plagued by lingering connotations of the widespread violence of the civil war of the 1980s, between the US-backed, right-wing Partido Democrático Christiano (PDC) of José Napoleon Duarte and the revolutionary, land-reforming Farabundo Martí National Liberation Front (FMLN). The war, exceedingly brutal, was a pitched, back-and-forth battle of scorched-earth and slain-cattle tactics that took a staggering toll on civilians, particularly at the hands of right-wing death squads estimated to have killed tens of thousands. By war's end in 1992, an estimated 75,000 people had been killed and countless others displaced; in the UN-brokered peace deal the FMLN became an opposition party and the government agreed to reforms.

In January 2001, an earthquake (7.6 on the Richter scale) devastated El Salvador, mangling infrastructure, destroying colonial buildings and wiping out whole neighbourhoods in hellish, deadly mudslides. Recovery, though slow, has been steady, and signs of ongoing reconstruction are everywhere, from fenced-off 18th-century churches to sparkling new spans along the Pan-American Hwy.

Despite the quake and a high crime rate (take precautions seriously) El Salvador is progressing steadily. The country, with the

A MAN WHEELS HIS BICYCLE IN THE GOLDEN AFTERNOON RAYS.

highest minimum wage in Central America, ranks among the top economic performers on the isthmus. El Salvador has embraced tourism, and the establishment of travel guards in the parks has helped make the parks safe again. Use common sense and caution, especially in San Salvador, but don't let El Salvador's turbulent past overshadow its modern-day offerings.

DEFINING EXPERIENCE

☼ Trekking with your government-appointed guide through the wilds of Parque Nacional Cerro Verde, bursting with native flora and migratory toucanets, jays, woodpeckers and hummingbirds, past the stunning deep-blue crater lake Lago de Coatepeque to the incredible vistas of Volcán Izalco, black and bare, and Volcán Santa Ana, rocky, smoky and cascading dramatically into its own crater.

RECENT FAD

☼ Surfing La Costa del Bálsamo. With waves packed in Costa Rica and word out about Nicaragua, Central America surfers in the know now angle toward breaks on El Salvador's Pacific coast such as Playas El Tunco (best left break), El Sunzal (longest

point break) and Punta Roca (best wave in El Salvador).

FESTIVALS & EVENTS

☼ Suchitoto Arts and Culture Festival; Suchitoto; February. Music, dancing, theatre, fine arts, good food and warm ambiance amid a lovely natural setting.

☼ El Salvador del Mundo; August. Carnivalesque celebration of 'Divine Saviour of the World' Jesus Christ, who's regaled with music, art, food and street parades countrywide.

☼ El Salvador Independence Day; September. Military pomp and marching parades mark El Salvador's celebration of Central America's 1821 declaration of independence from Spain.

WHAT'S HOT...

☼ Suchitoto. Largely abandoned during the civil war, cute, colonial Suchitoto ('the place of birds and flowers' in native Nahuat) has rebounded with the return of its inhabitants, who've developed an arts and culture scene unlike any in El Salvador. With cobblestone streets, an energetic town square, nearby Los Tercios waterfall and »

EL SALVADOR.

> " *We were on a beach in El Salvador and we wanted to get some chow, so we flagged down a bus (a typical Latino rainbow on wheels). There was positively no room. Buddy one managed to straddle the gearshift with the driver's hand between his legs on the 'stick', while I was on the step in the doorway. Buddy two had one foot in and the other out, hanging on to the open door. The ticket guy ended up hanging on the side of the bus, clutching the partition between two windows!* "
>
> - Jeremy Jensen, Germany

» public arts projects around town, here's the best base camp for exploring northern El Salvador's beguiling mountains or just hanging around town.

WHAT'S NOT...

- La Unión. Hot, drab, and chaotic, this commercial port town on the Golfo de Fonseca has little to offer travellers who aren't fascinated by container ships.

DO MENTION

- The friendliness Salvadorans often show. With so few travellers about, the national traits of hospitality and kindness are amplified by the presence of international visitors.

DON'T MENTION

- That Roman numeral '13' tattooed on your chest: street gangs are a way of life in Salvador, and violence is real. There are nine to 11 violent deaths in El Salvador every day, and 100,000 reported gang members across El Salvador, Guatemala and Honduras. Two of the biggest gangs, Mara Salvatrucha (MS-13) and Mara 18, are particularly violent, and recent news reports have tied them both to gangs in the USA and Al Qaeda terror cells.

RANDOM FACTS

- Once the heart of El Salvador's coffee country, Alegría has blossomed anew as the country's flower-growing capital.

- Tazumal, the 'pyramid where the victims were burned', comprises El Salvador's pre-eminent Mayan ruins, dating from 5000 BC. Joya de Cerén is the best preserved Mayan site in the country, a veritable time capsule yielding clues of daily life 1400 years ago as they are excavated from beneath heaps of volcanic ash.

- Hot but lovely, Isla Montecristo harbours hundreds of nesting pelicans and egrets, and offers canoeing and horseback riding, relatively rare in the country.

THINGS TO TAKE

- Sneakers: skip the hiking boots and slap on sturdy, quick-to-dry sneakers for hiking El Salvador's network of parks, mountains, volcanoes and coastlines. Socks optional.

- Decent clothes: Salvadorans pride themselves on their appearance – dingy duds win no points with the locals.

- Spanish phrasebook: English is spoken less here than in any other Central American country.

- US dollars. Make sure you're carrying small denominations (ones and fives).

HOT TIPS FOR TRAVELLERS

- Skirt the crowds to Parque Nacional El Imposible by hiking in the back way, through Tacuba, moderately strenuous and mostly downhill.

- Punta Roca in La Libertad gets nods as El Salvador's best wave, but surfers know El Sunzal, further west on La Costa de Balsalmo, as the longest and most attractive point break in the country.

- A paranoid, but brutally accurate background on the civil war, Oliver Stone's 1986 film *Salvador* features James Woods as a sketchy journalist watching the country's plunge into apocalypse.

THREE WORDS TO DESCRIBE THIS COUNTRY

- Under the radar

- Jay Cooke

MOST BIZARRE SIGHT! ★

Guns, guns and more guns: with up to a million illegal guns in circulation, and roughly 18,000 security guards working around the country, El Salvador is awash in firearms and gun shops are ubiquitous.

»»

AUSTERELY ATMOSPHERIC CELLS IN ÎLE ROYALE, THE LARGEST OF THE ÎLES DU SALUT.

- **POPULATION**
  182,400
- **VISITORS PER YEAR**
  10,000
- **UNIT OF CURRENCY**
  EURO (€)
- **COST OF A MUSHROOM AND CHEESE CREPE**
  €4.05 = US$5
- **CAPITAL**
  CAYENNE
- **LANGUAGES**
  FRENCH, CREOLE, VARIOUS NATIVE DIALECTS

⭐ THE SPACE AGE MEETS THE RAINFOREST. As if South America wasn't surreal enough, there's French Guiana (Guyane). This tiny country at the top corner of the southern half of the continent is a colourful riot of contrasts.

Columbus first sighted this coast in his travels, and Sir Walter Raleigh tried to find El Dorado in the region at the end of the 16th century. After much disputation, the whole region was finally divided between the English, the Dutch and the French. During the 19th century the French used the islands off the coast as a penal colony, where convicts were exiled in notoriously horrifying conditions. The prisons were formally closed in 1951 and the abandoned prison facilities, now dark and full of ghosts, are one of the tourist attractions.

Of the three resulting countries (Guyana, Suriname and French Guiana), this one is by far the most developed and the easiest to get to. This is mainly because it is the site of the Space Centre (Centre Spatial Guyanais), used by the European Space Agency to send satellites into space. The French pour millions into this colony and, as a result, the infrastructure and amenities are high quality – as long as you don't veer too far into the interior, that is. The thousands of personnel and troops employed in the Centre provide the main engine of the economy. Most of the country is undeveloped, a thick mantle of rainforest dotted with destitute villages. Most locals are employed in agriculture, fishery and forestry, and barely eke out a living.

A TAPESTRY OF CONTRASTS

French Guiana is an administrative district of France and part of the EU. So be warned – the prices are Parisian, especially for decent accommodation. Colonialism is alive and well here, and much of the landscape and conditions have remained unchanged for 150 years. The locals are deeply ambivalent about being part of France. On the one hand, they appreciate some of the advantages of French aid, such as health services and roads. On the other, they dream »

HOT TIP FOR TRAVELLERS!

French Guiana is expensive, but some places let you hang your own hammock for a fraction of the price of a room.

»

FRENCH GUIANA.

DRUMMERS PEPPER THE STREETS OF CAYENNE WITH LOCAL RHYTHMS.

» of independence. There have been violent struggles to this effect: the last such incident was in 1997, when the French quashed a civil insurrection, but things have been quiet since then.

This is a land of incredible ethnic diversity: there are Amerindian villages, Brazilians, Haitians, Indonesians, Chinese, Africans and even a village founded by Hmong refugees from Laos (Cacao). And then there's the foreign elite working at the Space Centre. The fauna is just as striking, consisting of monkeys, iguanas, turtles, macaws, piranhas and the black caiman.

Ecotourism is slowly taking off – ironically enough because the surge in mining activity is driving the development of roads and infrastructure. Gold mining and logging are making a comeback here, and environmental watchdogs are warning that the unrestrained exploitation of mineral and timber resources is severely endangering the environment in the area. Also, there has been strong evidence of mercury poisoning among native Amerindians in the area. Mercury is a toxic by-product of gold extraction; it is dumped into the water and absorbed by the fish, posing a risk to native communities who depend heavily on a diet of fish.

DEFINING EXPERIENCE
○ Dancing under the rain in the Cayenne Carnaval to the deafening sound of drums, swatting mosquitoes, and suddenly spotting a rocket taking off in the distance and disappearing into the night sky

FESTIVALS & EVENTS
○ Carnaval; held throughout the country but mainly in Cayenne; February/March. This is the most important festival in the country. The varied ethnic make-up of the country comes out to play in this colourful, almost pagan, celebration.

WHAT'S HOT...
○ The rainforest in December

WHAT'S NOT...
○ The mosquitoes

RANDOM FACTS
○ Without a doubt the most famous book set in French Guiana is *Papillon,* by Henri Charrière (published in 1970, and made into a movie starring Steve McQueen and Dustin Hoffman in 1973). Charrière was sent to Devil's Island in the 1930s, convicted of a crime that he

> **"** The Hmong village, on market day, is one of the wonders of South America. **"**
>
> - Yotam Ben Zvi, Israel

were smallholders, afraid that only rich farmers would be able to afford the GM bean and kick them out of business.

THINGS TO TAKE

- A torch and batteries
- Protection against sun, rain and mosquitoes
- A hammock

THREE WORDS TO DESCRIBE THIS COUNTRY

- Rainforest, multicultural, rockets

- Andres Vaccari

didn't commit. The book recounts his experiences as a convict, the brutality and inhuman conditions he had to endure for 13 years until, after many escape attempts, he made it to Venezuela. Although the book was a bestseller, Charrière was accused of fabricating the whole thing, and most critics agree that he made it all up.

- The unemployment rate in French Guiana is close to 25%.
- Of all the EU territories outside the European continent, French Guiana is the only one that is not an island.

HOT TOPIC OF THE DAY

- In May 2005 the first trial of genetically modified (GM) coffee in the world was sabotaged. The French government staged the experiment in Guiana because no coffee grows there, so the GM plant ran no risk of contaminating other plants. Scientists added a protein to the coffee bean that makes it lethal to insects but not to humans. The experiment was supposed to run for another two years. It's suspected the perpetrators

---

MOST BIZARRE SIGHT!

Bastille Day celebrations – a great event in Paris – in a Caribbean atmosphere

>>

MEXICO.
VITAL STATISTICS

- **POPULATION**
  106.5 MILLION
- **VISITORS PER YEAR**
  20 MILLION
- **UNIT OF CURRENCY**
  PESO
- **COST OF A STREET TACO**
  3 TO 8 PESOS =
  US$0.35 TO US$0.75
- **CAPITAL**
  MEXICO CITY
- **LANGUAGES**
  SPANISH,
  50 INDIGENOUS
  LANGUAGES,
  INCLUDING MAYA
  AND NAHUATL

SKELETON FOLK ART MAKES FOR A
SPOOKY STREET STALL.

★ BEYOND BEACHES & MARGARITAS. Historically, Mexican tourist brochures tended to emphasise cheap booze, deserted tropical beaches and tawdry handicrafts.

Thanks to international cinematic hits such as *Like Water for Chocolate*, curiosity has shifted to the country's rich archaeology, architecture, cuisine and cultural heritage.

Bolstered by an ambitious makeover of its Centro Histórico, Mexico City has become a jet-set destination for trendy shopping and hip nightlife. All told, the capital is in the midst of artistic renaissance, melding ancient civilisations with hypermodern sensibilities.

Tourism represents an ever-increasing share of Mexico's economy, nearly a 10th of its gross domestic product at last count. Family visits by Mexican expats account for most travel across the US–Mexico border, but non–North American visitors are increasingly catching the buzz. Due to the post–September 11 North American wariness about personal safety – and an odd notion of increased safety of travelling in numbers – cruise-ship arrivals are increasing by leaps and bounds. Thankfully, the tourism industry is diversifying to promote more

ecofriendly activities and visits to lesser-known provinces.

NOTHING NEW ABOUT THE NEW WORLD

Mexico's ancient Mesoamerican roots run deep. Today, much of what makes the country so intriguing emanates from the enduring spirits of aboriginal civilisations such as the Maya and Aztecs. Signs of their existence, present or past, resonate in seemingly every nook and cranny.

Mexico's mind-blowing mix of peoples and cultures mimics its diverse topography – it's a vast patchwork with something to fascinate even the most jaded globetrotter. The multifaceted cuisine is one of the world's most eclectic, earthy and creative. There's no better place to experience the intermingling of classes and cultures than in Mexico City's Zócalo (Central Plaza) on a Sunday afternoon. Otherwise, to witness the country at it's colourful best, catch a festival or celebration.

A COUPLE OF COCONUT FARMERS TAKE A BREATHER IN CHICHICAPA.

BORDERLINES: THE NORTH–SOUTH CLASH

Things are heating up along one of the world's longest borders. While the USA is debating potential amnesty and guest-worker policies, lawlessness and corruption are gripping Mexican border towns such as Nuevo Laredo, where federal agents patrol in lieu of trustworthy local cops. Meanwhile, in California and Arizona, volunteer militiamen have started their own vigilante border patrols. On both sides of the volatile frontier, activists are denouncing the record number deaths of would-be illegal immigrants.

Rivalries between drug cartels are escalating as they battle for control of lucrative smuggling routes in northern Mexico. Kidnappings for ransom are on the rise as well, as exemplified by the broad-daylight nabbing of soccer team Cruz Azul's Argentine coach by heavily armed men in Mexico City.

MAÑANA, MAÑANA

With term limits preventing the swaggering ex–Coca-Cola executive Vicente Fox from seeking re-election in July 2006, competition in Mexico's presidential elections promises to be fierce. Key issues will include human and labour rights, education funding and improving public health and social security.

For all its troubles, Mexico is relatively safe and hospitable. Any hostile sentiments are typically reserved for specific foreign governments and not directed at individual travellers. Even in the face of rampant modernisation, most of the country remains as charming and *tranquillo* (laid-back) as ever.

MOST BIZARRE SIGHT

☼ The Museo de las Momias in Guanajuato. It's the quintessential expression of Mexico's obsession with death; 100 exhumed, mummified corpses are on display.

RECENT FAD

☼ Postal democracy: a new law signed by outgoing Presidente Fox will allow Mexico's estimated 11 million emigrants to vote by mail in the 2006 presidential election.

FESTIVALS & EVENTS

☼ Festival Internacional de Cine: Expresión en Corto; Guanajuato; July. Edgy film shorts attract the luminary likes of Oliver Stone to this Unesco World Heritage city.

☼ Encuentro Internacional del Mariachi y la Charrería; Guadalajara; September. Big »

MEXICO.

> " Bored of sun and sand in gorgeous Bahías de Huatulco in Mexico, I was looking for an organized trip to see the surroundings. But no more gringos were around and the guy could not run the show just for us. So he suggested that we go to his home, pick up his wife and kids, and do the same tour by shared taxi. When we arrived at his place, lunch was ready – the kids had just hunted a yummy iguana that morning. As the guests, we got the best bit – the paws. "
>
> - Eva Sanchez Guerrero, Spain

» sombreros, melodramatic 'ay-eye-ay-ay' ballads, animated folk dancing and *haute couture* rodeo will consume Mexico's second city and vibrant cultural capital.

○ Sanmiguelada; San Miguel de Allende; September. This running-of-the-bulls festival kicks off with an artificial dawn cast by thousands of fireworks. Flower altars abound but machismo trumps all as traditional dancers from surrounding states compete until none is left standing.

○ Festival Internacional Cervantino; Guanajuato; October. The quixotic streets of the party-hearty university town are filled with performing artists, featuring many international troupes, all paying tribute to the literary spirit of Don Quixote and his bumbling sidekick Sancho Panza.

○ Día de los Muertos (Day of the Dead); November. Fantastic candy altars festoon cemeteries nationwide. Head to Mexico City, or the states of Michoacán or Oaxaca for the most passionate flair.

○ Festival de los Rábanos; Oaxaca; December. Folk artists decorate the main plaza with incredible sculpture and elaborate nativity scenes fashioned exclusively from radishes

the day before festive must-see Christmas-Eve processions.

WHAT'S HOT...

○ Hollywood setting up film studios in San Miguel del Allende and Baja California

○ *Nueva cocina mexicana* – sophisticated cuisine with earthy native flourishes

○ Hip urban hideaways in stunning restored colonial structures; secluded beachfront boutique resorts

WHAT'S NOT...

○ Massive, eco-insensitive coastal resort development

○ Driving at night without headlights; unsigned speed bumps

○ The Zapatistas – Subcomandante Marcos is rumoured to have left Chiapas

○ Espeaking espańglish – mashing-up English and Mexican is no longer supercool

RANDOM FACTS

○ Tortillas eaten daily: 1.2 billion.

○ Mexico ranks second in the world for kidnappings after Colombia.

○ More US expats reside in Mexico than in any other country in the world.

○ An estimated 15% of Mexico's indigenous people (upwards of seven million) speak 50 distinct dialects and little or no Spanish.

THINGS TO TAKE

○ Antidiarrhoeal drugs

○ Mosquito net and repellent

○ Photos of friends and family – only a child by your side is a better ice-breaker

HOT TIPS FOR TRAVELLERS

○ Verify ever-changing paperwork and document requirements.

○ Nortec Collective DJs blend dance/electronica beats with traditional Mexican *norteño* accordion and tuba riffs in their *Tijuana Sessions* series.

THREE WORDS TO DESCRIBE THIS COUNTRY

○ Sunny, sexy, *saboroso* (flavourful)

- *Andrew Nystrom*

HOT TOPIC OF THE DAY! ★

The US–Mexico border: 10 million Mexican migrants in the USA remit billions of dollars to their relatives each year

LITTLE GIRLS FROCK UP FOR THEIR FIRST COMMUNION IN EL CASTILLO.

★ WAR & REMEMBRANCE. Violence has rattled Nicaragua since European colonisation in the 1500s, when gold-thirsty Spanish colonisers destroyed the resistant capital, Managua.

A class rivalry resulted in battles between León and Granada in the 18th and 19th centuries, and in the 1850s the American scoundrel William Walker torched Granada when his bid to rule Central America by force was snuffed. US Marines landed in 1912, ostensibly to protect canal interests, but inevitably they were drawn into Nicaragua's internal politics, and aided the 1933 installation of Anastasio Somoza García's military dynasty.

Somoza's family dynasty supported US interests throughout the Cold War, reaping the spoils and repressing dissidence nationwide. The theft of international relief funds by Somoza and his cohorts after the 1972 Christmas Eve earthquake in Managua fuelled a rival movement, the Sandinistas, who fought the Somoza regime throughout the 1970s. When they eventually took Managua in 1979, President Anastasio Somoza Debayle abdicated and bailed out, leaving the Sandinistas in charge. US president Ronald Reagan launched the Contra war in the 1980s, a messy covert/overt battle pitting US-backed rebels against the Soviet/Cuban-sponsored government, a Cold War swan song that mired the country in war for a decade. With the demise of the USSR in 1989, stakes shifted, and in 1990 Violetta Chamorro was elected president, the US trade embargo was lifted, and the country started on its road to stability.

NATURE'S WRATH

Ma Nature hasn't made things easy – with its location along the Pacific Ring of Fire, Nicaragua's a hot bed for seismic turbulence. Earthquakes destroyed León in 1610 and Managua in 1972, the latter killing 6000, levelling 250 city blocks and leaving 300,000 homeless. In 1998 Hurricane Mitch stalled over Central America, dumping buckets »

HOT TOPIC OF THE DAY! ★

Fair Trade Coffee Tourism. A global glut in coffee beans has gutted the Nicaraguan market, causing prices to plummet and decimating agricultural communities. Help by joining the Global Exchanges Fair Harvest Exchange Program, 13–21 December (www.globalexchange.org).

A TRIGGER-HAPPY VOTER UNLEASHES HIS DISSATISFACTION ON THIS POLITICAL MURAL.

NICARAGUA.

» of rain, causing widespread flooding and seriously damaging the infrastructure of Nicaragua. In summer 2005, an earthquake measuring 6.3 on the Richter scale struck off Nicaragua's southwest coast rattling Volcán Concepción on Ometepe Island; it sent plumes of ash skywards and has caused confusion as to whether this portends a future eruption or not.

THE TEST BEGINS NOW

Despite centuries of turbulence, these days hope prevails more widely. Nicaragua has stabilised politically and is starting to develop its tourism industry as a way to strengthen the economy, which – as the second worst in the Americas – needs all the help it can get. As the biggest country in Central America, and one harbouring much of the isthmus's diversity within its borders, Nicaragua is well positioned for a travel boom; yet, for the moment it remains relatively unexplored. You can visit the country's protected parks and nature reserves, shop for local art and crafts or ride the sick Pacific surf breaks without contending with too many other travellers. Get there now, though, as word's getting out.

RECENT FAD

✪ Chugging along on the slow boat down Río San Juan, the sticky, steamy waterway in southeastern Nicaragua. Once targeted for development to carry trans-isthmus shipping traffic (it lost out to the Panama Canal), the river drains Lake Nicaragua into the Caribbean Sea and forms a winding border with Costa Rica. Lush and remote, with irregular boat services and few attractions beyond sheer nature, the route is drawing more and more intrepid travellers, who endure the heat and mosquitoes to access the primal, untapped Refugio Bartola nature reserve or continue downriver to San Juan del Norte, the dank settlement of 900 or so local characters, which truly feels like the edge of the world.

FESTIVALS & EVENTS

✪ Semana Santa; countrywide; March/April. Holy Week (the week before Easter) is widely celebrated with food and drink in this largely Catholic country; many consider León's celebration the grandest.

✪ Palo de Mayo; Bluefields; May. This pagan-themed springtime party celebrates rebirth, fertility and the end of the rainy

MOST BIZARRE SIGHT! ✪

The eerie ruins of El Centro, Managua, which was destroyed by the Christmas Eve earthquake in 1972 and never rebuilt

> " *Unforgettable: the little girl on the bus in Nicaragua who braided my hair when she saw my own clumsy attempts, pulled out two barrettes from her own hair and put them into mine.* "
>
> - Christiane Kabisch, Germany

season with costumes, parades and plenty of dancing around the maypole.

◎ Crab Soup Festival; Corn Islands; August. This festival marks the 1841 abolition of slavery in Nicaragua and is celebrated by cooking a huge vat of crab soup on the beach.

WHAT'S HOT...

◎ The Corn Islands' turquoise waters, coral reefs, white-sand beaches and thatched-roof bungalows provide a Caribbean-style contrast to the more well-trodden Pacific beaches; they make a quiet, relaxing retreat well worth the US$120 return air fare from Managua.

WHAT'S NOT...

◎ Sadly, San Juan del Sur. With cruise ships now docking here, the town's hipper underground days have started going the way of Phuket, Thailand.

HOT TIPS FOR TRAVELLERS

◎ Go north: the southwest is getting crowded, but the northern highlands are wonderfully undertravelled. Visits to Estelí, Jinotega, Matagalpa and the mountains reveal a different Nicaragua, at once welcoming and unhurried.

◎ Stow your inner Indiana Jones and avoid the Minas Triangle in northeastern Nicaragua; controlled by renegade bandits, it's truly a no-man's-land.

◎ The most obvious surf is in San Juan del Sur, but smaller beaches north and south of the town have much less bustle but most of the same conditions.

DO MENTION

◎ The outstanding works of poet Rubén Darío, from León. The 'Prince' of Spanish-American literature has inspired generations of Central American poets, writers, artists and thinkers.

DON'T MENTION

◎ Your perspectives or opinions on the Sandinistas and Contras. Wounds are still raw from the conflict; let your hosts broach the topics first.

RANDOM FACTS

◎ Johnny Cash and Merle Haggard dominate jukeboxes in the Caribbean port town of Bluefields, where nine radio stations blare reggae, salsa, calypso and country and western.

◎ Windsurfers beware: despite years of harvesting, freshwater sharks lurk in Lake Nicaragua.

THINGS TO TAKE

◎ DEET – mosquitoes run big in these parts and can carry some nasty viruses

◎ Baseball cards – score points with the local kids in this baseball-mad nation; bonus credit for Dennis Martinez, Nicaragua's greatest sporting hero

◎ Sunscreen – you'll need it on the coast, and you'll pay extra for it there

THREE WORDS TO DESCRIBE THIS COUNTRY

◎ Next big thing

- Jay Cooke

DEFINING ✪ EXPERIENCE!

After scoring a hammock at Masaya's Mercado Viejo, wandering Granada's palm-fringed colonial plaza, and bounding down the Pan-American Hwy by bus, you arrive in San Juan del Sur, where the backpackers, expats and surfers have gathered at sunset at the bars and beaches, rum drinks in hand to toast the sun setting on another day in Nicaragua's Shangri-La.

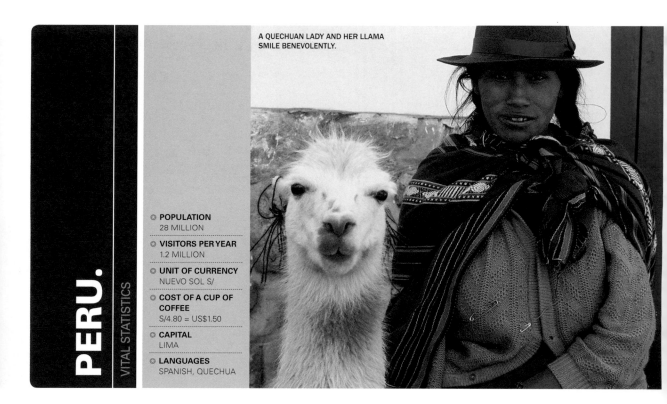

A QUECHUAN LADY AND HER LLAMA SMILE BENEVOLENTLY.

PERU.
VITAL STATISTICS

- **POPULATION**
  28 MILLION
- **VISITORS PER YEAR**
  1.2 MILLION
- **UNIT OF CURRENCY**
  NUEVO SOL S/
- **COST OF A CUP OF COFFEE**
  S/4.80 = US$1.50
- **CAPITAL**
  LIMA
- **LANGUAGES**
  SPANISH, QUECHUA

THE BENEFITS OF PONCHOS. Peru is often called the quintessential South American destination, evoking images of Andean mountains, fabled lost cities, panpipe players, llamas and, of course, the ever-fashionable and functional poncho.

But it's with this increasing familiarity with all things Peruvian that the country has lost much of its tough-travel edge, making it more attractive to people of all travel persuasions – from five-star high-enders to seasoned backpackers. Current figures show that the number of visitors to Peru is expected to rise by 6% over the next year, reinforcing the strong upward trend. Peru is also one of the countries on the World Travel Organization's list of Top Emerging Tourism Destinations. However, surging visitor numbers can often be a curse, spoiling the very things that made the destination popular in the first place, which is why the Peruvian government has tried to curb visitor numbers at its most well-loved sites. Nowadays, you can only hike the Inca Trail, the continent's top hiking route, as part of a licensed trekking group and there is a limit of 500 people on the trail per day. There are also potential plans to

temporarily close the trail for maintenance in the next few years. The number of daily visitors to Machu Picchu has also been restricted to 2500, although some argue that this number is still too high. Nonetheless, these are positive signs, which ensure the country's continued appeal to future poncho-loving generations.

'DEEPEST DARKEST PERU'?

Ever since Tintin and Snowy had a brush with the Incas, the country has been a must-see for young modern-day adventurers, making it ever-more popular by the year. Nowadays the country is synonymous with gringos flying to Lima, heading south to Nazca and Arequipa, making their way east to Lake Titicaca and then north to Cuzco and Machu Picchu. However, there are a few less-obvious routes for those who still dream of independent adventure. One of the best trips starts in

Chiclayo in northern Peru. From there, head east to Chachapoyas, which is a good base for visiting the fortress of Kuélap and many other remote archaeological sites, via either Jaén or Celendín. From Chachapoyas, scenic roads lead to Pedro Ruíz and Tarapoto, where there are opportunities to hike to high jungle waterfalls. The final gut-wrenching bus journey goes to Yurimaguas, where cargo boats leave for Lagunas and Iquitos. At Iquitos you can arrange boat trips that go deep into the heart of the Amazon Basin. This is certainly a trip for curious travellers, who want to sample wild, unpaved Peru. Don't expect comfort!

DEFINING EXPERIENCE
○ Watching the sun rise over Machu Picchu, the most strikingly familiar image in South America.

FESTIVALS & EVENTS
○ Carnaval; February/March. Held on the last few days before Lent, this holiday is often celebrated with water fights, so be warned. It's a popular fiesta in the highlands, with the Carnaval de Cajamarca being one of the biggest. It's also busy in beach towns, where the water is still warm.

○ Semana Santa; March/April. Holy Week (the week before Easter Sunday) is »

HOT TOPIC OF THE DAY!

While the Shining Path and Tupac Amaru guerrilla groups are now no longer a major threat in Peru, the country still has problems with violent crime and gang warfare. Coca production remains at a high level too.

FOR THE ADVENTUROUS

The variety of trails to trek, canyons to explore and dunes to surf is staggering. Here are a few ideas to keep the adrenalin surging:
○ Trekking and mountain biking around the Cordillera Blanca
○ Trekking the Ausangate Circuit alongside alpacas
○ Wandering in the Cañón del Colca, one of the world's deepest canyons
○ Trekking the Inca Trail to Machu Picchu
○ River-running on the Tambopata and Apurímac
○ Sand-boarding at Huacachina

PERU.

"

Peru has a way of enchanting your spirit.

"

- Heather Ayres, USA

MOST BIZARRE SIGHT! ★

The mystery behind the massive Nazca Lines, which are etched out in the desert, has baffled people for generations. The so-called 'astronaut' figure is probably the strangest of all.

» celebrated with spectacular religious processions; Ayacucho is recognised as having the best in Peru. Cuzco is also good for Easter processions.

○ Inti Raymi (Winter Solstice); June. Inti Raymi is the greatest of the Inca festivals. It's certainly the spectacle of the year in Cuzco and attracts thousands of Peruvian and foreign visitors. Despite its commercialisation, it's still worth seeing the street dances and parades, as well as the pageant held in Sacsayhuamán. It's also a big holiday in many of the jungle towns.

○ El Señor de los Milagros (Lord of the Miracles); October. There are major religious processions in Lima; celebrants wear purple.

RECENT FAD

○ Like many love potions, the latest one to catch on in Peru is odd. The drink is 'frog juice', made with honey and Titicaca frogs. The juicing itself is illegal, and the protection of frogs has been stepped up, but the practice still goes on.

DO MENTION

○ Football (*fútbol*) – Peruvians are crazy about the game

DON'T MENTION

The fact that Peru hasn't qualified for the football World Cup since 1982

RANDOM FACTS

○ Cuzco cathedral has a painting of the *Last Supper* featuring a guinea pig as the main course.

○ Apparently the 'ancient' stone penises at the Peruvian village of Chucuito are fake.

THINGS TO TAKE

○ Mosquito repellent

○ An extra bag for the acquisition of Peruvian headgear

○ Toilet paper

HOT TIPS FOR TRAVELLERS

○ Try to sit at the front of the bus if you're going on a long journey in Peru – even paved roads have potholes and you'll bounce far higher if you sit at the back.

○ Drink Inka Kola instead of frog juice.

THREE WORDS TO DESCRIBE THIS COUNTRY

○ An ancient realm

- *Heather Dickson*

A RURAL GAUCHO SMILING IN THE SADDLE.

- **POPULATION**
  3.5 MILLION
- **VISITORS PER YEAR**
  2 MILLION
- **UNIT OF CURRENCY**
  URUGUAYAN PESO
  (UR$)
- **COST OF A CUP OF COFFEE**
  UR$18 = US$0.75
- **CAPITAL**
  MONTEVIDEO
- **LANGUAGES**
  SPANISH,
  PORTUGUESE

⭐ LA VIDA NOT SO LOCA. Sandwiched between the two giants of South America, Argentina and Brazil, you'd expect Uruguay to suffer from a massive inferiority complex.

But Uruguayans seem comfortable with their country's reputation as the quiet, uneventful one. Many travellers take Uruguay as a welcome parenthesis after the intense, boisterous vibe of Buenos Aires or Rio de Janeiro. This is a place of picturesque colonial cities and an endless parade of beach resorts, a fertile expanse criss-crossed with pristine rivers, traditionally sustaining an economy of wheat and cattle. Its restful natural beauty lacks monumental landmarks (no breathtaking waterfalls, mountain ranges or sheer cliffs), but it offers an unspoiled landscape ideal for hiking, horse riding, fishing, biking or just lying about. Prepare to relax.

Uruguayans are hospitable, generous and easygoing. Despite the high rate of tourists per capita, visitors are still objects of curiosity. Uruguayans are delighted by the fact that people from distant parts of the world show an interest in their country. The only exception to this rule is Punta del Este,

which exists solely for tourism. Tourists have helped soften the blow of recent economic crises felt in Argentina and Brazil. Uruguay's weather is temperate; the summers are not too hot and the winters not too cold, and ecotourism and 'agrotourism' have emerged as major attractions. There are some great spots for whale-watching, and Isla de los Lobos is one of the most important reservations of sea wolves in the world. Also, you can stay in a comfortable hotel in the countryside and tour through carefully orchestrated reconstructions of a long-gone rural life (minus the gory bits).

The two major cities, Montevideo and Colonia, are quite small and their attractions warrant only a couple of days' stay. But the nightlife is quite good. Colonia is an open-air museum, showcasing Portuguese colonial architecture dating from the end of the 17th century and with streets crawling with vintage cars. Both cities offer plenty of »

HOT TOPIC OF THE DAY!

The rise of sensible, left-leaning governments throughout South America after decades of tyrannical military governments and failed neoliberal programmes that have plunged the region into ruin

OLD-WORLD CHARM
IN THE STREETS OF MONTEVIDEO.

URUGUAY.

» opportunities for indulging in that distinctly South American obsession with plazas, monuments, statues, mausoleums for famous heroes of the independence, statues, statues, plazas and statues.

Punta del Este is like another country in its own right. It's a famous beach peninsula that parties hard year-round, but particularly in summer. It attracts celebrities and upper-class socialites from Argentina and other nearby countries – they are almost as fascinating to watch as the native fauna. There are hotels, restaurants, bars, discos and night clubs galore. And if you stay awake late enough, you can watch the whales roam close to the coast from August to November.

At the other end of the spectrum are destinations such as Cabo Polonio, a fishing town 200km (124mi) up the coast from Montevideo. Surrounded by beaches and dunes, Cabo Polonio is accessible only by horse-drawn cart or 4WD. There are no cars, and only a few places have electricity and plumbing. These out-of-the-way destinations are attracting many tourists, but not enough to spoil the tranquillity. Yet.

Compared with the rest of South America, Uruguay has had a relatively stable political scene. For many decades it lived in a state of near civil war, but at least democratic elections were held regularly. A military dictatorship ruled from 1973 until 1985, imprisoning and murdering hundreds of people. Uruguayans are still digesting the legacy of those years, trying to establish the fate of the 'disappeared'. However, the scars of past dictatorships are not as visible to the traveller as in some other South American countries.

DEFINING EXPERIENCE

⊙ Sitting on a beach in Punta del Este in summer, waiting to spot a whale emerging from the pristine Atlantic waters, after being up all night dancing

FESTIVALS & EVENTS

⊙ Carnaval; February/March. It is not as spectacular as the one in Brazil, but at least you won't get mugged every two hours.

⊙ Semana Criolla; Montevideo; during Semana Santa, the week before Easter. It features rodeos and cattle and sheep exhibitions. You can watch the famous *payada*, in which two gauchos confront

URUGUAY.

> *In Montevideo (Uruguay) we went to a tango bar called Salu where the locals hang out and dance the tango. They show so much passion in their dancing, it was absolutely fantastic.*
> *It was great to see a 70-year-old bloke gliding gracefully across the floor with a young gal in his arms! We arrived at 10pm and before we knew it, it was 5am and we had learnt to tango!*
>
> *- Narelle & Gez, Australia*

- The name 'Uruguay' comes from Guaraní, the language of the native people of the region. It means 'river of the painted birds'.
- The first football (soccer) World Cup was held in Montevideo in 1930. In a country where more than 30% of people declare themselves nonreligious, soccer has rushed in to fill the gap.
- Maté is the national drink, a herbal brew native of that part of South America. It was first adopted by the Guaraní Indians, and reputedly has many advantageous health effects, although it has a high caffeine content.

DO MENTION
- That their culture is up to date and has no need to envy Europe. Uruguayans are proud of their culture. The country has nurtured formidable, world-class writers, painters and musicians

DON'T MENTION
- That Argentines dance the tango better

THINGS TO TAKE
- Fishing rod
- Swimwear
- Umbrella
- Some good books you've always wanted to read but never had the time
- A bicycle
- Digestive salts or equivalent – in case you overdo it with the *asado* (spit roast)

HOT TIPS FOR TRAVELLERS
- Uruguay is a very bicycle-friendly place. The locals love bike riding, and car drivers are used to it.
- You're advised to learn who Artigas was – the Uruguayan national hero. His image is ubiquitous. And the Uruguayans may be so flattered and impressed by your knowledge, you might even get a second serve of steak. On the house.

THREE WORDS TO DESCRIBE THIS COUNTRY
- Laid-back, beaches, football

- Andres Vaccari

each other, armed with guitars. Each improvises a series of witty rhyming verses, and the other responds, trying to outdo his adversary.

WHAT'S HOT...
- Siesta

WHAT'S NOT...
- Steven Seagal. Uruguay's Ministry of Education and Culture is considering legal action against the makers of *Submerged*, a recent Z-grade Hollywood production starring Steven Seagal. They allege the film portrays their country as a backwards banana republic, and claim they are rallying to protect Uruguay's national symbols and international image.

RANDOM FACTS
- One of the reasons why the Spanish showed interest in the Río de la Plata area is because of a legend that spread among the Indians. The legend spoke of a city, Trapalanda, made of pure gold and silver, and inhabited by immortal beings. The myth motivated dozens of doomed expeditions into Patagonia, well into the 18th century.

MOST BIZARRE SIGHT!

A gaucho in traditional costume, complete with whip and spurs, walking down the streets of Colonia talking on his mobile phone

USA.

VITAL STATISTICS

○ **POPULATION**
290 MILLION

○ **VISITORS PER YEAR**
46 MILLION

○ **UNIT OF CURRENCY**
US DOLLAR ($)

○ **COST OF A CUP OF COFFEE**
BREWED US$1.30;
ESPRESSO STYLE
US$2.45

○ **CAPITAL**
WASHINGTON DC

○ **LANGUAGES**
ENGLISH, SPANISH,
NATIVE AMERICAN
LANGUAGES

A BODY BUILDER SHINES AND FLEXES IN STARS AND STRIPES ON MUSCLE BEACH, LOS ANGELES.

⭐ **FORTRESS AMERICA.** It's been a perplexing time for the USA. The world's sole remaining superpower has had its global image battered out of shape over the last couple of years, as international support for the American-led War on Terror diminishes.

The Pew Research Center discovered – in a survey of attitudes in Western European nations – that even communist China has a more favourable image than the USA, and that generates an obvious knock-on effect as far as tourism is concerned. American travel-industry leaders have done the sums and they've reached a disturbing conclusion: the USA's poor public profile means that the country is haemorrhaging billions of dollars in tourism revenue.

Travellers have also been put off by increased security measures and visa procedures, which kicked into hyperdrive after September 11 and have continued apace after the Iraq war. 'Fortress America' has shut its doors even more tightly, and that's not going to change with the impending introduction of biometric facial-recognition technology for those wishing to enter the country. With iris scans, fingerprint scans and perhaps even voiceprint identification

due to become a reality, the onus could soon be on travellers to prove they are not a spy or a terrorist, particularly if they have a name similar to a known criminal, or if they happen to crack a joke about bombs while waiting to go through customs.

ONCE YOU'RE IN...

The good news is the travel industry is working hard to offset this negative image. Think of it as a tug-of-war between the government and the tourism authorities – instead of rope, they're tugging on a welcome mat and the winner gets to withdraw the mat from the country's doorstep or extend it as they see fit. There's also a sense that ordinary US citizens are keener than ever before to change the stereotype, particularly since the War on Terror is losing support even within the States.

Indeed, there's a lot to get excited about, but it's hard to sum up the appeal of the

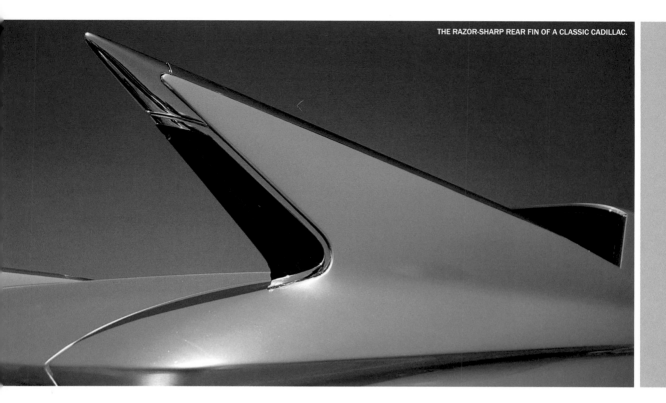

country in just a few paragraphs, for it's hardly a model of a unified culture. The USA is best thought of as a continent, with virtually each state and each city providing a world within a world. There's Las Vegas – glitzy and shot through with adrenalin; New York – rebuilding itself after September 11 and enhancing its cocky urban vibe; Hawaii – volcanic, tropical and far removed from mainstream American life; Los Angeles – Hollywood and all the rest; Yosemite National Park – shrine to the Great Outdoors; Alaska – the frozen frontier to the north…

JUST GO WITH THE FLOW
If all of that doesn't appeal, then consider the latest trend in US travel: nude tourism. The American Association for Nude Recreation (AANR) claims that nude tourism (as opposed to 'textile tourism' – for the clothed) is now a $400 million industry, with 50,000 AANR members and more than 250 clubs and resorts extolling activities such as nude hot-air ballooning and naked hikes by moonlight. Another popular pursuit is naked drive-bys, and no, that doesn't involve 'gang banging' in the buff – instead, hop on a tour bus and drive by celebrity homes, marvelling at the lives of the rich and famous as you feel the cool breeze on your skin.

Only in America – and only if you can get in.

RECENT FAD
○ Fad dieting. The No-Carbs Diet, the Super-High Protein Diet, the Beverly Hills Diet, the Cabbage-Soup Diet, the See-Food Diet, the Air Diet, the Mud Diet, the Fruit Diet, the Russian Air Force Diet – you name it, America has classed, contained and consumed it.

MOST BIZARRE SIGHT
○ Tom Cruise throttling Oprah Winfrey on primetime TV.

FESTIVALS & EVENTS
○ Super Bowl; various venues; late January. Football madness.

○ New Orleans Mardi Gras; New Orleans; February or March. Voodoo, excess and jazz. Early reports after hurricane Katrina suggest that the 2006 Mardi Gras will go ahead, but check before you go.

○ St Patrick's Day; countrywide; mid-March. Especially raucous in the Irish heartlands of New York and Chicago.

DEFINING EXPERIENCE! ✪

The road trip is still the ultimate expression of freedom in America – hire a car, put the top down, crank up your radio, and kick your hicks on Route 66…or something like that.

USA.

> " *Cave Creek is situated north of Scottsdale (Phoenix, Arizona). Only a 20-minute drive from town but you feel like you're in an Old West town. And in a way, you are. There are country bars with pool tables, live country bands and real cowboys. If you don't dance, that's OK because you'll love watching the pros swing and twirl – you will have a good time even if you don't like country music. You may even see horses tied up to the hitching posts outside.* "

– Susan Logan, Australia

» ○ The Kentucky Derby; Louisville; May. Horse racing's big event.

○ Independence Day; countrywide; July. Flag waving, patriotism, and fireworks.

○ National Hobo Convention; Britt, Iowa; August. For the itinerant at heart.

○ Redneck Games; East Dublin, Georgia; July. Events include the Mud-Pit Belly Flop, the Hubcap Hurl, Bobbing for Pig's Feet, the Dumpster Dive and the Armpit Serenade (in which competitors make farting noises using their armpits).

○ Burning Man; Black Rock City, Nevada; August or September. Get naked while participating in 'a temporary community dedicated to radical self-expression and radical self-reliance' – part of which includes 30,000 people getting off on the sight of a gigantic effigy of man burning.

DO MENTION

○ How friendly the locals are. Americans will love you for not swallowing the anti-Yank hype.

DON'T MENTION

○ The War on Terror – just to be on the safe side.

RANDOM FACTS

○ About a quarter of the American population has been on television.

○ In Natoma, Kansas, you can't throw knives at men wearing striped suits – apparently, it's been outlawed.

○ Americans purchase around $46 billion worth of diet products annually.

○ Since 1840, every American president elected in a year ending in a zero has either died during their term or has survived an assassination attempt. George W Bush was elected in 2000, and his fate is still waiting to be confirmed.

THINGS TO TAKE

○ An international driving licence – America demands to be seen by car.

HOT TIPS FOR TRAVELLERS

○ Summer is when American families take time out to explore their own backyard. Avoid the congestion of 290 million people milling about from state to state and visit the USA during autumn or early spring instead.

○ The hottest tip is to remember to tip – around 10%. Watch Quentin Tarantino's film *Reservoir Dogs* (1992) for an example of what happens when you don't.

THREE WORDS TO DESCRIBE THIS COUNTRY

○ Brash, patriotic, uncompromising

– Simon Sellars

ANGUILLA

Anguilla is truly, as they say, 'tranquillity wrapped in blue.' It's small and lightly populated, and the islanders are friendly and easy-going. The interior of the island is flat, dry and scrubby, pockmarked with salt ponds and devoid of dramatic scenery, but it is fringed by beautiful beaches, aquamarine waters and nearby coral-encrusted islets, which offer great swimming, snorkelling and diving. Anguilla has some of the finest beaches in the Caribbean: long strands of semisecluded miniparadise, with baby-soft sand and swaying palm-tree backdrops.

ANTARCTICA

Antarctica is spectacular, a wilderness of landscapes reduced to a pure haiku of ice, rock, water and sky, filled with wildlife still unafraid of humans. It is a land of extremes: the driest, coldest, most inhospitable and isolated continent on Earth. Antarctica is unique, and a journey here is like no other. Tourism has become Antarctica's growth industry – not mining or oil drilling, as many people once feared. Provided visits are properly managed, tourists may turn out to be one of the best assurances that this wilderness can remain (nearly) as pure as the driven snow. Let us hope!

ANTIGUA & BARBUDA

If it's sandy beaches with almost unbelievably turquoise water, sun and relaxation you're after, Antigua and Barbuda won't fail to deliver. It has great reefs and wrecks for diving and snorkelling. On neighbouring Barbuda you can track the island's fabled frigate birds and visit the Caribbean's largest rookery. Barbuda is a quiet, single-village island that gets very few independent visitors, mainly ardent bird-watchers and a few yachties enjoying its clear waters and tranquil beaches. Antigua is a touch more happening, but the pace is still deliciously slow.

ARUBA & THE NETHERLANDS ANTILLES

It's possible that Aruba and the Netherlands Antilles is the most concentrated area of multiculturalism in the world. Papiamento, spoken throughout the Netherlands Antilles, is testament to this fact – the language is derived from every culture that has impacted on the region, including traces of Spanish, Portuguese, Dutch, French and local Indian languages. The islands are diverse – there are Aruba's beaches, the cutesy houses of Curaçao, Bonaire's reefs, ruggedly steep Saba, Sint Maarten with its large resorts and casinos, and the delightfully slow pace of Sint Eustatius.

BAHAMAS

The Bahamas has successfully promoted itself as a destination for US jet-setters, and a lot of it is Americanised. Yet fishing is still the main livelihood for many and a gentle character prevails. There are still places among its 700 islands and 2500 cays to disappear into a mangrove forest, explore a coral reef and escape the high-rise hotels. The 18th-century Privateers' Republic has become the 21st-century banker's paradise, at least on New Providence and Grand Bahama. On the other islands – once known as the Out Islands but now euphemistically called the Family Islands – the atmosphere is more truly West Indian.

BARBADOS

There is a simple reason why Barbados is the Eastern Caribbean's most popular destination: the beaches are impossibly beautiful. However, the beaches are attached to a densely populated and heavily developed country. As the more intrepid visitor will discover, this well-oiled tourist machine has deeper cultural, historical and natural attractions, but you have to make an effort to get beyond the trappings of package tourism. While there remains an undeniable British influence, Barbados is West Indian to its core. The country is the source of classic calypso rhythms, a cuisine of breadfruit and flying fish, and world-famous rums.

BERMUDA

Visitors from the USA find this most isolated of island groups to be quaintly English, whereas Brits find it has an American flavour. Whatever your point of origin, you can't deny the island makes for a delightful getaway vacation. If you're looking for peace and quiet, Bermuda has pampering resorts to soothe your soul. Or perhaps you want to let loose. Jump on a motor scooter and let the wind whip through your hair. The island's surrounding coral reef offers memorable diving and snorkelling. Bermuda is sometimes erroneously associated with the Caribbean, which lies nearly 1600km (1000mi) to its south.

« BOLIVIA

Bolivia isn't called the Tibet of the Americas for nothing: it's the western hemisphere's highest, most isolated and most rugged nation. It's also South America's most traditional realm: the majority of the population claim pure Amerindian blood, and many maintain the cultural values and belief systems of their forebears. The geography of this landlocked, Andean country runs the gamut from jagged peaks and hallucinogenic salt flats to steamy jungles and wildlife-rich pampas. Surprisingly, it still falls below many travellers' radar, so unlimited opportunities for off-the-beaten-track exploration await in one of South America's most peaceful, secure and welcoming destinations.

CANADA

Canada's wild northern frontier has etched itself into the national psyche, and its distinct patchwork of peoples has created a country that is decidedly different from its southern neighbour. It's the sovereignty of Canada's indigenous, French and British traditions that gives the nation its complex three-dimensional character. Add to this a constant infusion of US culture and a plethora of traditions brought by immigrants, and you have a thriving multicultural society.

CAYMAN ISLANDS

The Cayman Islands are dotted with deal-cutting characters with briefcases and mobile phones, scuba divers in wetsuits and English folk checking the cricket scores. Scratch below the surface of condos and highrise hotels and you'll discover a distinct culture founded only a few centuries ago upon – and inextricably bound with – the sea. Towering underwater walls, shipwrecks and reefs have made the Caymans legendary among divers and snorkelers, and mile upon mile of pristine beaches and predictably glorious sunsets poll well with extreme-relaxation enthusiasts.

COSTA RICA

For decades, Costa Rica was a forgotten backwater, a country so laconic it couldn't be bothered having an army, even though it was sandwiched between Nicaragua and Panama. Then North American retirees discovered its charms and Costa Rica became hot property. The country is unique for its enlightened approach to conservation. More than 27% of the country is protected in one form or another, and over 14% is within its national park system. With its luxuriant rainforests, pristine white beaches, diverse wildlife, to-die-for coffee, relaxed hospitality and ecotourism, Costa Rica is definitely one of the destinations *du jour*.

CUBA

You can spend a lifetime uncovering Cuba's nuances – that's precisely why travellers can't stay away, discovering firsthand what makes this enigmatic island tick. In an amazing balancing act, Cuba is at once poor and broken, and rich and thriving. From the beat of the music echoing through towns and villages to the hustle of Havana's glorious, crumbling streets, Cuba challenges and enchants all who venture in. While Fidel's infrastructure has seen better decades and the food is, well, best not spoken about, the last great bastion of communism enchants with its intoxicating human spirit. Or was that the rum?

DOMINICA

Dominica is largely rural, uncrowded and unspoiled. It has a lush mountainous interior of rainforests, waterfalls, lakes, hot springs and rivers, many of which cascade over steep cliff faces en route to the coast. Apart from its natural splendours, including the highest mountains in the Eastern Caribbean, the island has an interesting fusion of British, French and West Indian cultural traditions, and is home to the Eastern Caribbean's largest Carib Indian community. What Dominica lacks in sandy beaches and all-inclusive resorts it more than makes up for in unspoiled rainforest, unique diving spots, vibrant live music and pride in a barely diluted Carib culture.

DOMINICAN REPUBLIC

Is there a better definition of paradise than the Dominican Republic's palm-fringed white-sand beaches, turquoise waters and rum-and-merengue-soaked nights? While there is no shame in spending a week pampering yourself at an all-inclusive resort (the DR is famous for these), this is a country of remarkable depth and grace, and it's well worth exploring. Santo Domingo offers architectural charm and historical gravitas, while the rugged mountain interior offers world-class rafting, trekking and wildlife-watching. Above all it's the Dominicans who make the DR tick: fun-seekers throw themselves wholeheartedly into neighbourhood parties, surfing contests, music festivals and *two* annual Carnival celebrations.

FALKLAND ISLANDS (MALVINAS)

Just next door to South America and Antarctica, the Falklands are British through and through. With only a few inhabitants (most are British military personnel), it's hardly Touristville. The remote islands briefly rocketed to international importance during the 1980s, when Britain took them back after an invasion by Argentina and everyone learnt their alternative name: Islas Malvinas. There's some amazing wildlife (penguins, seals and albatrosses for starters), and the windswept, treeless terrain has a curious attraction.

GRENADA

Grenada is a heady mix of idyllic tropical rainforests, fecund valleys, terraced gardens and rivers that fall away to white-sand beaches, bays and craggy cliffs. St George's, the beautiful capital, gives Grenada a small-town character, with a dash of dynamic sophistication. While Grenada island accounts for 90% of the nation's land and people, the country's smaller islands – such as Carriacou and Petit Martinique – are definitely worth a visit too. Both are just a short boat ride away from Grenada island and offer comfortable lodgings, beaches and a sublime laid-back tempo.

GUADELOUPE

Guadeloupe's shape inevitably invites comparison to a butterfly, with its two wing-shaped islands. The spirited blend of French and African influences goes straight to the heart of the Caribbean's Creole culture. As well known for its sugar and rum as for its beaches and resorts, the archipelago mixes modern cities and rural hamlets, rainforests and secluded beaches. There are nine inhabited islands to choose from, including Grande-Terre, Basse-Terre and Marie-Galant. Bustling Pointe-à-Pitre is the main hub, but the sleepy capital is on Basse-Terre's remote southwestern flank.

GUATEMALA

Although Guatemala is recovering from the wounds of military dictatorships and guerrilla warfare, it possesses a gritty determination to keep the glorious colours of Mayan culture flying. And what a wealth of masts it has to nail them to. Its volcanoes can seem the highest and most active, its Mayan ruins the most ruinous, its colonial cities the most historic, its jungles the most enigmatic and impenetrable, its coral reefs the most beautiful, and its flora and fauna some of the most unusual in the world. Guatemala is one of those rare destinations that rewards even the most jaded traveller.

GUYANA

Dutch and British colonisation made an indelible mark on Guyana, leaving behind a now dilapidated colonial capital, a volatile mix of peoples and a curious political geography. The country's natural attractions, however, are impressive and unspoiled, with immense falls, vast tropical rainforest and grasslands teeming with wildlife. If the government doesn't destroy the environment in a bid to pay off its huge foreign debt, it could be the ecotourism destination of the future. Adventure guides and resorts are on the increase, but it'll take advance planning to book a tour operator. Unfortunately, going it alone isn't always possible, affordable or safe.

HAITI

The modern world's first black-led republic, Haiti boasts a unique culture and an incredible artistic tradition. Its intensely spiritual people are known for their humour and passion, upheld in the face of poverty, civil strife, oppression and urban overpopulation. Their language, dance and music reflect a unique syncopation between the spiritual and material worlds. Haiti is not yet set up for the Club Med crowd, but the open-minded adventurer will find a country whose contradictions will linger in mind, heart and spirit. Just be sure to bring an open mind and a sense of humour.

HONDURAS

Honduras' slow pace, natural beauty and low-profile tourism make it particularly appealing to travellers (well-armed with insect repellent) who enjoy getting off-the-beaten track. Take your pick from the spectacular Mayan ruins at Copán, the long and lazy Caribbean coastline, the idyllic Bay Islands, the tropical rainforest of the Mosquitia region, colonial mountain towns, »

« the cool cloud forest of La Tigra National Park, and the manatees and birdlife in the country's protected coastlands, wetlands and lagoons. Travel in Honduras is easy, enjoyable and inexpensive.

JAMAICA

Pulsing with music and awash in the zesty smells of its singular cuisine, Jamaica is a destination for the senses. Travellers have long regarded Jamaica as one of the most alluring of the Caribbean islands and its beaches, mountains and carnal red sunsets regularly appear in tourist brochures promising paradise. Jamaica has a diversity that few other Caribbean islands can claim. Stray from the north coast resorts and you'll discover radically different environments and terrain. Or throw yourself into the thick of the island's life and experience the three Rs: reggae, reefers and rum.

MARTINIQUE

Martinique is a slice of France set down in the tropics, but the zouk music pouring out of bars is a reminder that Martinicans have a culture of their own, solidly based on West Indian Creole traditions. French may be the official language, but most locals speak Creole, which retains traces of the many tongues spoken by African slaves. Martinique's large towns feel like modern suburbs, but thankfully nearly a third of the island is forested. You can still find sleepy fishing villages, remote beaches and lots of hiking trails into the mountains.

PANAMA

Along the isthmus bridging the Americas, the wildlife and terrain of two continents meld to form the striking contrasts of Panama. Ocean, mountains and jungle set the stage for countless adventures. The little-visited nation has some of the finest birdwatching, snorkelling and deep-sea fishing in the Americas. Panama celebrates its Spanish heritage with colourful festivals, seasoned with the influences of the remaining indigenous groups and the West Indian culture of its black population. It's difficult to leave the country without feeling you're in on a secret the rest of the travelling world has yet to discover.

PARAGUAY

The tourist trail largely bypasses this small subtropical country, landlocked in the heart of South America, and therein lies much of Paraguay's charm. Paraguay is a subtropical rain forest decorated with metallic butterflies, exotic bird-filled wetlands and the Gran Chaco, a wild frontier, and has some of the friendliest and most unaffected people in the world. Conversing in a blend of Spanish and Guaraní that epitomises the country's unique cultural interweaving, the Paraguayans are most certainly the highlights of this Paraíso Perdido (Paradise Lost).

PUERTO RICO

Puerto Rican culture is a mixture of Spanish, African and Taíno traditions topped with a century-thick layer of American influence. Spanish is the island's main language, but people also use many English, Amerindian and African words. Roman Catholicism reigns, but is infused with spiritualism and folkloric traditions. The music keeps time with African *la bomba* and also 'Nuyorican' salsa hailing from *émigrés* in New York. Puerto Rico is uniquely a part of, and apart from, the US and the rest of the Caribbean. Its natural beauty lies in a blend of dark jungle, dry plains, steep mountains and azure seas.

SAINT KITTS & NEVIS

The islands of St Kitts and Nevis are two of the sleepiest places in the Caribbean, and agriculture is still a larger part of the economy than tourism. The islands have mountainous interiors, patchwork cane fields, salt ponds and deeply indented bays. The culture of the islands draws upon a mix of European, African and West Indian traditions. While three quarters of the population live on St Kitts, both islands are small, rural and lightly populated. St Kitts offers more resorts and nightlife, but also has retained much more of the Caribbean personality.

SAINT LUCIA

Resort developments on St Lucia have made this high, green island one of the Caribbean's trendy package-tour destinations, but it's still a long way from being overdeveloped. Bananas are still bigger business than tourism, and much of the island is rural: small coastal fishing villages give way to a hinterland of banana and coconut plantations folded within deep valleys topped by rich, mountainous jungle. Its most dramatic scenery is in the south, where the twin peaks of the Pitons rise sharply from the Soufrière shoreline. The rugged terrain continues offshore in a diving heaven of underwater mountains, caves and drop-offs.

SAINT VINCENT & THE GRENADINES
St Vincent and the Grenadines are well known to wintering yachties, aristocrats and rock stars, but not yet to most other visitors. The 30 islands and cays that comprise the Grenadines reach between St Vincent and Grenada and are surrounded by coral reefs and clear blue waters. Fewer than a dozen are inhabited and even these are barely developed. They are some of the region's best spots for diving, snorkelling and boating, particularly the uninhabited Tobago Cays. St Vincent and the Grenadines share traditional West Indian culture, giving it a multi-ethnic twist of African, Black Carib, French and British influences.

SURINAME
With a Caribbean feeling, Suriname is a unique enclave whose extraordinary variety of traditions derives from indigenous cultures, British and Dutch colonisation, the early importation of African slaves and, later, workers from China and indentured labourers from India and Indonesia. The country's greatest attractions are the extraordinary nature parks and reserves, notably the enormous World Heritage–listed Central Suriname Nature Reserve. Paramaribo, the vibrant capital, retains some fine Dutch colonial architecture, while enticing aromas waft from the streetside food stalls.

TRINIDAD & TOBAGO
While it has all the Caribbean properties – beaches, seafood, rum cocktails – the dual-island nation of Trinidad & Tobago rocks to its own steel-pan drum. It's as multihued as its people and sunsets, and embraces a national identity intensified by isolation, a patchwork history, politics and the ubiquitous beat of the music. Tobago is relaxed, slow-paced and largely undeveloped. Trinidad is a densely populated, thriving island with a cosmopolitan population and strong regional influence. It's made a name for hosting the loudest and wildest Carnival in the Caribbean, whereas on Tobago the reefs are calm and the beaches good.

TURKS & CAICOS
As part of the Caribbean, this British colony has many charms. The Turks & Caicos – oddly named and a little misshapen – is the often-neglected stepsister to the neighbouring Bahamas. Several islands are fringed with exquisite beaches and for divers there are several hundred miles of coral reef that make it a hot destination. Small cafés and bars doze in the daytime and awaken at sunset as boats return, with damp passengers talking of curious iguanas and gentle stingrays.

VENEZUELA
The common denominator that unites Venezuela is an overwhelming passion for life, love and sheer enjoyment. The country rocks to Latino, Afro and Caribbean rhythms that resonate with the energy of a people living for the moment. Venezuela is a land of incredible variety and epic proportions; it has snow-capped Andean peaks, Caribbean coastline, the legendary Amazon and wildlife-rich savannas. Angel Falls – the world's highest waterfall – plummets from a flat-topped *tepuis* rising vertically from the plains. With a culture as diverse as its geography, the Stone Age lifestyle of the indigenous Yanomami coexists with Caracas' striking modern architecture.

VIRGIN ISLANDS
A divided archipelago for more than 250 years, the Virgin Islands attract mariners and millionaires. With well-protected anchorages and a year-round balmy climate, this is the destination for luxury yachts and cruise ships. Despite busy shopping districts, spectacular beaches beckon and the rhythms of reggae or calypso swirl through the air. Tourist development has been limited by recognition of environmental problems, and the islands have different characters: while the US Virgin Islands have pursued the tourist dollar, the British Virgin Islands are keen to stay limey and out of the limelight.

>> ASIA.

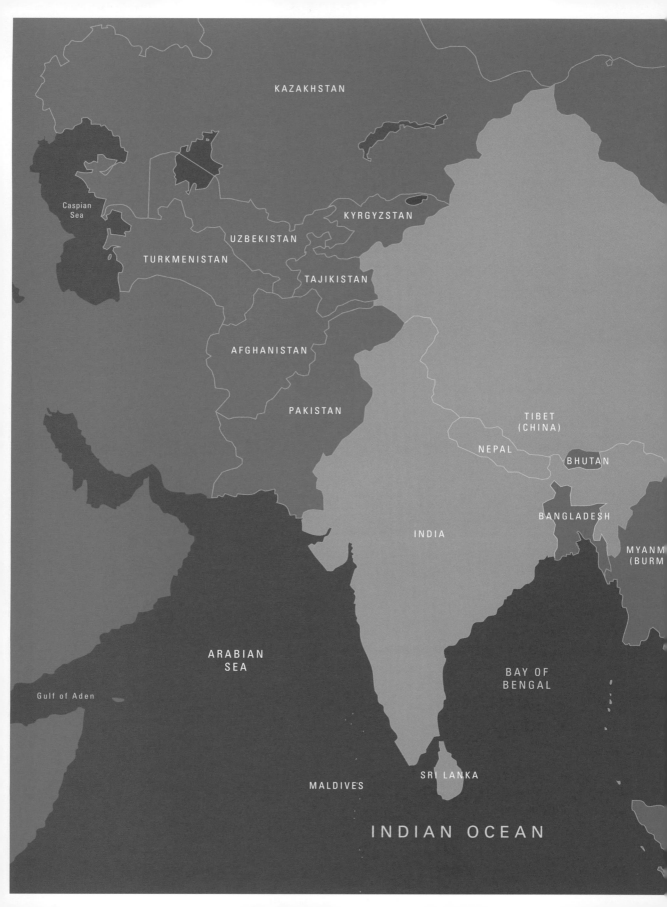

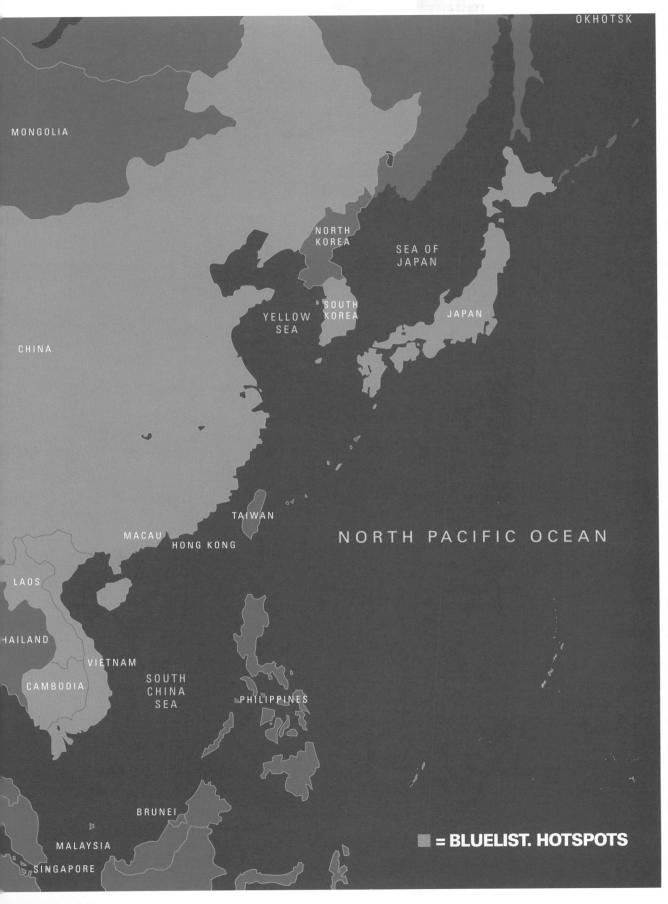

OKHOTSK

MONGOLIA

NORTH
KOREA

SEA OF
JAPAN

SOUTH
KOREA

YELLOW
SEA

JAPAN

CHINA

TAIWAN

MACAU

HONG KONG

NORTH PACIFIC OCEAN

LAOS

HAILAND

VIETNAM

SOUTH
CHINA
SEA

CAMBODIA

PHILIPPINES

BRUNEI

MALAYSIA

SINGAPORE

= BLUELIST. HOTSPOTS

A CHEEKY YOUNG GIRL IN THE VILLAGE OF BAVEL.

CAMBODIA.

ITAL TATI TIC

- **POPULATION**
  14 MILLION
- **VISITORS PER YEAR**
  1 MILLION
- **UNIT OF CURRENCY**
  CAMBODIAN RIEL (R)
- **COST OF A CUP OF COFFEE**
  2000R = US$0.50
- **CAPITAL**
  PHNOM PENH
- **LANGUAGE**
  KHMER

★ ROAD TO REHABILITATION. Even when Cambodia was the basket case of Asia, riddled with insurgency and awash with unexploded bombs, travellers came here to add a war zone to their list of visited countries.

It was lawless, edgy, even dangerous, but that was part of the appeal. Veterans of those days tell rowdy stories of drinking till dawn in the brothel-bars of Svay Pak while drunken cadres rattled machine-gun bullets into the night sky.

Since then, Cambodia has come back into the Southeast Asian mainstream, a logical step on from Thailand, livelier than Malaysia, edgier than Laos and less discovered than Vietnam. It has better historic relics than all of them in wonderful Angkor Wat and it still retains a tangible air of lawlessness and excitement, despite the end of the Khmer Rouge insurgency, falling crime figures and long overdue political reforms.

WAR AS A TOURIST ATTRACTION?
Predictably, part of Cambodia's unique appeal comes from the 1975–79 war. Man's inhumanity to fellow man holds a timeless, if macabre, fascination, and many of

Cambodia's major tourist attractions are battlefields, prisons and mass graves. Even if you eschew the gruesome sights of the Killing Fields, buildings and trees across Cambodia bear the scars of flying bullets and shrapnel, a constant reminder of the Khmer Rouge years and American bombing that still officially 'never happened'.

The social scars of war are just as visible. Hundreds of Cambodians are injured by landmines every year, adding to the growing army of amputees who beg for small change in tourist areas around Phnom Penh. It would be extremely unwise to leave the beaten path anywhere in Cambodia – if you can't see evidence that someone has walked there before you, don't even think about it!

Prostitution and violent crime are two more unwelcome legacies of the war years. However, the ready availability of firearms has created an unexpected tourist

A YOUNG MONK CONTEMPLATES LIFE AND POSSIBLY MOTORCYCLES ON A BOAT RIDE TO KRATIE.

opportunity – firing machine guns left over from the war. And yes, Cambodia is still as corrupt as it has always been – if you hire a motorbike or car, expect to pay regular bribes to traffic cops.

BANANA BUNCHES & SPIDER LUNCHES...

Another surprising draw for visitors to Cambodia is eating gross stuff – or at least, things that wouldn't immediately strike Westerners as a tasty snack. Popular options include fried spiders, baked frogs, duck chicks and *prahoc* (fermented fish crushed into a pongy grey paste by human feet).

Of course, Cambodia isn't all about 'out-there' experiences. It has peaceful Buddhist monasteries and ancient temples, lazy rivers and unspoiled national parks, fabulous food and an easily accessible traveller scene, plus some of the liveliest and most interesting markets in the region. The legendary Cambodian dope scene has largely disappeared; it was once possible to buy marijuana by the kilo in Phnom Penh's Russian Market, but these days you'll have to make do with bunches of bananas, rambutans and juicy dragon fruit.

DEFINING EXPERIENCE

◯ Arriving in the Bayon temple at Angkor Wat before dawn, with massive fruit bats swooping past your face, then watching the sun slowly illuminate 200 carved stone faces of Avalokiteshvara – it is serenity defined!

FESTIVALS & EVENTS

◉ Chaul Chnam Chen (New Year); mid-April. This is a three-day celebration that culminates in the ritual washing of Buddha statues. The biggest celebrations take place around Wat Phnom in Phnom Penh.

◉ P'Chum Ben; September–October. You can help Cambodians pay tribute to the dead during this 15-day festival. Khmers offer food, drink, money and even cigarettes to the dead, represented by local monks.

◉ Bom Om Tuk (Water Festival); November. Marks the reversing flow of the Tonle Sap river with three days of dragon-boat races, fireworks and a flotilla of burning boats.

◉ Angkor Wat Half-Marathon; Angkor Wat; November. One of the few international sporting events in Cambodia. Entry fees go to charities working with victims of landmines.

»

RECENT FAD! ✪

Walloping foreigners! Teenagers from wealthy Khmer families have taken to setting their bodyguards on people who rub them up the wrong way in Phnom Penh's bars. Unless you fancy scuffling with trained heavies, watch whose pint you spill.

CAMBODIA.

FROM THE ROAD

"

On the way through Cambodia, my boyfriend sat next to this local bloke who was so excited about sitting next to a tourist (we were in a relatively remote area) that he talked to us for the whole trip (seven hours!). We commented on his excellent English. He said that learning English used to be illegal, but he had an illegal book that he hid and it taught him everything he knew about the language.

"

– Katherine Bennell, Australia

» HOT TOPIC OF THE DAY

⚙ The much-touted Khmer Rouge Tribunal. Most of the leaders of the Khmer Rouge are still at large, despite the creation of a UN-backed tribunal to investigate crimes by Pol Pot's regime. The main problem is money – so far, the Cambodian government has managed to raise only 10% of the US$13 million needed to bring Khmer Rouge leaders to justice.

DO MENTION

⚙ Angelina Jolie. After years of promoting conservation in Cambodia, the *Tomb Raider* star was granted honorary Cambodian citizenship in 2005. The love affair between Cambodia and Jolie started in 2002, when the actress adopted an orphaned Cambodian boy with then husband Billy Bob Thornton.

⚙ Child prostitution. Cambodians tend to sweep the problem under the carpet, to the despair of nongovernmental organisations who are working to protect children from sexual exploitation. Foreigners can help by reporting dodgy behaviour on special anti–child prostitution hotlines.

DON'T MENTION

⚙ Bird flu. Although Cambodia has so far seen just two cases of the potentially deadly bug, poultry farmers worry that an outbreak will lead to mass slaughter of the nation's chickens.

RANDOM FACTS

⚙ Cambodia is 90% Buddhist but almost all of its historic sites – including Angkor Wat – are Hindu.

⚙ The Khmer alphabet has 74 letters.

THINGS TO TAKE

⚙ An umbrella and/or swimming trunks – large parts of Cambodia vanish under water during the annual monsoon

⚙ Earplugs, if only to stop the boom of Vietnamese pop from the bar next door

HOT TIPS FOR TRAVELLERS

⚙ For fabulously authentic Khmer lunches, head for the food stalls in Phnom Penh's markets.

⚙ Rent a motorcycle to explore the area around Phnom Penh – petrol is readily available on the road side and rental rates are amazingly cheap, even after you factor in the inevitable bribes to dodgy traffic cops.

⚙ Never leave the path. This may seem strange advice from a company that promotes independent travel perhaps, but the countryside is strewn with unexploded munitions.

THREE WORDS TO DESCRIBE THIS COUNTRY

⚙ Wild, water-logged, wonderful

– *Joe Bindloss*

A FAMILY AT THE LANTERN FESTIVAL, CAUSEWAY BAY, HONG KONG.

VITAL STATISTICS

○ **POPULATION**
1.3 BILLION

○ **VISITORS PER YEAR**
109 MILLION

○ **UNIT OF CURRENCY**
YUAN (Y)

○ **COST OF A BEER**
Y6 = US$0.75

○ **CAPITAL**
BEIJING

○ **LANGUAGES**
MANDARIN
(OFFICIAL),
CANTONESE,
VARIOUS REGIONAL
DIALECTS

CHINA.

FOLLOW THE DRAGON. Fast, brash and unpredictable – these three words describe perfectly the current state of the Middle Kingdom. Gone are the days of Mao suits and bicycles – they've been replaced with Cadillacs, hot pants and hip-hop.

Over the past two decades, China has undergone unbelievable social and cultural transformations. Today, the country is bursting with creative energy; everywhere you travel you'll see rampant construction, urban landscapes changing overnight and old buildings making way for the new. Development brings with it an array of headaches – pollution, rising crime and unemployment, just to name a few – but these negatives form only one part of modern China. With freer flow of information, a cacophony of fresh voices have emerged, challenging the way China is redefining itself in the 21st century.

China has been open to foreign visitors only since the late 1970s; however, it wasn't until the mid-1980s that an actual tourist industry began to take shape. Much of the country was off limits to foreigners and only those with the right permits were allowed to visit forbidden areas. Today, visitors are free to travel almost anywhere they please, though infrastructure in many areas still leaves much to be desired, especially in the interior. Getting around in China can be a hassle if you don't speak some Chinese, but with the 2008 Olympics on the horizon, the government plans to make larger cities more tourist friendly by increasing the number of English signs on the streets and in bus and train stations. Taxi drivers and policemen are being encouraged to learn English to help out tongue-tied, non-Chinese-speaking foreigners.

XANADU, WHERE ARE YOU?

Despite all the changes, traditional China is never far away, even if it's currently buried under layers of construction and dust. The Great Wall remains as impressive as ever and the Forbidden City retains its original splendour, drawing a steady stream of tourists through its gates every day. And »

HOT TOPIC OF THE DAY! ✪

Chinese companies trying to buy up overseas assets: China's thirst for foreign capital and technological know-how is generating fear and xenophobia among American politicians.

MEN AND THEIR MAH
JONG SQUARES.

CHINA.

» beyond the staple sights touted in travel brochures, there is a host of wonders that many visitors never see. China is populated by more than 200 ethnic minorities, and each has its own distinct set of customs and traditions. The country's geography is as varied as its people – in the southwest are lush paddy fields and mist-covered hills, while the northwest is home to the scorching sands of the Taklamakan Desert and the magnificent plateaus of Tibet. Catch a glimpse of traditional religious beliefs that lay dormant for years but are now making a comeback in China's sacred mountains. Wutai Shan (Mt Wutai), in Shanxi province, has been a Buddhist sanctuary for more than 2000 years and is one of China's holiest mountains. For the entire month of August, Buddhist rituals are acted out on Wutai Shan's remote mountain peaks,

MOST BIZARRE SIGHT! ⭐

Coal-mine tours. Don miner's overalls and a safety helmet and descend 90m underground into the coal mines of Jinhuagong, Shanxi province, which are notorious for their number of mining-related deaths each year.

»»

SCALING THE GREAT FIREWALL

China has more than the 100 million Internet users, second only to the USA in the number of people online. Most Chinese can now access foreign news and information, much like users in other parts of the world. Print and broadcast media are still tightly controlled by the government, but with the current online frenzy, officials are finding it futile to try and block so-called 'subversive' websites. Not that they haven't tried – the search engine Google has been cut off from time to time to prevent users from reading Jiang Zemin jokes that made it into top-10 search results.

The Internet is especially influencing Chinese youth, who spend hours in crowded Internet cafés playing video games, chatting and watching movies online. Internet addiction among teenagers has become such a serious problem that government-sponsored clinics have been set up to cure addicts. The most popular remedies include low-voltage shock therapy and intravenous fluids to regulate the brain. Using the excuse that Internet exposure at a young age can lead children down a path of crime and hedonism, the government lobs heavy fines at café owners who allow Internet access for minors.

> "
> *I was on the Great Wall of China. It started to rain but I was saved from a soaking by a group of Chinese teenage girls who shared their umbrella with me. Each of them also wanted to get their picture taken with me – a white-haired old lady. It is true that age is respected in China and I felt like a very important visitor.*
> "

- Christiane Kabisch, Germany

and foreigners are welcome to visit. It's experiences like these that will ensure a trip to China is truly special.

Napoleon once claimed that 'when China awakes, she will astonish the world'. Modern China, teeming with energy and rife with contradictions, has awoken. There's no better time to visit; the dragon's on the move and the world is watching.

DEFINING EXPERIENCE
- Exchanging text messages with a Tibetan monk you met in Shanghai while hiking to the top of the misty Yellow Mountains at dawn

FESTIVALS & EVENTS
- Haerbin Ice & Snow Festival; Haerbin; January–February. In northeast Heilongjiang province, this annual festival features enormous blocks of ice carved into whimsical sculptures and lit from within with coloured lights.
- Water Splashing Festival; April. The Dai people of China's Yunnan province celebrate their new year by throwing water on one another to ensure good luck and happiness for the coming year.

- Shanghai International Film Festival; Shanghai; June. The only international film festival held in China and a must-see red carpet event. More than 900 films from more than 60 countries will be showcased.
- Mid-Autumn Festival; late September or October. Marks the end of the harvest season. Families celebrate by lighting fireworks and eating moon cakes (sugary pastries filled with ground lotus or sesame seeds).
- Shanghai Biennale; Shanghai; September–November of even-numbered years. Artists from all over the world will participate in this contemporary (and at times controversial) art extravaganza at the Shanghai Art Museum.

DO MENTION
- The 2008 Olympics, a source of national pride for most Chinese and a chance for the government to prove China is on a par with the rest of the world.

DON'T MENTION
- The Tibet issue, a very bitter topic and one many Chinese feel sensitive about.

RANDOM FACTS
- China has more bird species than any country in the world.
- Umbrellas originated in China around AD 500.
- The first World Toilet Expo made its debut in Shanghai in July 2005.

THINGS TO TAKE
- Earplugs: the constant construction can be deafening
- Deodorant: nonexistent except in major cities

HOT TIPS FOR TRAVELLERS
- Don't forget to ask for a discount when checking into your hotel as prices can be slashed up to 50% during the low seasons.
- Always carry cash and travellers cheques – only top-end hotels, restaurants and shops take credit cards.

THREE WORDS TO DESCRIBE THIS COUNTRY
- Bold, brazen, capricious

- *Julie Grundvig*

HONG KONG.

VITAL STATISTICS

- **POPULATION**
  6.8 MILLION
- **VISITORS PER YEAR**
  21.8 MILLION
- **UNIT OF CURRENCY**
  HONG KONG
  DOLLAR ($)
- **COST OF A CUP
  OF COFFEE**
  HK$20 = US$2.60
- **LANGUAGES**
  CANTONESE,
  ENGLISH

OYSTER SAUCE IS AN INTEGRAL INGREDIENT IN MANY CHINESE DISHES – EVEN IN VEGETARIAN DISHES.

★ **IT WAS A VERY GOOD YEAR.** Hong Kong is proving itself the great survivor. Having weathered the stormy seas of economic meltdown and Severe Acute Respiratory Syndrome (SARS), Hong Kong's tourist industry has bounced back in a big way.

Some 21.8 million crowded into the former British colony in 2004, a 40% increase over 2003, the year Hong Kong's tourist industry collapsed under the weight of SARS. The surge spilled well into 2005, with an 11% growth during the first quarter, and that was before the opening of the city's newest attraction: Hong Kong Disneyland. While record numbers of foreign travellers have been pouring in, Hong Kong has also been flooded by tourists from mainland China, who accounted for slightly more than half of all tourists in 2004.

WHAT'S NEW?

Where do we start? The US$3.5 billion Hong Kong Disneyland, new for 2006, is just one of many developments that the tourist board is using to lure in more visitors. Also highly touted is the AsiaWorld-Expo, which will be the future site of concerts and conventions, as well as the newly christened Avenue of the Stars (Hong Kong's version of Hollywood's Walk of Fame) located on the Tsim Sha Tsui East Promenade. Leisure tourists may want to try the new 'Ngong Ping 360', a new Lantau Island tourist attraction that includes a 5.7km-long (3.5mi) cable car and a cultural village complete with a theatre, tea house and restaurants. Added to this are renovations at Victoria Peak and Stanley Waterfront, plus a world-class, multimedia sound-and-light show that ignites the Hong Kong waterfront on a nightly basis.

Always on the move, Hong Kong's next pet project is to develop itself as a port of call for cruise ships; plans are under way for the development of a new terminal dedicated to handling the expected influx of visitors by sea. And, getting in on the act, a flurry of hotel-building projects (including an ultraplush Four Seasons Hotel) are adding an additional 14,000 rooms to the city.

VISITORS STROLL INSIDE THE HONG KONG CONVENTION AND EXHIBITION CENTRE, GAZING OUT ONTO THE HONG KONG SKYLINE.

KEEPING IT REAL

While looking to the future, Hong Kong has forgotten neither its past nor its exceptional natural attractions. The territory is planning to turn the old Central Police Station, Victoria Prison and former Central Magistracy compound into a tourist attraction. Upgrades have been made at the Hong Kong Museum of Art. Meanwhile, the tourist board has teamed with local green teams to open up seven new hiking trails, as well as a Wetland Park in Tin Shui Wai. Bird-watchers will want to look out for the excellent and free *Hong Kong Bird Watching Map*, distributed at the airport and tourist offices. One of the most popular getaways is still the Giant Buddha at Po Lin Monastery on Lantau. For those who have already been, it's worth going back to see the newly installed 'Wisdom Path', a creative new attraction that features 38 inscribed planks that together form the 260-word Heart Sutra, a prayer articulating the doctrine of emptiness.

WHAT'S ON TAP

Making the most of these developments, the tourist board is rolling out 2006 as 'Discover Hong Kong Year'. The scheme will promote the new attractions by launching them in conjunction with trade shows, concerts and entertainment events. All this is creating a buzz in the air that some travellers may welcome. If, however, you're looking to get away from the crowds, you may want to try elsewhere.

DEFINING EXPERIENCE

○ Having just won a fistful of cash at the track, taking the Mass Transit Rail (MTR) to Nathan Rd where you slurp noodles and drink 'pearl tea' before blowing your winnings on a new wardrobe and the latest hi-tech gear.

FESTIVALS & EVENTS

○ Hong Kong Marathon; February; www.hkmarathon.com. This race draws nearly 30,000 runners.

○ Hong Kong Arts Festival; February–March. Hong Kong's most important cultural event is a month-long extravaganza of music, dance, film, drama and art events.

○ Hong Kong Rugby World Cup Sevens; Hong Kong Stadium; March–April. Probably the most anticipated event on the local social calendar, this three-day international rugby tournament has a real party atmosphere. »

HONG KONG.

> *This was my third visit to Hong Kong but the first time I had gone to the outlying islands, and all I can say is why didn't I go before? They are so different and so lovely (in a Hong Kong sort of way), quite Mediterranean if you ignore the occasional power station. We were bowled over by Cheung Chau, and we spent a second day on Lamma, which we loved even more.*
>
> - Ian Mackay, Australia

» ○ Winterfest; Central; late November–early January. Santa and his reindeer fly into Hong Kong for a series of concerts and events.

HOT TOPIC OF THE DAY

○ Young Hong Kongers are busily setting up forums and organisations to strengthen democracy in response to recent moves by Beijing to influence leadership control in Hong Kong.

HOT TIPS FOR TRAVELLERS

○ Hong Kong's official tourist website, www.discoverhongkong.com, has the latest details about events and tourist attractions. Personal Digital Assistant (PDA) users can download its leisure guide for free.

○ Visit the fishing village of Lei Yue Mun, where you can choose live seafood from the vendors and request that it be shipped to the restaurant of your choice, whereupon you tell the waiter how you want it prepared.

○ Take advantage of the newly launched Cultural Kaleidoscope, a scheme developed by the Hong Kong Tourism Board to get travellers more involved in local activities.

You can sail on a Chinese junk, join a feng shui tour of downtown, take a Chinese 'tea appreciation' class, or get some kung fu tips from martial arts instructors. All programmes are free. Check the aforementioned website for details.

WHAT'S HOT...

○ Bruce Lee. Despite being dead for more than 30 years, the kung fu master still holds a special place in Hong Kong's heart. A statue of the man was erected on the Avenue of the Stars in November 2005.

WHAT'S NOT...

○ Rickshaws. Tourist rickshaws were once found around the Star Ferry building in Central, though they seem to have disappeared of late.

○ Filth. Since the outbreak of SARS in 2003, Hong Kong has been obsessed with controlling the spread of disease. The result has been a much cleaner city.

DO MENTION

○ Your friend's latest outfit. Hong Kongers are very image conscious and like to be reminded that they are wearing the trendiest gear.

DON'T MENTION

○ The cramped living quarters. This is all too obvious.

RANDOM FACTS

○ Hong Kong's only Olympic gold medallist won his hardware as a windsurfer.

○ Hong Kong has more Rolls Royces per capita than any other city in the world.

○ Hong Kong is the world's busiest container port, handling 207 million tonnes of cargo annually.

○ Sixty percent of Hong Kong Island is designated national park.

MOST BIZARRE SIGHT

○ 'Wet Markets', where you can spot all manner of meat, organs and other unidentifiable parts of animal anatomy

THREE WORDS TO DESCRIBE THIS COUNTRY

○ Work, eat, shop

- Michael Kohn

THINGS TO TAKE!

Make sure you have a change of clothes respectable enough to get you into a few clubs. Dregs are often turned away at the door.

»

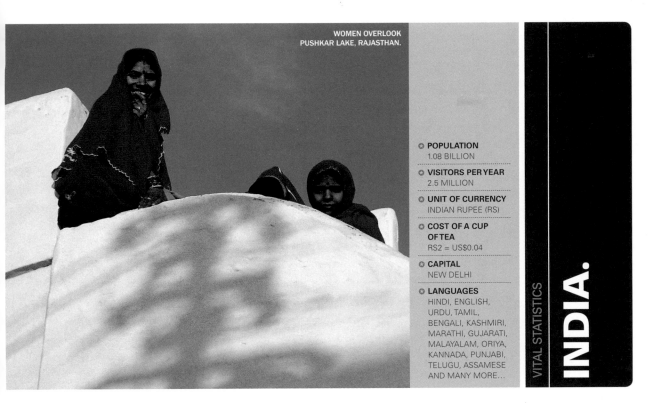

WOMEN OVERLOOK
PUSHKAR LAKE, RAJASTHAN.

VITAL STATISTICS

INDIA.

- **POPULATION**
  1.08 BILLION
- **VISITORS PER YEAR**
  2.5 MILLION
- **UNIT OF CURRENCY**
  INDIAN RUPEE (RS)
- **COST OF A CUP OF TEA**
  RS2 = US$0.04
- **CAPITAL**
  NEW DELHI
- **LANGUAGES**
  HINDI, ENGLISH, URDU, TAMIL, BENGALI, KASHMIRI, MARATHI, GUJARATI, MALAYALAM, ORIYA, KANNADA, PUNJABI, TELUGU, ASSAMESE AND MANY MORE…

⭐ **SIMPLY UNDERRATED.** India has long been something of a mystery to the travelling community. Among the travelati, everyone wants to have experienced India – and by 'experience', people mean 'endure'.

Indeed, the sages won't consider you a 'true traveller' unless you've passed out on the back of a camel, waited for days at a train station, had your passport and money stolen from underneath your trousers, and spent hours squatting in agony over a dubious hole in the ground.

Perhaps it's this vision of India that keeps it such a shockingly unvisited country. This may come as a surprise to the average Australian, British or Israeli backpacker, but India is far from overrun with travellers. With fewer than three million foreign tourists a year, India is dwarfed by such neighbours as Thailand, Indonesia and China. It's as though normal people are content to look at Taj Mahal postcards and watch tiger documentaries, leaving actually going there to intrepid adventurers who can brave the dangers and stoically endure the privation. And those who *do* visit often want nothing more than to perpetuate this image, for it makes them look that much cooler.

It's all bunk, of course. India is perhaps the greatest travel destination in the world. No doubt a lot of the stereotypes are true: it's steeped in tradition (not only is it impossible to swing a peacock without knocking over a temple, mosque or *gurdwara* – Sikh temple – but spirituality infuses ordinary Indians' daily lives like nowhere else on earth); it produces cheesy, poppy movies; the vast majority of people are desperately poor; and the food is absolutely terrific. But these days, you're nearly as likely to hook up with a film star in a nightclub as you are to get sick. Villagers may provide their email addresses or mobile phone numbers for you to keep in touch. And as for people cleaving firmly to traditional ideas about astronomy and numerology…well, OK; some things never change.

EMBRACE THE BEHEMOTH

The sleeping giant whose wakening has been predicted for decades is finally showing signs of stirring. Riotous and colourful as »

⭐ **HOT TOPIC OF THE DAY!**

Relations with the USA seem to be at an all-time peak. Everyone is talking about how the War on Terrorism is going to affect Indian–US relations…and relations with Pakistan.

HINDU PILGRIMS PREPARE TO WASH AWAY THEIR SINS IN THE SACRED GANGES ON DARBHANGA GHAT IN VARANASI.

INDIA.

» always, India is beginning to realise its true potential as a major 21st-century power. Religious tensions are at an all-time low, as symbolised by India's political trifecta: a Muslim president, a Sikh prime minister and a Christian head of the governing party. A liberalised economy, a government with renewed commitment to secularism, improved relations with Pakistan, a kick-ass cricket team and a new eminence on the world stage have combined to give Indians the feeling that they've finally *arrived*.

Everything is bursting at the seams, and Indians desperately want to share their new experiences with the rest of the world. Never before has the country been so accessible and so kind to the traveller. Rather than eroding Indian culture, globalisation has boosted the country's self-esteem, allowed its citizens to interact in exciting new ways, and blended with traditional elements to add new zest to an already spicy mix. The result is a nation that's fantastically rewarding to explore and all too easy to get lost in.

DEFINING EXPERIENCE
⊙ Enjoying tandoori chicken and a mango lassi on a budget hotel's rooftop overlooking sunset on the Taj Mahal while a Bollywood soundtrack competes with cows mooing, chickens clucking, rickshaw drivers arguing and a muezzin singing in the background.

FESTIVALS & EVENTS
⊙ Republic Day; January. If there's ever a good time to be in Delhi, this is it: jostle everyone else for views of the elephant processions and military sabre-rattling.

⊙ Holi; March. This Hindu festival is one of the world's most exuberant. When else will you get the chance to splatter your neighbour with paint or dyed water?

⊙ Rath Yatra; Puri; early July. Ever wondered where the word 'juggernaut' came from? Get a view of the gigantic temple car of Lord Jagannath making its annual journey in Puri and you'll never wonder again.

⊙ Ganesh Chaturthi; Mumbai (Bombay); August. He may not be one of the major Hindu deities, but the elephant-headed god of good luck, Ganesh, sure is popular – so popular, in fact, that even cynical Mumbaikers have dedicated an entire festival to him.

⊙ Diwali; October. Hinduism's answer to Christmas consists of five days of

> "
> *Indian time is affectionately known as 'rubber' time because it can be stretched. For example, according to official number one our bus would leave at 8.30am, but official number two said 8.15am. Our Lonely Planet said 8am, and the bus ended up leaving at 7.45am!*
> "

- Karan Kapur, United Arab Emirates

presents, parades, lamps and candies, as Hindus struggle to honour a host of gods and goddesses during this catch-all festival of lights.

- Eid-ul Fitr; October. This festival marks the end of Ramadan and the first sunlit meal for observant Muslims in 30 days.

- Camel Fair; Pushkar; November. If you wanted to swap your rucksack for a camel, here's the place: literally hundreds of thousands converge on hippy little Pushkar during this festival, creating a bizarre nomadic metropolis where every other living thing is likely to spit at you.

WHAT'S HOT...

- Nudity and public displays of affection – in the press. Ever since the conservative Bharatiya Janata Party (BJP) government got voted out in 2004, the Indian media have become racier and racier in their depictions of celebrity sex and other skin-toned themes. For the average Indian, who is deeply traditional when it comes to pressing the flesh, such behaviour is something to be gawked at (and possibly leered at in private).

WHAT'S NOT...

- Hrithik Roshan – he is *so* yesterday's star.

DO MENTION

- Anything to do with Indian cricket. Just pull up a familiar name (such as 'Sachin Tendulkar') and watch everyone in the room become your new best friend. You get extra points for being able to list teams the Indian side has recently defeated, and for mentioning India's long dominance of south Asian cricket. Starting a discussion about who's the hottest actor in Bollywood is never unfruitful either.

DON'T MENTION

- Politics or Pakistan. It's not that these are taboo topics – it's just that you want to be very, very mindful of your audience. Best to leave these subjects alone; there's so much more to talk about.

RANDOM FACTS

- Chess was invented in India, as was Buddhism. The former is much more popular in modern India than the latter.

- 'Bungalow', 'jungle' and 'cummerbund' are Hindi words.

- Unlike in Nepal, Indian cows are not afforded completely sacred status – in fact, India has begun selling cows to Pakistan for butchering.

MOST BIZARRE SIGHT

- Gleeful urbanites splashing each other with paint (the term 'wild abandon' comes to mind) during the festival of Holi

THINGS TO TAKE

- A passport brimming with the appropriate paperwork – once you're in the country, Indian bureaucracy will do its best to stymie you at every turn.

- A moneybelt or neck pouch – in fact, it's best to sew your belongings directly into your skin.

- Your iPod or other favourite diversion – those bus and train rides can be *looong*.

- A very, very flexible attitude towards life and everything about it. Trust us on this one.

THREE WORDS TO DESCRIBE THIS COUNTRY

- Thoroughly, insanely transcendent

- Vivek Wagle

HOT TIP FOR TRAVELLERS!

When travelling long distances by train, it's often worth the money to splurge on an air-conditioned, three-tier ticket. Most 'hard-core' travellers will scoff at your softness, but the air-conditioned carriages are roomier, less stuffy and less populated by men inclined towards sexual harassment.

JAPAN.

VITAL STATISTICS

- ⚬ **POPULATION**
  127 MILLION
- ⚬ **VISITORS PER YEAR**
  5 MILLION
- ⚬ **UNIT OF CURRENCY**
  YEN (¥)
- ⚬ **COST OF A CUP OF COFFEE**
  ¥350 TO ¥500 =
  US$3.25 TO US$4.65
- ⚬ **CAPITAL**
  TOKYO
- ⚬ **LANGUAGE**
  JAPANESE

TOKYO GOTHS GATHER AROUND HARAJUKU STATION EVERY SUNDAY TO PRIMP FOR TOURISTS, TEEN FASHION MAGAZINE PHOTOGRAPHERS, AND EACH OTHER.

⭐ **NAME THIS COUNTRY... When you think of Japan, do you think of a place that's too expensive to visit, too remote to get to and too difficult to get around?**

There must be a few of you, because Japan attracts just five million tourists per year, placing it in 33rd position in the 'World Tourism League' behind much smaller nations, such as the Ukraine, and the top attraction, France (with 76 million visitors annually).

But actually, it's shaping up to be a good time to visit Japan. Now that the Japanese economy is into its second decade of decline, the government is aching to redress the balance after years of neglecting tourism in favour of pumped-up banking and manufacturing sectors. While the rest of the world has been in the throes of a long-standing love affair with tourism, Japan now wants a piece of the action. Better late than never.

WISING UP TO THE WORLD

Current prime minister Koizumi is the first to bother with tourism, and he's pledged to get 10 million visitors per year into Japan by 2010. This is good news for travellers, because it means that a few crucial areas

will be rethought and redeveloped in the near future, such as the lack of foreign-language signage and information kiosks at airports and key tourist attractions. Japan also suffers from a surfeit of 1st-class hotels (two-thirds of Japan's visitors are on business trips), and there's a drive to increase the number of budget and midrange options. Tourist boards will be standardised, a relief for those travellers who find that the current system, split between multiple government agencies, means that information is often contradictory and out of date from region to region.

Japan is also starting to realise the marketability of its enduring influence on Western popular culture; there may come a day sooner than you think when Astroboy, Godzilla and *manga* (comic) museums take pride of place in tourism brochures alongside geisha girls, sake and Mt Fuji. Japan's rich tradition of incredibly diverse and colourful regional festivals is also being promoted, rather than an exclusive

focus on the hoary old national tradition
of cherry-blossom viewing. And the tourist
board is starting to push its attractions that
lie beyond the main island of Honshu – like
Okinawa, with a culture developed often
independently of mainstream Japanese life,
and Hokkaido, home of ice festivals, the Ainu
people and yet more untapped tradition.

THE SONG REMAINS THE SAME

But for those who already know and
love Japan, it's the same as it ever was;
the country, as always, is a glorious
contradiction, a sprawling, untameable beast
that consistently wrong-foots the unwary.
Sure, there's all that wonderful tradition –
samurai, geishas, the whole bit – but layered
over the top is a furious modernism, where
trends appear and disappear in months,
weeks – sometimes days. It's easy to forget
that Japan has had its borders opened to
the rest of the world for fewer than 150
years; it's had a lot of catching up to do,
and (in Tokyo, especially) the place seems
on permanent fast forward. Elsewhere, you
might stare in amazement at replica Statues
of Liberty that perch atop many business
hotels, or contemplate the surrealism of
the Seagaia Ocean Dome, a 140m enclosed

'beach', with its own ocean, under a
permanently blue, artificial sky.

Pack an open mind when you visit Japan.
Now, more than ever before, it's highly
advisable – for all sorts of reasons.

DEFINING EXPERIENCE

✿ Posing for a photo with a schoolgirl
who is dressed as Little Bo Peep while
listening to Japanese noise-punk band The
Boredoms on your iPod as a group of little
old ladies dressed in traditional kimono
race past you to catch the bullet train

FESTIVALS & EVENTS

✿ Wakakusa Yamayaki; Nara; January. The
ritual burning of the grass on Wakakusa
Hill, during which the whole 342m (1122ft)
hill is set ablaze.

✿ Hanami (Cherry-Blossom Viewing);
February–April. A beloved institution,
as Japanese of all persuasions gather to
celebrate the blooming of the country's
famous cherry blossoms.

✿ Hounen Matsuri; Komaki; March.

✿ Kanamara Matsuri; Kawasaki; late March
or early April. During this celebration
and Hounen Matsuri (above), two among

»

JAPAN.

"

Japan is known for its natural hot springs. It was on a cold winter's day that I decided to kick back and warm up in an outdoor hot spring bath. The difference in water and air temperature was lulling, and I soon drifted off to sleep. I woke when I felt scratching on the back of my head. Snow had started falling and several monkeys, apparently having the same idea as me, had hopped into my hot spring. And one of them was carefully looking for fleas, on me!

"

- Belinda Gribble, Australia

» Japan's many fertility festivals, giant wooden penises are paraded through streets to the local shrine.

○ Golden Week; April–May. This is the agglomeration of Green Day, Constitution Day and Children's Day.

○ O Bon (Festival of the Dead); July & mid-August. Lanterns are floated on rivers, lakes or the sea to signify the return of the dead to this world, supposedly to visit their relatives.

○ Tanabata Matsuri (Star Festival); July. This is a romantic festival based on an old legend concerning two lovers who lived in the Milky Way and turned into stars.

DO MENTION
○ The World Expo of 2005, a recent source of Japanese pride, seen by the nation as the perfect showcase for the country's new-found attitude towards its natural environment and towards the world outside of Japan.

DON'T MENTION
○ Japan's poor showing in the 2002 World Cup, which it cohosted with South Korea – it's still a sore spot.

RANDOM FACTS
○ The Japanese associate the number four with death, and therefore refrain from buying products in packs of four. You might occasionally find the number four missing from hotel room numbers.

○ In feudal Japan, women blackened their teeth to beautify themselves.

○ German prisoners of war during WWII are credited with introducing sausages to the Japanese palate.

○ Japan is the world's biggest manufacturer of zippers, with around a quarter of global production.

○ Japanese superstition teaches that if you whistle at night you'll be attacked by a snake.

MOST BIZARRE SIGHT
○ The Meguro Parasitological Museum in Tokyo, the world's only museum devoted to human and animal parasites.

THINGS TO TAKE
○ Cash – despite its technological prowess, Japan still hasn't fully embraced 'plastic money'.

○ A strong stomach: you'll need it for visiting the Meguro Parasitological Museum (see 'Most Bizarre Sight'), and in case you are offered one of Japan's more unusual regional dishes: raw whale sperm.

HOT TIPS FOR TRAVELLERS
○ Invest in a Japan Rail Pass, for slashed discounts on Japan's notoriously expensive rail system.

○ Check out Quirky Japan (www.quirkyjapan.or.tv) if you're 'tired of shrines and temples, reconstructed ferro-concrete castles and tea ceremonies'. As the site says, 'Japan, behind the conservative grey suits and formal bows, is a country quirkier than you can ever imagine'.

○ Visit the Japan National Tourist Organization website (www.jnto.go.jp) if you can't get enough of shrines and temples, reconstructed ferro-concrete castles and tea ceremonies.

THREE WORDS TO DESCRIBE THIS COUNTRY
○ Modern yet traditional

- Simon Sellars

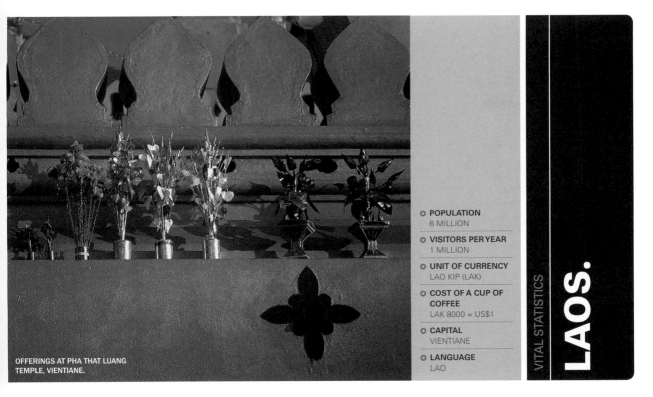

OFFERINGS AT PHA THAT LUANG
TEMPLE, VIENTIANE.

LAOS.

VITAL STATISTICS

- **POPULATION**
  6 MILLION
- **VISITORS PER YEAR**
  1 MILLION
- **UNIT OF CURRENCY**
  LAO KIP (LAK)
- **COST OF A CUP OF COFFEE**
  LAK 8000 = US$1
- **CAPITAL**
  VIENTIANE
- **LANGUAGE**
  LAO

SOUTHEAST ASIA'S 'OTHER LAST FRONTIER'. Laos has long held a special place in the hearts of travellers who find Thailand too touristy, Cambodia too risky and Myanmar too political.

The people are said to be the friendliest on earth – though this is also claimed, with some credibility, about the Burmese – and a long-running insurgency, coupled with a mildly paranoid communist government, has preserved large parts of the country in pristine condition. Don't be surprised if you hear people describing Laos as 'like Thailand in the 1960s'.

The big problem with travel in Laos has always been the roads – they're poorly maintained and frequently off limits due to rebel attacks. For years, the only way to get to large areas of Laos was by air on the cranky aircraft of the national carrier, Lao Airlines. You'll still have to gamble on Lao Airlines to reach many towns in the far north of the country, where poor weather conditions, mountains and a lack of fly-by-wire technology all add spice to the flying experience.

Luckily for nervous fliers, road travel is becoming an increasingly viable option with the decline of the Hmong insurgency. New areas are opening up all the time – the days when backpackers visited Vientiane, Vang Vieng, Luang Prabang and then went home are thankfully a thing of the past. Following a government change of heart in 2004, tourist visas should now be available on arrival at all border crossings from China, Cambodia, Vietnam and Thailand.

JUNGLE TEMPLES, TRIBAL TOTEMS AND INNER-TUBE FLOATING

Although visiting Laos is getting easier with each passing year, the attractions are the same as they've always been. The countryside is dotted with ancient temples and *wat* (monasteries), and the vast unspoiled forests offer some fantastic opportunities for ecotourism – including caving and kayaking through the Khammuan Limestone area and trekking to hill-tribe villages in the remote north of the country.

»

RECENT FAD!

Nightlife. Despite the best efforts of the communist government to stop the 'moral corruption' of Lao youth, bars and clubs are pushing back the official 11.30pm curfew – you can now drink until 1am at many nightclubs in Vientiane.

CHILDREN TAKE A SUNSET SWIM IN THE SONG RIVER, VANG VIENG.

LAOS.

» Don't come to Laos expecting a 24-hour, Thai-style party. Laos is a quiet backwater of a place and there's little to do in the evenings apart from sip Beerlao on the hotel balcony and pass the time of day with fellow travellers – of course, many people think this is a good thing! Even the main traveller centre of Vang Vieng is a sleepy, laid-back place, where visitors are more likely to drift down the river on inner tubes than hold full-moon parties.

It's also worth remembering that Laos is still suffering the after-effects of the Vietnam War. America bombarded the jungle with thousands of tons of munitions in a deluded attempt to nip the 'domino effect' in the bud and many areas of central Laos are still off limits due to unexploded bombs.

DEFINING EXPERIENCE
○ Watching dragon-boat races on the Mekong River, munching on tilapia grilled on lemon-grass skewers and sipping Beerlao, then finishing off lunch with a serving of inner peace at a village *wat*.

FESTIVALS & EVENTS
○ New Year (Bun Pi Mai); April. Along with other Buddhists in the region, the Lao celebrate by throwing huge quantities of water about the place. If you're around, head to Luang Prabang for elephant processions and costume dramas.

○ Bun Bang Fai (Rocket Festival); May. Pyros can join in the fun of this festival. Villagers engage in wild dancing, theatrical performances and the joyous launching of bamboo rockets into the sky to help initiate the annual rains.

○ Dragon-boat races; Mekong River near Vientiane; October. As part of the Bun Auk Pansa water festival, locals float thousands of offerings of flavours, candles and incense on the river at dusk.

DO MENTION
○ Lao rat. In June 2005, scientists discovered a previously unknown species of rodent for sale at a rural food market in central Laos. Closely related to the porcupine, this chubby rodent is the first new mammal family to be discovered anywhere in the last 30 years!

DON'T MENTION
○ Thai TV. As part of a campaign to reduce the influence of Thai culture on the

"

In far-flung northeast Laos the menu at one tiny restaurant offered field rat, bamboo mole, antlers (fresh or dried), bee larvae, squirrel and flying fox. When asked what rat tasted like our host replied 'like flying fox, very tasty'. 'What about squirrel?' I said. He made choking motions and told me, 'Not good, it's just for falang' (foreigners).

"

- Liz Pick, Australia

LAOS.

People's Democratic Republic, the Lao government banned Thai television in 2004. Owners of bars and restaurants that show Thai TV programmes can now be fined – good for the national identity, bad for viewers, who now have to make do with two channels of government propaganda.

HOT TOPIC OF THE DAY

- Hmong refugees. The ethnic Hmong people of northern Laos are still widely persecuted for siding with the USA before the 1975 revolution and Laos faces an ongoing antigovernment insurgency by Hmong guerrillas. Thousands of Hmong have fled across the border to Thailand since the communist takeover, but plans are now afoot to return many of the refugees to Laos. Before you write this off as someone else's problem, four Americans were arrested in 2005 for 'liaising' with Hmong rebels.

RANDOM FACTS

- The Lao kip is one of the most devalued currencies in the world – in 1979, there were 35 kip to the US dollar; today the kip is worth just 1/80 of a US cent.

Ninety million cluster bombs were secretly dropped on Laos by the American air force during the Vietnam War – more than the total number of bombs dropped on Japan and Germany in WWII.

THINGS TO TAKE

- Torch (flashlight), unless you fancy fumbling around for a match and candle every time the power fails.
- Mosquito repellent; they buzz and they bite all over the People's Democratic Republic.
- Thongs (flip-flops), or buy them locally for pennies. The Lao remove their shoes before entering houses and temples; don't get left behind by wearing lace-ups.

HOT TIPS FOR TRAVELLERS

- The former capital, Luang Prabang, is much more atmospheric than the current capital, Vientiane; even if you only have a short time in Laos, try to visit both.
- Dragon-boat races are held to celebrate religious festivals at many towns along the Mekong River, which marks the border between Laos and Thailand. Keep your ear to the ground as you travel around – there may be a boat race just a short *sǎam-lâaw* (pedicab) ride away.
- Head to riverside parks and boat jetties across Laos for a tasty lunch of grilled pork and river fish on lemon-grass skewers, served with pounded papaya salad and sticky rice.

THREE WORDS TO DESCRIBE THIS COUNTRY

- Beautiful Buddhist backwater

- Joe Bindloss

NEPAL.

VITAL STATISTICS

- **POPULATION**
  27.6 MILLION
- **VISITORS PER YEAR**
  379,000
- **UNIT OF CURRENCY**
  NEPALI RUPEE (RS)
- **COST OF A CUP
  OF COFFEE**
  RS 30 = US$0.40
- **CAPITAL**
  KATHMANDU
- **LANGUAGE**
  NEPALI
- **LITERACY**
  45%
- **WORKFORCE
  EMPLOYED IN
  AGRICULTURE**
  80%

ANNAPURNA 1 (8091M) GLIMPSED THROUGH
BUDDHIST PRAYER FLAGS, GHOREPANI.

TOURISM IN REVERSE. Soaring mountains, raging rivers, fascinating cultural diversity, a wealth of historical monuments, bargain basement travel costs and a staggering range of outdoor activities, not to mention some of the friendliest people on earth...

Once upon a time, these badges of distinction formed the basis for Asia's most abundant destination for budget travellers. This storybook land, however, seems not to be able to wake up from a nightmare of troubles that have plagued the country for nearly a decade.

The Maoist insurgency that uprooted Nepal's tranquil rural areas in the mid-1990s still burns deeply across the country. Fighting is sporadic, yet amazingly no foreigners have died in a conflict that has cost more than 12,000 Nepali lives. This fact has kept Nepal's tourist industry up and running, albeit at half speed.

ON THE BANDH WAGON
Bandh (general strikes) are the greatest inconvenience for travellers, as these can grind transport to a halt for days at a time. Tourists caught unawares have been left stranded in remote villages, so it's best to keep tabs on the situation. In the capital, keep a safe distance from political marches and student gatherings, as these sometimes dissolve into street battles between stone-throwing students and tear gas–firing police. Trekking across rebel-held areas poses few problems, save for the inconvenience of having to give a 'donation' for the privilege, usually around Rs 1000, about US$14. The belief in safe travel was somewhat shaken in April 2005 after two Russian trekkers were injured when a bomb exploded near their taxi in eastern Nepal. Such stories, along with travel warnings posted by the US Department of State and other international bodies, have sent tourist numbers sliding; tourism was down by 25% over the first half of 2005.

SKIP THE CROWDS
Nepal's tourist sector is unlikely to improve in 2006. Strongly worded travel warnings

GIGGLING VILLAGE GIRLS OF GHEMI PICNIC
ON THE ROCKS IN UPPER MUSTANG.

make it difficult to fully condone travel in the country, but if you're up for a little adventure, travelling in rural Nepal is actually quite safe and sane. You just need to bear in mind the local rules, namely obeying Maoists whenever you should meet them. (Thoughtfully, advance warnings are always given before buses are torched.) Travellers who do visit Nepal are rewarded with their pick of hotel rooms, great-value tours, uncrowded hiking routes and the odd Maoist trekking permit, a souvenir in itself.

DEFINING EXPERIENCE

- Paying a Maoist a 'donation' to trek into the Annapurna Range, then setting up camp, grilling up a yak steak and dal dinner, and having visions of a yeti clambering over the peaks before realising it's only the AMS (acute mountain sickness) that's playing tricks with your mind

RECENT FAD

- Trekkers have begun collecting Maoist travel permits. Stamped with images of Marx, Engels, Lenin and Chairman Mao himself, they make a nice addition to the scrapbook.

- Recent expeditions have been mounted to clean up the trash left on Mt Everest. Some 50 tonnes of refuse has been dumped there since 1950.

FESTIVALS & EVENTS

- Basant Panchami; February. If you fancy seeing a Nepali wedding, the best time to catch one is on this auspicious day. Festivals held throughout the country hold particular significance for students.

- Holi; March. This is not the sort of day you want to go out in your Sunday finest. During the festivities, coloured water is sprayed on everything that moves. Foreign tourists are not immune to the havoc and tend to be the most popular targets. Watch out!

- Buddha Jayanti; Lumbini; April. Celebrate the Buddha's birthday in his home town. This festival attracts pilgrims from across Nepal.

- Dasain; September–October. The atmosphere is somewhat subdued at Nepal's biggest festival as it's a family-oriented holiday. You may see gambling, colourful processions and the odd sacrificial goat.

NEPAL.

> *While white-water rafting in the Trisuli River in Nepal, a great crashing sound came from the cliffs above the river bank and a body fell down the cliff into the river. On closer inspection we found it was a dead cow pushed in by the locals. The guide put it very simply – 'holy cow, holy river'.*

- Don Byron, Australia

» HOT TOPICS OF THE DAY

- The Maoist insurgency, the struggling economy and the latest political crisis in Kathmandu are the talk of the day. And how about democracy? Nepal's King Gyanendra dismissed the government in February 2005 and now leads through absolute rule.

- No news is bad news. King Gyanendra's decision to end press freedom has led to the arrest of dozens of journalists. When reading local newspapers, bear in mind that censorship is now the law of the land.

RANDOM FACTS

- Eight of the 10 highest summits in the world are located in Nepal.
- Nepal is the world's only Hindu kingdom.
- In 40% of Nepali marriages, the bride is under 14 years old.
- More than 1200 climbers have reached the summit of Mt Everest. More than 180 climbers have died attempting it.
- The Nepali flag is the only national flag not rectangular in shape.
- Some 92 different languages are spoken in Nepal.

MOST BIZARRE SIGHTS

- The sea of red flags, each emblazoned with the communist hammer and sickle, proudly waved at Kathmandu political rallies – who says communism is dead?
- Cow dung when it's administered for medicinal purposes

THINGS TO TAKE

- A lightly loaded backpack – you'll need all the room you can spare after a Kathmandu shopping spree
- Diamox, to fend off the dull throb of AMS

HOT TIPS FOR TRAVELLERS

- In a bid to lure climbers back to Nepal, the tourism board has recently slashed the price of climbing permits; up to 50% for some mountains. For US$5000, a team of seven can make an assault on 11,090m (36,385ft) Kanchenjunga, the third-highest mountain in the world.
- Keep up with the latest student protests and *bandh* strikes by checking the online newspaper www.kantipuronline.com.
- The website www.nepal.com is loaded with links on Nepali news and information.

THREE WORDS TO DESCRIBE THIS COUNTRY

- Mountains, monasteries, Mao

- Michael Kohn

PORTRAIT OF A BEARDED MAN IN TRADITIONAL ROBES AND FUR HAT IN INSADONG-GIL, SEOUL.

SOUTH KOREA.

- **POPULATION**
  48 MILLION
- **VISITORS PER YEAR**
  5.8 MILLION
- **UNIT OF CURRENCY**
  WON (W)
- **COST OF A CUP OF COFFEE**
  W4000 = US$3.80
- **CAPITAL**
  SEOUL
- **LANGUAGE**
  KOREAN

★ A LAND OF MORNING CALM. Hypermodern yet soothingly green, the Republic of Korea is the quirkier side of northeast Asia. It's a chameleon-like country that has been transformed from rural to urban in four decades.

Now it's a technocratic culture hooked on the adrenaline of the new, and for the traveller this means a neon-infused culture with a firm grip on its ancient past.

The former Joseon dynasty capital, Seoul, has reinvented itself as a kid with too much energy. Construction sites reign supreme and the urban rush hour never ceases to amaze. Seoul has cheap and cheerful hot-fried-dough stands; *galbi* (beef-rib) palaces; and underground shopping centres. Add affordable taxis and a world-class subway and you've got a travel-friendly destination. A destination where nearly everything edible claims to be an aphrodisiac ('good for stamina') has to be good!

Seoul's entertainment precinct, Myeong-dong, dazzles with vitality, and university districts such as artsy Hongdae (Hongik University) redefine cool every hour with a passing parade of cutting edge–clad students. But South Korea is much more than dizzy high-rises, salary men and shop-till-you-drop malls. It's a country of mountains; a hiking haven with some of Asia's finest Buddhist temples. Most Koreans are outdoor junkies who love trading city sprawls for a dose of fresh air. Head for the hills at Songnisan National Park (which means 'Remote from the Mundane World Mountain'); explore Dadohae Haesang National Park, a marine archipelago of 1700 islands; or simply Zen-out at Seongnamsa, a stunning temple.

South Korea has a buoyant expat scene and its locals are a welcoming bunch, especially when there's a string of *soju* (vodkalike spirit) shots involved. Let the singing begin!

AN EMERGING DESTINATION

In 2003, 72% of international visitor arrivals were from the Asia-Pacific region. Increasingly, Taiwanese, Chinese »

MOST BIZARRE SIGHT! ★

The neighbourhood *bang* (room), also known as 'homes away from home'. These places are dedicated to videos, board games and computer games, and are usually filled with teenage boys. They're kitsch but cute.

COLOURFUL PAPER LANTERNS
HANG OUTSIDE A TEMPLE.

» and Japanese tourists are exploring this previously overlooked country. Despite high household debt, domestic-tourist numbers are also on the rise, aided by the formalisation of a five-day working week and the new bullet train, the Korea Train Express (KTX).

Often eclipsed by dysfunctional North Korea and its powerful siblings – China to the west and Japan to the east – South Korea is set to step out of the shadows in 2006. If South Korea is one thing, it's enthusiastic. And that's infectious.

FESTIVALS & EVENTS

◎ Lunar New Year; January. Every Korean will get into party mode during this three-day public holiday.

◎ Cherry Blossom Festival; Jinhae, Gyeongsangnam-do province; April. OK, South Korea doesn't like comparisons to Japan, but it knows a good blossom tree when it sees one.

◎ Buddha's Birthday; April. Lantern parades are the order of the day to say 'happy birthday' to the big guy. Crowds will weave in a glowing procession from Tapgol Park to Jogyesa, Seoul, on the weekend prior to the holiday.

◎ Mud Festival; Daecheon Beach; mid-July. Try your luck in the mud-wrestling contest.

◎ Cuttlefish Festival; Gangneung; August. Join in a catch-a-cuttlefish-by-hand competition at this more off-beat festival.

◎ Chuseok (Korean Thanksgiving); October 200. Perhaps not the best time to visit with 75% of Koreans heading home in droves during this holiday period.

MOUNTAIN HIGH

Koreans have long believed that the peaks and slopes of the peninsula's mountains are inhabited by *sansin* (mountain spirits). The mountains are a source of worship and prayer and are considered guardians of the nation. And while the industrial era has given birth to mountains of a new kind – monolithic buildings and downtown business districts – the mysticism of the mountains remains etched in the hearts and minds of every Korean.

SOUTH KOREA.

> "
> We went to a suburban bathhouse in Seoul. The sort of place tourists do not visit often. Different women guided us from place to place and showed us what to do. We hopped on these tables to have a full body scrub, very relaxing – until we hear laughing. We open our eyes to a large group of women gathered around us staring and pointing to one of our girls. I suppose they had never seen someone with red hair naked. It was one of the funniest and most relaxing experiences I have had on holidays.
> "
>
> - Jodie Egan, Australia

WHAT'S HOT...

- Dog-friendly restaurants
- Snow White complexions
- Anything designer: Louis Vuitton, Ferragamo, Dior
- Korean protest culture
- Learning English
- Digital cameras
- Spicy *kimchi* (pickled cabbage)
- Overseas travel

WHAT'S NOT...

- Shark and octopus restaurant aquariums
- North Korea's 'nukes' (nuclear weapons)
- The decline of small, family-run businesses
- The US push for South Korea to drop its screen quota (which guarantees all Korean cinemas screen local films for 106 days of the year)
- Hello Kitty
- Bear products used in traditional medicine
- Rounds of golf costing US$200

DO MENTION

- How much you love spicy Korean food

DON'T MENTION

- Comparisons to Japan – the South Koreans are over it! Reminding Koreans that their country was once a Japanese colony (it was dominated by the oceanic power from 1910 to 1945) or talking up the Americanisation of South Korea, won't go down well either.

HOT TOPIC OF THE DAY

- The unification of the Korean peninsula. In order to make it in the 21st century, the divided societies of capitalist South Korea and communist North Korea need to be reconciled.

RANDOM FACTS

- Out of a population of 48 million people, more than 36 million people carry mobile phones.
- The cult TV programme *M*A*S*H* made a black comedy out of the Korean War.
- Confucian hierarchy emphasises 'respect for your elders'.
- South Korea is the 11th-largest trading nation in the world.
- In rural Namhae County, a small hamlet known as 'German Village' is an attempt by local authorities to reverse the population decline. Cheap land and housing subsidies have been offered to any Korean who has lived in Germany for the last two decades. The result? An uncanny re-creation of German life where you would least expect it.

HOT TIPS FOR TRAVELLERS

- The time to head to South Korea is autumn (September to November) when the mountains are at their sunny best. Cherry blossoms and mild weather will greet visitors in spring (April to May).
- The Korean National Tourism Organization's comprehensive website (www.knto.or.kr) is worth checking out for all things South Korean.

THREE WORDS TO DESCRIBE THIS COUNTRY

- Orthodox, original, enigma

- Sarah Wintle

RECENT FAD! ⊗

Got a personal mini–home page? Nearly every techno-literate South Korean has one. A 'mini-hompy' (an online version of a house where personal photos and diaries are exhibited for the mass web audience) is so 'right now'.

»

FOR INDUSTRIOUS SRI LANKAN LOCALS, A BRAND NEW DAY HAS DAWNED...PRE-DAWN.

SRI LANKA.

VITAL STATISTICS

- **POPULATION**
  20 MILLION
- **VISITORS PER YEAR**
  560,000
- **UNIT OF CURRENCY**
  SRI LANKAN RUPEE
  (RS)
- **COST OF A CUP OF COFFEE**
  RS 40 TO RS 80 =
  US$0.40 TO US$0.80
- **CAPITAL**
  COLOMBO (SRI
  JAYAWARDENEPURA-
  KOTTE)
- **LANGUAGES**
  SINHALESE, TAMIL,
  ENGLISH

★ A SERENDIPITOUS DISCOVERY. The word serendipity, meaning a happy, unexpected surprise, comes from an old name for the tropical island of Sri Lanka – Serendip.

Despite its manifold cultural treasures, divine beaches and magnificent natural heritage, Sri Lanka hasn't had anywhere near the growth in tourist numbers that Thailand or Malaysia have seen. The tsunami of 26 December 2004 hit just when travellers were starting to return after more than 20 years of civil war between the majority Buddhist Sinhalese and the mainly Hindu Tamils of the north and east.

The long, bloody civil war has been largely in abeyance since 2001, though you'd be a brave person to predict a final peace settlement anytime soon. The conflict turns partly on a question of pride – whether the Sinhalese are the main culture or the Tamils have equal status with the Sinhalese. Wars involving pride, ethnic mythologies, visions of God-given superiority and a long list of grievances are not easily solved. The 2004 tsunami struck Sri Lanka hard, and its tourism industry harder than many sectors.

The beach resorts of the south and east are already recovering, though it will take longer to erase the memory.

Even with the current troubles, Sri Lanka is still a ridiculously beautiful place. Colombo may not be the Paris of the East but as Asian capitals go it's small, reasonably easy to get around and still has some gracious parks and colonial buildings. Technically the capital is at Sri Jayawardenepura-Kotte on Colombo's outskirts. The great Buddhist ruined cities and monuments of the northern plains such as Anuradhapura, Polonnaruwa and Sigiriya fully deserve their World Heritage listings – yet aren't as well known as Ayutthaya or Angkor Wat. The huge network of national parks includes some of the best in Asia, with great tracts of jungle and rainforest protecting elephants, sloth bears, leopards and sambar deer. The Buddhist majority (some 70% of the population, the rest being divided among Hindus, Christians and

»

Muslims) hold the protection of wildlife and nature as a sacred duty.

TOURISM 1970S STYLE

One of the many results of the civil war has been that a lot of Sri Lanka's tourism infrastructure has been stuck in a kind of time warp. The industry is still fixed on package tourism to the point that there have been sporadic calls for extra taxes on travellers who dare to book their holidays individually over the Internet. The coastal resorts and the tea-growing hill districts have many ageing 1970s-era package-tour hotels in need of renovation, and some restaurants still think that grilled fish with limp chips all smothered in tomato sauce is the Western traveller's idea of top nosh. Some fantastic new luxury resorts and boutique hotels have opened since 2000, but the budget and midrange end of the market would benefit from new businesses, owners »

MOST BIZARRE SIGHT!

The firewalkers and cheek-piercing penitents at Tamil religious festivals – don't try this at home

BUNGALOW LIFE

While the beach resorts are being rebuilt, it's a good time to explore the splendours of the Hill Country, where Scottish plantation owners (the 'wild men of the hills' as one colonial governor called them) laid out verdant gardens of tea bushes in the late 19th century. The houses, estates, clubs and golf courses they left behind are somehow even more British than Britain, a kind of folk memory of life back home. Hill towns such as Nuwara Eliya have splendidly stuffy old clubs such as the Hill Club, where guests must still wear jackets to dinner, and hotels and guesthouses with names like the Grosvenor, the Windsor, St Andrew's and the Rising Lion. Expect lots of heavy wooden furniture, hunting trophies in the billiards room, bed nets, doilies, delicious cups of hill-country tea and club sandwiches, with the peculiar thrill of the occasional leopard sighting and burst of Indian *filmi* music from the radio. The hill towns of the tea-growing areas are linked by a wonderful old train line, which putters between Kandy and Badulla, through Ella, Haputale and Nanu Oya, chuffing past tea gardens, waterfalls, dramatic escarpments overlooking the southern plains and the pyramid-shaped bulk of holy Sri Pada (Adam's Peak).

SRI LANKA.

> *We sat down to eat at a roadside restaurant in Sri Lanka. A cat was obviously interested but also anxious about something in the bushes. A waiter inspected and found two cobras, one with its mouth firmly clamped around the other, their bodies twisting as they fought. A guy wearing only a loin cloth appeared with a stick and thrashed the living daylights out of the snakes, picked up the creatures with his stick and carried them off. When we went back to our table, the cat was delicately eating off our plates.*

- Beverly Jones, Britain

RECENT FAD!

Baila music, a kind of Sri Lankan samba-calypso dance music introduced by African soldiers serving the Portuguese, is undergoing a revival.

» and ideas. There are enough good new B&Bs, beach bungalows and restaurants to satisfy travellers watching their rupees, but you have to be a bit choosy.

DEFINING EXPERIENCE
- Pedalling through the jungle-clad ruins of Anuradhapura's mighty temples, shrines and great domed dagobas (stupas; some 60m high), then retiring to the bungalow for an evening arrack (palm-sugar rum) and Ayurvedic ginger beer and watching the monkeys cavort in the trees

FESTIVALS & EVENTS
- Duruthu Perahera; Kelaniya Raja Maha Viharaya (Kelaniya Royal Great Temple), just outside Colombo; January full moon. A showcase for the rich Buddhist culture.
- Esala Perahera; Kandy; July or August full moon. A 10-day Buddhist pageant held in the Buddhist religious capital, with parades of caparisoned elephants, dancers, drummers and torch bearers.
- Deepavali (Hindu festival of lights); November. Tamil families light clay lamps and young scoundrels let off firecrackers.
- Any international one-day cricket match.

Sri Lankans love this peculiar British game with immense passion. All-rounder Sanath Jayasuriya and master spin bowler Muttiah Muralitharan are national heroes across all communities.

HOT TOPIC OF THE DAY
- Is the ceasefire between the Tamil Tigers and the government permanent or just a pause between hostilities?

DO MENTION
- The good traditional Sri Lankan cuisine. A more subtle variation on Indian cooking, it takes an age to prepare (up to two hours just for breakfast) but at its best it is superb.

DON'T MENTION
- The rights or wrongs of the Tamil Tiger insurgency. Locals often feel that outsiders simply can't understand.

RANDOM FACTS
- President Chandrika Kumaratunga is the daughter of not one but two former prime ministers.
- Sri Lanka has the oldest nature reserves in the world – the Buddhists set aside areas such as Mihintale for preservation as long as 2500 years ago.

THINGS TO TAKE
- Your own coffee – the local stuff is usually not very good
- A good raincoat – tropical downpours are frequent and drenching
- A torch (flashlight) – power cuts are not uncommon and the tropical night can be black indeed

HOT TIPS FOR TRAVELLERS
- For festival dates and more, check out the excellent national tourism site at www.srilankatourism.org.
- Sri Lanka is a major clothing exporter and there are some terrific bargains to be found in the surplus stores in Colombo – you can pick up a new season's style months before it reaches the high-street boutiques back home.

THREE WORDS TO DESCRIBE THIS COUNTRY
- Verdant, ancient, vexatious

- Richard Plunkett

A YOUNG MAN RUGS UP ON THE YARLUNG TSANGPO RIVER.

VITAL STATISTICS

TIBET.

- **POPULATION**
  2.7 MILLION
- **VISITORS PER YEAR**
  856,000 (700,000 ARE CHINESE)
- **UNIT OF CURRENCY**
  CHINESE YUAN (Y)
- **COST OF A BOTTLE OF LHASA BEER**
  Y4 TO Y8 = US$0.50 TO US$1
- **CAPITAL**
  LHASA
- **LANGUAGE**
  TIBETAN

★ BUSINESS IS BOOMING. Tourism in Tibet remains firmly in China's grip. When permit policies are relaxed and flight connections become reliable, tourists will flood into the country.

The opposite occurs upon the occasional tightening of regulations. The past few years, however, have seen a steady loosening of control and authorities promise that plans are afoot to do away with the permit system altogether (but don't hold your breath!).

Does China want tourists in Tibet? The answer is yes. Tourism helps defray the costs of China's costly presence on the plateau by subsidising some of its infrastructure projects. China has reopened and restored many monasteries damaged during the Cultural Revolution as it knows these are the main attractions to Tibet.

Do Tibetans want tourists? Absolutely, yes. While Burmese opposition leader Aung San Suu Kyi decries tourism for funding Burma's military junta, the Dalai Lama believes that when tourists visit Tibet they increase awareness of the Tibetan plight, as well as giving them the opportunity to learn something of its unique culture and history.

But there is a double edge to this sword. The upshot of all those tourists has been an influx of Chinese migrants eager to cash in on the tourist trade. Lured by promises of jobs and subsidies, these newcomers have taken much needed work out of the hands of native Tibetans. Chinese entrepreneurs have usurped local shop owners, hoteliers and tour operators. And in 2004 some 100 Chinese guides were sent to Lhasa to replace experienced Tibetan guides who had previously studied English in India.

For better or worse, the tourist trade has also played a significant role in reshaping towns and cities. Construction crews are racing to build hotels, roads and bridges. Some historic sites have been restored although many old homes in Lhasa have fallen to the wrecking ball. Unesco recently advised that all remaining historic buildings in Lhasa be protected; this declaration came in the wake of recent house demolitions in Shöl, the area below the Potala Palace. Nearby Potala Square, the most obvious addition to the city, was built in military-parade-ground fashion; perfectly placed »

RECENT FAD! ★

Young Tibetans are crowding into PC game centres to play the latest shoot-'em-up computer games.

AS ONE OF TIBET'S FIVE MOST SACRED LAKES, LAKE MANASAROVAR PROVIDES A DIVINE VISTA TO THIS PRAYER WALL WITH YAK HORNS.

TIBET.

» for hordes of mainland Chinese tourists to pose for snapshots. Surprisingly, it is these visitors who now make up the bulk of the tourist trade as Tibet becomes increasingly fashionable among China's rapidly expanding middle class.

Infrastructure development has made many hard-to-reach places more accessible, allowing for quicker, less-arduous travel. In 2007, the highly controversial train line between Golmud and Lhasa will be complete. Condemned by the Dalai Lama, this project seals Tibet's fate as an integrated part of China, and will only accelerate Han Chinese immigration policies. With the train line figuring to increase crowds you may want to plan a trip to Tibet in 2006. But if you're dead set on riding the world's highest train route, wait one more year.

Despite these rapid developments, travellers are still finding ways to get beyond the tourist gloss of Lhasa. Heading deeper into the plateau to nondescript monasteries is one way of beating the tourist rush. Getting off the beaten path also means trekking, and there is an ever-growing number of routes.

Of course, the biggest draw to Tibet is still the people. An undying devotion to their faith and to the Dalai Lama permeates everything, and it's hard not to get swept up in the mystical side of the country. Some travellers are coming away from Tibet disappointed at the obvious impacts of China's colonisation, but those who get to know a few Tibetans come to realise that their spirit is far from broken and that hope is still strong in their hearts.

WHAT'S HOT...
✪ Trekking. A decade ago few travellers were hiking in Tibet, but newly pioneered routes in Ü province are opening up a variety of adventurous options. The most popular hike is the four-day walk between Gandan and Samye monasteries, but you may prefer the legendary Mt Kailash.

WHAT'S NOT...
✪ Nangma. Three years ago these late-night entertainment clubs were hugely popular among Tibetans for their innocent show tunes and traditional dance routines. Lately, however, many have gone to seed, becoming fronts for prostitution and other criminal elements.

FESTIVALS & EVENTS
✪ Losar; February–March. This colourful holiday marks the start of the Tibetan

> "
> *Hitchhiking in Tibet is illegal according to the Chinese, scorned by nomads and cheap fun for locals and backpackers. That is until you notice that all people on the truck carry machetes which come closer to one's neck with every bump. After six hours of corrugated road, a fight broke out between two machete-wielding farmers as the truck rolled into the sunset. Blood began to pour and mantras were said but no-one dared intervene. What a relief when we finally reached the hot springs.*
> "
>
> – Lucy Hordern, Australia

TIBET.

New Year and includes theatre performances and activities centred on the monasteries.

- ✪ Gyantse Horse-Racing Festival; mid-July. Racing, archery and traditional dancing feature at this event.

- ✪ Nagchu Horse-Racing Festival; August. This is an authentic event that draws up to 10,000 nomads and their braying, stomping and bucking broncos.

HOT TIPS FOR TRAVELLERS

- ✪ Take a virtual tour through Tibet using www.tibetmap.com, an excellent website with downloadable maps and pictures of dozens of remote monasteries.

- ✪ Your approach to Tibet can make or break your trip. Coming by road from China, Tibet appears fresh, invigorating and spiritual; a great discovery at the end of a long journey. By comparison, travellers flying in from Kathmandu may feel jaded, having already done a virtual tour of Tibet in the bookshops of Thamel.

- ✪ Check www.tibetinfo.net (Tibet Information Network) for the latest Tibet news.

HOT TOPICS OF THE DAY

- ✪ The train line from Golmud and the changes it will bring to Tibetan society

- ✪ The Dalai Lama and his latest plans to reconcile with China: some are concerned that his more lenient stance goes too far in recognising Chinese sovereignty

DO MENTION

- ✪ The beauty of Tibet and the fortitude of its people

DON'T MENTION

- ✪ Politics. While you're in no danger, Tibetans can get in real trouble for discussing politically sensitive topics with foreigners.

RANDOM FACTS

- ✪ On 22 August 2003, 99 Chinese and Tibetan couples were married on the lake shores of Nam-tso, a publicity stunt organised by the TAR (Tibetan Autonomous Region) tourism department.

- ✪ Before heading off to Beijing, the Olympic torch will be carried to the top of Mt Everest in May 2008.

- ✪ The Dalai Lama was awarded the Nobel Peace Prize in 1989 in recognition for his nonviolent campaign to end China's occupation in Tibet.

- ✪ Around 1.2 million Tibetans have died as a result of China's policy of imprisonment, torture and execution.

- ✪ Tibet is the source of Asia's greatest rivers, including: the Yangtze, the Yellow River, the Mekong River, the Brahmaputra, the Indus and the Ganges.

THINGS TO TAKE

- ✪ A reliable pair of sunglasses and a back-up pair, plus sunscreen; UV rays are strong on the plateau

- ✪ Medicine to combat the almost inevitable cold, cough and sinus infection

- ✪ A down-filled sleeping bag if you plan to camp or at least a small dormitory sleeping bag for poorly heated hotels in rural areas

THREE WORDS TO DESCRIBE THIS COUNTRY

- ✪ Prostrate, meditative, contemplative

– Michael Kohn

MOST BIZARRE SIGHT!

Pool tables at truck stops on desolate highways

VIETNAM.

VITAL STATISTICS

POPULATION
82 MILLION

POPULATION OF HO CHI MINH CITY
6 MILLION AND COUNTING

VISITORS PER YEAR
3.5 MILLION

UNIT OF CURRENCY
DONG (D)

COST OF A GLASS OF BEER
1600D = US$0.10

CAPITAL
HANOI

LANGUAGES
VIETNAMESE, RUSSIAN, FRENCH, CHINESE, ENGLISH

TONNAGE OF BOMBS DROPPED ON VIETNAM
15 MILLION

NUMBER OF MOTORBIKES
9.4 MILLION

AMOUNT OF *NUOC MAM* (FISH SAUCE) PRODUCED PER YEAR
200 MILLION LITRES (53 MILLION US GALLONS)

THIS HMONG WOMAN OF SAPA TOTES THE LARGE SILVER HOOP EARRINGS POPULAR IN HER REGION.

EVERYBODY'S TALKING AT ME... If you still think of this country as 'Nam', envisioning brilliant green fields dotted with landmines, generations of people living in longhouses and suspicious police hiding in the undergrowth then you're in for huge surprise.

In the swing of Vietnamese history, war with America, communism and the Khmer Rouge have not affected this traditionally rural society as much as the current capitalist drive to succeed. The old ways still exist; in fact, the history-thick culture is what makes Vietnam so fascinating; it has some of the richest arts, food and dress traditions to be found anywhere in the world. However, tradition is also marketed on a T-shirt now, sold by young, tertiary-educated women with dreams of Ho Chi Minh City (HCMC).

The time to be in Vietnam is today, because tomorrow is the feeling in the air and it seems a terrible thing to miss out on. The under-30s, who make up an incredible 65% of the population, are looking towards a future in Hanoi and HCMC; it has taken only one generation to move from the horrors of war to the delights of spend, spend, spend. Because Vietnam's history is so close, the traditions that have kept this rich country going prevail, but are either incorporated into the tourist market or challenged at every step by a population who enjoys a steadily relaxing government, sexuality and lifestyle.

THE SECRET OF SUCCESS
Vietnamese people live, breathe and work business. The capitalist ideology was never so apt; the country has such a drive to survive and, beyond that, succeed. Claws sheathed and purring proudly, Vietnam looks set to become the new Asian 'tiger' economy. The country is also enjoying a budget-travel boom, where you can experience pristine beaches just before they turn into flashy resorts; misty-mountained village life just before the juggernaut tours get there; and elegant cities in the throes of a youth-fuelled cultural metamorphosis.

THE DILAPIDATED FAÇADE OF A HOUSE IN THE ARCHITECTURALLY HISTORICAL TOWN OF HOI AN, QUANG NGAI.

KEEP THAT ONE TO YOURSELF

Vietnam currently has more contagious bugs than a primary school in winter and many of them are a lot more complicated than a sniffly nose. Outbreaks of SARS and bird flu have recently been added to the cocktail of dengue fever, hepatitis, malaria, rabies, typhoid and tuberculosis. A trip to Vietnam means starting out like an inoculated pin cushion, so bear in mind as you bare your behind that there are a few more things to avoid now than fields of unexploded ordinance.

DEFINING EXPERIENCE

⚙ Clinging to the back of a motorcycle headed for the market with your head pressed to a stranger's back while HOT (High-Five of Teenagers) blasts from his headphones, and catching glimpses of school girls in pure white *ao dai* (Vietnamese national dress) and barely older girls with freshly plucked eyebrows, skin-tight clothes and bags of shopping packed into a photosticker booth.

FESTIVALS & EVENTS

⚙ Human chess *(co nghoi)*; Hanoi; January–February. Attractive, young, unmarried people from the village of Lien Xa are used as human chess pieces in the week following Tet (Vietnamese Lunar New Year).

⚙ Holiday of the Dead (Thanh Minh); April. Commemorates deceased relatives.

⚙ Elephant Races; Don Village; April–May. Set on even, treeless ground, this 2km race involves the audience banging gongs and blowing horns to encourage the elephants along.

⚙ Wandering Souls Day (Trung Nguyen); August. Offerings are made to the wandering souls of the forgotten dead.

⚙ Buffalo Fights; Do Son; September. After being secluded for more than six months, the six finest Do Son and Do Hai buffalo fight it out before collectors bravely try to capture the winner.

⚙ APEC; Hanoi; November. The Asia-Pacific Economic Coorporation forum will hold its 2006 summit in Vietnam, this year notably attended by US president Bush.

HOT TOPIC OF THE DAY

⚙ Whether to buy a traditional Vietnamese *ao dai* wedding gown or rent a Western one is the question on every future bride's »

VIETNAM.

FROM THE ROAD

> *I woke up to find men wedging up the bus wheels with bits of wood and stones, trying to lever us onto a tiny boat to transport us across the Mekong. Failing to drown us before we got to Vietnam, we walked to our new transport: a* tuktuk *full of live pigs in sacks, 10 of us sitting on the pigs in the heat of the April Asian sun. Still, we were being refreshed as the locals continued to throw buckets of water over us and the pigs to celebrate the new year.*

- Alison Knight, Britain

» lips. Current Vietnamese fashion says the latter although they are horrendously expensive and must be taken back after the big day.

WHAT'S HOT...
- Hotpot buffets (or 'standing' dinners)

WHAT'S NOT...
- Communism

HOT TIPS FOR TRAVELLERS
- Take an open mind and adventurous taste buds as everything that creepeth upon the earth can crawl onto any menu in Vietnam.

- Tourism information can be rather hard to find as most Web content relating to Vietnam involves the war. Try www .vietnamtourism.com for disordered but informative country info or www .thingsasian.com for a well-organised, micro traveller's version.

- Sky River, Ho Chi Minh City, whose slogan 'create your curiousness' is bound to spark yours with an exquisite collection of *ao dai*; check out www.skyriveronline .com.

- Saving face is as important as it always was in Vietnam and a lost temper can also mean a lost friend, business deal or enjoyable stay.

DO MENTION
- Shopping – dubbed as the new Singapore or Hong Kong, Vietnam has turned its traditional lacquered wares and ethnic clothing into nice little earners.

DON'T MENTION
- Vietnam's newly embraced capitalism in the light of the Vietnamese/American War over communism (especially if you're in town for the shopping).

RANDOM FACTS
- During Summer Solstice Day (Tiet Doan Ngo) human effigies are burned to satisfy the need for souls to serve in the God of Death's army.

- The traditional peasant prerequisites for a happy life are: obtaining a buffalo, a marriage and a house.

THINGS TO TAKE
- Great wads of dong – necessary for even the mildest of shopaholics

- Antibodies

THREE WORDS TO DESCRIBE THIS COUNTRY
- Dong-wrapped anticipation

- Laura Jean McKay

AFGHANISTAN

Landlocked Afghanistan has seen armies and empires, merchants and mendicants, poets and prophets come and go over millennia, and has recently seen more than its share of (ongoing) troubles. Images of a war-blighted landscape do not do justice to a country blessed with a stark natural beauty, venerable history and rich and diverse culture. It may be hard to believe now, but Afghanistan was once the ultimate destination on the hippy trail. Even though Afghanistan isn't on the news every night anymore, it's not a safe place to travel to.

BANGLADESH

Bangladesh may have had its share of floods, famines and cyclones but this visually stunning destination has much to offer. The world's most crowded country has friendly people, luxuriously fertile land, rich history, a broad mix of cultures and a tropical atmosphere that's unique to Bangladesh. Away from the noise and bustle of the capital, Dhaka, there are magnificently lush hills waiting to be explored, plus archaeological sites, the longest beach on the planet and cruises along the country's countless rivers. It is one of the last frontiers where genuine cultural interaction is not only possible, but unavoidable.

BHUTAN

Bhutan teeters between contemporary and medieval: monks transcribe ancient Buddhist texts into laptop computers, traditionally dressed archers use alloy-steel bows and arrows, and its farsighted leaders maintain Bhutan's pristine environment and unique culture. Since Bhutan's doors opened in 1974, visitors have been mesmerised by spectacular Himalayan scenery, impressive architecture and hospitable people. To see the best of Bhutan, spend a week or more on foot, trekking through the great forested wilderness that covers most of the country.

BRUNEI

The Islamic sultanate of Brunei is one of the world's smallest countries – and richest, thanks to its treasure-trove of oil. It's known chiefly for the astounding wealth of its sultan and for its tax-free, subsidised society. With alcohol virtually unobtainable, no nightlife or active political culture, it's certainly peaceful. The capital, Bandar Seri Begawan, has retained its fringe of traditional, river-dwelling stilt villages as an enduring vision of the past. Brunei makes its living efficiently plundering natural resources from underground, yet nearly 80% of the country is covered by pristine rainforest threaded by mangrove-lined rivers and walking trails.

KAZAKHSTAN

If you love remoteness, wide open spaces, lunar landscapes, long hypnotic train rides and horse sausage, you'll be in your element in Kazakhstan. But it's not all barren steppes – there's also cosmopolitan Almaty and the spectacular spurs of the Tian Shan and Altay mountains to explore. And if it occasionally seems that the landscape has been bombarded by nuclear explosions, well, that's because Soviet rocket scientists began using Kazakhstan as a sandpit in the late 1940s. With whole steppe cities being refashioned with new-found oil money and a pioneer spirit, Kazakhstan is a surprise and delight for visitors.

KOREA, NORTH

Many argue that the Democratic People's Republic of Korea is widely misunderstood in the West, whose media report a single view of the country as one intent on nuclear weapons proliferation for material gain. Behind Pyongyang's so-called gambit claims and brinkmanship – and appeals for a few moments alone in the spotlight – lies a warrior-like history fuelled by deeply complicated territorial battles and scrambles for sovereignty. Today you can visit North Korea on heavily controlled tours – just don't expect to talk to any locals.

KYRGYZSTAN

What Kyrgyzstan lacks in gracious buildings and fancy cakes, it makes up for with nomadic traditions such as laid-back hospitality, a healthy distrust of authority and a fondness for drinking fermented mare's milk. It is perhaps the most accessible and welcoming of the former Soviet Central Asian republics, and boasts the region's most dramatic mountains – the central Tian Shan and Pamir Alay ranges. Kyrgyzstan is doing more than any other Central Asian republic to encourage and simplify tourism.

MACAU

Macau: the Las Vegas of Asia? Quite likely, since casino revenues here are tipped to

« exceed those of Las Vegas' in 2006. Less than a decade since Portugal handed the territory back to China, the spirit of Macau has changed markedly. Low-cost airlines have sent inbound visitor numbers reeling. And a mammoth American casino has set up shop, hoping for a piece of the action. Thankfully, though, Macau's colonial-enclave appeal has not been lost: you can still stroll down cobblestone streets, admire the European architecture and feast on Portuguese cuisine, long a major draw for the ever-resilient Macau.

MALAYSIA

Malaysia has a marvellous knack for soothing your senses. The hassles here are few, the landscapes – from intensely beautiful islands and mountains to verdant forests and jungles – are appealingly diverse, and most of the inhabitants would have to be asleep to be more laidback. There's a heady mix of people – Malay, Chinese, Indian and the diverse indigenous tribes of Sabah and Sarawak in Borneo. Historical influences loom large in the stately colonial architecture of Georgetown (Penang) and Melaka, and the prosperous nation's love of progress is proclaimed in its gleaming, futuristic buildings.

MALDIVES

The Maldives is made up of hundreds of tiny islands, most of them bobbing only a few metres above sea level. If your idea of paradise is a tropical island with swaying palm trees, white-sand beaches and turquoise lagoons, then the Maldives will not disappoint. The Maldives were hard hit by the 2004 tsunami. The tourist industry in the Maldives has bounced back remarkably quickly and most resorts are open again, offering the full 'sun, sand and swaying palms' experience. Tourists are unlikely to encounter any major signs of damage. Divers will be pleased to hear that most of the Maldives' famous coral reefs escaped serious damage.

MONGOLIA

Mongolia occupies a special place in the minds of many dreamers, stirring up visions of the untamed: Genghis Khan and his hordes, and wild horses galloping across the steppes. Even today, outside of Ulaanbaatar you may get the feeling you've stepped into another century rather than another country.

The 'Land of Blue Sky' is a place where Siberian forests, rolling steppes, the vast Gobi Desert, glacier-wrapped mountains and crystal-pure lakes meet. It is an invigorating and exhilarating place to visit, and remains one of the last unspoiled travel destinations in Asia.

MYANMAR (BURMA)

Myanmar still wears its traditional longyi even as its neighbours abandon their saris for jeans, and in the countryside rice paddies are still farmed using water buffalo. These romantic images are a traveller's dream, but they exist in the presence of oppression and hardship. Myanmar is ruled by a harsh military regime, human rights abuse is widespread, and Myanmar has long been grounded by isolation and international fallout following the lockup of Aung San Suu Kyi. Would-be guests are advised to consider all sides of the 'should you go?' question before making plans to visit this fascinating country.

PAKISTAN

Media impressions of Pakistan are a jumble of Islamic fundamentalism and martial law. Sure, there are a few wild and woolly regions (most of which are either off-limits or require an armed guard to visit), but this is only one layer of an incredibly multilayered country. Pakistan offers some of Asia's most mind-blowing landscapes, extraordinary trekking, the spectacular Karakoram Highway, a multitude of cultures and a long tradition of hospitality. It's the site of some of the earliest human settlements and the crucible of two of the world's major religions: Hinduism and Buddhism.

PHILIPPINES

This is southeast Asia with an edge: 7106 islands; politicians as crooked as the pristine coastline; steaming jungles; scorching volcanoes, monolithic whale sharks; grinning card sharks; resolute treasure hunters; ex-head-hunters; and some of the last remaining pirates in the world. Flavoured by its Spanish and US colonial past, contemporary Philippine culture marks a unique convergence of Christianity, baseball caps and mystical spirits. This is a land where ancient rice terrace amphitheatres lie concealed in thick mountains, thousands of far-flung islands lie in wait for the intrepid explorer's beach towel, and the oceans boast world-class diving with a kaleidoscope of fish.

SINGAPORE

There are those who say Singapore has lost its soul in its transformation from colonial outpost to industrial powerhouse, but they couldn't be more wrong. A sultry heart beats beneath the big-city surface. This is an undeniably Asian city with a unique mix of Chinese, Malay and Indian traditions, where fortune tellers, calligraphers and temple worshippers are still a part of everyday life. Shopping and eating are national passions, and city pubs and clubs stay open for drinking and dancing until dawn. A primary rainforest in the centre of the island is a refuge from the bustle.

TAIWAN

Steeped in traditional Chinese culture, with influences from Japan and the island's own indigenous tribes, Taiwan is a destination full of surprises. Beyond the bustling metropolises are lush tropical landscapes, rushing rivers, hot springs and some of northeast Asia's tallest mountains. The island is a compact showcase of natural attractions and cultural jewels, with unexpected marvels around every corner – like a computer-generated Chinese watercolour. In the cities, experience some of the finest Chinese cuisine in the world, explore bustling night markets, attend a Taiwanese opera or relax in a traditional Chinese teahouse.

TAJIKISTAN

Travel in Tajikistan is a grade harder than most of Central Asia, but if you are ready to take things as they come, you are at the cutting edge of adventure. Once part of the Persian empire, Tajikistan is a patchwork of self-contained valleys and regional contrasts, with a shared pride in a cultural heritage that is claimed as the oldest and most influential in the Silk Road region. The Pamir region is easily the country's highlight, with peaks dwarfing anything found outside Nepal. Despite a violent period following independence from the Soviet umbrella, today most of Tajikistan is stable.

THAILAND

Follow your eyes, but trust your heart. Thailand is a land of pleasant contradictions. Lose yourself in the cool mist of a mountain-top trail trod by post–Stone Age cultures or in the smoky haze swirling around the world's tallest hotel. Jaw-dropping natural beauty, eye-catching architecture, an intricately woven culture and downright fabulous cuisine all lure more visitors here than to any other country in Southeast Asia. The devastating tsunami in 2004 could not hold back the Thais for long; all areas are up and running again.

TURKMENISTAN

A fascinating desert republic, Turkmenistan is a mysterious and wild straggle of deeply mystical civilisations. Most of the country consists of an inhospitable lunar-like desert called the Karakum, which conceals unexploited oil and gas deposits, set to become one of the biggest prizes in the contest for Central Asia's mineral wealth. Turkmenistan is sparsely populated and its people, the Turkmen, are only a generation or two removed from being nomads. Despite successive governments bent on modernisation, Turkmenistan is a spiritual and traditional land, largely trapped in time.

UZBEKISTAN

Double land–locked Uzbekistan lies at the heart of Central Asia, sealed off from the world by mountains and deserts, and sharing borders with all five of the other 'Stans. This is the land of the ancient Silk Road and Alexander the Great's conquests. Such a crossroads could not be anything but a cultural melting pot, and so Uzbekistan boasts a proud artistic history and diverse culture, exemplified by cities such as Samarkand and Khiva. Travel to areas bordering Afghanistan, Kyrgyzstan and Tajikistan and the eastern region is unsafe.

ASIA.

SNAPSHOTS.

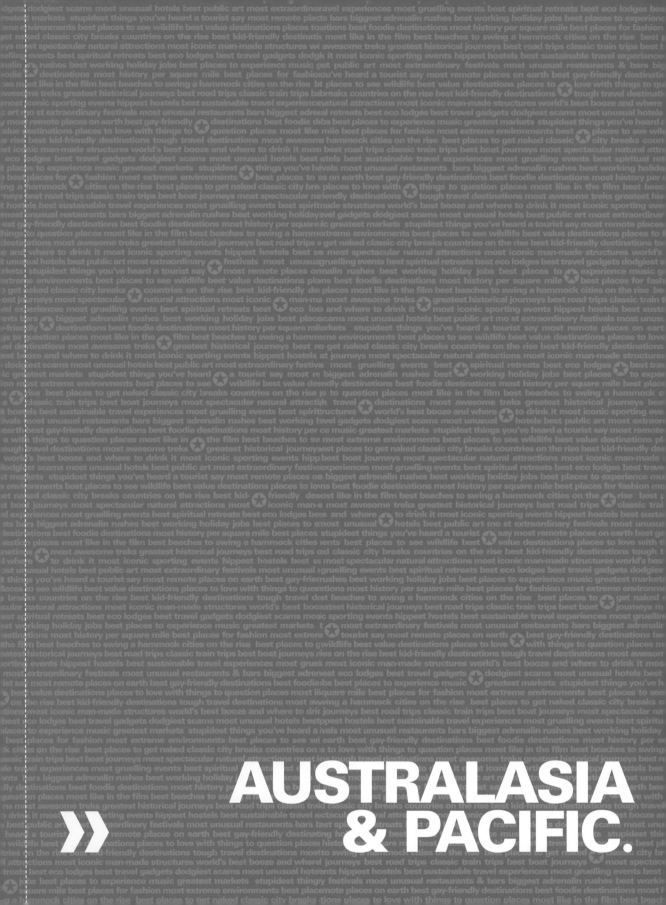

AUSTRALASIA & PACIFIC.

MICRONESIA

MARSHALL
ISLANDS

KIRIBATI

NAURU

SOLOMON
ISLANDS

Solomon
Sea

TUVALU

SAMOAN
ISLANDS

COOK
ISLANDS

TAHITI &
FRENCH
POLYNESIA

Coral
Sea

VANUATU

FIJI

TONGA

NEW
CALEDONIA

PITCAIRN
ISLAND

SOUTH
PACIFIC
OCEAN

TASMAN
SEA

NEW
ZEALAND

■ = BLUELIST. HOTSPOTS

AN INDIGENOUS MARKET PERFORMER WORKS BENEATH A TYPICALLY AUSTRALIAN EXPANSE OF BIG BLUE SKY.

AUSTRALIA.

VITAL STATISTICS

- **POPULATION**
  20 MILLION
- **VISITORS PER YEAR**
  5 MILLION
- **UNIT OF CURRENCY**
  AUSTRALIAN
  DOLLAR ($)
- **COST OF A CUP
  OF COFFEE**
  A$3 = US$2.30
- **CAPITAL**
  CANBERRA
- **LANGUAGE**
  ENGLISH

A BRAVE NEW WORLD. The Land Down Under has always been popular with travellers from the Asia Pacific region – New Zealanders make up Australia's biggest tourism market, followed by the Japanese – but less so with other parts of the world.

Now, though, with the increase in global travel, tourists from elsewhere are starting to sit up and take notice, and a large part of that is due to the proliferation of relatively inexpensive flights to what was once a pricey long-haul destination. Within Australia, budget airlines have also sprung up, offsetting the pain of travelling around such a massive continent. But what really attracts all of these groups is the realisation that Australia offers the flamin' lot: good food and fine wine, a unique indigenous culture, idyllic beaches and national parks, outback minimalism, and a couple of inimitable urban experiences – cultural Melbourne and hedonistic Sydney.

FALLING IN LINE

The fastest-growing world-travel niche belongs to ecotourism. A major industry survey uncovered some interesting stats: two-thirds of participants stated that travel increased their respect for other cultures,

while almost half said that exposure to another culture encouraged them to travel responsibly. Ecotourists look to hands-on activities to increase their awareness, and Australia's natural environment is ideal: go camel riding in the Simpson Desert; tour the Northern Territory with an Aboriginal guide, discovering wildlife, rock art and bush tucker along the way; stay at an 'ecolodge', surrounded by wilderness, in the tropical far north. Such locations provide the backdrop to another emergent travel trend, albeit one that might be at odds with ecotourism: destination weddings. Put a little love into your life – and nab the perfect photo op – by saying your vows in a tropical forest in Cairns. Just don't throw confetti on the fragile forest floor.

It's worth bearing in mind though, that not so long ago, Australia was considered a cultural backwater, the butt of many a joke. Aussie comedian Barry Humphries compared living in Australia with 'going

TWO DOGS HANG OUT IN THE BACK OF A 'YOU BEAUT' UTE, MENA CREEK.

to a party and dancing all night with one's mother'; Jerry Seinfeld proclaimed Melbourne to be the 'asshole of the world'. Now, Melbourne is a serial winner of the 'world's most liveable city' award and Australia is all things to all people.

It's amazing what a little hype can do.

DEFINING EXPERIENCES
- ✪ Eating damper under the stars at dusk while drinking in the serene outback beauty of Uluru (Ayers Rock)

- ✪ Throwing up at a barbecue after a few too many beers and sausages

FESTIVALS & EVENTS
- ✪ Gay & Lesbian Mardi Gras; Sydney; March. Gay, garish and absolutely massive.

- ✪ Adelaide Arts Festival; Adelaide; March.

- ✪ Commonwealth Games; Melbourne; March. Commonwealth nations gather in »

MOST BIZARRE SIGHT!

Shane Warne's hair transplant (see 'Don't Mention')

SCHAPELLE: NOW YOU SEE HER, NOW YOU DON'T

Australia loves a fad – the populace is quick to embrace and even quicker to discard, especially when the craze surrounds a public figure. They call it the 'tall poppy syndrome' – grow too tall, get cut down – and there's no greater illustration of this than the plight of Schapelle Corby, a 27-year-old Queensland beauty student caught with 4.1kg (9lb) of marijuana in her bag at Bali's Denpasar airport in October 2004. Corby has tearfully, repeatedly claimed her innocence, suggesting the dope was planted by Australian baggage handlers. Whether she's guilty or not is anyone's guess – there's equal evidence on either side – but whatever the case, her plight sparked off a media fixation that pretty soon became a national obsession. Corby was alternately glorified, demonised, sexualised and vilified by all and sundry until her sentence was handed down by the Indonesian courts: guilty. At the time of writing, the appeals process was still under way, but Corby is now in real danger of being totally discarded by the fickle Aussie media in favour of something even more sensational: a poker-playing dog, no doubt, or a cat that can flip burgers while riding a unicycle.

»

> *Whilst spending some time in an Aboriginal town in northern Australia, I went fishing with an Aboriginal man. We were walking along in the water when he suddenly said: 'Better get out, there's a croc'. We quickly made our way out of the water. After a while he decided it wasn't a salt-water (people-eating) croc but rather a fresh-water one and therefore 'safe' to swim with, so we went back in. We got within 3m (10ft) of the croc before the man realised that the 'croc' was a lily pad.*

- Hannah Eames, Australia

HOT TOPIC OF THE DAY!

In the outer suburbs of Newcastle, near Sydney, a spate of frozen chickens falling from the sky had the locals scratching their heads as they repaired smashed roofs, windows and car bonnets. Bizarre theories were put forth. Some say birds plucked the chooks from garbage dumps, dropping them from the heavens when they became too heavy; others say a crazed madman with a grudge fired them from the hills with a homemade bazooka. The mystery was never solved.

» Melbourne to battle it out for sporting gold, silver and bronze.

- Womadelaide; Adelaide; March. Womadelaide is an outdoor world-music festival.

- Australian Goanna-Pulling Championships; Wooli; April. Participants squat on all fours, attach leather harnesses to their heads and engage in cranial tug-of-war.

- Melbourne International Film Festival (MIFF); Melbourne; July. Recently MIFF has had a distinct Southeast Asian focus.

- Darwin Beer Can Regatta; Darwin; July. Featuring a regatta of boats made entirely from beer cans.

- Stompen Ground Festival; Broome; September or October. Celebrating Aboriginal art and culture.

- Melbourne Cup; Melbourne; November. A massive horse-racing carnival.

DO MENTION

- Australia's contribution to aid relief in the Southeast Asian areas devastated by the recent tsunami. This is a source of Australian pride and has strengthened the bond between Australia and the region (although that bond was threatened by hysterical members of the public after Schapelle Corby was sentenced by an Indonesian court; see the boxed text).

DON'T MENTION

- Shane Warne, famous Australian cricketer, and Russell Crowe, famous 'Australian' (he was born in New Zealand) actor. These bad boys spent 2005 throwing phones at people and sending lewd text messages to women, and by the end of the year, the Australian public had grown thoroughly sick of their antics.

RANDOM FACTS

- Australia is home to the world's biggest earthworm (*Megascolides australis*), found in Gippsland, Victoria.

- Australians buy between 200,000 and 300,000 lawnmowers per year.

- New South Wales has such a bad locust problem that a recent cookbook advocated easing the plague via consumption.

- Melbourne's Monash University named a species of dinosaur *Qantassaurus* after the national airline, Qantas.

THINGS TO TAKE

- A sense of humour and a thick skin – you might get the 'piss ripped out of you' by an Aussie, which, translated, means they might make fun of you a little bit

- A healthy appetite: the grub's pretty good (as are the grubs; see 'Random Facts')

- High-strength sunscreen if travelling to the northeast coast; warm clothes if travelling to the southeast coast

HOT TIPS FOR TRAVELLERS

- Australia is really big – if you want to see it all, give yourself around 12 months.

- 'Rugby' means rugby union, 'league' means rugby league, 'football' means Australian rules and 'soccer' means football.

- Explore Tasmania, with its beautiful wilderness areas, a vibrant arts scene and a very relaxed, unique outlook on life.

THREE WORDS TO DESCRIBE THIS COUNTRY

- Vast, laid-back, dry

- Simon Sellars

A STATUE OF THE VIRGIN ATOP EAST TIMOR'S HIGHEST POINT, MOUNT RAMELAU.

VITAL STATISTICS

EAST TIMOR.

○ **POPULATION**
998,000

○ **VISITORS PER YEAR**
N/A

○ **UNIT OF CURRENCY**
US DOLLAR ($)

○ **COST OF A CUP OF COFFEE**
US$1 TO US$2

○ **CAPITAL**
DILI

○ **LANGUAGES**
PORTUGUESE, TETUN, BAHASA INDONESIA, ENGLISH

★ THE LESTE FRONTIER OF ASIA. Timor Leste is the poorest country in Asia and the newest nation in the world. Given that it has only recently emerged from the trauma it endured under years of Indonesian occupation, there are few places that are as untouched by tourism as East Timor.

Its psyche was born of revolution, and now in its infant years it is upping its efforts to make the most of its resources: oil, coffee and natural splendour that could invigorate even the most travel-weary wanderer. If ever there was an uncontested truth about this complicated country, it's this: Timor's an underrated travel destination.

The coast road (the only one in East Timor that is possible to traverse without a 4WD) traces the ocean across the breadth of the country, petering out in the last 8km (5mi) into an unpaved smattering of rocks that eventually spill out onto the white sands of Tutuala Beach at the easternmost point of the island. The winding road takes you through ever-changing, other-worldly terrain: carpets of rice fields stretching out to the ocean, meandering water buffalos and villages full of people who smile and wave. With unscathed diving and snorkelling sites, surprising ethnic diversity

and a history that's being written on a day-to-day basis, this island is ripe for adventure.

DILI DALLYING

The capital city of East Timor is Dili – an unassuming town that has no traffic lights and more potholes than people. The contrasts and contradictions that are rife throughout the country all collide in this crazy capital. In the heart of town, you can look across the tranquil ocean towards Atauro island, with the coast curving away indefinitely to the left and the Christ statue on your right. But turn around to face Dili and you are reminded at once of the recent tragedies that this city has endured; burnt-out concrete-skeleton buildings still remain, looking more like tombstones than shops and homes.

The mountains start immediately where the buildings stop, carving their way »

RECENT FAD! ○

Car accessories. Inside every taxi is a dense jungle of dangling plastic hearts and air-fresheners. Decorative mirrors are suction-capped across the dashboard and posters of American pop stars adorn the roof.

PERFORMERS BATHED IN
GLORIOUS BRONZE LIGHT DURING
A TRADITIONAL TIMORESE DANCE.

EAST TIMOR.

» upwards in all sorts of brave shapes and bold greens. They're what the expats call the 'real East Timor' whenever they need to remind themselves of why they're in Dili.

DEMOCRAZY

After enduring years of international apathy about the injustices occurring in Timor Leste, the nation now has to withstand a bombardment of international goods, people and ideas.

Foreigners, who are all trying to help pave Timor's rocky road to democracy, parade down the streets of Dili in indistinguishable UN vehicles. There are Vietnamese hair salons, Brazilian nightclubs and Portuguese restaurants. If the influence of Australia's proximity and presence isn't evident enough in the number of bars touting Foster's beer, think of the dive sites with names such as 'Bob's Rock' and 'Jim's Crack'.

Timor's full of ambiguities and surprises. It's the sort of place where embassies send text message to their respective nationals, advising them to 'flee' because of a 'situation'; it's a place that shelters evacuees from off-shore oil rigs during cyclones; and a place where apparitions of the Virgin Mary are commonplace, and tsunami hoaxes have the Dili's entire population seeking refuge in the mountains.

A mere two-hour plane ride from Australia, East Timor is a hop, a skip and a world away.

FESTIVALS & EVENTS

⚙ In addition to Catholic events, there are various public holidays commemorating landmark dates:

⚙ Independence Day; May. Commemorates East Timor's independence, gained in 2002.

⚙ Referendum; August. Commemorates the referendum of 1999.

⚙ Liberation Day; September. In remembrance of the original Liberation Day in 1999.

⚙ Santa Cruz Day; November. Marks the massacre of 1991.

WHAT'S HOT...

⚙ Tropical weather

⚙ Diving in fertile coral reefs

⚙ Restaurants serving seafood on the waterfront

FROM THE ROAD

"

Most of East Timor's countryside remains untouched by commerce and it provides a good escape from the tourist locations. The landscape is stunning and you will inevitably be greeted by curious looks and cheers from the local children excited to see foreigners passing through.

"

-Hana Mijovic, Indonesia

WHAT'S NOT...
- Tropical diseases
- Driving on unpaved roads
- Restaurants boasting dog on their shopfront

HOT TOPICS OF THE DAY
- The relationship between the church and the state
- The dispute over who is entitled to the oil in the Timor Sea
- Bringing to justice the perpetrators of human rights violations in 1999

DO MENTION
- Timor's beautiful countryside, proud history, bright future and right to its oil.

DON'T MENTION
- The events of 1999; don't surrender your sensitivity to inquire about lost loved ones.

RANDOM FACTS
- In 1994, Australian activist Kirsty Sword met and fell in love with jailed resistance fighter, Xanana Gusmão. She is now the first lady of an independent East Timor.
- Among East Timor's resident reptiles is a species of dragon lizard that can glide through the air between trees for up to 50m (164ft).
- One of the major buyers of East Timorese coffee is Starbucks.

MOST BIZARRE SIGHT
- The view from the top of Mt Ramelau: if you're standing on the top of this highest peak in Timor (2963m, or 9721ft) on a clear day, you may be able to see both the north and south coasts.
- The main street of the capital city: truckloads of flags, fists and slogans speeding down crumbling roads lined with burnt-out buildings and swanky coffee shops.

THINGS TO TAKE
- Mosquito repellent
- Snorkelling gear
- Low expectations of good roads and accommodation options

HOT TIPS FOR TRAVELLERS
- Do some preplanning; outside Dili there are few places to stay and no petrol stations.
- Read James Dunn's *East Timor: A Rough Passage to Independence* so you can see the country in context.
- Make sure your insurance policy covers you for evacuation in the event of civil unrest or medical emergency.
- Never trust a street sign.

THREE WORDS TO DESCRIBE THIS COUNTRY
- Poor, proud, promising

- Marika McAdam

DEFINING EXPERIENCE!

Standing at a political rally in a forest of Fretilin flags with old men wearing traditional dress and Che Guevara T-shirts and dancing in jubilation – you intermittently throw your fist in the air and shout 'Democracia!'

A LONE TREE AGAINST A SUBLIME VIOLET SUNSET IN IPAN.

GUAM + NORTHERN MARIANA ISLANDS.

VITAL STATISTICS

- **POPULATION**
  150,000 (GUAM);
  80,006 (NORTHERN MARIANAS)

- **NUMBER OF MILITARY PERSONNEL & THEIR FAMILIES**
  23,000 (GUAM)

- **VISITORS PER YEAR TO GUAM**
  1 MILLION PLUS

- **UNIT OF CURRENCY**
  US DOLLAR ($)

- **COST OF A CUP OF COFFEE**
  $3

- **CAPITAL**
  HAGÅTÑA (GUAM)
  SAIPAN (NORTHERN MARIANAS)

- **LANGUAGE**
  ENGLISH, CHAMORRO, JAPANESE, KOREAN

★ JOIN EVERYONE AND THEIR TOUR BUS. If the terms 'package tour' and 'duty free' don't send horrified shivers up your island-loving spine, then Guam and the Northern Mariana Islands may be for you.

Jutting out of the northern Pacific Ocean and the Philippines Sea, these volcanic tips (some of which are still active) boast crystal waters, military bases and tourists a plenty.

Once branded Islas de los Ladrones (Islands of Thieves) after a bartering misunderstanding between Spanish explorers and the indigenous Chamorro (the Chamorro exchanged food and water for their take of the Spanish ship's contents), the islands themselves have been subject to copious thievery over the centuries. Ping-ponged from Spanish Jesuits to German businesses, then cleared for the Japanese sugarcane industry, the region was almost bombed out of the water in WWII by Japan and the USA, who has retained government. The Northern Marianas have been promoted as 'America's best-kept secret' and, indeed, they are used as a US military sanctuary and were a CIA base until the 1960s. Now that the secret is out, the islands are renowned for Saipan's sweat-shop industry, Guam's duty-free status and their firm place on Asia's tour hit-list for public holidays. The fact that you can still get traditional dishes flavoured with *finadene* (spicy sauce) and glimpse Chamorro and Carolinian culture is a miracle and a tribute to the recent efforts to restore the islands' identities.

The two seasons in Guam and the Northern Marianas, dry and wet, do not mean that you need that extra jumper – the temperature hovers at an exquisite 27°C (81°F) all year. Saipan is listed in the *Guinness Book of World Records* as having the world's most equable temperature, however, the increasing number of typhoons and the occasional earthquake tend to shake this status somewhat.

DEFINING EXPERIENCE
- Standing in a shallow lagoon off Coco Island waving money to flag a lift with a

passing privet boat while a Japanese tour-chain boonie stomp (hike) passes through the wilderness behind you and military helicopters practise manoeuvres and hack the air overhead.

FESTIVALS & EVENTS

- Tagaman Triathlon; Northern Marianas; mid-May. A serious 2km (1.2mi) swim, 60km (37mi) cycle and (not-so-fun) 15km (9.3mi) run for the fanatical fit.

- Malojloj Fiesta; Guam; May. Any conversation with a local at this time of year will probably involve an invite to this wild, three-day block party.

- Liberation Day; Guam and Northern Marianas; July. The entire population hits the streets for parades, food and entertainment.

DO MENTION

- Guam's return to Chamorro pre-Spanish village names

RANDOM FACTS

- Guamians boast the world's largest K-mart, open 24 hours a day, seven days a week.

- All nine species of Guam's unique birds have been devoured to extinction by the accidental introduction of the brown tree snake.

- Tinian, Northern Marianas, holds the dubious reputation of being the take-off »

RECENT FAD! ✪

October is wedding season in Guam with thousands of Asian brides and grooms flocking to exchange vows and receive duty-free gifts in swanky hotels overlooking the water.

BEFORE COMPLAINING THAT IT SUCKS...

Think carefully before slapping at a mosquito during your stay. According to Northern Mariana legend, female mosquitoes are the product of a wingy young lady who was killed by her husband after discovering that, while he had been running around trying to please her, she was doing the dirty. After dumping her body in the water, her blood curdled and produced mosquitoes. Thus, when mosquitoes whine and suck blood they are only making a belated effort to become human again.

GUAM + NORTHERN MARIANA ISLANDS.

FROM THE ROAD

> *Several different cultures – Chamorro, Philippino, Japanese, Korean, Chinese, to name but a few – have settled in Guam, creating an idyllic Asian microcosm.*
>
> - Nicole M Reynolds, USA

HOT TOPIC OF THE DAY!

The Northern Mariana Islands recently became the first US territory to receive Approved Destination Status from the People's Republic of China. As a result, 30,000 Chinese tourists visited the Northern Marianas in the 2004–05 financial year, making a change from the standard US-military and Japanese-holiday presence.

» site for the aircraft that dropped the atomic bombs on Hiroshima and Nagasaki.

- Latte stones are not a unique place to rest your coffee but magnificent stones carved by the ancient Chamorro and dotted throughout the Northern Marianas.

MOST BIZARRE SIGHTS

- The revolving statue of Pope John Paul II in Hagåtña, Guam
- Walking – a certifiably insane act in the eyes of the people of Guam
- The atomic bomb pits near Saipan, Northern Marianas

THINGS TO TAKE

- Pockets full of US cash and travellers cheques – needed and accepted throughout the region
- Sunscreen, sunglasses and a hat

HOT TIPS FOR TRAVELLERS

- Avoid the islands during traditional Japanese holiday seasons (Christmas to New Year, Golden Week and Obon) – not only will you have to sleep in the streets, it will be crowded and noisy out there.
- The miscellaneous guide to everything Guam, www.guam.net, is a work in progress which promises to be 'very exciting for people on and off-island'. Old Guam (http://old.guam.net), however, is up and thriving with postcards from paradise, the empty but hopeful 2006 calendar of events and some very unusual Guam-related links.
- A more detailed view can be found at www.guam-online.com, unbecomingly marketed at US 'military (personnel) with orders to Guam'.
- The beautiful Marianas Visitors Authority site is worth swimming around in for a good while; visit www.mymarianas.com.

THREE WORDS TO DESCRIBE THIS COUNTRY

- Metropolis of Micronesia

- Laura Jean McKay

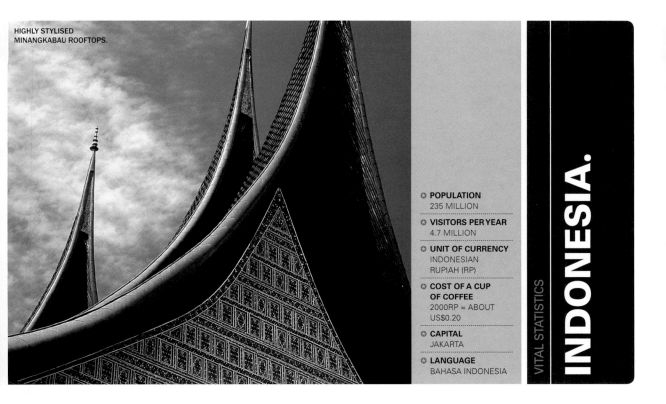

HIGHLY STYLISED
MINANGKABAU ROOFTOPS.

INDONESIA.

VITAL STATISTICS

- **POPULATION**
  235 MILLION
- **VISITORS PER YEAR**
  4.7 MILLION
- **UNIT OF CURRENCY**
  INDONESIAN
  RUPIAH (RP)
- **COST OF A CUP
  OF COFFEE**
  2000RP = ABOUT
  US$0.20
- **CAPITAL**
  JAKARTA
- **LANGUAGE**
  BAHASA INDONESIA

PEACEFUL TRADITIONS, PROBLEMATIC PRESENT. It's not for nothing that Churchill decried democracy as 'the worst form of government, except for all the others that have been tried'.

More than seven years after the deposing of Soeharto and his military dictatorship, Indonesia has yet to regain its footing. Living in almost unimaginably widespread country, with distinct populations dispersed among scattered islands, Indonesians are struggling to support their nascent democracy, endure the growing pains of social upheaval, and live peacefully with each other the whole while. Pitted against them are disturbing cultural and economic forces that threaten to bring hidden tensions to the surface at any time.

The good news is that Indonesia's most fundamental traditions act to hold its people together. The islands have always been a place of staggering diversity, both in the natural world (with more animal and plant species than Raffles could ever shake a Singapore Sling at) and in the cultural realm, with Islam the newest primary ingredient in the archipelago's *rendang* curry of influences. The deeply Muslim nation's two main tourist sites are temples of Hinduism (Prambanan) and Buddhism (Borobudur). Its Pancasila (Five Guiding Principles) are bound by the notion of unity in diversity. Its people run the gamut from Arab-influenced Acehnese on Sumatra to the nomadic fisherfolk of Papua (formerly Irian Jaya). And its landscape…well, how much do you want to know about mind-blowing beaches and lava-spouting volcanoes?

It sounds like a traveller's paradise – and it should be. But things are no longer so simple. Democracy has brought long-submerged issues into the public domain. In the days of Soeharto, people were too frightened to talk about such things as corruption and separatism. Now that Indonesians can choose (and censure) their leaders, they have found a voice with which to express their long-pent-up disapproval. Social change has not yet brought about economic progress. Political corruption »

HOT TIP FOR TRAVELLERS!

If you're bargaining for wares, use the Jakarta slang *enggak* (pronounced vaguely as it looks, but also as though you're trying to dislodge a bit of steak from your oesophagus) to mean 'no', rather than the standard *tidak*. It'll give you more cred. The word 'bankrupt' (pronounced 'bahn-kroo') also helps.

INDONESIA.

A SITA DANCER STRIKES A POSE BEFORE A TEMPLE DOOR.

» is still rampant, and hardly a day goes by without a high-profile scandal on the front page of the *Jakarta Post*. Frightened by their government's slow and cautious reaction to the December 2004 tsunami that all but destroyed the province of Aceh, the people are more restive than ever. The tension of the 2002 Bali bombings lives on, as sporadic terrorist attacks continue to plague the islands.

All this has made Indonesia an iffy proposition for many travellers, who have begun staying away from the archipelago. From 2002 to 2005, international tourism declined each year, resulting in economic crisis for many communities that depended on foreign visitors. The US, UK and Australian governments, fearful of attacks on Westerners, have begun warning their citizens against travelling to Indonesia.

A POSITIVE BACKLASH

Such worrisome trends have, however, begun jolting Indonesians into action. After every terrorist attack, support for violent, extremist factions declines. In an almost unheard-of twist, hotels are beginning to lower rates for foreign visitors, attempting to draw back international business. Recent visitors to Indonesia have commented on how grateful entire communities seem at being 'honoured' by guests. It appears as though the majority of Indonesians recognise that their well-being is tied inextricably with the rest of the world, and they are beginning to do all they can to welcome the world back to Indonesia.

DEFINING EXPERIENCE

✿ Sipping a cocktail out of a coconut shell and curling your toes into the sand at Kuta Beach, Bali, while hawkers try to sell you satays, cheap jewellery and massages

FESTIVALS & EVENTS

✿ Nyepi (also known as Caka New Year); March. The whole island of Bali comes to a stop in order to celebrate Balinese New Year – in fact, preparations begin the previous day and the hangover continues for at least a day or two.

✿ Idul Fitri (also known as Eid-ul Fitr); October. This festival is one the end of Ramadan. All restaurants open and people chow down ravenously.

✿ Hari Natal (Christmas Day); December. Despite the predominantly Muslim

INDESIA.

"
When I arrived in a village on a small island in Indonesia, the people all came to meet me. I was trying to talk to the people, but nobody in the village spoke English, so we had to communicate with our hands. There was no hotel or hostel, and I ended up getting a room at the local prison.
"

- Luka Benedik, Slovenia

population, Indonesians enjoy celebrating Christmas. Exchanging presents and throwing parties is common.

WHAT'S HOT...
- Political corruption – again

WHAT'S NOT...
- Tsunamis, terrorism and Tien Soeharto

HOT TOPIC OF THE DAY
- Indonesians are almost as abuzz as Australians about the treatment of foreigners who may have committed drug crimes on the islands. An example is the incarceration of Australian Schapelle Corby, who was sentenced to 20 years in prison after having been found with a large amount of marijuana in her baggage. The majority of Indonesians support strong drug laws and accept their sometimes harsh court system as a necessary defence against the evils of drugs.

DO MENTION
- Food and sports (especially international sports – don't forget to mention table tennis and badminton) are always great

initial topics. They're also a lot more fruitful than talking about the weather: Bahasa Indonesia doesn't have enough synonyms for 'hot' and 'humid'.

DON'T MENTION
- The topic of Acehnese independence (probably not anytime soon) or East Timorese independence (still a source of debate and rancour) are probably best avoided.

RANDOM FACTS
- Indonesia is the world's largest archipelago, with more than 17,000 islands (more when the tide's low).
- More Muslims live in Indonesia than in any other country.
- More people die as a result of volcano eruptions in Indonesia than in any other country.
- Bahasa Indonesia is a manufactured language based on Malay, which was the language of traders and not the primary tongue of almost any Indonesian back when the country gained independence (officially 1945, really 1949). It has no tenses, moods, conjugations or declensions. An easy A in language class.

THINGS TO TAKE
- Lightweight clothes that cover the arms and legs completely and let your skin breathe. They'll keep the sun off but also get you entry into mosques and other holy places.
- Earplugs – an indispensable companion for sleeping through neighbours' drunken fights or zealous roosters' predawn alerts.
- All the medicine you think you'll need.
- Outdoor gear – it's tough to find good raincoats, mosquito repellents (especially for the monster mutated mosquitoes you're bound to run into) or camping stuff.

THREE WORDS TO DESCRIBE THIS COUNTRY
- Masked, brave, expansive

- Vivek Wagle

MOST BIZARRE SIGHT!

Watching Balinese men beat the crap out of each other with sticks the week after Idul Fitri. It's traditional, or so they say...

NEW ZEALAND.

VITAL STATISTICS

- **POPULATION**
  4 MILLION
- **VISITORS PER YEAR**
  2.4 MILLION
- **UNIT OF CURRENCY**
  NEW ZEALAND
  DOLLAR ($)
- **COST OF A CUP OF COFFEE**
  NZ$3.50 TO NZ$4.50 ≈
  US$2.40 TO US$3.10
- **CAPITAL**
  WELLINGTON
- **LANGUAGES**
  ENGLISH, MAORI

THE BOILING WATERS OF CHAMPAGNE POOL, THERMAL RESERVE.

PASSION FOR PURITY. Thanks to the trilogy of award-winning films by Kiwi director Peter Jackson, who found Middle Earth at the end of the earth and writ it larger than any promotional marketing could, travellers the world over have been flocking to New Zealand.

The country's enchanting natural wonders – rumbling volcanoes, spewing geysers, deep-fissured fjords and soaring snow-shrouded peaks – infuse the soul, reinvigorating and inspiring it. It's no wonder then, that many New Zealanders are passionate about keeping New Zealand nuclear-free and GM-free, and are fervently against whaling. Domestic politics is progressive among both the Pakeha (European-descent New Zealanders) and tangata whenua (people of the land), and the Maori Party, which launched in July 2004, looks set to become a key political player in New Zealand.

GET IN QUICK...
If not for its remote geographical location, New Zealand would be in greater danger of being strangled by the tourism hand that feeds it (tourism recently surpassed dairy as the nation's number one industry). By 2010, New Zealand's Tourism Research Council forecasts that the country will receive more than three million international visitors in a calendar year, which will mean that the number of visitors each year rivals its population.

New Zealand's compact size – a couple of weeks' travel top-to-bottom will give you a decent gander at the place – and its favourable exchange rate make it an unbeatable backpackers' destination, with arguably the world's best-equipped and best-value hostels, and a plethora of pristine places to pitch a tent. The tourist tide won't stem anytime soon, and the challenge now for New Zealand is maintaining that purity that is a huge part of its attraction.

...AND GET AWAY FROM IT ALL
New Zealanders are mad about outdoor

ALPINE GUIDES AMID AN
EXQUISITE ICE CAVE.

activities, and, with such a beautiful backyard, it's not hard to see why. Surfers can find secluded beach after secluded beach of surfable breaks – strap a board to the roof of your car and head to Northland's breathtaking beaches: Ninety Mile Beach, Ahipara, Mangawhai Heads and Cape Reianga; or try Gisborne, Piha or Raglan. Land-lovers can pull on a pair of boots and connect with locals on farmstays. There's solitude galore for trampers (trekkers) or try rafting the wild, rushing rivers or skiing/snowboarding the slopes. Urbanites can party till the wee hours in New Zealand's nightlife capital of Wellington or at lower-key joints such as the Grand Hotel in Helensville, a choice little pub out of Auckland that showcases up-and-coming local bands. While Queenstown might teem with revellers in peak season, less than a couple of hours away are villages like Wanaka, with its cosy bars, open fireplaces and entertaining characters. Yep, you can definitely still find your own corner of this 'Middle Earth'.

DEFINING EXPERIENCE
☺ After a sunset surf at Langs Beach near Waipu, perching on hay bales around a bonfire under a full moon, drinking Hawke's Bay Cabernet Sauvignon Merlot, and listening to the sound of the waves and the chilled roots/reggae/pop of Trinity Roots/Katchafire/Bic Runga

FESTIVALS & EVENTS
☺ New Zealand Sevens; Wellington; February; www.sevens.co.nz. This is the best two-day party anywhere! Costumes, rugby and beer – what more could you want? (Though it could be said *any* rugby game is an event in New Zealand.)

☺ New Zealand International Arts Festival; Wellington; February–March; www.nzfestival.telecom.co.nz. New Zealand's capital ups its already sizable cultural quotient with international performing artists at this festival.

☺ Golden Shears Sheep-Shearing Contest; Masterton; March.

☺ Pasifika Festival; Auckland; March; www.aucklandcity.govt.nz/whatson/events/pasifika. The South Pacific's largest art and culture celebration is free.

☺ Queenstown Winter Festival; Queenstown; July. Ten days of partying will make sure you don't feel the cold.

RECENT FAD! ☺

Possum fur and possum skin has become a fashion item in New Zealand. Even the most ardent animal lovers are all for eradicating these rogue marsupial pests, who are threatening the country's treasured forests by devouring 7 million tonnes of native trees' new growth each year. Possum-skin lingerie or possum-fur shoe insoles, anyone?

»

> *Fruit and vegetable shops line the back roads of New Zealand. The honesty system applies, which works very well. There's a box for you to put the payment for what you want to buy. Prices are low and the produce couldn't be fresher.*

- Mick Barrow, Australia

» HOT TOPICS OF THE DAY

- Curbing coastal development
- Maori land claims, particularly the debate over nationalising the public foreshore and seabed; this issue was a political football during the 2005 election
- The impact of migration
- The lack of a decent public-transport system in Auckland

HOT TIPS FOR TRAVELLERS

- For info on farmstays, head to www.ruralholidays.co.nz; or look into 'Wwoofing' (Willing Workers on Organic Farms; www.wwoof.co.nz) for food and board in exchange for labour.
- Surfers can drop in on www.surfing.co.nz for surf reports and the local low-down.

DO MENTION

- New Zealand's home-grown success stories: from stalwarts Neil and Tim Finn and Peter Jackson, to the avant-garde creations of fashion designers Karen Walker, Zambesi and Kate Sylvester
- The rugby, if New Zealand wins (especially against Australia)

DON'T MENTION

- Sheep jokes (they've herd…sorry heard 'em all before)
- The rugby, if New Zealand loses (especially to Australia)

RANDOM FACTS

- Sheep outnumber humans in New Zealand by approximately 10:1.
- 'God Save the Queen' is still officially the national anthem, although 'God Defend New Zealand' or the Maori war chant immortalised by the All Blacks, the haka, is more commonly performed.
- More than 10,000 women in New Zealand play rugby.

THINGS TO TAKE

- Fearlessness – for the endless extreme sports
- A wide-lens camera – to capture the panoramic scenery
- Sea sickness tablets/wristbands – for the interisland ferry crossing

THREE WORDS TO DESCRIBE THIS COUNTRY

- Adrenaline-inducing, awe-inspiring, aware
  - *Catherine Le Nevez*

MOST BIZARRE SIGHT! ★

New Zealand has an obsession with 'big things'; the Big L&P (Lemon & Paeroa) bottle in Paeroa honours the country's national fizzy drink, which was invented here in 1904 using local mineral water.

A GROUP OF YOUNG BOYS POSE ON A
TROPICAL BEACH ON SAVAI'I ISLAND, SAMOA

- **POPULATION**
  160,000
  (INDEPENDENT
  SAMOA), 58,000
  (AMERICAN SAMOA)

- **VISITORS PER YEAR**
  105,000

- **UNIT OF CURRENCY**
  TALA (ST;
  INDEPENDENT
  SAMOA)
  US DOLLAR ($;
  AMERICAN SAMOA)

- **COST OF A CUP
  OF COFFEE**
  ST3 = US$1.10

- **CAPITAL**
  APIA (INDEPENDENT
  SAMOA)
  PAGO PAGO
  (AMERICAN SAMOA)

- **LANGUAGE**
  SAMOAN, BUT MOST
  SPEAK ENGLISH

STRADDLING THE 171ST MERIDIAN. 'Paradise' is a word used by pretty much anyone trying to sell a holiday. The Samoan islands is one of the few places where the word can be used with sincerity.

They're home to pristine beaches traversing blue lagoons, native jungles with secluded waterfalls and crystal waters showing off some of the world's finest and most accessible coral reefs. Yes, the clichés abound, but they are true – and all in this small cluster of volcanic islands that is the Samoan islands.

Natural beauty can mean big money and like most of their neighbours in the Pacific with a small economy and few other natural resources, tourism counts for a lion's share of the national income. The Samoan islands have contentedly stayed off the bandwagon of development and package tours and gone along on their own merry way, business (or pleasure) as usual. But don't let size or tranquillity fool you, there are abundant bars and clubs, mostly in Apia, which is also the home of many a café and restaurant offering a diverse range of cuisine.

Samoa is an essential stamp in any serious surfer's passport, but it's no place for a novice (who doesn't want to leave in traction). For those of us not endowed with the passion and skill for crushing waves, there is ample to keep amused: snorkelling or canoeing around plentiful lagoons is high on the list for many travellers. When you tire of the water (yeah, right!) you can head for the gorgeous O Le Pupu-Pu'e National Park on 'Upolu or the National Park of American Samoa on Tutuila.

The author Robert Louis Stevenson spent the last four years of his life here and is quoted as saying of his hosts; *'they are easy, merry, and leisure-loving… Song is almost ceaseless'*. If that doesn't sound like a good time, I don't know what is.

UNCLE SAM & THE KIWIS
After Samoa's long history as one nation, the international politics of the 20th century chopped it in halves: Samoa or independent Samoa to the west and American Samoa to »

HOT TOPIC OF THE DAY!

Global warming (no pun intended) and rising sea levels are monumental challenges for the Samoan islands, with such a high proportion of the community barely above sea level. There are ongoing studies into a variety of contingency plans.

A *PAO-PAO* BOAT POWERS INTO THE SUNSET, VAISALA BEACH.

» the east. To cut a long story short, on 17 April 1900 all the chiefs of the eastern islands signed a deed of cession, putting the region under the jurisdiction of the US navy. Later, in 1905 it officially became known as 'American Samoa'. During the build-up to WWI, Britain was getting antsy about German interests in the area and put the hard word on New Zealand to take the western islands of Samoa under its wing. This wasn't popular with native Samoans and by the early 1960s independence was won.

CYCLONES & OTHER STORMS

On average a cyclone strikes every 10 to 15 years; the early '90s saw two – cyclones Ofa and Val – cause devastating damage. In combination with the daunting clean-up, a taro blight in 1993 wiped out the islands' staple crop. The Samoan islands have weathered the recent global and regional political troubles quite well. More tourists chose Samoa in the wake of a coup in Fiji in 2000, while independent Samoa was relatively unaffected by significant changes in global tourism following the September 11, 2001 attacks on New York. Though fewer people have been taking overseas holidays, a larger proportion are choosing quieter destinations. The 2002 bombing in Bali also pushed Samoa up the list for most people wanting a tropical holiday.

RECENT FAD! ✪

None really – hey if your home looked like this would you bother with sticker booths or Personal Digital Assistants?

FROM THE BEGINNING

It is believed the Samoan islands were initially settled by folk from Fiji and Tonga about 3500 years ago. Aside from a few run-ins with the neighbours (in AD 950 the Tongans had a short-lived notion of settling on Savai'i), Samoans have lived as one nation of many villages. Europeans started passing through in the mid-1700s, and by 1820 quite a few, mainly escaped convicts and retired whalers, had settled in Apia. By the late 1800s trade routes and fisheries had generated a great deal of international interest in the area. Britain, Germany and the USA very nearly came to fisticuffs; one Samoan chief described it as 'three large dogs snarling over one small bone'.

> *I was out riding on my motorcycle one Sunday in Samoa and stopped to ask for directions. It was nearly noon and after the father of the house had showed me where to go, he invited me in for lunch. Being in a family home with complete strangers, communing over food the mother had spent all morning preparing was a humbling feeling.*
>
> - Leah Oehlert

DEFINING EXPERIENCE

- After testing your nerve with the natural waterfall slide down the Papasee'a Sliding Rock into a jungle pool, jumping in your hired 4WD and heading to the beach for an afternoon of kayaking and snorkelling

FESTIVALS & EVENTS

- Independence; independent Samoa; June.

- Teuila Festival; Apia; first week of September. Named after Samoa's national flower, this is a week-long festival showcasing all that is Samoan: traditional games, canoe and *fautasi* (longboat) racing, traditional dance, music, handicraft displays and even tattooing.

- Palolo Rise; October & November. In the days following the full moons. The *palolo* is a sea worm and the 'rise' is its spawning season. Locals greet this time of year with zeal as the worm is regarded as a great delicacy.

DO MENTION

- Traditions. Samoans are warmly open to visitors that are respectfully curious about their culture and are more than happy to take the time to tell some of their ancient tales.

DON'T MENTION

- Japan's economic assistance and the strings that could be attached. This includes Samoa's vote regarding international whaling.

RANDOM FACTS

- Missionaries had an easier job than expected as Samoan and Christian creation myths bear uncanny similarities. Also, a legend involving Nafanua, the war goddess, prophesied that a new religion would find a stronghold on the islands.

- In the late 1800s, Germany, the USA and Britain each had warships in the port of Apia, all having been offered use of the harbour in return for protection. Their sabre-rattling came to an ominous end on 16 March 1889, when the harbour was struck by one of the world's worst cyclones.

- Coconut trees live to more than 70 years of age and will produce about 60 coconuts a year. It's estimated that 800 products are derived from coconut oil.

THINGS TO TAKE

- Pack thongs (flip-flops), baggy shorts and insect repellent.

- Toiletries can be unpredictable, rather expensive and worth packing rather than buying them when you arrive.

HOT TIPS FOR TRAVELLERS

- Leave your haggling prowess at home, the price asked is the one you're expected to pay.

- Chill out on Sundays; most Samoans are church-going and frown on raucous behaviour on Sundays.

THREE WORDS TO DESCRIBE THIS COUNTRY

- Tropically, blissfully shipwrecked
  - Robert Harding

MOST BIZARRE SIGHT!

During the 'Palolo Rise' (see Festivals & Events left) the spawning waters look like green vermicelli soup. Most Samoans have their favourite recipe, though some connoisseurs pluck them straight from the water to consume raw.

COOK ISLANDS

Wafer-thin cays and far-flung atolls, blue lagoons and superb reef snorkelling, white-sand beaches and verdant volcanic mountains, a slow pace and friendly people – what's not to like about the Cook Islands? Lascivious dancing and beer bashes in the bush have survived years of missionary zeal. Rarotonga, the gorgeous main island, has densely forested mountains. The isolated islands of the northern Cooks receive almost no visitors, except for the occasional delighted yachtie. Get yourself stranded on an outer island and hope your return-trip freighter doesn't come back any time soon.

FIJI

Lapped by warm azure waters, fringed with vibrant coral reefs and cloaked in the emerald green of the tropics, Fiji is a paradise seeker's dream come true. Its sun-soaked, white-sand beaches and resorts are bliss, but only a slice of the country's allure. The diving and snorkelling mecca also has rugged highland interiors that offer stunning landscapes, remote villages and treks through extinct volcanic craters. Giant waterfalls plunge through rainforest in well maintained reserves while archaeological sites dotted throughout the country allude to Fiji's mysterious past. Fiji is an interesting blend of Melanesian, Polynesian, Micronesian, Indian, Chinese and European influences.

KIRIBATI

Blessed with billions of stunning fish swarming over myriad coral reefs and plenty of WWII wrecks, Kiribati (pronounced kiri-bahs) is a hidden island paradise in the Pacific Ocean. The atolls are scattered on either side of the equator so the weather is dependably warm. Modernity is slowly rearing its head, but locals still welcome travellers as rarely seen curios. There are few organised activities on offer, though it's not hard to find diving and game fishing with local people, and the less adventurous will find idyllic beaches are never far away.

MARSHALL ISLANDS

The Marshalls are made up of more than one thousand flat coral islands of white-sand beaches and turquoise lagoons. Like other Pacific paradises there's spectacular diving, lush tropical greenery and beautiful beaches. The Marshallese people retain many of their pre-colonial crafts and traditions, especially on the outer islands. Sadly, many of the Marshallese still struggle with the after-effects of the 20th-century's Atomic Age. Bikini Atoll is the most famous of the nuclear-testing sites of the 1960s, though inhabitants of other islands also suffer from radiation poisoning. Many islands remain too contaminated to be resettled or visited.

MICRONESIA

There's something to be said for a country that has tried to outlaw ties and baseball caps. Despite being firmly tied to the USA's economic and political apron strings, each of the four island states has maintained its own culture: Kosrae remains a casual backwater; Pohnpei a jungle paradise; bright, bubbly Chuuk attracts divers with its sunken WWII wrecks; and unconventional Yap is a traditional centre, famous for its massive stone money. One of the Federated States of Micronesia's sources of income is selling its internet domain name (.fm) to radio stations.

NAURU

Nauru was once the rich kid of the Pacific, wealthy through phosphates. But now the stocks of bird poop have been exhausted, mining has utterly destroyed the landscape, and the island survives on handouts from Australia in return for hosting a detention centre for asylum seekers. With fresh water, vegetables and power in short supply, and a new detention centre being built on Christmas Island, Nauru's future is in the balance. On a positive note: a colourful reef dotted with sunken WWII wrecks surrounds the island, and makes great diving.

NEW CALEDONIA

Kanaks and *café au lait*, blackbirding and barrier reefs, Melanesian massacres and *menus du jour* – New Caledonia exemplifies that one person's bread is another person's pain. It's still very much a colony of France, and the motherland has sent in the marines more than once to keep the local population from rioting. Political unrest aside, New Caledonia attracts divers and tourists who flock to experience the diverse landscapes of sunny beaches, rugged mountains, rolling plains, cool forests and lush tropical vegetation. With a nod to local custom and an open mind, a trip to New Caledonia will be unforgettable.

PALAU

The Republic of Palau is becoming a byword for an underwater wonderland, showcasing Micronesia's richest flora and fauna, both on land and beneath the waves. It's a snorkeller's paradise, with an incredible spectrum of coral, fish and sumo-sized giant clams. Blue Corner is Palau's most popular dive. There's a good chance this bounty will survive, as Palauans are active on environmental issues, particularly regarding overtourism, overfishing, erosion, litter and pollution.

PAPUA NEW GUINEA

Papua New Guinea is a raw, remarkably untamed land, filled with great mountain ranges, mighty rivers and stunning beaches, and five million people living much the way they have for thousands of years. PNG can be a dangerous place, but it's not as bad as commonly perceived. You could get unlucky, but very few people do and if you use common sense you're more likely to be smothered in smiles than encounter difficulties.

PITCAIRN ISLANDS

The Pitcairn Islands are not on any international air routes and getting there is strictly for the determined, but that can be precisely the attraction. Beautifully green and lush, and with a population you could easily seat in a city bus, tiny Pitcairn is most famous as the hideaway settlement for the notorious HMS *Bounty* mutineers. With points of interest with names like John Catch-a-Cow and Bitey Bitey, the antiquated language of the mutineers' descendants is an attraction in itself.

SOLOMON ISLANDS

The Solomons is a stunning archipelago of pristine beaches, atolls, lagoons and reefs where the simplicity of life is an attraction in itself. It's hard to imagine that not so long ago the ancestors of today's friendly and laid-back islanders were head-hunting cannibals. Ancient arts are still practised and WWII debris is strewn across the country. This is a famous dive destination with its colourful reefs, underwater topography and sunken war wrecks. Despite a paradisiacal setting, the Solomons has suffered from ethnic conflict and the areas of Guadalcanal and Malaita continue to experience a breakdown in law and order.

TAHITI & FRENCH POLYNESIA

Don't just fantasise about tropical islands dotted with palm trees and aquamarine lagoons; they really do exist. In Tahiti and its neighbouring islands the air is heavy with not only tropical humidity but also romance and history. People come to French Polynesia to live it up in stylish resorts, scuba dive in lagoons teeming with tropical fish, gorge on the unique mix of French and Polynesian cuisine and, basically, experience a little French chic mixed with South Pacific charm. Escape to the place that inspired Paul Gauguin and Robert Louis Stevenson.

TONGA

Tonga has long beguiled and enchanted travellers with its rich cultural heritage, friendly people and awe-inspiring natural beauty. The modern world has crept into the kingdom with LA gangster wear more common than traditional waist mats on the streets of Tongatapu; this very conservative country struggles with inevitable change. Only its outstanding natural splendour remains constant – from the rainforests of 'Eua, the beaches of Ha'apai and the waterways of Vava'u to the magnificent diving throughout the country's waters.

TUVALU

If hustle and bustle don't appeal, Tuvalu might just be the place. Time moves at its own pace in this tiny Pacific nation. With just a handful of tourists a year, you're likely to have the beach to yourself. The tiny group of islands and atolls, however, are seriously endangered by rising sea levels caused by global warming, so you'd better be quick.

VANUATU

An independent country for only 25 years, Vanuatu is a land of volcanoes and lush forests, with a kaleidoscope of cultures and more than 100 indigenous languages. The ni-Vanuatu, are among the most welcoming people in the Pacific. A snorkellers' and divers' mecca, there are countless coral reefs and the world's largest diveable WWII shipwreck: the SS *President Coolidge*. Port Vila is the bustling hub of tourism, but the more remote islands offer an insight into a complex culture and hard-to-beat natural beauty.

EUROPE.

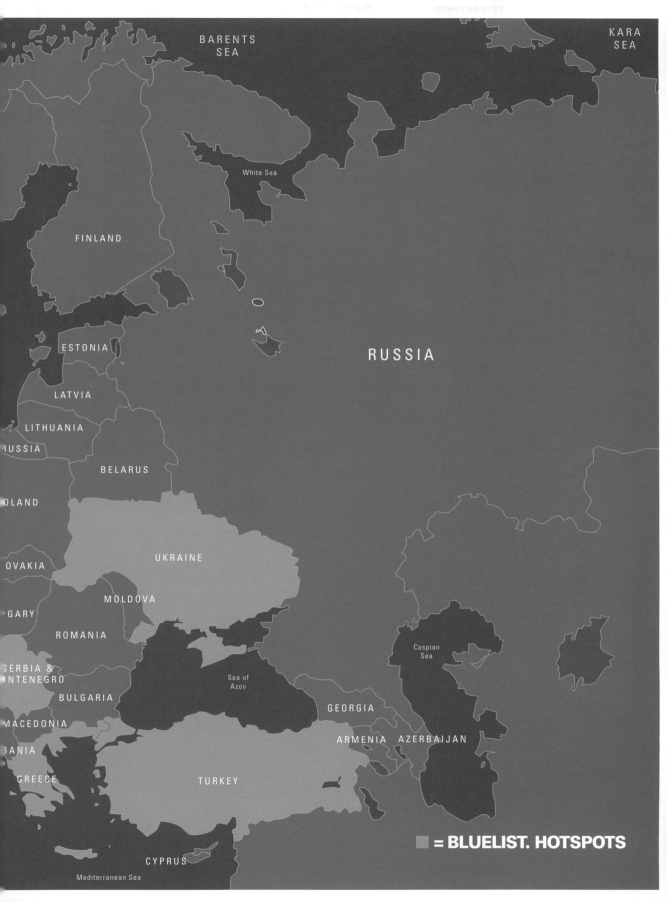

CROATIA.

VITAL STATISTICS

⊙ **POPULATION**
4.4 MILLION

⊙ **VISITORS PER YEAR**
4 MILLION

⊙ **UNIT OF CURRENCY**
CROATIAN KUNA (KN)

⊙ **COST OF A CUP OF COFFEE**
10KN = US$1.71

⊙ **CAPITAL**
ZAGREB

⊙ **LANGUAGES**
CROATIAN, SERBIAN, ITALIAN, SLOVENIAN, HUNGARIAN

DRESSED IN BLACK, AN ELDERLY WOMAN PROVIDES AN AUSTERE BACKDROP TO HER WHIMSICAL POSIES FOR SALE, KORČULA.

★ **NEVER SAY NEVER AGAIN.** Croatia was recently tipped to be Europe's hottest tourist destination, topping all sorts of polls and winning all sorts of awards, although by the time you read this, Antarctica will probably be the 'new Croatia', given the fickle nature of travel trends.

Beyond the hype, Croatia has always been feted as one of Europe's most stunning jewels, with its 1000km (620mi) stretch of Adriatic coast, inspiring (though rocky) beaches and more than 1000 idyllic islands to choose from. Unsurprisingly, by the end of the 1980s, 10 million visitors a year were swarming to this Eastern-bloc country that looked, felt and even smelt like the Mediterranean, but came at a fraction of the price of Spain, Italy or France. But the love affair suffered coitus interruptus in 1991 when Croatia, then part of Yugoslavia, declared independence while its Serbian enclave, Krajina, declared itself independent of Croatia. All hell broke loose for the next five years as civil war erupted, and heavy fighting decimated many lives and a large chunk of the Croatian countryside.

When a ceasefire was declared in 1995, Croatia went off the world stage for the better part of a decade, re-emerging in recent times with war scars healed and a robust tourist infrastructure in place. Now, travellers are being lured back to that sublime coastline and the giddy thrill of hopping between olive-grove and lemon-tree encrusted islands, accompanied by the type of sun-ripened, old-world charm that's rapidly becoming scarce in Europe's overpopulated, overdeveloped west.

ATTRACTIVE, ADRIATIC & AFFORDABLE

Croatia might not be as much of a bargain as the rest of Eastern Europe, but it's relatively affordable compared to out-of-control Western Europe, and wafting over everything is that dreamy Adriatic airiness, a pungent blend of Italian, Austrian, Slavic and Mediterranean influences. Along the Dalmatian coast you'll find some outstanding seafood, as well as a range of organic produce (Eastern Europe's standard

»

PRETTY PASTEL-HUED SHOPS IN CAVTAT, DUBROVNIK.

meat-and-potatoes diet is a real no-no here). Meanwhile, Italian is an official language on the Istrian peninsula and German is often a second language in the interior. So much for Yugoslavian dictator Tito's dream of Slavic unity: Croatia always was a bubbling cauldron of exotica that had no place behind the Iron Curtain.

Another 'tick' on the discerning traveller's list is Croatia's position at the nexus of Europe: train connections from Zagreb radiate out to Germany, Austria, Italy, Hungary, Slovenia, Bosnia-Herzegovina and Serbia & Montenegro, while ferries link the nation with Italy and Greece.

All up, Croatia today is probably much like an old-timer's nostalgic remembrance of cheap, carefree Greece in the 1970s, before rampant price increases swept down from northern Europe like an infected mushroom. But Croatia has 1185 of its own beautiful islands, islets and reefs – so who needs Greece?

DEFINING EXPERIENCE

- ◎ Sunbathing naked on a secluded island under a lemon tree while feasting on »

FROM BYRON TO MADONNA (VIA BONO)

Croatia's shifting status can be measured by the type of celebrities it attracts. In the 19th and 20th centuries, it was the playground of a cultured few who were 'in the know'. The romantic walled city of Dubrovnik was a haven for poet Lord Byron and playwright George Bernard Shaw, and later for writers Agatha Christie, who honeymooned there and in Split, Vladimir Nabokov, who spent many summers in Opatija, and James Joyce, who taught English in Pula.

Much later, during the height of the 'Homeland War', you couldn't get a proper celeb here for love nor money – the only big names to pay any attention to the region were bleeding-heart do-gooders like Bono. But now that Croatia is back on the map, who should turn up? None other than Madonna and Guy Ritchie, name-checked by the tourist board as recent visitors (along with the Sultan of Oman). That might tell you something about the 21st century, so get in quick – before more faded stars jump on the bandwagon.

RECENT FAD! ◎

Mobile phones: Croatians have more mobile phones (2.3 million) than they do fixed lines (1.8 million).

" *Croatia has come back with a vengeance as a great holiday destination. Good food and wine, beautiful people and beautiful scenery. I return every time I go to Europe – it's very addictive!* "

- Mark Vukoss, Australia

» *burek* (Turkish-style pie), sausage-and-potato casserole and mushroom soup with buckwheat and listening to 'turbofolk' music

FESTIVALS & EVENTS

- ✪ Dubrovnik International Film Festival; Dubrovnik; late May.

- ✪ International Children's Festival; Sibenik; first week of July. Promotes the 'aesthetic education of children and youth' with puppeteers, filmmakers, actors, poets and musicians.

- ✪ Split Summer Festival; Split; mid-July–mid-August. Pop music, exhibitions, opera, concerts, dance and street theatre.

- ✪ Dubrovnik Summer Festival; Dubrovnik; July and August. Classical music, theatre, concerts, opera and dance presented on a series of open-air stages.

DO MENTION

- ✪ How stylish the locals are. A point of local pride and possibly a reaction against the West's continual stereotyping of Eastern European fashion: ill-fitting suits, bad haircuts etc.

DON'T MENTION

- ✪ The rights or wrongs of Croatia's 'Homeland War'. Not even Croats can agree on this one.

RANDOM FACTS

- ✪ The necktie originated in Croatia 350 years ago; it was first worn by the military.

- ✪ The first ballpoint pen (later patented by Biro) and working parachute were invented in Croatia.

- ✪ Shakespeare's *Twelfth Night* used Dalmatia as its setting.

MOST BIZARRE SIGHT

- ✪ The mummies of Vodnjan: these desiccated remains of centuries-old saints whose bodies mysteriously failed to decompose are considered to have magical powers.

THINGS TO TAKE

- ✪ Rubber footwear: for wading into the water along the rocky coast

- ✪ Highest-rating sunscreen

- ✪ Coffee: to offset the Croatian brew (which might be a shock to those coming from the West)

HOT TIPS FOR TRAVELLERS

- ✪ Take the advice of the tourist board: 'Local gossip is saying that the people of Split are the best and most passionate lovers in Croatia'.

- ✪ Some remote areas still contain landmines, including the Danube region in eastern Slavonia and Krajina. Make sure you don't stray into fields or abandoned villages.

THREE WORDS TO DESCRIBE THIS COUNTRY

- ✪ Hottest tourist destination

- *Simon Sellars*

HOLIDAYMAKERS KICK BACK ON THE NORTH NORFOLK COAST.

VITAL STATISTICS

ENGLAND.

- **POPULATION**
  51 MILLION
- **VISITORS PER YEAR**
  21 MILLION
- **UNIT OF CURRENCY**
  BRITISH POUND (£)
- **COST OF A CUP OF COFFEE**
  £0.50 TO £2 =
  US$0.88 TO US$3.50
- **CAPITAL**
  LONDON
- **LANGUAGE**
  ENGLISH

STRONGER THAN EVER. For years the English have enjoyed the popular pastime of putting themselves, their towns and their country down, so much so that an illustrated book entitled *Crap Towns* has been flying off the bookshelves in the last few years.

However, things have definitely started to change. England's traditional façade of timeless rural scenery, obsessive politeness and innumerable tea cosies is beginning to crumble under the weight of a new image: frantic urban regeneration, cutting-edge cities, and a new-found cosmopolitan attitude that reaches far beyond the London boroughs and has everyone – locals and tourists alike – demanding better quality and service.

Couple all this with the country's defiant attitude and refusal to scurry for cover after the London bombings in July 2005 and England suddenly seems to be riding the crest of a wave. General economic stability and the capital's successful 2012 Olympic bid only serve to support the theory that England is stronger than ever, more united in its approach, more proud of its achievements, more positive about the future and staunchly unwilling to let anyone take that confidence away.

TEACHING AN OLD DOG NEW TRICKS

As if given a taste of how things could be, discerning punters now expect standards to be on a par with anywhere else in Europe and, after years of flatlining, the tourist industry in England has finally cottoned on and leapt into the 21st century.

The crippling chintz, swirly carpets and faded velvet of rural B&Bs that were once the preserve of blue-rinse holiday makers have given way to a new brand of trendy accommodation options in all price brackets. The quality of food has changed enormously too and, although you'll have no problem finding a greasy spoon for a cholesterol-ridden lasagne and chips, there's a wealth of gastro pubs, gourmet restaurants and glorious delis taking over the streets of England's cities and rural towns. US-based *Gourmet Magazine* has gone as far as to say that London is 'The best place to eat on the planet', while 14 of the 50 Best Restaurants »

RECENT FAD!

Cosmetic surgery: the number of procedures undertaken in Britain rose by 60% in 2004.

MAKE SPRAY WHILE THE SUN
SHINES IN PICCADILLY CIRCUS.

ENGLAND.

» in the World for 2005, as voted for by *Restaurant* magazine's panel of industry experts, are in England. Even the schools are getting in on the act with celebrity chef Jamie Oliver spearheading the campaign for healthier school dinners.

COMING OF AGE

So it seems England is coming of age, finally balancing the picturesque rural villages of honey-coloured cottages, thatched roofs and rose gardens against equally seductive boutique hotels, trendy restaurants and some of Europe's edgiest clubs. It's your choice whether to take in a lazy afternoon tea complete with clotted cream and strawberries; traipse across the hills in search of ruined castles and medieval abbeys; lope from one giant outdoor music festival to another; or take your place in the stands to watch some of the world's finest footballers battle it out on the pitch.

England is an incredibly diverse destination with scenery that bounds from wild, windswept beaches to snow-capped peaks and buzzing cities with vibrant nightlife. It has history by the truckload and now a delicious sense of a country that is brimming with pride and eager to show its best secrets to the world. Visit now to taste the passion, the pride and the new-found sophistication.

DEFINING EXPERIENCE

○ Hiking across the hills and moors, enjoying that glorious break in the clouds causing magnificent shards of light to illuminate the stone cottages and majestic fens, before stumbling through the door of a thatched pub to dry out by a roaring fire and down a pint of the landlord's finest ale

FESTIVALS & EVENTS

○ University Boat Race; Putney; April. The annual clash between Oxford's and Cambridge's top rowing teams and one of the most popular English sporting events of the year.

○ Queen Elizabeth's official 80th birthday celebrations; countrywide; June 2006. The Queen's actual birthday is in April but special commemorative events are planned throughout the country in June.

○ Henley Royal Regatta; Henley-on-Thames; first week of July. This five-day rowing festival attracts the champagne-swilling, the rich and the beautiful.

"

In the summer of 1995 my friend and I – both of us teachers – were in Dorset, England, determined to walk wherever we went. We walked into Tolpuddle the day of the yearly celebration of the Tolpuddle Martyrs, the original (in the world) union members! A teachers' union invited us to walk with them and we did, supporting union efforts around the world, we felt, now knowing about the difficulties of the first unionists. What a crazy thing to walk into, in a mild little flowery country-side in June!

"

- Lynn Chong, USA

ENGLAND.

- The Proms; London; mid-July–early September. This is a massive classical music festival culminating in a triumphant, flag-waving night at the Royal Albert Hall.

- Reading and Leeds Festivals; August. Some of the country's largest rock, pop and dance music festivals; in the absence of Glastonbury in 2006 they'll be bigger than ever.

WHAT'S HOT...
- Awareness bracelets

WHAT'S NOT...
- Crazy Frog ring tones

HOT TOPICS OF THE DAY
- Immigration and asylum
- The state of the government (a perennial complaint)
- World Cup 2006

MOST BIZARRE SIGHT
- A bundle of black pudding (a sausage of congealed pig's blood) swaddled in ladies tights (stockings) being hurled at a stack of Yorkshire puddings 7m (20ft) off the ground. The World Black Pudding Throwing Championship takes place annually on the second Sunday in September in the village of Ramsbottom near Manchester and celebrates the ancient rivalry between Lancashire and Yorkshire.

DO MENTION
- London's plans for the 2012 Olympics

DON'T MENTION
- The introduction of the euro or the European constitution unless you can handle a tirade from a nation of tabloid-informed Eurosceptics

RANDOM FACTS
- Britons drink more than 165 million cups of tea every day.
- Percy Shaw, a Yorkshire man, invented the cat's eye in 1933.
- The world's most widely supported football club is Manchester United with a total of 152,000 paid-up members and 45,000 season ticket holders.

THINGS TO TAKE
- An umbrella or raincoat: no-one comes here for the weather
- A taste for real ale
- Comfortable shoes for all that rambling over dales and hills and through those glorious National Trust properties

HOT TIPS FOR TRAVELLERS
- See the cities then hire a car and lose yourself on the stunning back roads of Dorset, the Cotswolds, the Lake District or the Yorkshire Dales.
- Queue patiently at every opportunity and never try to push ahead, and if you're not walking up the escalator stand to the right.
- For comprehensive information on all things English visit www.bbc.co.uk.

THREE WORDS TO DESCRIBE THIS COUNTRY
- Diverse, dynamic, damp

- Etain O'Carroll

THE VALLÉE BLANCHE, CHAMONIX VALLEY.

FRANCE.

VITAL STATISTICS

- **POPULATION**
  60.6 MILLION
- **VISITORS PER YEAR**
  76 MILLION
- **UNIT OF CURRENCY**
  EURO (€)
- **COST OF A CUP OF COFFEE**
  €1.20 TO €5 = US$1.40 TO US$6
- **CAPITAL**
  PARIS
- **LANGUAGES**
  FRENCH, CATALAN, BASQUE, BRETON, CORSICAN

TOP DOG. Artists, designers, writers and philosophers have flocked here for centuries making France an epicentre of European art and culture. The lifestyle, scenery and sybaritic pleasures that attracted them have also made it the world's favourite tourist destination.

France is the undisputed king of tourism, attracting more visitors than any other country and yet doing so without resorting to crass attractions or needless commercialism.

On top of this the French are so enamoured by their own image that 90% of holidays taken by the French are domestic. For the rest of us, bombarded with images of the Eiffel Tower, the Arc de Triomphe, the Louvre and the Moulin Rouge, it's easy to feel like you already know the country, but in reality the iconic images of Paris are just the tip of the iceberg.

France is such a diverse country that it easily justifies its global position as tourism leader. It's a seductive place with an intoxicating mix of rural chateaux, lavender fields, poplar-lined roads and romantic cities. The food lives up to its wonderful reputation, the museums and galleries are packed with some of the world's finest artworks and the scenery is simply stunning.

UNEASY TIMES

Below the glossy surface, France isn't looking so good. Support for President Jacques Chirac is at an all-time low and the man hotly tipped to succeed him, Nicolas Sarkozy, is far from popular. The economy is troubled, a social crisis is looming and the French themselves are beginning to feel a little agitated. Public life seems to be lacking direction since the French rejected the EU constitution and lost the bid for the 2012 Olympics. Once at the heart of EU political life, France now wonders where it fits in; the agricultural subsidies on which the country relies are under threat and, without the impetus of a major sporting event to prepare for, capital projects have been put on hold.

In Paris, stifling bureaucracy rather than lack of investment has been blamed

ATTACK OF THE 6000FT MODEL, CANNES.

for François Pinault's decision to abandon a refurbishment of the huge Renault Museum and instead locate his vast contemporary art collection in Venice. Either way it was a major loss for the city. Add this to the French love of going on strike, wine harvests being affected by global warming and record droughts that have prompted a ban on the filling of swimming pools in many municipalities, and the French are wondering if even their much-needed tourist industry is under threat. This general malaise isn't helped by elevated oil prices and rising inflation and many fear the country may soon begin to slip into depression.

CULTURAL DEBATE

French culture may seem robust to the rest of the world, but the French are worried that it is being increasingly threatened. Recent measures to preserve French culture include restrictions on the use of English-language words in advertising and restrictions on airtime given to foreign music on national radio stations.

France has always prided itself on its openness and its welcoming attitude towards immigrants; however, in recent times this attitude has been called into question. The ban on the use of religious symbols in state schools was largely seen as an attempt to forbid Muslim girls from wearing a *hijab* (headscarf). Fears of terrorism have led to the tightening of regulations by the Minister of Interior, which has prompted the dramatic French to complain that their country is now a police state where fines are issued to everyone at the drop of a hat.

For the visitor though, these issues rarely impinge on that quintessential French holiday experience. After all, this is the country that virtually shuts down for the month of August when everyone is *en vacances* (on holiday). The nation that loves to love, strike, smoke and grumble is still a potent mix for any visitor. The question is whether it's still such a great place to live.

DEFINING EXPERIENCE

⚙ Breakfasting alfresco on freshly baked baguettes, some fine camembert and a bowl of strong coffee, followed by a short shopping spree for designer labels – accompanied by your Yorkshire terrier (in matching outfit, of course) – and a late lunch at a chic streetside *brasserie* (restaurant)

»

FRANCE.

"

At a pension in Aix-en-Provence, I took a room which included breakfast. The first morning at the breakfast table, I found that breakfast consisted of hard-crusted French bread left over from the previous evening's meal and a small juice glass half filled with white wine. Simply dunk the bread in the wine for a 'fruity' healthful breakfast and stay buzzed all day just like the owner!

"

- Thom Sacco, USA

» RECENT FAD

- The *cinq à sept* (five to seven) after-work cocktail hour has become the civilised way to socialise over a few drinks before returning home to the family.

FESTIVALS & EVENTS

- Bordeaux Wine Festival; June–July. The wine hub of France hosts local food and wine sampling, a giant public banquet, free concerts, fireworks and wine-barrel racing.

- Tall Ships Race; St Malo; July. The 50th anniversary of the Tall Ships Race will take place in 2006 following its original course from St Malo to Lison with a large fleet of historic boats.

- Bastille Day; July. France commemorates the storming of the Bastille in 1789 and the start of the French Revolution with fireworks, free concerts and street festivals all over the country.

- Paris Plage; mid-July–end of August. Some 3km (2mi) of the quays on the Right Bank of the Seine in Paris are turned into a giant beach, complete with white sand, palm trees, sunbeds and parasols.

- Nancy Jazz Pulsations; mid-October. Nancy's thriving festival covers all jazz-influenced music from ska and blues to progressive jazz.

- 24 Heures du Mans; Le Mans; June. A famous 24-hour car endurance race with teams of three drivers.

DO MENTION

- World Cup 2006. Can the French crawl back to glory?

DON'T MENTION

- Immigration, asylum and racism – no-one in France wants to admit there is any problem with this issue

- The state of the social-security system and the plans to reform it

RANDOM FACTS

- The French consume an average of 60L of wine per person per year.

- Between 8am and 8pm, the music played on French radio stations must not contain more than 40% by foreign artists.

- Frogs are now a protected species in France and frogs' legs are now imported – mainly from Indonesia.

- The metric system was invented by the French Academy of Sciences in 1790.

THINGS TO TAKE

- A penknife for cutting up the brie on all those afternoon picnics

- Your best clothes – keeping up with the French fashionistas is a tough act

HOT TIP FOR TRAVELLERS

- Keep up to date on all things French at www.franceguide.com.

THREE WORDS TO DESCRIBE THIS COUNTRY

- Sophisticated, seductive, romantic

- *Etain O'Carroll*

MOST BIZARRE SIGHT! ✪

Paris Roller night: every Friday night from 10pm to 1am a group of up to 20,000 skaters make their way around Paris on a 20km to 30km (12mi to 20mi) route. Join in if you can skate and brake.

A WONDERFUL WHITEWASHED STREETSCAPE ON SANTORINI, THE CYCLADES.

VITAL STATISTICS

GREECE.

○ **POPULATION**
10.7 MILLION

○ **VISITORS PER YEAR**
13 MILLION

○ **UNIT OF CURRENCY**
EURO (€)

○ **COST OF A CUP OF GREEK COFFEE**
€2 = US$2.40

○ **CAPITAL**
ATHENS

○ **LANGUAGE**
MODERN GREEK

THE BEST OF BOTH WORLDS. Much is made these days of how very modern – and European – Greece has become. Athens has a sparkly new airport and metro, and the whole country got a bit swept up for the Olympics.

The locals themselves seem to have developed sophisticated tastes – designer sunglasses, ecru-coloured couches and an interest in reinvented traditional cuisine, for example, are must-haves in this newly arrived material world.

But though times are changing, much of the population is, thankfully, too old to be bothered changing with them. It is still possible to visit Greece and feel as though you've arrived via time machine instead of aeroplane – ancient ladies in black walk miles to tend their vegetable gardens, and old men while away the hours playing backgammon at their favourite café, or *kafeneio* (male-only coffee house), on the village square. And even though an EU-funded road-building blitz has transformed many of the country's potholed dirt tracks, the majority of vehicles travelling on these brand-new two-lane blacktops are donkeys, mules and flocks of sheep with bells on.

So the really good news is that, despite all the incursions of the modern world, the quintessential charms of Greece – spirited people, unspoilt villages, sumptuous countryside, glittering glassy seas, quaint candle-lit chapels and lively tavernas offering up fragrant herb-laden dishes – are not in the least depleted. All of these things can be found just about everywhere, just a few feet from your beach umbrella.

DEFINING EXPERIENCE

○ Anything involving the sea: skimming across Santorini's caldera in a speeding *caique* (small boat) at sundown; eating freshly caught, charcoal-grilled fish at a beachside taverna; floating naked on the Aegean's lakelike salty waters

FESTIVALS & EVENTS

○ Easter; March/April. Easter is the most important event on the Orthodox calendar. »

RECENT FAD! ⊛

Sampling the country's infinite range of ouzos, especially those from the island of Lesvos (also known as Mytilini). For a novelty souvenir, bring home a little bottle of Mini, which features a cheerleader-style girl in a miniskirt on its label.

A FISHING BOAT MOORED OFF THE
SOUTH COAST OF CRETE.

GREECE.

Prime spots to experience Easter in all its glory are Patmos, where there's a ritualistic washing of the disciples' feet on Maundy Thursday; Crete's Agios Nikolaos, where an effigy of Judas is burned; and Arahova, which celebrates in grand style with uphill races for the elderly.

- ✪ Eurovision Song Contest; Athens; 18–20 May 2006.
- ✪ Posidonia Cup offshore yacht race;

Faliron Bay, Piraeus; June. This event is big news internationally in shipping and yachting fraternities. The race is followed by the Posidonia Exhibition, a biennial showcase of shipping news, products and services.

DO MENTION
- ✪ The Elgin Marbles (a section of the Parthenon 'stolen' by Britain and now on display in the British Museum) and you'll

ON A WINNING STREAK?

While the jury's still out on whether or not Greece will ever manage to recoup any of the €11 billion it splashed out for the 2004 Olympic Games, there is no doubt that the money spent on public works gave the country a massive leg up into the 21st century. Athens' efficient metro and tram service and new airport, for instance, were long overdue and the Olympics provided the motivation for the government to get its act together. Aside from the big wins of the Olympics (disgraced runner Kostas Kederis and huge debts aside), Greece surprised all and sundry with victories in the UEFA (Union of European Football Associations) Euro 2004 soccer competition and the 2005 Eurovision Song Contest.

Although increased tourist numbers were supposed to flow on predictably after the Olympics, rising prices and other less-tangible factors seem to be sending many travellers elsewhere, especially to Greece's nemesis, Turkey. The government is now pouring millions of euros into upgrading top-end hotels and extolling the benefits of playing golf (of all things) on Greek soil. Perhaps the march of progress will erase the visitor's chance of encountering what remains of traditional Greek culture sooner than we think.

"

My first time in Santorini we arrived very early morning – it was still dark. My friend drove us up to Imerovigli from the port with his motorbike – I had no idea (not even seen a photo) what the place looked like, and all I could see was blackness around me. He took me to a spot and we waited for the sun to rise over the caldera – the most unforgettable experience and view!

"

- 'fLUffYbinks', Thorn Tree

RANDOM FACTS
- Greeks consume more olive oil per capita than any other nationality – a whopping 26L each year.
- Tree trunks are often painted white with lime to deter ants.
- According to an old law passed in 1911 that is still valid, the punishment for stealing a beehive or a sheep is exile.

THINGS TO TAKE
- Sunglasses, sunhat and sunscreen
- Sensible shoes, and flip-flops for traversing hot sand
- Mobile phone (buy a local SIM card for 20)

HOT TIPS FOR TRAVELLERS
- For delicious food prepared with love, head to the countryside – little *kafeneia* and tavernas may only have a couple of dishes languishing in the oven but they are sure to be sensational.
- Island-hopping by ferry can be a wonderful way to explore Greece, but beware of constructing an overly ambitious itinerary based on timetables found in guidebooks and on websites – there is no definitive source for ferry timetables and they are always in flux. Flexibility is the key component of your island-hopping holiday; if you can, go where the wind takes you…
- Between 2pm and 5pm most shops close for the siesta, even in the cities; in rural areas all goes quiet and the locals take a nap. Any attempt to get things done during siesta will quickly become frustrating, so take a cue from the Greeks and use this time to relax.
- Don't enter a church or chapel unless you're appropriately dressed – that means long pants for men and covered shoulders and knees for women – and do not go behind the iconostasis.

THREE WORDS TO DESCRIBE THIS COUNTRY
- Chaotic, seductive, addictive

- Brigitte Barta

rouse a predictable – and justified – response defending Greece's claim to this archaeological treasure.

DON'T MENTION
- Contentious Macedonia and be careful about discussing Albania. Even though many Albanians are now well assimilated in Greece, there is still some racist hysteria about their presence in the country.

WHAT'S HOT…
- Arabian nights: anything and everything to do with the Orient – Indian décor, Middle Eastern cuisine, Turkish baths, belly dancing and even Eastern thought – is all the rage.

WHAT'S NOT…
- US foreign policy: Greeks are often fiercely anti-American, especially in relation to events such as the bombing of Kosovo and the invasion of Iraq. These sentiments go a long way back – there is a widely held belief the US interfered in Greek affairs during the bitter Civil War and that there was suspicious CIA involvement in the military coup that took place in 1967.

MOST BIZARRE SIGHT!

Mt Athos, the picturesque third prong of the peninsulas of Halkidiki, is no ordinary holiday spot. For a start, it's off limits to all females – and that even includes nanny goats. Home to a collection of 20 Orthodox monasteries, each looking like a spectacular medieval castle frozen in time, the peninsula is one of the largest spiritual havens on earth.

GREENLAND.

VITAL STATISTICS

- **POPULATION**
  56,375
- **VISITORS PER YEAR**
  32,000
- **UNIT OF CURRENCY**
  DANISH KRONE (DKR)
- **COST OF A BEER**
  DKR25 TO DKR40 =
  US$3 TO US$7
- **CAPITAL**
  NUUK TOWN
  (GODTHÅB)
- **LANGUAGES**
  GREENLANDIC,
  DANISH

SMILING INUIT WOMEN IN TRADITIONAL, EMBROIDERED COSTUME.

AN EMERGING TRAVEL DESTINATION. So you've stayed in Sweden's ice hotel, been to Santa's place in Lapland and survived Reykjavík's *runtur* pub crawl. But, hold on, don't hang up your thermal undies quite yet – now it's time for some real Arctic adventures.

Ice-covered, remote Greenland is the stuff of legendary explorers and *Boy's Own* stories, inspiring colossal trips and even bigger tales. This, the biggest noncontinental island on earth and 80% covered in ice, is the land that saw off the Vikings.

It's never been overrun, giving those people who *have* clung to its coastline barely a subsistence living. So why on earth would you visit now? Greenland is pricey, with most visitors' money being swallowed up by transport (there are very few roads). It's tough and has a tendency to be rather chilly. But for size, space and jaw-dropping amazement, it's on its own. Photogenic villages with painted wooden cottages huddle around the coast, interspersed with vast swathes of frozen tundra. Icebergs patrol the coast, dramatically calved from vast glaciers. Fjords dot the landscape, hemmed by spiky peaks.

Greenlandic travel has long been restricted to cruise ships plying the south coast or expensive specialist tours for the sort of people who think nothing of scaling a mountain before breakfast. But the country is slowly becoming more accessible to travellers, with an improving network of tourist offices, increased transport to and from the island and better accommodation and facilities. Make no mistake, Greenland is still no holiday resort, and you should expect to be at the mercy of nature's plans rather than your own timetable. But travel here is more possible than ever before.

DRIED FISH & MOBILE PHONES

Greenland is an island of contradictions that show its speedy modernisation. People clutch a mobile phone in one hand and dried fish in the other. Satellite dishes sit next to curing seal ribs on city balconies. The Home Rule government is working towards

increased separation from Denmark, but this brings dilemmas of its own. Moving towards all-Greenlandic schools would assert independence, but could make it difficult for students to get further education or work outside Greenland. And crucially, Greenland is economically dependent on Denmark, receiving around DKr3,000,000 (around US$10,000) per year in subsidy for every man, woman and child on the island. The Inuit have long relied on a subsistence income from hunting and fishing, and suffered from EU limits on fishing and crashing cod stocks in the 1980s. Greenland Tourism (the Greenland tourist board), founded only in 1991, is trying to supplement this traditional income with sustainable travel and tourism. This is no small task in one of the world's most fragile ecosystems, where local culture and wildlife are vulnerable to outside change. There is extensive research into the effects of climate change and the rate at which Greenland's ice sheet is melting; at places like the Akullit Peninsula it's possible to see global warming in action. Greenland's harsh environment may be just as likely to harm you as you it; nonetheless, if you do visit, tread lightly.

FESTIVALS & EVENTS

- ☻ End of the polar night celebrations; January–February. Relieved celebrations mark the return of the sun after its sojourn below the horizon.

- ☻ World Ice Golf Championship; Uummannaq; March. Golfers play on a white 'green' with red balls, frosty fingers and polar bears at this event.

- ☻ Nuuk Snow Festival; Nuuk; March or April. Artists from around the world make the grown-up version of snowmen at this festival.

- ☻ Dog-sled races; villages north of the Arctic Circle; March or April.

- ☻ Arctic Circle Race; Sisimut; early April. Hardy skiers battle it out in this tough 160km (100mi) race.

- ☻ Festival of Art & Music; Qaqortoq; late June or early July.

- ☻ Arctic Marathon; Nuuk; August.

- ☻ A social and political Inuit gathering and pop festival, held in July, is expected to be revived in 2006 in Aasivik (Summer Settlement).

DEFINING EXPERIENCE! ★

Dog-sledding frozen tundra to Norse ruins lit by the midnight sun, nibbling on dried fish and pretending to be an intrepid explorer

»

GREENLAND.

" *It was a fantastic experience - we were lucky enough to see an unbelievable display of the northern lights in Nuuk in mid-September. The whales around Disko Bay were also an amazing sight.* "

- Alex Pollitt, Britain

HOT TOPICS OF THE DAY

- Climate change
- How to deal with social problems among the local population
- The renewal of the US military's lease of the air base at Thule in 2004, which may be used as part of the 'Star Wars' defence system

HOT TIPS FOR TRAVELLERS

- Silence is perfectly normal to Greenlanders and a lack of conversation indicates comfort rather than unease.
- Greenland's pubs can be fun, raucous, rough or a combination of the three. Keep your eyes and ears open as the night progresses!
- Read *Miss Smilla's Feeling for Snow* by Peter Høeg, the most famous novel about Greenland, or *Last Places – A Journey in the North*, by Lawrence Millman, which is an entertaining account of Greenland.

DO MENTION

- Greenland's bid for FIFA (International Federation of Football Association) to recognise it as a separate nation to Denmark

DON'T MENTION

- Don't talk about hunting and whaling without researching the subject thoroughly – read Finn Lynge's *Arctic Wars*, *Animal Rights*, *Endangered Species* and Kjeld Hansen's *A Farewell to Greenland* for both sides of the story.
- Don't expect to be asked to widen the local gene pool – all those stories of wife-swapping are just that (mostly).

RANDOM FACTS

- Around 80% of the country is covered in ice.
- The depth of Greenland icecap is 3085m (10,120ft).
- Disko Bay's 'bergy bits' – smaller-than-iceberg–sized chunks – are chipped into cubes and exported to Europe and Japan to chill drinks. That scotch you order in a Tokyo pub may contain 25,000-year-old cubes from the frozen heart of Greenland's icecap and the air that fizzes out as they melt has been trapped since long before anyone ever heard of smog alerts.

MOST BIZARRE SIGHTS

- Midnight sun
- The aurora borealis
- Exploding icebergs

THINGS TO TAKE

- Toasty-warm clothes
- A strong stomach for sampling *kivioq* (small birds left to rot in hollowed-out seal carcasses)
- Patience for coping with changeable travel plans

THREE WORDS TO DESCRIBE THIS COUNTRY

- Not particularly green

- *Sam Trafford*

AN ATLANTIC PUFFIN WITH A BEVY OF SAND EELS IN ITS BEAK.

ICELAND.

⭐ **SNOWMOBILES, SCHNAPPS AND LAVA.** It's a tad ironic that one of Europe's most popular destinations for a party weekend has some of the highest alcohol prices in the world.

Still, where else can you bar-hop all night without seeing the sun go down, then go skinny-dipping in a natural swimming pool heated by a volcano? Iceland has been one of Europe's favourite weekend breaks for yonks, and its appeal shows no signs of diminishing with age. It's certainly one of the most unusual destinations within three hours' flight of Western Europe – if you ask almost anyone you find in the street, they'll say they want to come here.

In fact, the physical numbers of people visiting Iceland are comparatively small by the standards of international tourism – partly a factor of the painful cost of living, which places Iceland way up there with Japan and Norway in the list of most expensive holiday destinations. Then again, the whole nation has a population smaller than many European towns, contributing to a wonderful sense of escape and isolation.

Beaten by the waves of the north Atlantic, Iceland is a country of wild open spaces and empty black-sand beaches, of sapphire-blue glaciers breaking into the ocean and rainbows thrown up by waterfalls as they hammer through tortured lava flows. The interior of the island is a living geography lesson – superheated water boils up from the ground, hot enough to cook an egg, and plumes of sulphurous steam emerge from fumaroles, mud pots and vents all across the landscape.

When you tire of the volcanism – and the eggy pong that comes with it – you can pull back to Reykjavík, one of Europe's most human-friendly cities. Though small, the Icelandic capital lives like a European metropolis, with theatres, opera houses, Viking-theme restaurants, galleries full of conceptual art and some of the best and busiest bars in Scandinavia. At weekends, the famous *runtur* (literally 'round tour' »

»»

DETTIFOSS WATERFALL IS THOUGHT TO HAVE THE GREATEST FLOW VOLUME OF ANY WATERFALL IN EUROPE.

ICELAND.

» pub crawl roars through central Reykjavík and party people blow budgets bigger than national deficits drinking through the perpetually light summer nights.

Come morning, you can clear your head with a blast of spray from a blowhole on a whale-watching tour or settle your stomach with one of the most unsettling national cuisines in Europe – pressed testicle cake, anyone? However, it's essential to budget for a blow out, or you may find yourself subsisting on petrol-station hot dogs and alcohol-free lager while the party you can't afford to join rages around you!

A DELICATE BALANCE...

Icelanders have never liked being told what to do and the nation has a long history of ignoring international opinion and treading its own idiosyncratic path. Several recent decisions by the Icelandic government have raised eyebrows around the world, most famously the limited resumption of whaling in 2003. The granting of Icelandic citizenship to the fugitive chess champion Bobby Fischer in 2005 also caused a stir, particularly in America, where Fischer faces criminal charges for breaching international

sanctions against Slobodan Miloševiç's Yugoslavia. Both events caused ripples in the tourism industry, but for now at least, it seems that visitors are willing to forgive Iceland's more eccentric traits. However, the effect of whaling on the whale-watching industry remains to be seen.

DEFINING EXPERIENCE

☼ Dining on *hákarl* (rotten shark) and *brennivin* (Icelandic schnapps) then camping on a black-sand beach at the foot of a volcano, watching the aurora borealis and listening to the wind howling through the lava flows

FESTIVALS & EVENTS

☼ Food and Fun festival; Reykjavík; February. World-famous chefs compete head to head at Reykjavík restaurants – the goal is to prepare the best imaginable dish using only Icelandic ingredients.

☼ Reykjavík Arts Festival; Reykjavík; May. The 2005 festival focused on visual arts, but in 2006 it is set to return to a more familiar line-up of theatre, music and dance.

☼ Icelandair Horse Festival; Vindheimamelar; July. Expect mini- horse

---

MOST BIZARRE SIGHT! ☆

The Icelandic Phallological Museum in Reykjavik – the only museum in the world to display a complete collection of preserved penises from every mammal in a single nation

»

"

Believe it or not, you can dive in Iceland. There are several dive sites available. Advanced or dry-suit experience is required as the water stays at a chilly 3°C (37°F). One such dive site is at Þingvellir National Park. You can navigate your way through caverns in fresh water where visibility is over 20m (66ft).

"

- Chris Louie, USA

races, show-jumping and pint-sized dressage at this biannual festival.

○ Cultural Night; Reykjavík; August. Reykjavík brings out the cultural big guns – bars and restaurants host all sorts of recitals, performances and exhibitions.

○ Reykjavík Jazz Festival; Reykjavík; late September. Click your fingers to jazz heavyweights.

○ Iceland Airwaves Music Festival; Reykjavík; October. Rock out at this boisterous festival.

DO MENTION

○ Plate tectonics. Icelanders are deeply proud of the awesome volcanic power beneath their feet, which drives everything from pollution-free power stations to the Icelandic tourism industry. And this despite a series of devastating volcanic eruptions, including the explosion of the volcano Grímsvötn under the Vatnajökull glacier in 2004.

DON'T MENTION

○ Whaling. Iceland banned whaling in 1989, but so-called 'scientific whaling' resumed

in 2003. Although most Icelanders support whaling, there is little local demand for whale products – Icelandic consumers snapped up less than a quarter of the whale meat produced in 2004. Sadly, foreigners pointing out this rather glaring inconsistency are unlikely to win friends in Iceland's bars.

RANDOM FACTS

○ Iceland consumes more Coca-Cola per capita than any other nation.

○ Icelanders don't have family names. Second names in Iceland are formed from the father's first name, followed by 'son' or 'daughter' – eg Gunnar Gunnarson (Gunnar, son of Gunnar).

THINGS TO TAKE

○ Waterproofs or a brolly – rain in Iceland arrives unexpectedly and in biblical proportions

○ Your photo ID – only people aged 20 or older can drink alcohol or hire a car

○ A sleeping bag – made-up beds in hostels and guesthouses cost an arm and a leg; you can save a fortune just by providing your own bedding

HOT TIPS FOR TRAVELLERS

○ Buy a Reykjavík Tourist Card for free admission to most of Reykjavík's museums, galleries and thermal swimming pools, plus attractions in nearby Hafnarfjörður.

○ Rent the movie *101 Reykjavík* – this heart-warming tale of a Reykjavík slacker who impregnates his mother's lesbian lover is a helpful introduction to the way Icelanders see the world.

○ Hire a car – Iceland is chock full of glaciers, volcanoes and geysers and all are free if you can make your own way there.

THREE WORDS TO DESCRIBE THIS COUNTRY

○ Surreal, self-reliant, thirsty

- Joe Bindloss

ICELAND.

RECENT FAD! ✪

The oldest, ahem, leisure activity known to humanity. For some reason, Icelanders are procreating at an unprecedented rate – Iceland currently boasts the highest birth rate in Europe.

ITALY.

VITAL STATISTICS

- **POPULATION**
  58 MILLION
- **VISITORS PER YEAR**
  36.7 MILLION
- **UNIT OF CURRENCY**
  EURO (€)
- **COST OF A CUP OF COFFEE**
  €0.90 TO €2.50 =
  US$1 TO US$3
- **CAPITAL**
  ROME
- **LANGUAGES**
  ITALIAN, FRENCH,
  GERMAN, SERBIAN,
  CROATIAN

AN OLD-FASHIONED BEACH BOX
ON VENICE'S LIDO BEACH.

ETERNAL CHIC. Perhaps it's the giant sunglasses, chichi dogs and backside-hugging trousers that ooze Italian style or maybe it's just that innate cat-walk gait that Italians seem to have. Either way, it's hard not to feel a little unkempt by comparison.

Couple this trivial inadequacy with the Italian *ars vivendi*, or art of living, the year-round attractions, the stunning scenery and the heady mix of media and politics, and it's enough to make most tourists go weak at the knees.

Italy can be overwhelming. It screams with style and jet-set glamour, it's endowed with some of the world's finest works of art, it's littered with architectural treasures and home to some of the earth's finest food. The country hardly needs any other reason for a visit, but with low-fare airlines now flying into more and more regional airports, and low-cost internal flights from companies such as AlpiEagles and Meridiana, it has never been easier, or cheaper, to get to, or around, Italy.

PUTTING ON A BRAVE FACE

Once you arrive you'll soon realise that the fortune Italy has amassed in priceless artworks and architecture over the centuries is finally getting the makeover it deserves. All over the country buildings are clad in a shroud of scaffolding as the crumbling grandeur that has for so long been an essential part of Italy's character is cleaned up and repaired. Those gaping cracks are being shored up, the tiled ochre roofs are being fixed and centuries-old frescos are being retouched.

Despite this apparent push to restore some of Italy's finest works to their original condition, the country's economy is in the doldrums. Business is badly depressed and visitor numbers are stagnant. And although the hoteliers and restaurateurs will be very glad to see you, don't expect beaming service smiles everywhere you go. Much of the blame for the dreary economic outlook is placed on the shoulders of slippery prime minister Silvio Berlusconi, the man no-one admits they voted for. As his parliamentary

A FRIENDLY GAME OF FOOTBALL
ON THE BANKS OF THE ARNO.

term draws to a close, political debate is intensifying and in mid-2005 one minister even suggested a return to Italy's former currency, the lira, as a solution to the nation's economic woes. This perennial distrust of Berlusconi and his government means that upcoming elections in 2006 should prove an interesting battle ground.

THE PASSION AND THE GLORY

Most Italians are hoping that 2006 will be the year for Italy to make its mark on the world in other ways. Sport, a major Italian obsession, is in for a big year. The baroque city of Turin is hosting the Winter Olympic Games in February, when 2500 athletes and up to 10,000 journalists are expected to flock to the city for the games and the glorious après-ski. Once the games finish and the snow melts all thoughts will turn to football as the national team prepares for another attempt at winning World Cup glory.

DEFINING EXPERIENCE

✪ Sitting outside a traditional café in a Renaissance piazza, dressed in the latest Versace catsuit, sipping an espresso as the pigeons peck at your feet and you watch the world go by

FESTIVALS & EVENTS

✪ XXth Winter Olympic Games; Turin; 10–26 February 2006. Turin hosts 17 days of all things fast and frozen on the slopes and rinks.

✪ Viareggio Carnival; Tuscany; February. One of Italy's most spectacular carnivals features huge papier-mâché puppets poking fun at politicians and public figures.

✪ Venice Carnival; February. The most famous of Italy's street parties consists of 10 days of masked, costumed merriment in and around 'the world's most beautiful drawing room'.

✪ Settimana Santa (Holy Week); April. The week leading up to Easter is celebrated with solemn processions, Passion plays and a candle-lit walk through the Colosseum led by the Pope.

✪ Cantine Aperte; May. Free access to vineyards across Italy is granted to sommeliers and wine-tasting fans. The festival generally includes exhibitions of local handicrafts and performances by folk musicians and dancers.

✪ Palio delle Quattro Antiche Repubbliche Marinare (Regatta of the Four Ancient

RECENT FAD! ✪

An Italian company has launched a 'talking wine label', which comprises a chip implanted in the bottle telling you where the wine comes from, how to enjoy it and what food it should accompany.

»

ITALY.

FROM THE ROAD

> *It was about 8pm. In Sorrento we found a secluded swim area... Jumped in, swam out about 20m (65ft) all the while the cliffside slowly revealing the cityscape behind it. The sun was setting and casting a magnificent reflection on the coloured buildings set on the hillsides. I'll never forget it.*

- 'jagwire'

» Maritime Republics); Pisa; June. This annual race is between the four historical maritime rivals of Pisa, Venice, Amalfi and Genoa. The festival rotates between the cities each year.

○ Il Palio; Siena; July & August. This thrilling but dangerous race on horseback round the city's main piazza is preceded by a parade in traditional costume.

WHAT'S HOT...
○ Enormous designer sunglasses

WHAT'S NOT...
○ Ferrari's Formula One performance

DO MENTION
○ Food: the Italians' love affair with food brings out some of the best conversations

DON'T MENTION
○ Ferrari's dismal Formula One performance
○ The Mafia

RANDOM FACTS
○ The Arabs introduced spaghetti to Sicily as early as 1150 and today Sicilians eat 42kg (93lb) of pasta per person each year.

○ Despite the Vatican's ruling on contraception and cash incentives from the government for larger families, Italy's birth rate is the lowest in Europe, with only an estimated 8.89 births per 1000 in 2005.

○ Dr Giorgio Fischer, a gynaecologist from Rome, invented liposuction in 1974.

THINGS TO TAKE
○ Modest clothes to gain access to the country's thousands of superb churches

○ A phrasebook to help interpret menus and communicate with locals outside the main tourist hot spots

○ Cash: smaller shops, hotels and restaurants often don't accept plastic and a surprising number of major attractions accept only hard currency for admission fees

THREE WORDS TO DESCRIBE THIS COUNTRY
○ Chic, cultured, contagious

- *Etain O'Carroll*

HOT TIP FOR TRAVELLERS! ★

Don't dream of driving a hire car without comprehensive car insurance and the minimum excess. It makes dealing with those excitable Italian drivers so much easier.

»

HAYMAKING ON MOUNTAIN RAJAC.

★ THE NEW, NEW, NEW CZECH REPUBLIC. Want to make a bet on the next big thing in European tourism? Five years ago you'd be called a surrealist comedian if you picked Serbia & Montenegro.

Once the old Yugoslavia started falling apart in the early 1990s this Balkan federation had its name dragged through mud, war and NATO bombing until strongman Slobodan Miloševiç was finally booted out and sent to a war-crimes tribunal in The Hague. But what a difference a few years make. Pleasure cruisers are plying their trade along the Serbian stretch of the Danube, some hot new rock festivals are livening up the summer season, Belgrade's hedonistic nightlife is attracting attention and the divine Adriatic coastline of Montenegro is drawing in sun lovers looking for Croatian-style coastal beauty without the crowds or costs.

Serbia is a largely agricultural country of rolling hills and mountains, in the south petering out into the pancake-flat plains along the Danube River. Not many tourists venture beyond Belgrade at present, but the wineries and World Heritage–listed monasteries of Fruška Gora near the Art

Nouveau city of Novi Sad are gaining in popularity. Novi Sad also has the wild Exit Music Festival in July, whose 2005 line-up included the White Stripes, Carl Cox and veteran riffage monsters, Slayer. Southern Serbia has the ski resorts of Zlatibor and Kopaonik and a number of classic medieval Orthodox monasteries as well. Serbia's main attraction though is Belgrade, a Moscowlike melange of 19th-century buildings, gloomy fortresses and stunningly brutal Communist-era carbuncles. It's gritty but lively, and the nightlife is exhausting. Young Serbs manage to party all night at apartment-block bars, underground clubs and on river barges and still stagger to work in the morning. The city also has a magnificent array of museums, galleries and ridiculously cheap classical-music concerts, plus the splendour of the ancient Kalemegdan Citadel where the mighty Sava and Danube Rivers meet. Belgrade is becoming a major crossing point »

RECENT FAD! ◉

River-boat revelry: Belgrade's overflowing party scene has spread to river barges on the Danube and Sava Rivers

ENJOYING THE PEBBLED
BEACHES OF MONTENEGRO.

» for travellers heading east into Romania and Bulgaria, south into Macedonia and Greece, west to Croatia and north to Hungary. Transport links are excellent.

Montenegro's capital Podgorica is raw communist grey (in about 50 years or so it'll be acclaimed as a perfect example of 1960s poetry in concrete), but the rest of the country is a gem. The old capital Cetinje is tucked up high on a mountain where the old prince-bishops of 'black mountain' (the literal translation of Montenegro) managed to keep their heads above the Ottoman Empire. The vast Lake Skadar is perfect for bird-watching, the stunning Durmitor National Park sits on the lip of the 1.3km-deep (0.8mi) Tara Canyon, and there is a clutch of quaint little resorts along the mountainous Adriatic coast. The Bay of Kotor is southern Europe's greatest fjord, and boasts gorgeous old walled towns such as Herceg Novi and Kotor. Further south along the hairpin coastal-mountain roads (like something from a sports-car advertisement) there's peaceful Budva, the port of Bar and the long clean beaches of Ulcinj. Montenegro seems to be more at peace with its religious diversity than some of its neighbours. Some churches even have

two altars – one Catholic and one Orthodox. There are also plenty of medieval mosques and Sufi shrines in this compact, rugged little country.

Kosovo has never been acclaimed as much of a tourist drawcard – it's mostly a windswept highland plain – but the old Ottoman provincial capital of Prizren has a charming old quarter and some fine mosques. The Serbian monasteries of Patrijaršija and Decani outside Peja boast wonderful frescoes.

ANOTHER DIVORCE?

The big question is, will the federation last in its present form? The junior partner, Montenegro, will hold a referendum on independence early in 2006, and it looks like being a close-run thing. Another region, Kosovo, has been a UN protectorate since 1999, and the majority Albanian Muslim community is itching for full independence from Serbia. Kosovo, however, is something of a holy land for nationalist Serbs (and there are a lot of these) and the UN doesn't seem too keen on granting Kosovo full self-government just yet. The chances of renewed conflict over Kosovo are slim at present, but given the past 100 years of simmering

SERBIA + MONTENEGRO.

> " *The Serbians were the friendliest of the South Slavs I encountered. Many spoke good English and were very hospitable. Some would take the opportunity of meeting a Westerner to launch into 'look what NATO did to us' propaganda but they do clearly differentiate between governments and people.* "
>
> - Timo Stewart, Finland

conflict interspersed with violent eruptions here, you just never know.

DEFINING EXPERIENCE
- Climbing up the winding steps to the old walls above Kotor in Montenegro and taking in the views of southern Europe's biggest fjord, then walking back down again for a well-deserved dinner of fish, salad and wine at a cosy wood-lined restaurant in the Old Town

FESTIVALS & EVENTS
- International Wine Festival; Belgrade; March. Good grief, another excuse to imbibe alcohol in the biggest party town in the Balkans. It also has lots of food and music.
- Exit Festival; Novi Sad; July. It's the hardest-rocking summer music festival in Eastern Europe.
- Beer Festival; Belgrade; August. A celebration of fermented barley, hops and alcohol-affected dancing.
- Guča Brass Band Festival; last week of August. It's so uncool it's kind of cool – a real Serbian county knees-up.

DO MENTION
- The good local wines and spirits. Serbs and Montenegrin farmers take great pride in their home-brewing skills, and the flavour and alcoholic head kick of plum brandies in particular must be treated with respect.

DON'T MENTION
- The war(s). Serbs in particular suffered deeply in the post-Yugoslav wars yet seem to get no sympathy for being on the 'wrong' side. The refugees from Kosovo, Bosnia and Croatia deserve better.

RANDOM FACTS
- Serbian inventor Nikola Tesla, the original mad scientist, was a rival to Thomas Edison and died while trying to perfect a 'death ray'.
- Belgrade is one of Europe's oldest cities, with evidence of settlement from over 6000 years ago.

THINGS TO TAKE
- A crash course in the Cyrillic alphabet – most signs in Serbia and Montenegro use Cyrillic rather than the Latin alphabet
- Cash and ATM cards rather than travellers cheques

HOT TIPS FOR TRAVELLERS
- Watch the movie *Black Cat, White Cat* before you go to Serbia. This rambling tale of a gypsy clan captures the country's freewheeling spirit perfectly.
- Want to lift your nose at people who think Croatia is the latest thing in seaside holidays? Laugh haughtily and head for Montenegro's ravishing coast instead.

THREE WORDS TO DESCRIBE THIS COUNTRY
- Fractured, underestimated, addictive
  - *Richard Plunkett*

HOT TOPIC OF THE DAY!

Yet More Balkan States: Montenegro will hold a referendum on independence in 2006, and the UN protectorate of Kosovo looks more like gaining full independence every year. If both do, that'll be seven countries born out of the old Yugoslavia.

SLOVENIA.

VITAL STATISTICS

- **POPULATION**
  2 MILLION
- **VISITORS PER YEAR**
  1.2 MILLION
- **UNIT OF CURRENCY**
  TOLAR (SIT)
- **COST OF A CUP OF COFFEE**
  200 SIT = US$1
- **CAPITAL**
  LJUBLJANA
- **LANGUAGES**
  SLOVENIAN, CROATIAN, SERBIAN, GERMAN, ENGLISH

DRAGON BRIDGE (ZMAJSKI MOST, 1901) IN LJUBLJANA.

WHO MADE WHOM? To the outside world, Slovenia suffers from an identity crisis. For a start, it's endlessly confused with Slovakia, a situation exacerbated by the infamous bushwhacking it suffered in 1999 when George W Bush, then the governor of Texas, referred to the Slovenian foreign minister as Slovakian.

It's also sandwiched between Italy, Austria and Hungary, and invariably gets overshadowed by its flashier neighbours. And it's a former Yugoslavian republic so people tend to make a few assumptions: that it's stalled in some kind of communist time warp, and that it was ravaged by the Balkan Wars in the same fashion as other former Yugoslavian republics.

But get a load of this: Slovenia is a beautiful, peaceful country – affluent, affable and free of strife. It suffered just 10 days of fighting during the bitter wars of independence in 1991, and since then has been left to quietly go about its business while Bosnia, Serbia and Croatia raised hell on earth. It's unsurprising, then, that Slovenians just shrug their shoulders at the Western world's ignorance, all the better to kick back and enjoy their grand heritage, rolling fields of green, breathtaking mountains and the luscious capital, Ljubljana.

CLEAN & GREEN

Over the past few years, the buzz in the travel industry has anointed Ljubljana as the 'new Prague'. That's a somewhat dubious honour – aside from it being sheer advertising doublespeak, it perpetuates the myth that Slovenia has no identity of its own. Nonetheless, it's also a timely reminder of just what makes the capital so special. Actually, the comparisons are immediately apparent. Both cities are long-standing crucibles of intellectual and artistic activity – enjoying an attendant, bohemian café society – and both are blessed with remarkable, baroque architecture and elegant cobbled streets. But Ljubljana is without the hordes of lager louts,

THE SHADOW OF A LANTERN DRAWS
ACROSS THE AFTERNOON.

Champagne Charlies and Hooray Henrys that now seem to plague Prague. Instead, it's clean, green and well worth your time.

Elsewhere, Lake Bled is an absolute must-see. In its midst is a small islet with a stunning castle dating from 1111; the backdrop is the Julian Alps, a jaw-dropping, eye-rubbing vista of snow-capped mountains. Slovenia shares the Alps with its illustrious geographical neighbours, and that gives rise to another hoary epithet – it's also known as 'Little Switzerland'.

In the wash up, Slovenia is neither Slovakia nor Switzerland; it's a glorious entity in its own right, a kind of European interzone – historically aligned to the east but always looking to the west – contented with its lot and happy with what it's got: style, beauty, grace and charm in abundance. In fact, you may want to keep the place a secret (even if we obviously can't), and you wouldn't be the only one: Slovenia receives fewer visitors now than it did before the Balkans wars, but the number is slowly increasing.

DEFINING EXPERIENCE

✪ Submerging yourself in boiling thermal waters after a solid day of skiing, with a bottle of Cviček (a renowned dry red wine from Posavje) while watching the sun setting behind an 11th-century castle. (Music by Laibach optional.)

FESTIVALS & EVENTS

✪ Kurentovanje; Ptuj; February. Slovenia's most popular Mardi Gras celebration.

✪ Summer Puppet Festival; Ljubljana; June–September. This is held at the magnificent Ljubljana castle, and companies from all over Europe come to stage shows. Western Europeans are very good at this art, which is sadly dying everywhere else.

✪ International Summer Festival; Ljubljana and Bled; July–August. This is the top event in the calendar, an international fest of music, street theatre, dance and everything in between.

✪ Cows' Ball (Kravji Bal); Bohinj; mid-September. Eating, drinking and folk dancing to celebrate the return of the country's cow population to the valleys from high pasture.

HOT TOPIC OF THE DAY

✪ The issue of citizenship for nationals of former Yugoslav republics, who were wiped from population records and

»

RECENT FAD! ✪

'Balkans Parties', where crowds of young Slovenes dance and drink to old nationalist 'Yugo-rock', sung in Serbian or Croatian. This weird trend among teenagers (who are too young to be nostalgic about the old days of Slavic unity, or to remember the horrors of the conflict) is difficult to explain. But it's catching on.

SLOVENIA.

FROM THE ROAD

> *On the Ljubljana–Zagreb road or, more exactly, on the very border, is the divided Slovenian-Croatian village of Bregana. Here the border goes right through a restaurant, which gives you the option of having your meal in either country or, if you prefer, in both countries at the same time. You can also play billiards over the state border, but you have no option as far as the toilet is concerned – there is only one toilet and that's on the Slovenian side.*

- Rolf Palmberg, Finland

» stripped of Slovenian residency shortly before Slovenia joined the EU in 2004. It's a bit of a blow to the country's long-held tradition of liberalism.

WHAT'S HOT...
○ The culture project in the Metelkova Ulica, Ljubljana. Formerly an army barracks, this sprawling complex has now been converted into a commune space for artists and alternative lifestylers.

WHAT'S NOT...
○ Balkan nationalism

RANDOM FACTS
○ Each year, Slovakia sends around 600kg (1323lb) of wrongly addressed mail back to Slovenia.

○ Laibach is the German name for Ljubljana, imposed during Nazi occupation. It's also the name of a controversial Slovenian electronica/rock band, infamous for their coolly detached Teutonic look at Western culture.

○ It is believed that Slovenians invented skiing. The oldest known mention of this sport dates from the 17th century, and places its birth on the slopes of the Bloke Plateau in Notranjska. Fittingly, national hero Davo Karničar was the first human to race down Mt Everest on skis in one single, uninterrupted stretch, in 2000.

○ A brass plaque in Ljubljana's train station commemorates James Joyce's one-night stay in the city on 19 October 1904. It fails to mention that Joyce and his partner Norma Barnacle were on their way to Pula and caught the wrong train.

DO MENTION
○ The success of the local film industry, which has embraced co-production with its former Yugoslavian neighbours as part of the healing process. The Oscar-winning *No Man's Land* was filmed in Slovenia, while the short film *(A)torzija* won the Golden Bear at the Berlin Film Festival, as well as the European Film Academy Award.

DON'T MENTION
○ George Dubya

○ EU membership – Slovenians are divided on the matter

THINGS TO TAKE
○ Thermal underwear: skiing is Slovenia's most popular sport

○ A keen palate: Slovenia lies on the same latitude as Burgundy or Bordeaux, and some say its sparkling wines are second only to the French.

○ Binoculars (for looking at mountains and architectural details)

HOT TIPS FOR TRAVELLERS
○ Stay at a 'tourist farm' with a real, live rural family, help out with chores and receive home-cooked meals in return.

○ Heal yourself: Slovenia may not have a lengthy Adriatic coast like Croatia, but it does have thermal spas, all, supposedly, with individual health-giving properties.

○ Apparently, some care should be taken drinking the tap water. Preferably, drink bottled mineral water.

THREE WORDS TO DESCRIBE THIS COUNTRY
○ Scenic, charming, peaceful

- Simon Sellars

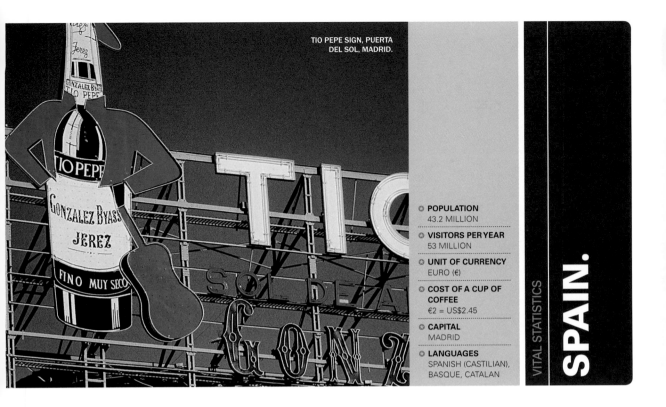

TIO PEPE SIGN, PUERTA DEL SOL, MADRID.

VITAL STATISTICS

SPAIN.

- ⊙ **POPULATION**
  43.2 MILLION
- ⊙ **VISITORS PER YEAR**
  53 MILLION
- ⊙ **UNIT OF CURRENCY**
  EURO (€)
- ⊙ **COST OF A CUP OF COFFEE**
  €2 = US$2.45
- ⊙ **CAPITAL**
  MADRID
- ⊙ **LANGUAGES**
  SPANISH (CASTILIAN), BASQUE, CATALAN

⭐ THE REINVENTION OF SPAIN. Think of Spain and most people think of that simple and singularly successful recipe of sun, sand and sangria. Think again.

Yes, if you're northern European and accustomed to patchy and altogether unsatisfying summers, the prospect of sunning yourself on 'Europe's beach' for a couple of weeks in August must be hard to resist. Follow the urge and you won't be alone – more than 53 million people visit Spain every year and it's not hard to see why. Lazing by an enchanted curve of the Mediterranean with a glass of fine Spanish wine in your hand, all the while surrounded by white-washed houses and the languages of the world, is indeed one of world travel's finest moments. And yes, crazy, frenetic and utterly infectious nightlife – few countries know how to party like Spain – and cities with traffic jams at 4am on weekdays have always been, and remain, part of the mix. Throw in some of Europe's most delicious and innovative food, supercheap flights and the uniquely Spanish excesses of flamenco

and bullfighting and it's difficult to imagine another European destination that offers more.

But Spain is so much more than 'just' *sol y playa* (sun and beach), which is just as well. After decades of selling Spain as a summer destination for shivering northerners, Spain has suddenly discovered that the beaches of Eastern Europe may just be cheaper. While still welcoming wholeheartedly the Ibiza party-goers or the beach bums of the Costa del Sol who've been coming here for decades, Spain's tourism authorities have finally caught up with their compatriots who've reinvented themselves into one of Europe's most modern and sophisticated countries.

The discerning traveller's reasons for visiting Spain are legion, from stunningly diverse landscapes and some of the finest art galleries in the world – the Prado in Madrid, the Guggenheim in Bilbao, the Picasso Museum in Malaga – to the »

HOT TOPIC OF THE DAY! ⊛

Gay marriage: homosexual unions were legalised in 2005 and while the majority of Spaniards support the move, a vocal minority suggests that conservative Catholic values can still run deep.

SPAIN.

DOMINO PLAYERS HIT THE TILES ON BARCELONETA BEACH, BARCELONA.

» architectural treasures of Barcelona, Granada, Cordoba and Seville, all of which are infused with Spain's polyglot heritage. This other side of Spain has always been there but it has been far too often bypassed in the rush to the beach.

You've got to hand it to the Spanish. Just three decades ago, Spain was a dictatorship in the thrall of one of the world's longest-serving fascists (General Francisco Franco cast his shadow over Spain from 1938 until his death in 1975). And, since the 1970s, Spain and its tourist industry have lived with the ever-present threat of terrorism – whether from the home-grown Basque group ETA or fanatics of the fundamentalist Islamic variety. But Spain hasn't flinched and has instead simply gone about its business, in the process becoming one of the most tolerant and liberal societies in Europe. Amid such upheaval, what holds it all together is Spain's capacity for remaking itself, each generation making the country new with its own particular version of the good life. This is, after all, the country that produced men like Pablo Picasso, Antoni Gaudí and Salvador Dalí, whose visions of the world were unlike any other.

FESTIVALS & EVENTS

- Las Fallas; Valencia; March. The all-night parties and daytime fireworks spectaculars of Las Fallas earned Valencia the title of Europe's noisiest city.

- Semana Santa; week leading up to Easter; March/April. This ritual in which hooded participants gather for eerie night-time processions dates back centuries.

- Fiesta de San Isidro; Madrid; May. This festival signals the start of summer with bullfights, parades and concerts.

DO MENTION

- Spain's transition from dictatorship to democracy. Spaniards have long had something of an inferiority complex and love to be told that they're as modern as any European.

DON'T MENTION

- ETA terrorism. International Olympic Committee member and Monaco monarch Prince Albert II asked about it during the final stages of Madrid's failed 2012 Olympic bid and hasn't been forgiven by Spaniards.

SPAIN.

" *We were visiting Granada, Spain, and managed to bribe a guard into letting us spend the night in the room Washington Irving stayed in as he wrote* The Alhambra. *We were locked in overnight, with no chance of getting out until the morning. If we were discovered, the guard would deny knowing us. We managed to sneak out the next morning when the gates were opened for the tourists, and we wandered out among the rest of the visitors. That night is a memory to treasure forever!* "

- Jeffery McCreary, USA

RECENT FAD

- Overseas travel: unlike their parents' generation, young Spaniards can't get enough of seeing the world, hence the long queues in travel agencies.

- Immigration: it was not until 1991 that more people came to live in Spain than left it and Spain now receives more immigrants every year than any other European country.

MOST BIZARRE SIGHTS

- The annual spectacle of grown (and often inebriated) men stumbling through the narrow, cobblestone streets of Pamplona pursued by 600kg (1323lb) bulls during the Running of the Bulls (6–14 July)

- Thousands of people pelting each other with tomatoes during Buñol's La Tomatina festival on the last or second-last Wednesday in August – it has no apparent purpose but is riotously fun

RANDOM FACTS

- Spain's new socialist government, which took office in 2004, matched the world record by having equal numbers of male and female cabinet ministers.

- According to the Organisation for Economic Co-operation and Development (OECD), Spain is the second-noisiest country after Japan.

- With an average altitude of 660m (2165ft), Spain is the second-highest country in Europe after Switzerland.

- Spaniards spend more money per capita on food than any other Europeans.

- More than 30 million people annually attend up to 17,000 bullfights across Spain, during the course of which 40,000 bulls are killed and 150,000 Spaniards are employed.

THINGS TO TAKE

- Highest-rating sunscreen and a hat

- A money-belt to ward off pickpockets on big-city metros and in tourist areas

- Warm clothes – Spain's high inland plateau is known for its 'nine months of winter and three months of hell', so come prepared for chilly (actually, downright freezing) winter nights

- A big appetite – Spanish food is a revelation based on the basic principle of taking the freshest ingredients and interfering with them as little as possible

HOT TIPS FOR TRAVELLERS

- According to legend, every Spaniard carries in his or her pocket a letter from the king which reads: 'This Spaniard is entitled to do whatever he or she feels like doing.' There are limits but not many.

- Believe the recent tourist slogan for Madrid which says, 'If you're in Madrid, you're from Madrid' – the Spanish capital is arguably Europe's most open and welcoming city.

- Spaniards rarely eat lunch before 2pm or 3pm and restaurants rarely re-open in the evening before 9pm (when you'll be the only person there).

THREE WORDS TO DESCRIBE THIS COUNTRY

- Welcoming, proud, fun-loving

- Anthony Ham

DEFINING EXPERIENCE!

Perching on a stool in a noisy bar in Seville's Barrio de Santa Cruz with a glass of Rioja wine in one hand, a plate of tapas before you, a bullfighting poster on the wall beside you and a flamenco performance rising up from a neighbouring tiled courtyard

DEEP SKI TRACKS CHANNEL TOWARD THE BRITTANIA HUT ABOVE SAAS FEE.

SWITZERLAND.

VITAL STATISTICS

⊙ **POPULATION**
7.25 MILLION

⊙ **VISITORS PER YEAR**
11 MILLION

⊙ **UNIT OF CURRENCY**
SWISS FRANC (COMMONLY SHORTENED TO SFR – THE OLD TERM; AND INCREASINGLY TO CHF – THE INTERNATIONALLY STANDARDISED ABBREVIATION)

⊙ **COST OF A CUP OF COFFEE**
CHF3.20 = US$2.50

⊙ **CAPITAL**
BERN

⊙ **LANGUAGES**
SWISS-GERMAN (NORTH, CENTRAL AND EAST), FRENCH (WEST), ITALIAN (SOUTH), RHAETO-ROMANIC (SOUTHEAST). ONLY ONE CITY, BIEL-BIENNE, IS OFFICIALLY BILINGUAL; THE REST ARE UNILINGUAL BY REGION.

★ **A LAND-LOCKED ISLAND NATION.** Switzerland – 'Confœderatio Helvetica' or CH – might be smack-bang in the middle of Europe, but that's never stopped it from running its own show – with Swiss-timepiece precision – despite its neighbours' political, military and economic decisions.

RECENT FAD! ⊛

M-Budget parties (www.mbudget-party.ch, in French, German and Italian). After initial consumer wariness, Migros supermarkets' lime green–packaged home-brand products have gained a cult following (demand outstrips supply for the M-Budget energy drink, big time) and spawned M-Budget parties with hip DJs, and snacks and soft drinks laid on.

This rarefied country of iridescent powder-coated peaks, crystalline lakes, rural mountainside villages, sophisticated cities and a reputation for banking has banked on its own future by remaining separate from the EU (at the same time as continuing to headquarter numerous international organisations) and retaining its own currency.

At a June 2005 referendum, however, 55% of Swiss voters did agree to enter the EU's Schengen Treaty area, removing passport controls at internal European borders. At the time of writing, an implementation date had yet to be set, but when it comes to pass the treaty will make Switzerland more accessible to travellers who previously needed a separate visa to enter, which led to travel agents in regions such as Asia advising their clients to bypass Switzerland in favour of other European destinations. It's a boon for the tourism industry, which now ranks third in the country behind the engineering and chemical industries, and employs 5.2% of the Swiss workforce, generating CHF22 billion annually.

SWITZERLAND ON A SHOESTRING?
The currency issue is an altogether different one: by not adopting the euro, Switzerland is perceived as prohibitively expensive, which isn't far off the money. In part it's because financiers worldwide keep their savings in Switzerland and so have an interest in keeping the currency strong; and partly because even lower-rung jobs attract relatively high salaries, which is good for the standard of living and low crime rate, but detrimental for its tourist image, particularly among budget travellers.

But it is possible to experience Switzerland on a fraying shoestring. Swiss

COW IN CONTEMPLATION: SWISS ALPS.

public transport costs can be kept in check with various discount-fare passes. Free bicycle rental is available at many city train stations. Switzerland rivals New Zealand for some of the best value-for-money backpacker hostels in the world (check out www.swiss backpackers.ch). You'll save a fistful of francs in winter by staying half an hour off the mountain and taking the bus and train up to the slopes. In summer, trekking the myriad of mountain trails for glorious see-forever vistas is free.

DEFINING EXPERIENCE
- Water skiing on Lake Geneva in the morning, riding the little train ASD (Aigle–Sépey–Diablerets) and replenishing with Lindt chocolate to ski the Alpine summit-ringed Les Diablerets glacier in the afternoon, before dipping Zopf bread into a drizzling fondue in your shuttered wooden chalet as the sun sets over the mountains

FESTIVALS & EVENTS
- Polo World Cup on Snow; St Moritz; January. The sport of kings in suitably champagne surrounds.
- Glacier Kiss; Flims; April. Snow-vehicle race proving there's a fine line between bravery and sheer madness.
- ART; Basel; June. Prestigious modern and contemporary art fair.
- Montreux Jazz Festival; Montreux; July. Stellar international blues, jazz and gospel acts.
- Bike-in cinema at Nidau castle; Biel-Bienne; July–August. The Swiss version of a drive-in.
- Street Parade; Zürich; August. Now bigger and wilder than its inspiration, Berlin's Love Parade.
- Inferno Triathlon; Thun; August. Hardcore swimming/race-biking/mountain-biking/ running.
- Museums' Long Night; Zürich; September. Get cultural until dawn.
- Jungfrau Marathon; Interlaken; September; www.jungfrau-marathon.ch. Four thousand runners ascend 42km (26mi) from 565m (1854ft) to 2110m (6923ft).

HOT TOPICS OF THE DAY
- The national air carrier, Swiss (formerly Swiss Air, which was grounded in 2001

»

HOT TIP FOR TRAVELLERS!

Hit the hay – literally. For an atmospheric sleep Heidi-style, *Schlaf im Stroh* (Sleep in Straw; www.schlaf-im-stroh .com) lets you bunk down in more than 200 farmers' haylofts when their cows graze the summer pastures, for around CHF20 per night including breakfast (showers, if available, may cost an additional couple of francs). BYO sleeping bag.

> "
>
> *I met Ernesto my Guatemalan lover in the year 2000 while travelling Central America; 10 days after we fell in love I went back to Australia. Ten months later we ended up in Switzerland together, four months later we found out I was pregnant. Our daughter was made in Switzerland and discovered with a home pregnancy testing kit in a pension in Tarragona, Spain. My baby was born in Australia, she is half Greek, half Guatemalan, living in Australia.*
>
> "
>
> - Maria Strofalis, Australia

MOST BIZARRE SIGHT! ✪

The award for most bizarre sight is a two-way tie between a larger-than-life (3m or 10ft) Freddie Mercury punching a defiant fist into the air on the shores of Lake Geneva in Montreux (Queen produced their final album, *Made in Heaven*, in Montreux' Mountain Studios); and the cosmic star-shaped Mystery Park in Interlaken, which interprets the mysteries of the world including the Egyptian Pyramids, Mayan calendars and alien contact with humans, based on the writings of the park's creator, Erich von Däniken.

» and went into liquidation the following year). Now that Germany's Lufthansa has bought the majority of shares, the Swiss are worried they'll lose their intercontinental Zurich hub (and worse, that they'll lose their iconic Swiss cross on the planes' tails).

⚙ Switzerland's geopolitical role in Europe and the EU. It includes work agreements with new members, the Eastern European countries.

⚙ The construction of the 57km (35mi) Gotthard rail link – the world's longest tunnel, opening 2012 – and the 34km (21mi) Lötschberg Tunnel (opening 2007). This will allow Switzerland to raise taxes for EU trucks using the snowy mountain roads.

WHAT'S HOT...
⚙ Zurich. It's been recognised as the city with the highest quality of life worldwide for the fourth year in a row; with a sizzling nightlife scene.

⚙ Swiss Army goods. Now that the army's been scaled back, Heimatwerk stores (www.heimatwerk.ch) sell clothing and items made from salvaged Swiss Army materials.

⚙ Freitag bags (www.freitag.ch). The Swiss are going mad for these bags, made from recycled truck tarpaulins, with straps fashioned from the trucks' seatbelts.

WHAT'S NOT...
⚙ Free use of marijuana. Switzerland's 2003 general elections saw a big shift to the right after many years of liberal tendencies (although marijuana was never 'officially' legalised), something that's now out of the question (so you'll still have to head to the Netherlands).

DO MENTION
⚙ Tennis ace Roger Federer's prowess

⚙ Praise for Switzerland's vast variety of cheeses

DON'T MENTION
⚙ Swiss banks laundering money (creative accounting takes place elsewhere these days)

⚙ The recent Bergier report (which asserted that Switzerland could have sheltered more refugees during WWII), as many Swiss feel they did all that was possible during those traumatic times

RANDOM FACTS
⚙ Cuckoo clocks are actually a German invention.

⚙ Australia and New Zealand might dispute who invented pavlova, but meringue was invented in Meiringen in Switzerland's Berner Oberland.

⚙ The teensy ½ franc is smaller than a 20 centimes/*Rappen* coin – a legacy of when it was the smallest silver denomination (everything smaller was copper). Though now made from alloy, it's still exactly half the weight of a franc.

⚙ Completely surrounded by Swiss territory but not of it are the towns of Büsingen (Germany; with side-by-side German and Swiss phone boxes) and Campione (Italy).

THINGS TO TAKE
⚙ As little as possible when trekking – you'll feel every kilogram of baggage on those inclines

THREE WORDS TO DESCRIBE THIS COUNTRY
⚙ Uplifting, unfettered, *über*-efficient
- *Catherine Le Nevez*

A STREET MARKET TEA SELLER IN BOSPHOROS

VITAL STATISTICS

TURKEY.

- **POPULATION**
  70 MILLION
- **VISITORS PER YEAR**
  18 MILLION
- **UNIT OF CURRENCY**
  TURKISH LIRA (TL)
- **COST OF A CUP OF COFFEE**
  TL0.50 TO TL1 =
  US$0.40 TO US$0.80
- **CAPITAL**
  ANKARA
- **LANGUAGE**
  TURKISH

OH I DO LIKE TO BE BESIDE THE SEASIDE. Long the weeping bridesmaid of Mediterranean megatourism, Turkey has at last arrived in the big league.

In 2004 a record 18 million tourists visited, mostly northern Europeans happy to sun themselves in the delightfully tacky resorts of the southwestern coast – though Chinese and Russian visitors are also making their presence known. The main attractions are the glories of imperial Istanbul and the big resorts of Kuşadasi, Bodrum, Marmaris, Antalya and Alanya, all fed by major airports. For the discerning traveller the big resort towns have little to recommend themselves besides nice weather and menus in eight different languages, but obviously they must be doing something right. The curious thing is that you rarely have to travel far to find a lovely little seaside resort without the touts and identical hotels. Close to Marmaris there's Datça and Bozburun, near Bodrum there's Ören, and near Antalya there's Çirali. There are dozens of similar less-visited resorts to be enjoyed along Turkey's Aegean and Mediterranean coasts. Here you can really get a feel for Turkish hospitality; a genuine warmth, kindness and eagerness to please that can't fail you set you at ease.

Turkey's biggest attraction is Istanbul, an imperial capital for 1500 years. The country's largest city boasts a magnificent harbour, palaces, bazaars, great shopping and every East-meets-West cliché imaginable. The skyline of minarets above the great Ottoman mosques never fails to impress. Growing air links to Istanbul's modern Atatürk airport brings in swelling numbers of weekenders to sample the city's fine restaurants, boutique hotels, nightclubs and limitless wealth of historic delights.

Another of Turkey's great assets is its enormous number of archaeological sites – it has something like 40,000 of them. Again, the tour buses pick a handful to swamp and leave dozens of equally impressive sites to custodians who spend most of their days

MOST BIZARRE SIGHT!

The distinctly phallic 'fairy chimneys' of Cappadocia – pillars of soft volcanic rock topped by harder capstones

»

»

MEN ENJOYING OKEY, A TILES
GAME, IN ISTANBUL.

TURKEY.

» fishing or tending bees. One such site near Antalya is spectacular Termessos, a well-preserved 2000-year-old city high up in the mountains. Sagalassos, a little further north, is being painstakingly rebuilt by a team from the Belgian University of Leuven, and in summer students give free guided tours. The cave churches of Göreme in Cappadocia are well known, but few people ever visit the incredible Alahan monastery near Karaman. There is more freedom of exploration for visitors to these Turkish archaeological sites than you'll find at similar sites in European countries – you'll rarely see signs asking you to stick to a specific route. However, while exploring it pays to watch out for hidden underground water cisterns.

Turkish touts are legendary, and can be relentless in popular destinations such as Sultanahmet in Istanbul and Marmaris where you may find you're the owner of a carpet you never dreamed you needed. Buying a carpet in Turkey often involves hours of discussion and litres of tea served in tulip-shaped cups – you'll be slowly hypnotised into exposing your credit card! It can get tiring after a while, but if you've just arrived in a town and don't really feel like exploring more museums, bazaars, Turkish baths or ruined cities it certainly helps fill an afternoon!

EVER MORE TO EXPLORE

Eastern Turkey is quite different from the western part of the country. It's drier, more mountainous, poorer and more traditional. Speaking basic Turkish is more of necessity in this area. Since the Kurdish insurgency died down in the late 1990s, more adventurous travellers have been exploring the wonders of Lake Van and the living museum towns of Şanliurfa, Mardin and Diyarbakir. The wet and rainy Black Sea coast is somewhat marred by overdevelopment, but the rafting and hiking opportunities of the Kaçkar Mountains are splendid. For a real frontier experience, hire a car and head into the jaw-dropping gorges and wild forests of the Toros Mountains at the eastern end of the Mediterranean – even intrepid Turkish travellers barely know about this region. Right at the edge of Turkey is the haunting ruined Armenian city of Ani, once secluded in a Cold War security zone, and nearby are the soaring peaks of Mt Ararat, where – according to legend – Noah landed.

"

When we crossed the Turkish border from Tehran (Iran) to Istanbul (Turkey), the women on our bus lifted their veils, revealing make-up and fancy hairstyles. Before we'd gone half an hour into Turkey, all the women had returned from the back in skirts and Western clothes. But most changed of all was the faces of the people – everyone was smiling and talking.

"

- Mick Barrow, Australia

DEFINING EXPERIENCE
- Taking a three-day *gület* (yacht) cruise on the Mediterranean Coast, drinking Efes beer and eating freshly grilled fish, stopping to swim in isolated coves and visiting coastal archaeological sites

RECENT FAD
- Cola wars: Coca-Cola is facing a challenge from local beverage Cola Turca, buoyed by shrinking affection for the USA and, paradoxically, a really cool series of ads starring Chevy Chase.

FESTIVALS & EVENTS
- Camel Wrestling Championship; Selçuk; January. More of a comedy event than real pile-driving camel action – two angry bull camels face off in a ring, one then turns and runs into the crowd…
- Kirkpinar Oil Wrestling; Kirkpinar; third week of June. Traditional Turkish wrestlers cover themselves in olive oil and fight for honour, accompanied by traditional drumming, at this festival.
- Aspendos Opera & Ballet Festival; Aspendos; mid-June–early July. Classical music and fluffy tutus liven up the near-perfectly preserved Roman amphitheatre of Aspendos near Antalya.
- Congress Cup Cirit Competition, Erzurum; July. Cirit is a classic Turkish sport, with two teams on horseback trying to hit each other with wooden javelins. There are several competitions in eastern Turkey but the Erzurum competition is the main event.

DO MENTION
- The fresh and tasty Turkish food. Turkey is a huge agricultural exporter, and much of the food is organic because farmers can't afford or don't need pesticides and agro-industrial chicken plants.

DON'T MENTION
- Anything to do with tax inspectors. Turks live in dread of these heavy-handed bureaucrats, because tax evasion is an essential part of life for nearly every business.

RANDOM FACTS
- The world's biggest chandelier (the size of a car) is in the Dolmabahçe Palace in Istanbul.
- The 'Turkish' fez is in fact North African and hasn't been worn in Turkey since the 1920s.

THINGS TO TAKE
- An iPod or Discman – the music played on Turkish buses can be very repetitive
- Highest-rating sunscreen – it's very expensive here

HOT TIPS FOR TRAVELLERS
- Be aware that many of the carpets and most of the brocades and exotic fabrics on sale in souvenir stores are actually imports from Pakistan and India.
- For the very best Turkish hotels check out the Small Hotels of Turkey website (www.nisanyan.net). It was created by choosy hoteliers Sevan and Mujde Nisanyan.

THREE WORDS TO DESCRIBE THIS COUNTRY
- Asian yet European

- Richard Plunkett

HOT TOPIC OF THE DAY! ⊛

EU membership: Turkey has been trying to join since 1959, and now that it has finally been accepted for membership the Turks don't seem so keen anymore.

»

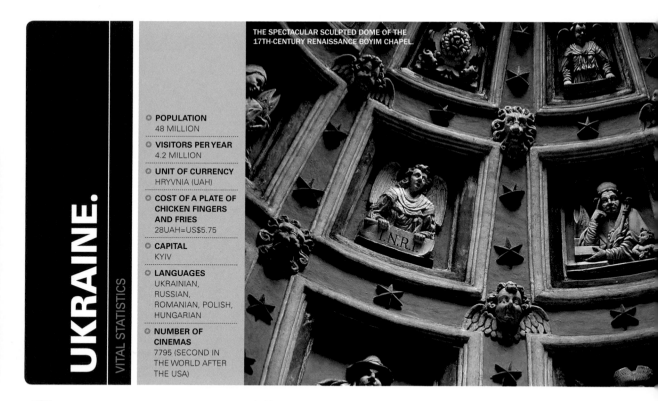
THE SPECTACULAR SCULPTED DOME OF THE 17TH-CENTURY RENAISSANCE BOYIM CHAPEL.

UKRAINE.

VITAL STATISTICS

- **POPULATION**
  48 MILLION
- **VISITORS PER YEAR**
  4.2 MILLION
- **UNIT OF CURRENCY**
  HRYVNIA (UAH)
- **COST OF A PLATE OF CHICKEN FINGERS AND FRIES**
  28UAH=US$5.75
- **CAPITAL**
  KYIV
- **LANGUAGES**
  UKRAINIAN,
  RUSSIAN,
  ROMANIAN, POLISH,
  HUNGARIAN
- **NUMBER OF CINEMAS**
  7795 (SECOND IN THE WORLD AFTER THE USA)

THE COMEBACK KID. Ukraine is one of the most talked about spots in Europe right now. The Ukrainian spirit has not soared this high since the 10th century, when Kyivan Rus was one of the mightiest states in Europe, an economic and learning centre that would become an important foundation of Russian culture.

There is still a long road ahead, but the enthusiasm is contagious. The Ukrainians, or 'Ukes', can hardly believe it themselves. They have had an appalling time in the last 100 years. In the 1930s Stalin wiped out seven million Ukrainians with his engineered famines, then executed or sent to forced labour camps millions more. By the end of WWII, nearly half the population of Ukraine had lost their lives.

Ukraine is the site of the infamous Chornobyl nuclear disaster of 26 April 1986, which marked a critical turn in the country's relations with the Soviet government. After disentangling itself from the crumbling Soviet empire in the early 1990s, Ukraine went through a difficult economic crisis. Most officials in charge of the presumed democratic government were in fact leftovers from the old communist guard. Corruption and nepotism abounded,

and still have not been completely extirpated.

Things came to a head with the so-called Orange Revolution, when hundreds of thousands of Ukrainians flooded the streets to protest the outcome of the November 2004 elections, in which Prime Minister Viktor Yanukovych was declared winner. The elections had been rigged, corrupted, and there were reports of voters being physically intimidated. The numerous supporters of the opposition candidate Viktor Yushchenko wore an orange ribbon or item of dress; orange was the colour used in his election campaign. After a tense standoff, the Supreme Court ordered a new round of elections, and Yushchenko scored the majority of the votes.

This historical popular revolt is widely regarded as the beginning of a new era. However, it might be a while before the

AN ORTHODOX PRIEST HEARS CONFESSION AT THE KYIV CARE MONASTERY.

sinister circus of post-Soviet politics (with its shadowy cast of corrupt officials and gangster capitalists, its mafia-style networks of cronies, and the suspicious serial 'suicides' of prominent figures and journalists) fades into history. There have been rumours of a plot to assassinate Prime Minister Yulia Tymoshenko (who recently ranked third in the *Forbes Magazine* list of most powerful women in the world).

While the hangover of history washes out of the system, you can join the party. Take advantage of the cheap food and drink, trek through the Carpathian Mountains, enjoy the Gothic and Byzantine wonders, stroll through the cosmopolitan port city of Odesa, and lounge about on the coast of Crimea by the Black Sea – which was formerly the favourite holiday spot for the Russian communist aristocracy and dubbed the 'Soviet California'. But please don't remind the Ukrainians of that.

DEFINING EXPERIENCE
☺ Drinking pepper vodka (a Ukrainian speciality) and throwing snowballs at the last remaining stature of Lenin in Kyiv's main thoroughfare

FESTIVALS & EVENTS
☺ Kyiv Days; Kyiv; May. Citizens celebrate the founding day of their city with music and folk art performances.

☺ National Virtuoso; Lviv; May. Expect music and theatrical performances focussing on national themes at this month-long event.

☺ KaZantip; Popovka village, near Yevpatoriya (Crimean Peninsula); July–August; www.kazantip.com. This month-long, nonstop dance party features DJs from Moscow, St Petersburg and Kyiv. People camp out on the festival grounds or on the nearby beach for this huge techno extravaganza.

WHAT'S HOT...
☺ The Orange Revolution

WHAT'S NOT...
☺ Tourists buying kitsch communist paraphernalia (such as CCCP T-shirts)

RECENT FAD
☺ Guided tours through the abandoned site of the Chornobyl nuclear power station are popular. You can don

»

UKRAINE.

"

In Kyiv two men in military uniforms checked my passport. They said my visa was not valid and I had to pay $50 or go to prison. When I refused to pay I was locked up for a night. I went back to Vienna (where I worked) and wrote an article. After the article was published, the Ukrainian ambassador invited me for dinner. He apologized and offered me a lifelong visa for Ukraine. I accepted (he was really polite and the food was awesome) but I haven't been back.

"

- Georgios Axarlis, Greece

HOT TIP FOR TRAVELLERS ★

If you want to know more about the history of the country, *Ukraine: A History*, by Orest Subtelny, is the best place to start. *Letters From Kyiv*, by Solomea Pavlychko, is an eyewitness account of the political and economic upheavals during 1990–91.

» protective clothing and a radiation-measuring device and amble through this haunted postapocalyptic landscape – or you can learn all about the tragedy from the safe distance of the Chornobyl Museum in Kyiv.

DO MENTION
○ That Nikolai Gogol was Ukrainian

DON'T MENTION
○ That Nikolai Gogol was mad

HOT TOPIC OF THE DAY
○ The extravagant lifestyle of Andriy Yushchenko, son of President Viktor Yushchenko, who drives around in a BMW and has a platinum-encased mobile phone. Andriy apparently also owns the copyright on products that use the symbols of the Orange Revolution: mugs, T-shirts, badges and anything emblazoned with the trademark inverted horseshoe or 'Tak!' (meaning 'Yes').

RANDOM FACTS
○ Ukraine won the 2004 Eurovision Song Contest with 'Go Wild', an entry by the amazing Ruslana, who swirled on the stage like a Cossack version of Xena the Warrior Princess. The 2005 Eurovision was held in Kyiv, and the Ukrainian entry was 'We Won't Stand This – No', by Greenjolly. This song was the unofficial anthem of the Orange Revolution.

○ When an explosion blew up the fourth reactor at Chornobyl's nuclear station in 1986, the Soviet Government covered up the disaster. The locals did not find out what had happened until many days later. To this day, the number of fatalities is not known. The official Soviet figure was 40. The UN estimates it was 15,000.

○ By the 15th century, war and plague had wiped out much of the population in the Ukrainian steppes. The place became a refuge for serfs and discontents escaping Catholicism and Polish oppression. These people came to be known as *kazaky* (Cossacks), a Turkic word meaning 'free man'. They acquired a fearful reputation by fighting off the Tatars and the Turks.

THINGS TO TAKE
○ Presents for everybody

THREE WORDS TO DESCRIBE THIS COUNTRY
○ Friendly, reserved, religious

- *Andres Vaccari*

ALBANIA

This pint-sized, sunny slice of Adriatic coast has been ground down for years by poverty and blood vendettas, but Albania now manages to pack a wild punch of traditional Mediterranean charm and Sovietstyle inefficiency. It's a giddy blend of religions, styles, cultures and landscapes. The visitor will find a warm and sincerely hospitable country with fantastic nature, breathtaking mountain landscapes and long sandy white beaches by the clear blue sea.

ANDORRA

Tiny Andorra comprises just a handful of mountainous landscapes and meandering rivers – but it has some of the most dramatic scenery in the Pyrenees, not to mention the best (and cheapest) skiing. There are plenty of good hiking opportunities in the high, remote parts of the country, away from the overdevelopment and heavy traffic that plague Andorra's towns.

ARMENIA

Fate placed Armenia at the point where the European and Middle Eastern continental plates collide, with a resulting mix in fortunes. History has seen Armenia suffer at the hands of conquering armies passing through – Roman, Persian, Arab, Ottoman Turk and Russian. These factors define the Armenians, who are fiercely proud of their language, culture and homeland. Armenia's landscapes span bare rocky highlands, mossy hornbeam and oak forests, stony pastures, gorges cut through layers of volcanic rock, and Lake Sevan's vast blue eye. Distinct seasons run from icy winters to hardened summers; spring's bloom and the long autumn days are ideal.

AUSTRIA

Austria is a land of mountains and impressive architecture with an unrivalled musical tradition that even the *Sound of Music* couldn't sully. Vienna is the capital, hub of the country's musical life and littered with beautiful buildings. Music, art and architecture reach baroque perfection in Salzburg, Mozart's birthplace. However, if baroque palaces, sparkling mountain vistas and Danube cruises don't do it for you, Austria does have another side: the modern-art Museums Quarter in Vienna, the architecturally adventurous Kunsthaus (arts centre) in Graz and the Bergisel tower in Innsbruck are just a few exciting developments in recent years.

AZERBAIJAN

Azerbaijan is exotic by the standards of its neighbours – it's clear that while Georgia and Armenia look to Europe, Azerbaijan is very much part of Asia. Its history and scenery are equally dramatic – from Albanian churches and Baku's old walled city to the extraordinary beauty of the High Caucasus Mountains and the lush plantations of tea covering the hills of the south. Visiting the country takes creativity and imagination as there is almost no traditional tourist industry outside Baku and a few mountain resorts, although a deeply ingrained sense of hospitality makes visiting any area hugely enjoyable.

BELARUS

Geography has played a major role in the history of Belarus, as the low-lying country straddles the shortest route between Moscow and the Polish border. The land has consequently been ravaged by war and controlled by Soviet dictatorship, but has emerged a survivor. A welcome detour from the madding tourist trail, there's more to see in Belarus than you might suspect. Wide stretches of unbroken birch groves, vast forested marshlands, and wooden villages amid rolling green fields give it a haunting beauty. Belarusians fully deserve their reputation of being warm, interesting, cultured and eloquent people.

BELGIUM

Despite being home of the EU, Belgium's spotlight on the European stage remains a little dim, but only because its people are rarely boastful. Belgium has more history, art and architecture packed inside its tiny borders than many of its neighbours, and it claims some of Europe's finest medieval cities: Antwerp, Brussels, Bruges, Ghent and Leuven. Belgians have a keen sense of the good things in life – they know how to eat well, they make some of the world's best beers and there's no need to introduce their chocolate.

BOSNIA & HERCEGOVINA

Sandwiched between Croatia and Serbia, the small country of Bosnia and Hercegovina is characterised by stunning mountain scenery »

« with swirling green rivers and a meld of Eastern and Western cultures. Despite the destruction of much of its heritage during the devastating war of the 1990s, progress since then has been substantial and Bosnia and Hercegovina shows proud resilience through its scars. Gorgeous Sarajevo is coming back to life, but unfortunately access to much of the glorious mountain scenery is still limited due to mines and unexploded ordnance.

BULGARIA

Since the early 1990s Bulgaria has morphed into a more modern version of itself, winning hearts with its surprising beauty and cultural oddities. It attracts tourists with its cheap skiing, beach holidays on the Black Sea coast, bustling capital Sofia, dramatic mountains, havenlike monasteries, Roman and Byzantine ruins, and excellent coffee. In the villages you can still find folk who ride a donkey to work, eat homegrown potatoes and make their own cheese – the difference now is that dinner is eaten in front of a satellite TV.

CYPRUS

Cyprus is a blend of Turkish and Greek, Muslim and Christian influences, viewed through the perspective of 9000 years of constant invasion. Crusader castles rub shoulders with ancient vineyards, frescoed monasteries overlook citrus orchards, and sandy, sunsoaked feet tread Roman mosaic floors. Where you go in Cyprus depends on whether you are a sun-worshipper or a culture vulture. Politically, Cyprus has remained a divided island since 1974 and, although unity is on the EU's agenda, the wounds caused by 30 years of division will not be easily healed.

CZECH REPUBLIC

There's nothing more to the Czech Republic than Prague, right? Think again! Granted, the Golden City does exert a siren pull, but when you tire of its cobbled streets, strike out into the rich and varied landscapes of Bohemia and Moravia – the two lands that together form the Czech Republic. Spruce forests, craggy hills, genteel spa towns and fairy-tale castles beckon. If you haven't tested the spas at Karlovy Vary, admired the enchanting beauty of medieval Český Krumlov or taken in the dramatic landscapes around Labe, then you haven't really seen the Czech Republic.

DENMARK

Cute and compact, Denmark is a harmonious blend of the old and the new. It boasts a compelling mix of lively modern cities, historic towns, rolling farmland, graceful beech woods and sleepy islands full of medieval churches, Renaissance castles and pretty harbours. Copenhagen, Scandinavia's largest and most cosmopolitan capital, is a compact but world-class destination with superb museums, a vibrant cultural life and a burgeoning bar, café and restaurant scene. Danish society stands as a benchmark of civilisation, with progressive policies, widespread tolerance and a liberal social-welfare system.

ESTONIA

This former Soviet Republic has undergone a rapid transformation since independence. The influence of modern technology co-exists happily with a people that are strongly connected to nature, and whose land – almost half of which is forest – is home to countless traditions and folk tales. Apart from the obvious charms of the capital Tallinn, the country boasts a combination of low population and stretches of fabulous nature. Estonia is the pretty little country that could – and did! Its subtle, quiet charms weave their way into your heart before you're aware of it.

FINLAND

Sleek and sophisticated Helsinki is home to Scandinavia's hottest nightlife and continues to grow as a city-break destination. The north boasts midnight sun, the aurora borealis, fast-paced dog sledding and or course Santa's post office (only for those who've been good, of course!). But much of the rest of the country's serenely beautiful, unspoilt wilderness is relatively undiscovered by tourists, making it a must for modern explorers.

GEORGIA

Wherever you enter Georgia your first impression is likely to be of beauty – steep cliffs with waterfalls pouring down to the turquoise waters of the Black Sea, the snow-capped Caucasus Mountains to the north, and the wild semidesert of the east. Tourist facilities in this newly independent nation are challenged by Western standards, but as a visitor you'll be fêted, fed, watered and made to sing and dance, all in incomprehensible Georgian, one of the world's most unusual languages. The warmth you'll experience here will help you understand why Georgia remains a highlight of many people's travels.

GERMANY

Germany nearly made our shortlist. Why? Well, if you think this place is all about beer halls and lederhosen, you've barely scratched its surface. The capital, Berlin, is one of the most exciting cities in Europe – cutting-edge architecture, world-class museums, legendary nightlife. Magnificent Bayreuth hosts a renowned Wagner Festival and Unesco-listed Bamberg is famous for its brewery-restaurants – who needs Munich's boisterous, boozy Oktoberfest? Get beyond the cities, too, and explore the breath-taking countryside: snow-capped alpine mountains, forest-fringed lakes and majestic rivers – none more dramatic than the Rhine, meandering sinuously through a craggy landscape strewn with ancient castles.

HUNGARY

As piquant as the paprika it's famous for, and as romantic as the Roma music that inspired Béla Bartók, Hungary offers visitors a taste of Europe's heart and soul – but at half the price of anywhere in Western Europe. Budapest is the star attraction, fabulously located on the Danube and rich in Art Nouveau and baroque architecture. Outside the capital are ancient castles, rejuvenating spas, Roman ruins, Turkish minarets, and exquisite lake and vine country. Now that Hungary has joined the EU, the time is more than ripe to go.

IRELAND & NORTHERN IRELAND

The Celtic Tiger has a definite limp and Europe's model economy is nowhere near as booming as it was in the '90s, but there are still as many reasons to visit Ireland as there are Irish theme pubs in the rest of the world. Slate-toned lakes, green pastures, ragged coastline and peaceful mountains, bundles of history and the legendary warm welcome still draw devoted followers. It may attract more visitors each year than its number of residents, but finding solitude and serenity is as easy as ever.

LATVIA

You'll never believe it shed its Russian stranglehold less than two decades ago as it has a serenity and charm rarely found elsewhere in Europe. Latvia's capital, Riga, is the biggest and most vibrant city in the Baltics. Great day-trips from Riga include the coastal resort of Jurmala, the Sigulda castles overlooking the scenic Gauja River Valley, and the Rastrelli Palace at Rundale. Latvia's less-travelled roads are equally rewarding, from the dune-lined coast and historic towns of the Kurzeme region in the west to the remote uplands of the east.

LIECHTENSTEIN

Liechtenstein is sandwiched snugly between Austria and Switzerland, Liechtenstein's domineering elder sibling. The Swiss franc is the legal currency and border regulations are necessary only on the Austrian side. A cross-country walk takes on a new meaning, as Liechtenstein measures a mere 25km (15mi) north to south and 6km (3.5mi) west to east. Head to the hills: there are numerous hiking trails offering spectacular views of craggy cliffs, quaint villages and lush green forests.

LITHUANIA

Possibly the Baltic countries' finest weapon of mass attraction – lovely Lithuania is a treasure-trove of unspoilt natural beauty, magical coastline and cobbled baroque cities. Rebellious, quirky and vibrant, Lithuania owes much to the rich cultural currents of central Europe. It once shared an empire with neighbouring Poland that stretched from the Baltic almost to the Black Sea. Its capital Vilnius, praised as the 'New Prague', boasts a baroque Old Town that is the largest in Eastern Europe.

LUXEMBOURG

Lilliputian Luxembourg makes up in snazz what it lacks in size. The beautiful countryside is dotted with feudal castles, deep river valleys and quaint wine-making towns, while the capital, Luxembourg City, is often described as the most dramatically situated in Europe. Luxemburg's people are proud of their heritage: the nation's motto is inscribed everywhere throughout Luxembourg City – *Mir wëlle bleiwe wat mir sin,* 'We want to remain what we are'. After a visit, you're sure to hope they do.

MACEDONIA

Macedonia is a real treat for travellers, especially those who like open spaces, majestic mountains, fantastic lakes and

»

« soaring waterfalls, spiced up with outdoor activities such as trekking, skiing or swimming, and stirred with a rich helping of culture along the way. Up-and-coming capital Skopje is a kicking little city with good nightlife and a buzzing youth scene – for crazy nights out if you overdose on the healthy life.

MALTA

Its warm climate, scenic coastline and reasonable prices have earned Malta a package-holiday reputation, but look beyond the beaches and there's a 5000-year history to explore. Apart from the rich history, Malta also offers beaches, bars, bustling Mediterranean life, friendly locals, a passion for *festas*, water sports and excellent opportunities for scuba diving.

MOLDOVA

One of Europe's smallest yet most divided nations, Moldova is a country of multiple personalities. The nation claims some of the most fertile soil in the former Soviet Union, with forests and vineyards stretching to every corner of its landlocked borders. Yet the natural splendour of Moldova conceals a population torn by political and ethnic tensions. Civil strife has given rise to two break-away republics: Transdniestr and Gaugauz. With a history as colourful as its landscape, Moldova is an intriguing place to visit; a post-Soviet enigma waiting to be unveiled.

MONACO

Tiny, glamorous Monaco, covering a mere 1.95 sq km (0.75 sq mi), is a fantasy land of perfectly groomed streets, lush gardens, chic boutiques and opulent 19th-century pleasure palaces. Most of the people who dwell here are drawn by the sun, glamorous lifestyle and tax-free income. This is the playground of Europe's elite, a country where Lady Luck might clean you out at the casino one day and put you on the Grimaldi guest list the next. It's a glittering, preening, swanking opportunity for people-watching perfect for amateur anthropologists.

NETHERLANDS

Amsterdam hogs the limelight – rightly so – but gable-spotters won't be disappointed if they find themselves in Haarlem, Leiden or Delft. Trendy Rotterdam, meanwhile, has a modern city-scape – by turns vibrant, astonishing and ugly (but memorable) – with a crackling nightlife to rival that of Amsterdam. Den Haag (The Hague), home to the government, has an air of genteel wealth. And when it comes to the landscape, the Dutch have turned a liability into an asset – its iconic windmills hint at the system of dykes and pumps that keep the sea at bay in this below-sea-level land.

NORWAY

There's no getting round it – Norway is an expensive destination. But whether you visit for adrenalin-fuelled thrills or leisurely cruising the coast and islands, Norway's sweeping fjords, white-timbered villages, vast Arctic tundra and rugged peaks will leave you as breathless as would a shot of *aquavit*. There's always tomorrow to save…

POLAND

Poland is a country of striking contrasts: contemporary city slickers fill the capital, Warsaw, while in the countryside horse-drawn carts negotiate peaceful lanes. Poland's relatively undeveloped coastline, with its attractive, sandy beaches, and the rugged mountains of the south are sure to delight visitors, and there are plenty of off-the-beaten-track destinations to discover. Nestled in the heartland of Europe, Poland has been both a bridge and a front line between Eastern and Western Europe. Today the country has bounced back from the turmoil of the 20th century and has quickly modernised since the demise of communism.

PORTUGAL

Portugal's reserve, especially when compared with its exuberant neighbour, Spain, conceals a quiet confidence. Savouring life slowly is a Portuguese passion, and much of the best pleasures are humble: traditional folk festivals; simple, honest food drowning in olive oil; music that pulls at the heart strings, recalling past love and glory; and markets overflowing with fish, fruit and flowers. The landscape is wreathed in olive groves, vineyards and Unesco World Heritage sites, while Portugal's delightfully laidback capital, Lisbon, is an architectural time warp, with Moorish, medieval, Manueline and Art Nouveau riches.

ROMANIA

This 'final frontier' country may be a living museum to Europe's lost ways, but it's also boldly strutting into the future. Straddling the rugged Carpathian Mountains, Romania offers an extraordinary kaleidoscope of cultures and sights, including majestic castles, medieval towns, superb hiking and skiing. Bucharest has a charm and nightlife all of its own. Romania's greatest asset is its diversity, both off the beaten tourist track and well and truly on it.

RUSSIA

Winston Churchill famously described Russia as a 'riddle wrapped in a mystery inside an enigma', and this remains an apt description of a place most outsiders know very little about. A composite of the extravagant glories of old Russia and the drab legacies of the Soviet era, Russia is a country that befuddles and beguiles but never bores. Russia is an essential and fascinating destination for anyone wanting to see another side to the European continent in all its awkward, mysterious glory. Moscow and St Petersburg are two of Europe's biggest cities, and are as dissimilar as it is possible to imagine.

SAN MARINO

San Marino is the world's oldest surviving republic, not much bigger than two or three suburbs strung together. You could think of San Marino as just another kitsch theme park: you can take pictures of the republic's soldiers, buy local coinage, send mail with San Marino stamps and admire the 'genuine reproductions' of medieval relics. But San Marino has its own distinctive flavour and proud identity, boasting some of the most stunning views of the Adriatic.

SCOTLAND

Given the long list of influential Scottish inventors and scientists, you'd think that the Scots would have come up with something to tame the weather. But, as comedian Billy Connolly said, 'there's no such thing as bad weather, only the wrong clothes'. Scotland, like a fine malt, is a connoisseur's delight – a mix of history, culture and arts, festivals galore, feisty people and a wild and beautiful landscape – it should be savoured slowly. It's a place that changes with the seasons, offering something new each time you visit.

SLOVAKIA

Slovakia has fared less well than the Czech Republic since the couple's 'Velvet Divorce' in the early 1990s. Domestic, not international, tourism forms its main source of tourist income. But this is starting to change – visitors are drawn here for the stunning landscapes of the Carpathian and Tatra mountains, great for walking, trekking, skiing and mountain-biking. The capital Bratislava is emerging from its frumpy, communist-era chrysalis to take on the trappings of a booming free market.

SWEDEN

Weekend-breakers may have discovered the hip bars and high design offered up by the tangled back streets of Stockholm, but the rest of Sweden is still waiting to blow people's preconceptions. For every cliché about Ikea, Abba and porn, there's an island accessible only by boat on the archipelago or a wooden cottage in the rolling, lake-studded hills of Dalarna. Further north, there are few spectacles in life more extraordinary than the northern lights, and nothing cooler than a schnapps at the world's original ice hotel.

VATICAN CITY

The world's smallest sovereign state, the Vatican City is the central authority of the Catholic Church, a fact which pervades every street, brick and grain of sand within its borders. Whether you want to check out the sheer volume of art treasures stored here, get in to see the Pope or simply take advantage of the tranquil atmosphere, the Holy See inspires awe in its visitors for good reason.

WALES

With its craggy sculptures of stone and ruined castles rising above the valley mist, otherworldly Wales is where legend and history merge. Lose yourself in the timeless scenery laced with waterfalls, lakes and jagged peaks, winding roads and sandy beaches. Tour villages with tongue-twisting names and gorge yourself on medieval castles and ruins, or join the adrenaline junkies searching for the ultimate thrill. After years of environmental degradation, Wales is carefully guarding its natural landscape and historical architecture. The best way to appreciate the Great Welsh Outdoors is by walking, cycling or canal-boating.

MIDDLE EAST
» & NORTH AFRICA.

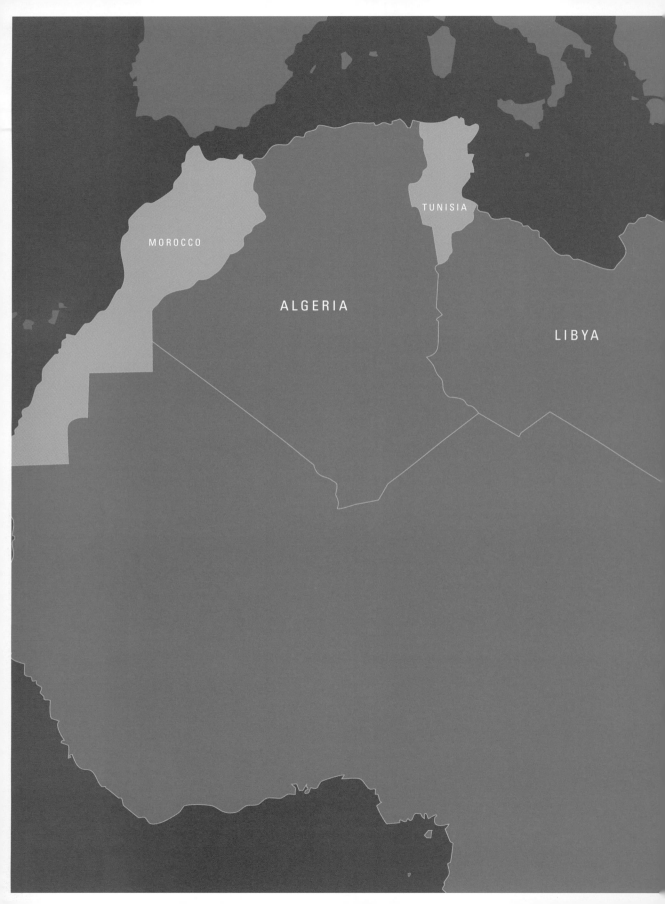

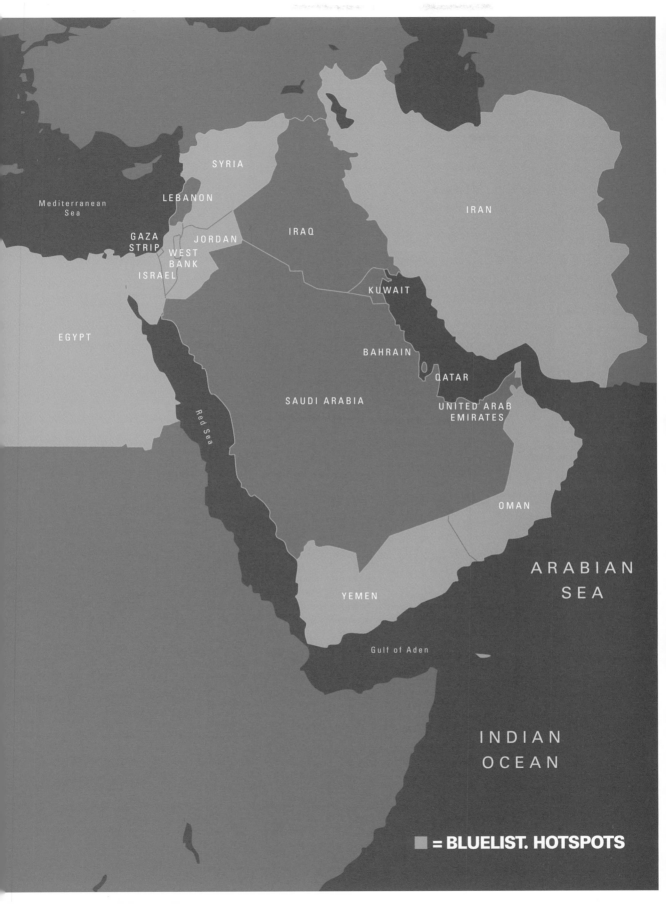

A SUFI FROM THE EGYPTIAN HERITAGE DANCE TROUPE.

EGYPT.

VITAL STATISTICS

- **POPULATION**
  74.9 MILLION
- **VISITORS PER YEAR**
  4.9 MILLION
- **UNIT OF CURRENCY**
  EGYPTIAN POUND
  (E£)
- **COST OF A CUP OF COFFEE**
  E£2.50 = US$0.45
- **CAPITAL**
  CAIRO
- **LANGUAGE**
  ARABIC

A CACOPHONY OF VOICES. If Cairo is the 'Mother of the World', then Egypt is its crossroads, a short hop from Europe, with one foot firmly planted in the Middle East and the other resolutely tapping to an African rhythm.

Egypt has always been all things to all people. It was occupied but never really conquered by such luminaries as Alexander the Great and Napoleon. It drew adventurers as diverse as Agatha Christie and Thomas Cook. Even as Egypt reinvents itself every day, not one ounce of its universal appeal has diminished. Indeed, no matter how many people visit Egypt every year, its mysteries ensure that it is, and will always be, a destination with cachet.

If you were schooled in the erudite halls of academic archaeology, the Pyramids of Giza, Luxor's Valley of the Kings and Karnak Temple, and Abu Simbel will be some highlights among many of Egypt's splendid Pharaonic heritage. If your apprenticeship was served amid the after-dark hedonism of the Mediterranean, the Sinai Peninsula's Red Sea Coast with its vibrant resorts and undersea wonders will appeal. Egypt's spectacular sights are countless – just ask Unesco, who have inscribed more Egyptian sights on their World Heritage list than any other country in the Middle East or Africa.

For all its wonders, Egypt has always been as much an idea as a place. In its modern manifestation, Egypt is the place to take the pulse of the Middle East. You'll soon discover that this pulse is racing, propelling the Middle East forward with its contradictions. It is at once elegantly sophisticated (Alexandria) and more clamorous than any place in the world (Cairo). In places like Siwa Oasis, where life proceeds at a tempo unchanged in centuries, time seems to trail off into the unfathomable Sahara Desert. Egypt is defiantly modern – it's the Middle East's capital of cinema, the leviathan of Arab pop and home to the Middle East and North Africa's largest pool of moneyed middle class. At the same time it is the touchstone of tradition – Islamic scholarship here determines trends across

PRAYER SESSIONS IN A LANEWAY, LUXOR.

the region, impoverished villagers till soil as in days of old and craftsmen's hammers pound out a subsistence living. This country also has its own share of geopolitical intrigue. Egypt is Israel's friend, but you'll often wonder whether this friendship is estranged as Egypt's beleaguered government balances upon the tightrope that separates its people from their Palestinian brothers and sisters, the government's American benefactors and its troublesome neighbours.

Egypt's contrasts and juxtapositions make this a country impossible to define, with the exception of one enduring theme. This is a country where life is lived at full volume, from roiling marketplaces and persistent touts to heartbreakingly beautiful calls to prayer from the country's mosques. More than that, it's a place of extremes, with travellers as susceptible to the rage of terrorists – the attack on hotels in Sharm al-Sheikh in July 2005 killed almost a hundred – as to disarming hospitality by ordinary Egyptians who would rather not eat themselves than see you go hungry. Egypt is as confronting as it is compelling, the place where all the hope and alienation of the region has taken root and found full voice.

DEFINING EXPERIENCE
☼ Sailing aboard a slow felucca (sailing ship) up the timeless waters of the Nile River as the temples of ancient Egypt slide past on the riverbank, the clamour of Egyptian diva Umm Kolthum wails from a nearby village and a call to prayer wafts out across the palm trees underneath which run children demanding 'one pen, one pen'

FESTIVALS & EVENTS
☼ International Book Fair; Cairo; January. This is the Middle East and Africa's largest book fair.

☼ Ascension of Ramses II; Abu Simbel; February. This is the first of two dates each year (the other is at the Birth of Ramses; October) when the sun penetrates into the inner sanctuary of the temple at Abu Simbel, illuminating the statues of gods within. It showcases all the pomp and ceremony of Egypt's premier king.

DO MENTION
☼ Quite early in negotiations mention that you won't sell your wife or daughter no matter how many camels you're offered. »

RECENT FAD! ★

Internet chat, text messaging, satellite TV and all things technological that enable young Egyptians to escape the watchful eye of their parents and the government

»»

FROM THE ROAD

> *I use Lonely Planet's quip about Cairo traffic – 'chariot race from* Ben Hur *with Peugeots' – regularly; an utterly breathtaking experience. Everyone should have a 30-minute peak hour taxi ride in Cairo once in their life!*

- Colin Youl, Australia

HOT TOPIC OF THE DAY! ⭐

What will happen after President Hosni Mubarak moves on? Will his family follow the path of Syria and Jordan and plant a dynasty? Or will an Islamic government arise? And, while we're at it, when will ordinary Egyptians finally get a say in their own future?

» DON'T MENTION

- The dress sense of young Egyptian men. Above all, the shirts – psychedelic patterns of brown and orange are not unusual – are what will catch the eye and hold it longer than you'd like. But always remember, *they* think they're cool.

HOT TIPS FOR TRAVELLERS

- When choosing a hotel, make sure it is at least 500m from the nearest mosque unless you want a melodic but utterly disorienting 4.30am wake-up call.

- If life on the Egyptian road gets too much, head for Dahab, a backpacker's paradise where everyone stays for twice as long as they planned.

- If a tout or tour guide takes you to a shop, the price of whatever you buy will include his or her commission.

- Ignore Cairo touts who tell you that the hotel of your choice is full, has closed down or has burned to the ground – it isn't and it hasn't.

RANDOM FACTS

- So great was Umm Kolthum's hold over the hearts of the Arab world that the coup which brought Muammar Gaddafi to power in neighbouring Libya on 1 September 1969 was delayed so as not to clash with an Umm Kolthum concert.

- Egyptian novelist Naguib Mahfouz won the Nobel Prize for Literature in 1988.

- Al-Azhar in Cairo is the world's oldest surviving university.

- According to the Torah, Bible and Quran, Moses received the Ten Commandments atop Mt Sinai, which is accessible from Dahab.

- Amr Diab, the chic king of Egyptian pop, is the Middle East's highest-selling artist.

MOST BIZARRE SIGHT

- Movie scouts touring the cafés around Cairo's cheap hotels in search of backpackers looking to earn a bit of cash for a day's work as an extra in an Egyptian movie

THINGS TO TAKE

- Ear plugs: sleeping amid the Egyptian clamour can be a challenge

- Either Ahdaf Soueif's *The Map of Love* or *In the Eye of the Sun*: stunning novels that capture the essence of modern Egypt's struggle between past and present

- A short-wave radio: you can pick up the BBC World Service on various frequencies, including AM 1323 in Alexandria, the Europe short-wave schedule in Cairo and the Middle East short-wave schedule in Upper Egypt

- A small size-three football: Egyptians love football and kids will quickly stop asking for pens and join any game you start

THREE WORDS TO DESCRIBE THIS COUNTRY

- Ancient, awe-inspiring, marvellous

- Anthony Ham

PLUMES OF SMOKE FROM A WATER PIPE IN ESFAHAN

VITAL STATISTICS

IRAN.

- **POPULATION**
  69 MILLION
- **VISITORS PER YEAR**
  1.3 MILLION
- **UNIT OF CURRENCY**
  IRANIAN RIAL (IR)
- **COST OF A FRUIT MILKSHAKE**
  IR3500 = US$0.40
- **CAPITAL**
  TEHRAN
- **LANGUAGES**
  PERSIAN (FARSI), TURKIC, TURKIC DIALECTS

✪ BEHIND THE VEIL. You should exercise extreme caution when travelling to Iran. There have been a number of bomb attacks recently, most of them arising from internal politics leading to the presidential elections in June 2005.

On 12 June 2005, at least 10 people were killed and dozens injured after bombs went off in cities across the country. There have also been hostile demonstrations outside the British embassy, and Westerners have been the target of kidnappers in the southeast of the country. The borders with Afghanistan, Pakistan and Iraq are particularly risky.

Prior to the US-led occupation of Iraq, and before the War on Terror spread a pervasive veil of paranoia about all things Middle Eastern, Iran was a popular destination for Western tourists. After the death of the Ayatollah Khomeini in 1989, and as the country emerged from a crippling and pointless war with Iraq, Iran began to open up to international visitors again. At the moment, Iran is locked into a protracted diplomatic struggle over its intentions to start a nuclear programme which Iran claims is strictly for energy purposes. In June 2005, after eight years of reformist struggle, a new president was elected: Mahmoud Ahmadinejad, a self-professed conservative who is determined to push ahead with the country's nuclear ambitions.

Iran is home to the Persians, one of the greatest civilisations the world has ever seen. The Persian people have occupied this region for the last 2500 years and their culture has absorbed and endured takeovers by almost everybody, greatly changing and growing in the process. Cyrus the Great first established the Persian Empire in 550 BC by snatching the throne of the Medes, one of the ruling Aryan tribes in the region. The ruins of Persepolis, the magnificent city founded by his successor Darius, are the highlight of any visit to Iran. Then Alexander the Great came. Then the Parthians. And then Ardashir, who founded the Sassanian empire. The Arabs stormed into Persia in AD 640 and established Islam as the cultural lifeblood of a new empire. Yet, a seemingly endless list »

RECENT FAD! ✪

'Pinglish', a mixture of English and Persian that teenagers use to compose text messages on their mobile phones

THE ALBORZ MOUNTAINS HAVE ABOUT 70 PEAKS OF MORE THAN 4000M HIGH.

IRAN.

» of wannabe empire builders kept pouring in: the Turks, the Mongols, and, more recently, the British and the Russians. Throughout this turmoil, some cultural features remained remarkably intact. The Persian language, for example, has hardly changed in 10 centuries.

Thanks to the relentless propaganda circulated in the Western media, the name 'Iran' is likely to conjure up the image of a bunch of sinister mullahs in beards making bombs, staging public beheadings and chanting 'Allah is great, Death to the West'. In 2002 US President George W Bush famously branded Iran part of an 'Axis of Evil'. This did not improve the situation.

Beneath the hysteria and misinformation, the real Iran presents a very different face; it is a sophisticated and truly breathtaking country. For many years now, Iranians have been poised on a razor's edge between ancient traditions and the contradictions of modernisation. A casual walk through downtown Tehran reveals the struggles and contrasts at the heart of contemporary Iranian society.

Iran's form of government is a theocracy; it's ruled by a president, a Council of Guardians ensuring that laws and social practices adhere to Islamic principles, and the Islamic Consultative Assembly (the legislative arm). The rules are strict and the punishments harsh. For instance, recently two young men were publicly executed for having homosexual relations. Visitors from the West (especially

OLDER THAN JESUS

Zoroastrianism is the earliest religion in the world to continue to the present day. It predates Judaism, Christianity and Islam, and deeply influenced each of these faiths. The preacher Zoroaster (Zarathustra or Zartosht) spread his message around the Irano–Central Asia region around 1400 BC. His philosophy was the first to postulate a single God who created all things, the notion of good and evil, and paradise and hell. Also, Zoroastrians were the first to picture angelic beings with wings and haloes, a tradition later copied by Christian iconographers.

> *I recently travelled to Esfahan. The coffee shop behind my hotel is one of the few places in the city where the local teenagers can go to eat ice cream and smile bashfully at their best friend's sister across the table. The whole experience was a great treat.*

- Katharine Shepherd, Britain

1934, when Reza Shah changed it to its modern name.

- Iran produces 53% of the world's pistachios.

- The famous Iranian mathematician and poet Omar Khayyam calculated the year to be 365.2 days, preceding the modern calendar by 500 years.

WHAT'S HOT...
- Iranian cinema, which has been attracting a lot of international attention in the past few years

WHAT'S NOT...
- 'Axis of Evil' rhetoric

HOT TOPIC OF THE DAY
- The tense nuclear policy standoff

DO MENTION
- The immense Arabic contribution to the history of mathematics and astronomy

DON'T MENTION
- The War on Terror

THINGS TO TAKE
- Sunscreen and hat

- Items of female hygiene (such as tampons, shampoo etc)

- American dollars – somewhat ironically these are widely accepted and traders prefer them over any other currency

THREE WORDS TO DESCRIBE THIS COUNTRY
- Generous, intricate, sensuous

- Andres Vaccari

female visitors) must familiarise themselves with certain rules of conduct and codes of dress. But this is not too hard, and the rewards are worth it.

The present regime does not count with the universal approval of Iranians. A generation of young people born after the heyday of the Islamic Revolution are clamouring for greater freedoms, and making their voices heard. Beneath the government's anti-Western rhetoric, the people of Iran are friendly, hospitable, and highly cultured. Unlike many Westerners, they know how to discriminate between people and the views of their governments.

Only the future can tell which way the balance will tip.

DEFINING EXPERIENCE
- Watching a flock of brown and green bee-eaters take flight from among the ruined columns of Persepolis and into a cloudless noon sky

RANDOM FACTS
- The name Iran refers to the Aryan (meaning 'of noble origin') tribes that settled in the area around 1600 BC. The region was known as Persia until

HOT TIP FOR TRAVELLERS!

It is imperative that you familiarise yourself with the rules and customs and that you try not to offend anybody.

ISRAEL+ WEST BANK & GAZA STRIP.

VITAL STATISTICS

- **POPULATION**
  6.9 MILLION, 3.8
  MILLION IN THE WEST
  BANK AND GAZA
- **VISITORS PER YEAR**
  1.6 MILLION
- **UNIT OF CURRENCY**
  ISRAELI SHEKEL (NIS)
- **COST OF A CUP OF COFFEE**
  12NIS = US$2.50
- **CAPITAL**
  JERUSALEM
  (DISPUTED)
- **LANGUAGES**
  HEBREW, ARABIC
- **AGING LEADERSHIP**
  ISRAEL'S PRESIDENT
  IS 83 AND ITS PRIME
  MINISTER IS 78.
  PALESTINIAN LEADER
  MAHMOUD ABBAS
  IS 70.

AN ORTHODOX JEW PRAYS UNDER THE SHADOW OF THE MENORAH IN THE OLD CITY OF JERUSALEM.

BACK FROM THE BRINK. When Ariel Sharon and Mahmoud Abbas shook hands in Sharm al-Sheikh in February 2005, officially ending the second *intifada* (literally, the 'shaking off'), Israel and the Palestinian Territories dusted off their collective cobwebs and prepared for the tourist boom.

Tour operators started booking out hotels and El Al's phones were ringing off their hooks. This was all the more improved when the US lifted its warning against travel in Israel. Over the first half of 2005 tourist numbers were up by 30% compared with 2004, but there was still a long way to go to reach 1999 levels (tourism fell by 75% during the 2001–04 *intifada*). Most tourists come from Britain, France, Italy, Germany and the US, the bulk being package and group tours. Independent travellers and backpackers have been slower to respond but are certainly on the rise. How long the influx continues is entirely dependent on the security situation – another string of bombings will almost certainly cause a reversal of fortunes.

21ST-CENTURY DIGITAL BOY

The lull in tourism by no means sent Israel's tourist board to sleep. On the contrary, a number of tourist sites and places of historical interest have been renovated, expanded and improved, thanks to Israel's hi-tech prowess. Multimedia adventures, cable cars, sound and light shows and thrill rides are a few of the gimmicks being used. While this may sound off-putting to those travellers who prefer DIY adventures, several of these attractions certainly merit consideration. Check out the interactive theatre at Caesarea National Park; here a holographic King Herod answers your questions and a hi-tech theatre allows you to 'tour' the ancient city during different periods of its history. A similar upgrade has been bequeathed to the Jerusalem Archaeological Park & Davidson Center, which sports an impressive film showing a reconstruction of the Second Temple.

A WOMAN KICKS BACK IN THE DEAD SEA WATERS.

Tourist sites in the West Bank are likewise clambering out of their slumber; Jericho in particular is being primed for an increase in visitors, thanks to a new tourist complex and cable car up the Mount of Temptation. Other parts of the West Bank are still the Wild West, and visiting places like Nablus, Bethlehem and Hebron will involve crossing checkpoints, ID checks, bag searches and changing vehicles en route. It's unorthodox travel to say the least but worth it to see the state of Palestine-*in-utero*.

SHOULD YOU GO?

Despite the 2005 ceasefire, Israel and Palestine still have quite a few details to hash out before a genuine peace can be established. Bombings, shootings and protests still occur so it's necessary to keep abreast of the situation. Casual tourists will experience few problems as long as they steer clear of demonstrations and hotbeds of violence such as Gaza (which is totally off-limits to tourists anyway). Those who do visit Israel now will find the timing good; tourist areas are not yet overrun and accommodation is still discounted. Land borders with Jordan and Egypt are also a breeze, so it's easy to wedge a trip to the Holy Land between the pyramids and Petra.

DEFINING EXPERIENCE

☼ A security guard probing you with his metal detector outside a bus station while a group of Heredi men nearby silently read their scriptures, oblivious to shouts and slogans of marching peacenik demonstrators as they head towards a wall of heavily armed teenage soldiers, who, if you asked them, would rather be in Ko Samui.

FESTIVALS & EVENTS

☼ Eilat International Film Festival; March; www.eilatfilmfest.com.

☼ Holy Week; Jerusalem; April. This week-long occasion commemorates the Passion of Christ. Events leading up to the death of Christ are re-enacted, masses are held and the faithful partake in ritual processions.

☼ World Pride; August. A massive gay-pride parade and festival.

☼ Red Sea Jazz Festival; Eilat; August.

☼ Tel Aviv Love Parade; August. This massive street and beach celebration will attract up to 250,000 party people decked out in flesh and body paint.

»

ISRAEL+
WEST BANK & GAZA STRIP.

FROM THE ROAD

> *In Israel, where many marriages are arranged by the parents, I met a woman in search of a bride for her son – and agreed to marry him. We celebrated our silver wedding anniversary last year.*

- Judith Rachmani, Israel

» WHAT'S HOT...
- Wine-tasting tours in the Golan Heights
- Avant-garde films
- Tel Aviv Maccabee basketball team
- Castro Men clothing
- Palestinian hip-hop
- Little yarmulkes

WHAT'S NOT...
- Working on a kibbutz
- Settlement building
- Trips to the Sinai
- Approval ratings for Sharon and Abbas

HOT TIPS FOR TRAVELLERS
- There are so many unique hostels and Christian hospices in Jerusalem that it's worth staying in two or three just for the experience; try one in East Jerusalem, one in the Old City Muslim Quarter and one near Jaffa Gate.
- Cairo and Damascus are more famous as places to study Arabic, but there are also opportunities in East Jerusalem. Ask at the British Council (31 Nablus Rd, Jerusalem; issa.faltas@ps.britishcouncil.org).

HOT TOPIC OF THE DAY! ⊛

Where to from here? Few Israelis are confident that Mahmoud Abbas has the power to fully crack down on terrorism. Even fewer Palestinians believe Sharon is serious about peace. Optimism for a peaceful resolution runs low but the conflict still makes for heated discussion.

- Look out for the publication *This Week in Palestine* or check its website, www .thisweekinpalestine.com, for the latest Palestinian news and views.

DO MENTION
- Israeli-born actress Natalie Portman and Euroleague basketball champions the Tel Aviv Maccabee. Another good ice breaker is the army; all Israelis are happy to detail where and how they served their term. Among Palestinians and Israeli Arabs, mention star football players Abbas Suan and Walid Badir who scored key goals for Israel during the 2005 World Cup qualifying matches.

DON'T MENTION
- Your extremist political views. Keep them silently tucked away until you've got a really good grasp of the situation on the ground. Jokes about the Holocaust are also a big no-no.

RANDOM FACTS
- Israel exports about 10% of the world's military equipment.
- During Israel's first years of existence, Albert Einstein was offered its presidency. Needless to say, he declined.
- The future state of Palestine already has a national motto: May God Protect My Country.
- The English words 'map', 'napkin' and 'apron', originate in the Hebrew language.

MOST BIZARRE SIGHTS
- The Separation Wall where it cuts through towns, villages and, in some cases, backyards
- Railway and bus stations on Sunday mornings when they are packed with M-16–toting soldiers heading back to base

THINGS TO TAKE
- A set of decent clothes for clubbing in Tel Aviv
- For women, an ankle-length skirt; it will allow you to blend in better in Jerusalem
- An open mind

THREE WORDS TO DESCRIBE THIS COUNTRY
- Middle East conflict

- *Michael Kohn*

YOUR CAMEL AWAITS – ALTERNATIVE TRANSPORT AROUND THE RUINS OF PETRA

VITAL STATISTICS

JORDAN.

⊙ **POPULATION**
5.5 MILLION

⊙ **VISITORS PER YEAR**
1.3 MILLION

⊙ **UNIT OF CURRENCY**
JORDANIAN DINAR (JD)

⊙ **COST OF A CUP OF COFFEE**
JD0.50 = US$0.70

⊙ **CAPITAL**
AMMAN

⊙ **LANGUAGES**
ARABIC, ENGLISH

⊙ **NUMBER OF CAMELS**
18,000

★ **A FEW EVENTFUL MILLENNIA.** Given the volatile situation in the Middle East, travelling to Jordan should be approached with caution. It is advisable to steer well clear of the borders with Israel and Iraq, which have been the site of sporadic violence in the last two years.

Jordan is touted as a potential terrorist target by many international watchdogs. The last attack was in April 2003, and since then Jordanian security forces have foiled several terrorist plans. Avoid public demonstrations, political gatherings and places with a high concentration of tourists. Of course, this is not always easy or realistic. Check the news from the region and the updates on the official travel advisories before making your decision.

Jordan has so far been the safest place in the Middle East. It has managed to stay out of the conflicts that have engulfed the region, thanks in part to the skilful negotiations of King Hussein. Jordanians are very friendly; everywhere you go, people will be eager to help you, invite you into their homes and offer you myriad cups of tea. It is rude to refuse. This selfless generosity stems in part from very ancient

traditions. For instance, in the world of the ancient Greeks, Zeus was the god of hospitality, and to turn away strangers was one of the highest offences. It was also rumoured that gods wandered the countryside disguised as beggars, knocking on doors and punishing severely those who refused them.

Virtually every ancient civilisation has passed through Jordan and left its slice of history, including the Sumerians, Hebrews, Egyptians, Babylonians, Greeks, Romans, Crusaders and Ottoman Turks. Throughout all these upheavals, the desert Bedouins have watched empires come and go and have managed to hold on to their land and way of life.

There is no shortage of things to see in Jordan, including many Biblical sites. Jordan's capital Amman is a modern and cosmopolitan metropolis, with up-to-date »

MOST BIZARRE SIGHT! ✪

Tourists lying on the beach by the Dead Sea covered in the rich mud of the area, which is apparently very good for the skin

»»

BEDOUIN MEN FROM WADI RUM.

JORDAN.

» infrastructure and amenities. It makes a great base to explore the rest of the country. Some of the best-preserved ruins in the Middle East are in Jordan, including famous Petra, a colossal city hewn out of rock, and the ancient Roman city of Jerash. Visit these places and you'll feel as though you've stepped back in time; the history is palpable. During the 20th century, the Middle East has been carved up into its modern configuration of nation-states; but trekking through the deserts and abandoned cities of the region makes you realise how arbitrary these divisions are. It's tempting to cast your mind back and imagine the fault-lines of all those ancient empires that once ruled over these cities, seas, and red sands. During their heyday, those empires also seemed invincible and eternal. In the difficult times we live in, this thought comes as something of a consolation.

DEFINING EXPERIENCE
○ Having tea in a Bedouin's tent after a camel ride through the desert of Wadi Rum

FESTIVALS & EVENTS
○ Dead Sea Ultra Marathon; Amman–Dead Sea; April. People from dozens of countries take part in this marathon to raise funds for patients suffering from neurological diseases, and to spread a message of peace and international cooperation.

○ Jerash Festival; July; www.jerashfestival.com.jo. The theatres of the ancient city of Jerash open to the public in this two-week international festival, which features music, poetry, dance and theatre.

WHAT'S HOT...
○ The Jordan Valley in July

WHAT'S NOT...
○ US foreign policy

HOT TIP FOR TRAVELLERS
○ The most important piece of advice is to familiarise yourself with the traditions and customs of this Arab nation, observe and respect them at all times.

RANDOM FACTS
○ Although the population is mostly of Islamic faith (mostly Sunni Muslims), Jordan is officially a secular state.

○ Due to a high evaporation rate, the waters of the Dead Sea are so high in minerals

> *A friend and I met a couple of guys in Jordan who drew us a map of how to enter the ancient city of Petra before sunrise. So there we were, all alone watching the beautiful sunrise over the tombs and caves in Petra. It was so unreal and nobody else were there.*
>
> - Ingela Johansson, Sweden

○ A headscarf, the best protection from the sun

THREE WORDS TO DESCRIBE THIS COUNTRY
○ Timeless, stunning, sandy

- Andres Vaccari

JORDAN.

and salinity that your body floats, and sinking or drowning is near impossible.

○ In Tell al-Kharrar you can visit the site where, allegedly, Jesus was baptised. The Israelis, however, claim that the site is on *their* side of the border.

○ TE Lawrence (aka Lawrence of Arabia, 1888–1935) was an upper-class English archaeologist who supported the Arab Revolt during WWI. Leading an army of 100,000 Arabs, he defeated the Ottoman Turks at Aqaba, in the south of the country. Today Aqaba is a popular beach resort, the only one of its kind in Jordan.

HOT TOPICS OF THE DAY
○ The Israeli-Palestinian conflict
○ The War on Terror

DO MENTION
○ That you hope for peace

DON'T MENTION
○ George W Bush

THINGS TO TAKE
○ Light, loose-fitting clothing that you can layer when it gets colder

THE VILLAGE OF AIT BENHADDOU IS ONE OF THE BEST PRESERVED KASBAHS IN THE ATLAS REGION.

MOROCCO.

VITAL STATISTICS

- **POPULATION**
  31.7 MILLION
- **VISITORS PER YEAR**
  4.2 MILLION
- **UNIT OF CURRENCY**
  MOROCCAN DIRHAM (DH)
- **COST OF A CUP OF COFFEE**
  DH5 = US$0.55
- **CAPITAL**
  RABAT
- **LANGUAGES**
  ARABIC, BERBER, FRENCH

BRIDGE OVER TROUBLED WATERS. In this post–War-on-Terror world (yes, we know it's not over), Morocco is a country whose time has come.

Morocco is both a bridge between peoples and a crossroads of history – in other words, it's long been accustomed to welcoming the world to its shores and not even the spectre of terrorism can throw this wonderful country and its even more wonderful people off their stride. After September 11 and terrorist bombings in Casablanca in 2003, the number of tourists visiting the country dropped dramatically. For those of you who didn't come because you thought it wasn't safe – in which case we assume you won't be visiting London, Madrid or New York any time soon either – it is, quite simply, your loss. At a time when bridges between cultures are more important than ever, Morocco is at once wholeheartedly African, proudly Middle Eastern and a slice of Europe grafted onto the African mainland. Not to mention as safe as anywhere else in the world.

For the comfort or security conscious, Morocco is reassuringly European (well, almost) in its tourist infrastructure, security measures and the attitude among locals that the best way to combat terrorism is to join with the peoples of the world in friendship. You'll find this latter quality in abundance – hospitality is an enduring hallmark of Moroccans. On the doorstep of Europe it may be and many of Europe's values it may share, but follow the aroma of spices or the rhythmic beat of a craftsman's hammer down a labyrinthine lane of one of Morocco's medieval bazaars, and you'll soon be transported into an altogether more exotic world.

AFRICA'S GATEWAY

A Moroccan sojourn will add depth, cachet and a whole new dimension to your travels and, best of all, it's an easy add-on to a European journey – if you're in London, Morocco is closer than both Athens and Istanbul. As you fly over that narrow stretch of water that separates Africa

SLOWLY DOES IT ACROSS THE IMMENSE SAND DUNES OF ERG CHEBBI NEAR MERZOUGA.

from Europe, remember that these same waters, so tranquil from above, tell a wholly different travel story from your own. Every year untold numbers of illegal immigrants attempt the crossing to Spain in leaky boats. Many make it, many more don't and some even die in the attempt. Their story is both tragic and courageous, a salutary lesson that travelling in someone else's country is a privilege not open to everyone.

Europe may tower over Morocco to the north, but Africa presses equally close from the south. The Sahara Desert – the world's largest – looms large above Morocco, offering in equal measure founts of inexpressible solitude, the untold beauty of nature's erotically sculpted sand dunes and a challenge to cross the sands. Reach the other side and you'll find yourself deep in Africa and what could ultimately be the journey of a lifetime.

Whether you're on your way north or south, Morocco's many charms – including the incomparable clamour of Marrakesh's night market, the dizzying other-worldliness of the Fès medina, the mud-brick fortresses of the Atlas Mountains, and the laid-back and super-cool port of Essaouira – will make it a destination you'll never forget.　»

SOMETHING FAMILIAR ABOUT THIS PLACE...

If you're into movies, a sense of *déjà vu* will be your constant companion on your Moroccan journey. *Othello*, starring Orson Welles, was filmed in Essaouira, while Alfred Hitchcock decided that nowhere but Marrakesh would do for the backdrop to *The Man Who Knew Too Much*. Fast forward to more recent times and the trend continues – *Lawrence of Arabia*, *Alexander*, *Gladiator*, *The Sheltering Sky*, *Jesus of Nazareth*, *The Last Temptation of Christ*, *Asterix* and *Hideous Kinky* were all filmed, at least in part, in Morocco.

Alongside this galaxy of superstars, however, is one glaring omission: not one second of *Casablanca*, perhaps the most famous movie supposedly set in Morocco, was filmed in Morocco, nor did Humphrey Bogart or Ingrid Bergman ever set foot in the country.

MOROCCO.

> "*If you get the chance, visit Chefchaouen in the Rif Mountains. We split up our bus trip from Fès to Tangier by staying in this beautiful mountain village for a night. After the hustle and bustle of Fès it was a welcome relief. The people are chilled, you don't get hassled as much and the blue-washed streets and houses are unlike anywhere else we saw.*"

— Simon Kenny, Britain

MOST BIZARRE SIGHT! ✪

The starting line of the Marathon des Sables, otherwise known as the Sahara Marathon. From 7 April 2006 in Ouarzazate, around 600 runners embark on the world's toughest foot race – 243km (150mi) over six (or, for some, seven) days. Even the race's website (www .saharamarathon.co.uk) describes the event as 'a world of lunatics and masochists'. If you thought the starting line was bizarre, you should see the finish line.

» DEFINING EXPERIENCE

○ Catch a breeze on an Essaouira rooftop overlooking an expansive sweep of beach and surrounded by Berber, Portuguese and French architecture, while listening to lounge music wafting up from the downstairs bar which is filled with artists from across the world.

RECENT FAD

○ French is the language of chic, as cool, world-wise and successful young Moroccans begin returning home, reversing the decades-long trend of Moroccans emigrating to Europe – these recent returnees plan to remake Morocco in their own image.

FESTIVALS & EVENTS

○ Festival of World Sacred Music; Fès; June. This festival attracts world-class acts to perform in the acoustically rich palaces and old homes of Morocco's most venerable city.

○ *Gnawa* & World Music Festival; Essaouira; June. Showcases jazz, local *gnawa* and music and art from across Africa.

○ Festival of Folklore; Marrakesh; June. An infectiously chaotic clamour of street performances by Morocco's premier acts.

DO MENTION

○ How safe you feel. Ever since September 11 and the terrorist bombing of Casablanca, Moroccans are desperate for the world to love and trust them again and you'll make their day by telling them that you do both.

DON'T MENTION

○ The Western Sahara. Ever since 1975 when an extraordinary march of 300,000 unarmed Moroccans took the territory, Moroccans won't hear a word spoken against their occupation, no matter what the UN or the indigenous Sahrawis say.

RANDOM FACTS

○ Numerous writers and painters have been inspired by the Moroccan light, among them Henri Matisse, William Burroughs and Paul Bowles.

○ If you feel old in Morocco, it's because one-third of the population is under 15.

THINGS TO TAKE

○ Warm clothes for crisp (or downright freezing) desert nights

○ English-language reading material as you won't find a lot in Moroccan bookshops

○ No fixed date for returning home – you'll only want to stay longer

○ Sleeping pills to counteract the caffeine-hits from so much tea and coffee that will be 'forced' upon you by friendly people

HOT TIPS FOR TRAVELLERS

○ Although the situation is improving, until it stabilises across the border in Algeria you'd be well advised to remain on the Moroccan side of the frontier.

○ Be patient at all times – everything does happen but it does so in its own time.

THREE WORDS TO DESCRIBE THIS COUNTRY

○ Exotic, colourful, intense

— *Anthony Ham*

JUST CHILLIN' WITH MATES AT THE FOOD STUFF SHOP.

ABDULLAH BIN NASER BIN MOHD.AL-JAFRI TRAD.
FOOD STUFF

⭐ **FRIENDLY PORT IN A STORM.** With the current political climate in the Persian Gulf, people have become a bit twitchy about visiting the Gulf States, but Oman is one place where you can experience traditional Islamic hospitality without the accompanying threat of international terrorism.

In fact, the attitude of the Omanis towards foreigners tends to be one of benign paternalism – just witness the way passing *jebbali* tribesmen stop to help hopeless foreigners who get their 4WD jeeps stuck in the sand.

Although Oman has its share of shopping malls and tacky roundabout sculptures – golden coffeepots and gilded eagles seem to be favourite subjects – the sultanate has largely escaped the relentless modernisation that has reduced the charm of other oil-rich states in the region. Even on the pristine highways that crisscross the desert, the *Arabian Nights* vision of Arabia is never far away. You may see it silhouetted against the sunset on camel back on a rocky desert ridge or plodding cheerfully through the dunes in sandals and *dishdasha* (traditional white Arabic robes), kilometres from the nearest human habitation.

Lately, there have been rumbles of discontent in the sultanate, but Oman has so far avoided the anti-Western sentiment seen elsewhere in the region, despite being a major regional base for British armed forces. Much of the credit for Oman's political stability goes to the benign leadership of Sultan Qaboos bin Said, who wields absolute power, yet uses it to produce the kind of people-friendly policies more commonly associated with fully-fledged Western democracies.

KHANJARS, SAND STARS, COFFEE-BARS...

Tourism in Oman is a relatively new phenomenon – until recently, visitors needed an invitation from a resident of Oman or a local hotel to even set foot in the country. Things have become much easier since the introduction of conventional three-week »

»

OMAN.

A MAN PREPARES FOR A CAMEL RACE IN BIDYA.

» tourist visas, which have opened up this fascinating desert nation which has changed little since medieval times, yet still manages to be accepting, rather than fearful, of modernity and foreign influences.

The major cities of Muscat and Salalah have all the amenities you would expect from an oil-rich Gulf State – slick international hotels, fast-food outlets, coffee shops and shopping malls. But stroll through the atmospheric *souqs* (markets) and you'll find white-robed traders selling camels, coffee, dates, incense and *khanjars* (traditional Omani daggers), much as they did in Old Testament times, when Ubar (near Salalah) was the main centre for frankincense production in the ancient world.

Tourism to Oman is based on the four pillars of forts, oases, beaches and wadi bashing (driving 4WD jeeps up the gorges of seasonal rivers that descend from the Omani mountains). Hikers can trek through date-palm and frankincense groves to ancient stone villages in the hills, and history buffs can act out *Arabian Nights* fantasies in desert forts across the sultanate. Jeep safaris to the sand dunes of the Empty Quarter are another popular diversion. Then there are the beaches – pristine, sandy and surrounded by the immaculate coral reefs of the Arabian Sea. It's a little like Egypt must have been before the arrival of mass tourism.

Although Oman has more for tourists than most of its Gulf neighbours, budget

CAMEL RACING GETS THE HUMP

Despite the Islamic proscription on gambling, Omanis are obsessed with camel racing. Owners of fleet-footed ships of the desert compete for cars and cash prizes at bandy-legged races throughout the Sultanate. Unfortunately, the sport has a shadier side – many of the jockeys are child slaves, sold to the camel stables by destitute families in poor Muslim nations such as Sudan, Bangladesh and Pakistan. Antislavery campaigners have brought the sport into such disrepute that many Gulf States are now planning to switch to robot jockeys to escape accusations of child abuse.

> "
> *If you're in the Nizwa region and have a 4WD, a trip to the plateau of Jebel Shams (about 2000m above sea level) is certainly a highlight of a journey to Oman. It is the second deepest canyon in the world after the Grand Canyon and really spectacular.*
> "

- Siegfried & Regina Peer, Austria

travellers will find that tourist dollars don't go far in the sultanate. You can save some money by eating at local restaurants but most hotels fall into the luxury category and you'll need a healthy wad of cash to hire a 4WD, join a diving safari or charter a speedboat to an idyllic desert beach.

DEFINING EXPERIENCE
- Sipping on Arabic coffee with Bedu tribesmen and watching the pink dawn light spread across the sea of sand

FESTIVALS & EVENTS
- Khareef Festival; Salalah; July–August. Forty-eight days of folk dances and cultural extravaganzas celebrate the arrival of the annual monsoon, which briefly transforms this small corner of the sultanate from dusty yellow to lush green.
- Eid al-Fitr; October. This festival celebrating the end of Ramadan is the biggest festival in the country. Huge feasts are held for up to a week following the sighting of the first new moon.
- Camel-racing season; October–March. Races are held in *wilayats* (administrative districts) across Oman.

Trained camels compete in strict age categories to win cash prizes and luxury cars for their owners.

DO MENTION
- Camel racing. Races between highly trained 'ships of the desert' are a national obsession – Oman even has its own Directorate General of Camel Affairs.

DON'T MENTION
- Does it need saying? As elsewhere in the Muslim world, the Iraq war is guaranteed to get hackles up.
- Don't openly question the sexuality of the Sultan. Outside Oman, it is widely accepted that Sultan Qaboos is gay, but nobody – and we mean *nobody* – talks about it within the sultanate.

RANDOM FACTS
- Most of Oman obtained electricity in 1970.
- Slavery was only abolished in Oman in 1975.

THINGS TO TAKE
- A hat and sunblock – only mad dogs and Englishmen underestimate the desert sun
- A mask and snorkel – the undersea world in Oman is one of the best-kept secrets in the Middle East and basking sharks and hammerheads are regular visitors

HOT TIPS FOR TRAVELLERS
- Get some four-wheel driving experience before you visit – wadi bashing by 4WD is one of the most popular activities in the sultanate.
- If possible, avoid Oman during Ramadan; locals strictly adhere to the daily fast and foreigners can be fined for eating, drinking or smoking in public during daylight hours.
- Always ask permission before taking photos – Omanis follow an ancient form of Islam and taking photos of living beings is taboo.

THREE WORDS TO DESCRIBE THIS COUNTRY
- Traditional, tolerant, timeless

- Joe Bindloss

OMAN.

MOST BIZARRE SIGHT! ✪

Camel racing. The sight of normally sedate camels engaged in racehorselike feats of exertion is as surprising as it is bizarre.

SYRIA.

VITAL STATISTICS

- **POPULATION**
  18 MILLION
- **VISITORS PER YEAR**
  2.8 MILLION
- **UNIT OF CURRENCY**
  SYRIAN POUND (S£)
- **COST OF A CUP OF COFFEE**
  S£50 TO S£75 = US$1 TO US$1.50
- **COST OF A GOOD QUALITY SWORD**
  FROM S£2500 = US$50
- **CAPITAL**
  DAMASCUS
- **LANGUAGE**
  ARABIC

TWO SIDES TO EVERY STORY. Syria has been in the news an awful lot lately, but mostly for the wrong reasons. And Syrians are none too pleased with the recent public portrayal of their country.

How would you feel if the world's last superpower lumped you in with Iraq and North Korea? With the rash of recent media attention it's only natural that most people think Syria is crawling with terrorists, but the press usually only tells a one-sided story when discussing the country. Even the US State Department admits 'the Syrian Government has not been implicated directly in an act of terrorism since 1986'. That's not to suggest the government is entirely noble – far from it. Its human rights record is appalling and it certainly could be doing more to stop violence in the region – but visitors have little to fear in Syria.

AXIS OF FRIENDLINESS

While the media debate and distort Syria's present, visitors are mostly thinking about the past. The Egyptians, Phoenicians, Assyrians, Persians, Greeks, Romans, Mongols, Ottomans, French and many others have left their marks here over the past 12,000 years, making today's Syria a virtual open-air archaeological museum. Palmyra, one of the Middle East's must-see attractions, encompasses stunning ruins from several of these cultures. Other attractions include Krak des Chevaliers, which Lawrence of Arabia called 'the finest castle in the world', Bosra, which holds arguably the best-preserved Roman amphitheatre, and Damascus, which claims to be the world's oldest continuously inhabited city.

But the most cherished aspect of your visit is sure to be the people. Despite anger over a meddling West, Syrians can differentiate the government from the governed, and they will be eager to get to know you. You'll be viewed not as a visitor, but as a guest, and people you meet only briefly will often invite you to their home for food and tea. It's even quite common for a total stranger to pay your bus fare.

INSIDE THE UMAYYAD MOSQUE WITH THE LEGENDARY TOMB OF ST JOHN THE BAPTIST.

This combination of history and hospitality has given Syria the greatest percentage increase in tourists in the Middle East and the seventh-largest increase in tourists in the world in recent years. That's not to say it's overrun with tourists – far from it: except for a few top spots, you're still unlikely to see more than a handful of other visitors – but tourist numbers will continue to increase. Just in the first half of 2004 package tour-group numbers from Western countries increased by more than 50%. Now is your chance to see the country before everyone realises what a great travel destination Syria is.

DEFINING EXPERIENCE
- Smelling sacks of spices, seeing camel heads hanging in butcher shop windows, hearing the muezzins' lyrical calls to prayer, tasting a hookah full of apple-tinged tobacco, and feeling the waves of cobblestone through the soles of your shoes as you wander aimlessly across the Old City *souqs* of Damascus and Aleppo

FESTIVALS & EVENTS
- Eid al-Adha (Feast of Sacrifice); January and, because Islam uses a lunar calendar, again in December. During this three-day religious holiday people slaughter sheep (in honour of Abraham's willingness to sacrifice his son) and share the meat with their neighbours.
- Good Friday; March/April. Syrian Christians visit at least seven churches on this day.
- Eid al-Fitr; October. This huge, joyous feast ends the month-long Ramadan fast.

WHAT'S HOT...
- Trekking among the Dead Cities

WHAT'S NOT...
- Getting too close to the Iraqi border

RECENT FAD
- It has become popular to stick around for a while. In the past most travellers just hit a few Syrian highlights as they followed the classic overland journey between Istanbul and Cairo, but these days people are making Syria their primary destination. Rising prices in Turkey are making some backpackers look at Syria as an alternative while others are just catching wind of what Syria has to offer. »

SYRIA.

> "
> We were on a bus in Syria, on our way to a castle called Krak des Chevaliers and started talking to Mary. We weren't sure where to get off the bus and Mary told us we should follow her as she lived near the castle. She asked us home for a drink and to meet her family. After giving us lunch Mary told us she'd take us on a tour of Krak des Chevaliers. We spent the afternoon learning about the history of the castle, and then went back to Mary's for dinner. It was an absolutely amazing day.
> "

- Brett Shearer, Australia

HOT TIP FOR TRAVELLERS! ✪

Do not visit Palmyra on a day trip from Damascus. As one of the world's great historic sites, the ruins deserve more than an afternoon. Plus going at sunrise lets you explore with virtually nobody else around and the soft, warm, morning light will make your photos spectacular.

» HOT TOPIC OF THE DAY

- ✪ Syria is entering a brave new world via the Internet. It took a long time for Syria to get online. The first public Internet shops didn't open until 2000 and back then one hour's access cost a day's salary for the average worker. Recently prices have dropped enough to allow far more people to get information the government would rather they did not have.

RANDOM FACTS

- ✪ Mark Twain travelled to Damascus in 1867 as part of a long voyage to Europe and the Holy Land. The journey was recounted in *The Innocents Abroad*, his best-selling book during his lifetime.

- ✪ Glass blowing was invented in Syria in the 1st century BC. Legend has it that glass itself was invented here about 2500 years earlier.

- ✪ Christians make up 10% of the population.

- ✪ The beautiful village of Maalula is one of the last places where Aramaic, the language of Jesus Christ, is still spoken.

- ✪ Your pet hamster's last wild relative probably lived near Aleppo.

DO MENTION

- ✪ Your travels. And not just where you've been in Syria. Increasingly Syrians dream of visiting other countries and they will enjoy discussing your other adventures because for the time being, travelling vicariously is the best most people can do.

DON'T MENTION

- ✪ Anything negative about Bashir al-Assad or his government. With thousands of secret police at work, the streets still have ears.

MOST BIZARRE SIGHT

- ✪ The Shrine of John the Baptist: the large, green-domed shrine in the prayer room of Umayyad Mosque in Damascus contains what is supposedly the prophet's head.

THINGS TO TAKE

- ✪ Torch (flashlight) for exploring ruins
- ✪ Your passport with no evidence of a visit to Israel, so you won't be turned back at the border
- ✪ Swimsuit for the *hammams* (bathhouses)
- ✪ Student ID for huge discounts on admission fees at most museums and historic sites

THREE WORDS TO DESCRIBE THE COUNTRY

- ✪ Friendly, ancient, emerging

- Tim Brewer

A NOMAD DRIVES HIS MOTLEY HERD OF SHEEP ONWARD IN THE JERID REGION OF SOUTHERN TUNISIA

VITAL STATISTICS

TUNISIA.

⊙ **POPULATION**
9.9 MILLION

⊙ **VISITORS PER YEAR**
4.8 MILLION

⊙ **UNIT OF CURRENCY**
TUNISIAN DINAR (TD)

⊙ **COST OF A BEER**
TD1.5 TO TD2 =
US$1.15 TO US$1.55

⊙ **CAPITAL**
TUNIS

⊙ **LANGUAGES**
ARABIC, FRENCH

✪ A MIRAGE ON THE MEDITERRANEAN. Tunisia is a place that never goes out of fashion. At a time when the tourism in Islamic nations has been in decline, the government of Tunisia has undertaken a remarkable effort to offer tourists a welcoming and safe environment.

So far Tunisia has kept its promise, and the tourists are coming in record numbers. Whereas Algeria and Libya, its neighbours on the North African coast, have had a troubled reputation, Tunisia has managed to stay relatively stable. The reasons for the constant tourist flow are also pragmatic. Tourism is a significant source of revenue for the economy. The country is hospitable and the cities have a first-class infrastructure that has been expanding in recent years.

It is not surprising that countless Hollywood films (such as *The English Patient* and a few of the *Star Wars* films) have used the natural beauty of Tunisia as a backdrop for romantic tragedies and intergalactic dramas. Tunisia is exotic and otherworldly, a unique slice of climates, landscapes and history. The Greeks, the Romans and the Arabs have left their prints, and the French ruled from 1881 to 1956. The landscapes range from desert to the pristine Mediterranean. Tunisia evokes a sense of timelessness, and often surprises the visitor with unexpected epiphanies. It is a place of ancient cities, awesome temples and museums, whitewashed walls and splendid mosaics. Highlights include the surreal Berber architecture, the museums and mosques, the coliseum in El Jem, the ruins of Dougga and the remains of the once-resplendent city of Carthage. Learning about the history and culture of this place greatly adds to the enjoyment of it.

With a lot to do and see in a relatively small place, Tunisia caters to both the adventurous and the lazy. And incredibly enough, it also caters for all budgets. You can do Tunisia on a shoestring or on a George Lucas budget.

DEFINING EXPERIENCE
⊙ Eating couscous with tender lamb spiced with *harissa* (chilli paste), accompanied by »

RECENT FAD! ✪

Star Wars **tours, which take you through the locations of the films**

»»

LIGHT AND SHAD
TREES AND SAND

TUNISIA.

» wine, looking over the ruins of Carthage into the Mediterranean, and – is that a mirage, or the ghost of a Phoenician ship cruising the waters?

FESTIVALS & EVENTS

- Festival of the Sparrow Hawk; El Haouaria; May. Now here's an interesting premise for a festival: birds migrating north for the European summer pass through a place called El Haouaria (on the shores of Cap Bon) before leaving the country. Every year about 150 local falconers show off their skill at training sparrow-hawks and female peregrine falcons. They catch the birds on their migratory path and train them to become hunters. There's a three-day festival, complete with singing, drumming and celebrations, in which the best hawks are pitted against one another in hunting competitions. The animals are kept until their relatives return in the autumn and are then released. The timing of the festival depends on the harvests and the rhythm of the seasons, so contact the Tunisian Tourist Office (www.tourism tunisia.com) for precise time and location closer to the date.

- International Festival of Carthage; July–August. Carthage's amphitheatres host an eclectic showcase of music, ballet and theatre. The festival also includes modern fusions of traditional music with jazz and electronica, and is bound to deliver a few pleasant surprises.

- International Festival of Symphonic Music; El Jem; July–August. A tasty festival of classical music, with outfits from all over the world, takes place in the ancient city of El Jem.

WHAT'S HOT...

- Local wines are acquiring a very good reputation. They are sold in closed-off areas of supermarkets, so as not to offend Muslim sensitivities.

WHAT'S NOT...

- Wearing a Luke Skywalker costume in the desert while touring the *Star Wars* sites

RANDOM FACTS

- Hannibal (247–183 BC) is one of the most famous military figures in antiquity. He was a Carthaginian general who early in life swore an eternal hatred of Rome, and spent the rest of his life giving them

> **"** *Port el-Kantaoui has to be seen to be believed. We counted more than a hundred hotels, cheek by jowl, each capable of housing some 3000 guests. Tunisia has become the new 'Spain' for Europeans and is now also a popular destination for Eastern Europeans seeking the sun in winter. What an incongruous sight: topless buxom mamas from Ukraine sunbaking next to slight Tunisian Islamic women complete with scarf and veil.* **"**
>
> - Leslie Burnett & Ruth Pojer, Australia

terrorist networks in the region. However, international watchdogs draw attention to the poor human rights record of the present government, which seems to be using the War on Terror to crush dissent.

THINGS TO TAKE
- Sun and wind protection
- Sunscreen
- Swimwear

HOT TIPS FOR TRAVELLERS
- Don't forget to haggle with market traders and stall owners; never pay full price.
- If you want to check out the latest news, there's an English news service online (www.tunisiaonline.com). Remember that the media are heavily censored by the government; to get the other side of the story, check the Human Rights Watch site (www.hrw.org/wr2k3/mideast8.html).

THREE WORDS TO DESCRIBE THIS COUNTRY
- Ancient, hospitable, stable

- Andres Vaccari

one headache after another. His most famous feat was to lead an army of 50,000 men and 40 elephants across the Alps, after which he defeated the Romans and occupied northern Italy. None of the elephants and very few of the men survived the tough trip. Ironically enough, we now know of Hannibal because of the Romans, who admiringly recorded his military accomplishments.

- Carthaginian civilisation thrived between the 6th and 1st centuries BC and challenged the Greek and Roman Empires in the Mediterranean. Carthage itself was approximately 16km (10mi) north of Tunis, the present capital.

- Tunisians had a major role in the establishment of the Union of the Arab Maghreb in 1989, a political and economic North African bloc embracing Algeria, Libya, Mauritania, Morocco and Tunisia.

HOT TOPIC OF THE DAY
- The tentative position of Tunisia in the political landscape of the region. Tunisia has been trying to remain neutral, while also acting as a mediating force. It acted decisively in dismantling

MOST BIZARRE SIGHT!

The Berbers are an indigenous North African tribe that fashion dwellings underground, carving them out of the soft rock; the result is one of the most striking, dreamlike architectural styles ever conceived.

OTHERWORLDLY TOMBS SPIKE THE AINAT SKYLINE.

YEMEN.

VITAL STATISTICS

- **POPULATION**
  21.5 MILLION
- **VISITORS PER YEAR**
  90,000
- **UNIT OF CURRENCY**
  YEMENI RIYAL (YR)
- **COST OF A
  NO-FRILLS MEAL**
  YR543 = US$3
- **CAPITA**
  SAN'A
- **LANGUAGE**
  ARABIC
- **LIFE EXPECTANCY**
  59 YEARS (MEN); 61
  YEARS (WOMEN)

SULTANS, SPICES & SERIOUS ARMS. Dubbed by the Romans as 'Arabia Felix' or 'Happy Arabia', Yemen is old-school Arabia unlimited, stretching from the cool mountains to the Red Sea.

Sultans are swingin' in luxurious pads that'd make your jaw drop, exquisite spires wend from ancient mosques, multistorey buildings of stone and clay line the streets, and the *souq* is where it's at to stock up on jewellery, incense and machine guns at this jivin' junction of the ancient spice route. As arms beside the *adas* (lentils) might suggest, Yemen is a volatile nation, with tourist kidnappings a frighteningly regular occurrence. However, the overall kindness to outsiders that pervades in this still very tribal society is overwhelming. After years of fighting, the modern Republic of Yemen emerged in 1990, when traditionalist North Yemen and Marxist South Yemen unified; fighting broke out again in 1994, but the separatist southerners were defeated and the Republic remained. In the present political climate of legitimate danger, fear and, let's face it, paranoia, foreign agencies are on high alert and recommend that

travellers to Yemen stick to the capital San'a and don't venture elsewhere. Wherever you go and whatever you decide, use your noggin and stay informed.

CHEWING THE FAT WITH SOME QAT

If you're a fellow, it's likely you'll be asked 'Do you chew?', and if you say yes, you'll soon find yourself with other fellows, chewing the qat plant to pass away a few hours of the afternoon. This stimulant is said to provide a mild chatty buzz, and while it certainly brings people together, its addictive nature brings with it social and economic problems. As a strictly gender-based society, it is unlikely you'll be invited into a qat den as a female. However, local ladies, possibly as curious of you as you are of them, are likely to engage you in the friendly talk of the day down at the *hammam* (bathhouse). There, on the inside, the barriers are down and the cloistered female society is open, at

MEN RELAXING AT A STREET STALL SELLING
JAMBIYAS (TRADITIONAL CURVED KNIVES) IN SAN'A

least for a couple of hours of chatting and soaking up the steam.

DEFINING EXPERIENCE

○ Dating back to before the 1st millennium BC, Yemen's old capital Ma'rib was once the hub of the ancient kingdom of Saba, and is purported to be the Queen of Sheba's old stomping ground. While the pace has certainly slowed down in recent millennia, Ma'rib is now the perfect place to head to for a piece of old Old Yemen…and it's quite literally in pieces. Most of the village is in ruins, but there are exquisite remnants of old temples, such as Mahram Bilqis (Temple of Bilqis; built before 800 BC in honour of the sun god), remnants of the Great Dam of Ma'rib and an assortment of small-windowed mud buildings. You'll encounter desolate landscapes and desperate poverty, but it is well worth the trip: the archaeology is simply stunning. Be warned that accommodation and eateries are scarce – you may wish to sign up for an organised tour rather than brave it by yourself.

FESTIVALS & EVENTS

○ Eid al-Adha (Feast of Sacrifice); January and, because Islam uses a lunar calendar, again in December. Beginning on the 10th of the Hajj, the month of pilgrimage to Mecca, this Islamic festival takes place over several days.

○ Victory Day; July. This is a national holiday commemorating the end of the 1994 War of Unity.

○ Eid al-Fitr; October. A three-day feast marks the end of Ramadan.

NOT-SO-HAPPY SNAPS

Watch out what you photograph: anything military-related is a no-go, as are airports. Never photograph Yemeni women unless they specifically request it (highly unlikely). If you ask, it will be awkward. Young Yemeni boys and girls, however, will show-pony with the best of them. Still, it might be best to ask their parents for permission first.

> *Yemen is unique to the Arabian Peninsula. It is certainly worth a visit and now is perhaps the best time to go, when it's still unspoilt by tourists and petrol dollars. It's like going back 500 years and a unique travelling experience.*
>
> - 'Grkguy', Greece

RANDOM FACTS

- Legend says the old city of San'a was founded by Shem, son of Noah.

- The recently introduced death penalty for kidnapping has acted as a much-needed deterrent.

- No ambulance service exists in Yemen – make your emergencies not too urgent!

- Like men travellers, women travellers should dress conservatively, but do not need to cover their heads.

- Cash up! Credit cards are virtually useless.

- With many places in Yemen off-limits, you may find yourself convoyed to and fro by a military escort.

- Home to one of the world's highest birth rates, the average Yemeni woman bears seven children.

- The major industries in Yemen are oil, cotton, leather and food processing.

MOST BIZARRE SIGHT

- Perched in your hotel room or while standing on your tippy-toes you're likely to spot a hidden Eden or two behind the high mud and stone walls in old San'a. In the middle of the city, these gardens are for respite and function, often growing fruit and vegetables (that once supplied the city). Unless you get in the good books of the people living in adjoining houses or leaders of neighbouring mosques, it's unlikely you'll be able to get a closer look.

THINGS TO TAKE

- A few handy rolls of toilet paper

- A ready supply of necessary medicines (with a note of explanation from your doctor)

HOT TIPS FOR TRAVELLERS

- If you've been to Israel at any time, don't come a-knockin' at Yemen. Any evidence of having travelled to Israel will result in a flat-out refusal of entry.

- The climate varies dramatically; April to May and September to October are probably the best times to go, overall.

THREE WORDS TO DESCRIBE THIS COUNTRY

- Modern-day *1001 Nights*

- Samone Bos

» Independence Day; November. This day commemorates the birth of the People's Republic of Yemen.

RECENT FAD

Western students are increasingly travelling to Yemen to study Arabic, particularly post–September 11. While the primarily non-English-speaking nation provides students with an opportunity to fully immerse themselves in the language, the Yemeni dialect is considered closer to the Modern Standard Arabic (Fusha) than Egyptian, Lebanese or Syrian Arabic. Unlike Cairo or Damascus – traditional foreign student hubs of the Middle East – the nightlife in Yemen is very limited, so for the studious swat and easily swayed alike, there is little distraction from the task at hand.

WHAT'S HOT...

A cooling brew of mint tea

WHAT'S NOT...

A cooling brew of beer – alcohol is illegal

DON'T MENTION

Beware with whom you discuss the War on Terror: you might strike the wrong chord.

ALGERIA

Despite continued political violence and a history of instability, Algeria is beginning to show signs of a more secure, positive environment. Independent travel can still be difficult here, so outside the cities travellers are better off joining an organised tour to see such sights as the dunes of the Sahara and majestic Atlas ranges.

BAHRAIN

A fascinating and diverse place, Bahrain offers travellers an easy and hassle-free introduction to the Persian Gulf. There are alleyways to explore, coffeehouses in which to sit and watch the world go by, magnificent desert landscapes, basket weaving with palm leaves and every kind of souk your shopping heart could wish for.

IRAQ

In its long and rich history Iraq has played host to great civilisations. Recent history has been less kind: the dictatorial reign of Sadaam Hussein, war with Iran and Kuwait, trade embargoes after the Gulf War and the US-led invasion in 2003 have all taken severe tolls, resulting in food and medicine shortages and ongoing social and economic problems. Iraq is one of the most dangerous places on earth and must be considered off-limits to tourists.

KUWAIT

With the 1990–91 Gulf War a fading memory, Kuwait is once again the prototypical Persian Gulf oil state. Walking around Kuwait City, it is hard to imagine the destruction of just a decade ago. There has been an obsessive, meticulous re-creation of the country's pre-invasion appearance. Liberation brought a new kind of openness to Kuwaiti life and for those looking for a relaxed entry into the Muslim world, Kuwait offers opportunities to wander around souks, mosques and other sandy traces of bygone Bedouin days.

LEBANON

Coolly combining the ancient with the ultramodern, Lebanon is one of the captivating countries in the Middle East. It is a place of contrasts with a powerful mix of cultures and traditions. There are soaring mountains and deep valleys, bikini-clad beach goers and women in head-to-toe chadors. After 15 years of destruction following the civil war in 1975, its recovering infrastructure offers plenty of welcoming opportunity to discover its ancient cities, popular ski resorts, memorable cuisine, Islamic architecture and Roman ruins.

LIBYA

The word is out: Libya is the latest travellers' hotspot. Obscured from Western view for the last 30 years under Colonel Gaddafi, the country has recently begun courting international tourism. With one foot in Africa, another in the Arab world and a history of Italian occupation, Libya presents travellers with a somewhat beguiling façade. Ripe for discovery are Libya's incredible hospitality, beautiful desertscapes, well-preserved classical ruins, prehistoric rock art and palm-fringed oases. There will be a total solar eclipse in early 2006.

QATAR

Travel to this thumb-shaped country in the Persian Gulf and you'll find a land of ritzy hotels, ancient rock carvings, enormous sand dunes and distinctive architecture. You can catch troops of traditional dance performers wearing costumes resplendent with jewellery. There's the opportunity for amazing desert excursions, or if greenery and shade are what you're after, you can stroll along the lovely 7km (4mi) coastal corniche in Doha.

SAUDI ARABIA

Once an exclusive club for the chosen few, such as pilgrims bound for Mecca, oil sheiks from Texas, contract workers and the odd asylum-seeking dictator, Saudi Arabia now welcomes visitors on special visas. The cost is stiff, the restrictions intimidating, but the thrill of just being there is unbeatable. Delights for the intrepid, moneyed traveller include ancient souks, antiquities half-buried in the desert, a Biblical sea and the heady taste of Arabian hospitality.

UNITED ARAB EMIRATES

The United Arab Emirates has transformed themselves into an Arabian success story through a mix of oil profits, stability and a sharp eye for business. Visitors are attracted by beaches, deserts, oases, camel racing, Bedouin markets and the legendary duty-free shopping of Dubai, all packed into a relatively small area. Dubai is the Singapore of the Gulf, with bustling harbours, gigantic shopping malls and bold architecture.

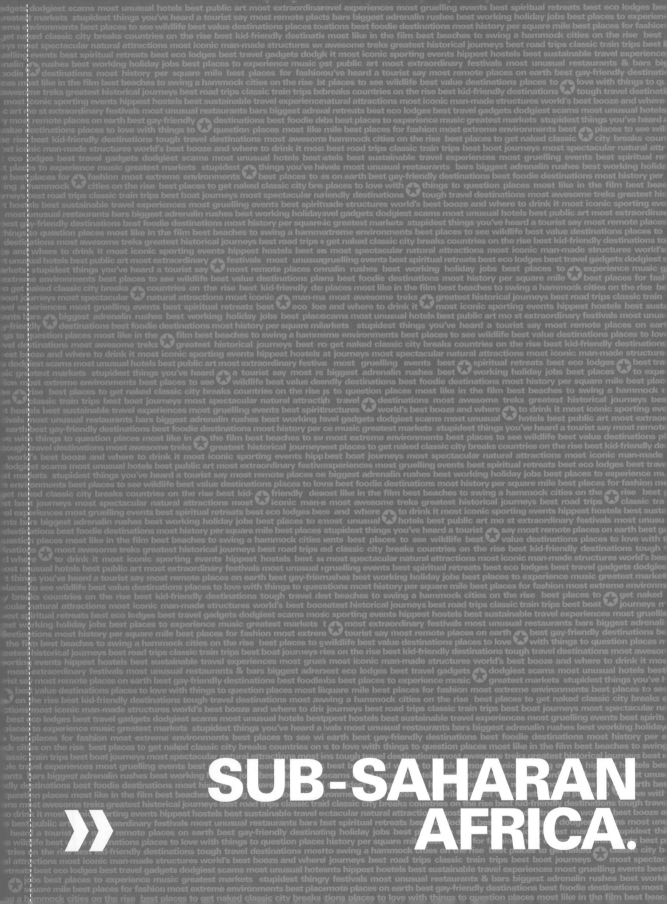

SUB-SAHARAN AFRICA.

»

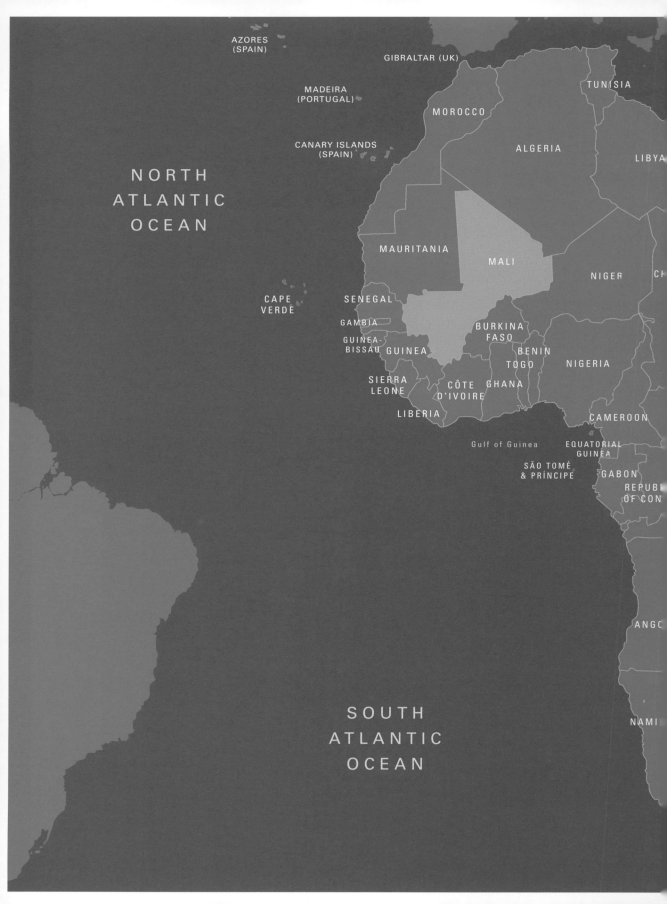

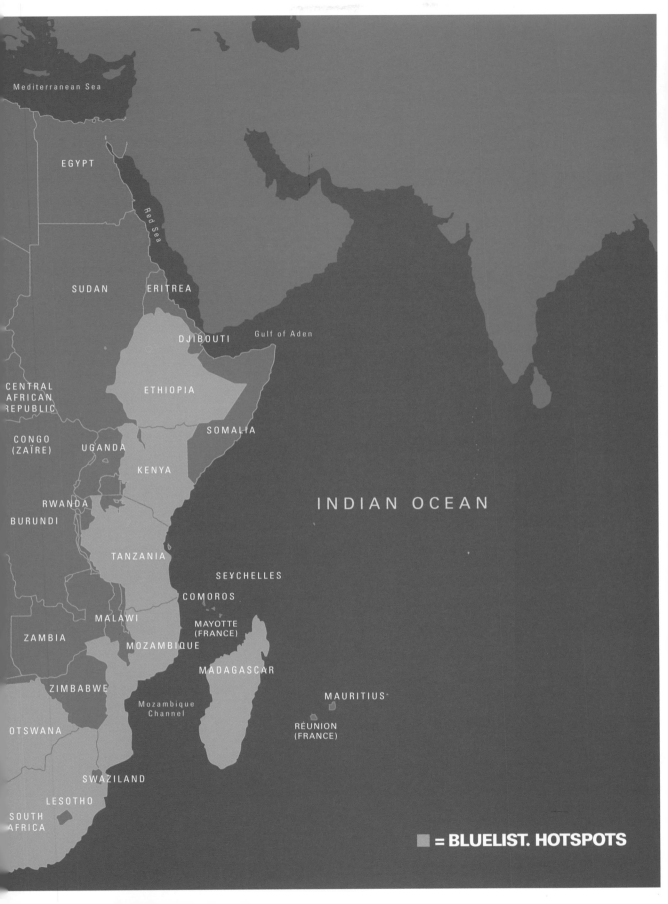

Mediterranean Sea

EGYPT

Red Sea

SUDAN

ERITREA

DJIBOUTI

Gulf of Aden

CENTRAL
AFRICAN
REPUBLIC

ETHIOPIA

SOMALIA

CONGO
(ZAÏRE)

UGANDA

KENYA

RWANDA

BURUNDI

INDIAN OCEAN

TANZANIA

SEYCHELLES

COMOROS

MALAWI

MAYOTTE
(FRANCE)

ZAMBIA

MOZAMBIQUE

MADAGASCAR

ZIMBABWE

Mozambique
Channel

MAURITIUS

RÉUNION
(FRANCE)

OTSWANA

SWAZILAND

LESOTHO

SOUTH
AFRICA

= BLUELIST. HOTSPOTS

BOTSWANA.

VITAL STATISTICS

○ **POPULATION**
1.8 MILLION

○ **VISITORS PER YEAR**
900,000

○ **UNIT OF CURRENCY**
PULA (P)

○ **COST OF A BEER**
P5 = US$0.95

○ **CAPITAL**
GABORONE

○ **LANGUAGES**
ENGLISH, SETSWANA

○ **LIFE EXPECTANCY**
39 YEARS (MEN); 40
YEARS (WOMEN) –
A TRAGIC REFLECTION
OF THE AIDS
EPIDEMIC

THE DISTINCTIVE VICTORIAN-INSPIRED
DRESS OF THE HERERO WOMEN WAS
ENFORCED BY GERMAN MISSIONARIES.

A LAND-LOCKED NATION OF DIAMONDS & PERILS. Deep in the heart of Africa and teeming with wildlife – elephants, lions, cheetahs and hippos, et al – Botswana is a land-locked landscape of sweeping savannas, salt pans and wetlands and the Kalahari Desert.

Home to three of the world's richest diamond mines, Botswana is definitely Africa's most economically thriving nation. The opulence of white ice and all that glitters certainly doesn't help the estimated 40% of locals afflicted by HIV in the horrific AIDS epidemic that has swept the continent (Botswana's infection rate is the second highest in the world behind Swaziland).

FIRM BUT FAIR?
Botswana is a peaceful country and its government is considered a free and fair multiparty constitutional democracy; it's a far cry from the despotism and corruption of some other African nations. In the Apartheid years, Botswana provided asylum to South African refugees and anti-apartheid activists, though did find itself in a bind as a result of its reliance on South Africa's monetary might, and overshadowed by the Afrikaans' monstrous military. The country's sympathy towards its

troubled neighbouring nations extended to Zimbabwe in the early 2000s when it endured hordes of needy and destitute Zimbabwean refugees. Today though, gun patrols and an electric fence act as Botswana's no-nonsense buffer between the two nations.

ECONOMY & ECOLOGY
With the foresight of self-preservation, both economically and ecologically, the government's tightly reined upmarket brand of low-impact tourism is the dish of the day here. So, if shoestring's your thing, you might have a problem exploring Botswana, as most accommodation and safari tours cater to the Heidi Klum–bejewelled style of Birkenstock.

DEFINING EXPERIENCE
○ Whack on your favourite pith helmet and head out to Chobe National Park, Botswana's wildlife wonderland. There, you'll cackle with jackals, warble with

CRUISING DOWN THE OKAVANGO DELTA IN A MEKORO, A CANOE DUG OUT FROM EBONY OR SAUSAGE TREE LOGS.

THE NO 1 LADIES' DETECTIVE AGENCY

Alexander McCall Smith's novels in the charmingly light-hearted series The No 1 Ladies' *Detective Agency* are all set in Botswana's capital, Gaborone. The protagonist, Mma 'Precious' Ramotswe is the first woman detective in Botswana and through her adventures readers can glimpse what life is like in Botswana. Some serious issues are explored, but mostly the subject matter is as fluffy and sweet as a scone at high tea. Titles in the series include the following:

- *The No 1 Ladies' Detective Agency* (1999)
- *Tears of the Giraffe* (2000)
- *Morality for Beautiful Girls* (2001)
- *The Kalahari Typing School for Men* (2002)
- *The Full Cupboard of Life* (2004)
- *In the Company of Cheerful Ladies* (2004)

warthogs and chinwag with cheetahs for the ultimate *Out of Africa* experience.

RANDOM FACTS

- Seretse Khama was Botswana's first elected president in 1965; the British Empire granted the country independence the following year.

- Botswana is home to an estimated 120,000 elephants – the old joke 'How do you fit four elephants in a Mini?' is upsized here.

- Botswana's economy magically transformed when diamonds were discovered outside of Orapa in 1967.

- Mokolodi Nature Reserve is home to Botswana's wonderful white rhino; it was reintroduced from South Africa and is now breeding in the reserve.

- Mashatu Game Reserve is also known as the 'Land of the Giants', and rightfully so. Not only is the reserve home to Africa's largest cat and tallest tree, you'll also find the world's largest land mammal, tallest land mammal and largest flying bird.

- No visa is required for citizens of the USA and most European and Commonwealth countries (check ahead). Visitors need sufficient funds and an onward ticket.

- Botswana has more snakes than you can spit at, but three types of snake that can spit that you! The country is home to 70 species of snake.

»

RECENT FAD!

'Expeditions' or 'Eco-Cruises' are all the rage. At the top end of the tourism market, superliners are steaming to Africa and coaching inland for a whistle-stop at Botswana. While you sip your piña colada somewhere around the South Atlantic Ocean, Captain Stubing, Julie, Isaac, Gopher and the gang clear the parquetry dance floor to screen educational programmes that'll bring you up to speed on local flora, fauna and geology.

»»

BOTSWANA.

> *Travelling overland through Botswana we made a pit stop in Maun, at a restaurant/movie house that was once a metal factory. Most of the interior décor, including a huge spider, had been made from scrap metal. We got chatting with the owner and he said we could camp behind the restaurant for free if we would design a zebra pattern in one of the corridors there. We agreed and had so much fun we stayed for nearly two weeks. This was in 1999 and apparently the zebra corridor is still there.*

- Deirdre Whelan, USA

HOT TOPIC OF THE DAY!

In June 2005, eminent feminist Gloria Steinem and a posse of 30 protesters picketed the opening of a De Beers' diamond store in New York City. They were opposing De Beers' forced (and reportedly violent) eviction of bushmen from their Kalahari Desert homes to make way for more, what they termed, 'blood diamonds'.

» FESTIVALS & EVENTS

- Maitisong Festival; Gaborone; April. This is Botswana's biggest annual festival of performing arts.
- Sir Seretse Khama Day; July. Celebrations are held to honour the first president of Botswana.
- President's Day; July. Botswana takes the day off to party.

DON'T MENTION

- The plight of the San people (inhabitants of Botswana for more than 30,000 years) is a touchy subject among locals. These tribespeople are subject to displacement and discrimination as they are shooed away from their land and livelihood.
- In June 2005, on the command of President Mogae, Australian professor Ken Good was deported as he was considered a threat to national security due to his links to humanitarian organisation Survival International. Mogae has since described the international interest generated as a 'Big hullabaloo over the deportation of a single, solitary white man'.

WHAT'S HOT...

- The government's stringently controlled ecotourism, which protects the pristine environment and wildlife
- Serious bling – diamonds are some girls', most rappers' and the Botswanan economy's best friend
- The government's recent nationwide Prevention of Mother-to-Child Transmission programme

WHAT'S NOT...

- The HIV epidemic – 40% of the population is presently afflicted by the virus
- Serious poverty – 46% of Botswana's population lives under the poverty line
- Wildlife officials purportedly beating and torturing Kalahari bushmen for suspected hunting

MOST BIZARRE SIGHT

- Heat mirages over the steaming and austerely white Makgadikgadi Pans: as earth becomes sky becomes earth, you'll see things appear and disappear and flocks of ostriches flying, only to remember later that they're land birds

THINGS TO TAKE

- Bring cash, cash and more cash. In remote rural areas, things move slowly: you may need to set aside an entire morning for a visit to the bank.
- Need we say it? Bring condoms if you intend on having sex, and, if you need them, bring your own syringes.

HOT TIPS FOR TRAVELLERS

- Don't wear your good shoes – Botswana is the place for the intrepid well-versed traveller who won't mind stepping in the Little Brown Jobs (or Big Brown Jobs – elephants, you see) that litter the landscape.
- Avoid the August gusts when hot winds turn much of Botswana into a dustbowl.
- *History of Botswana* by T Tlou and Alec Campbell is *the* history of Botswana.

THREE WORDS TO DESCRIBE THIS COUNTRY

- African Disneyland unlimited

- Samone Bos

A KARO BOY OF THE OMO VALLEY PROUDLY WEARS BODY PAINT IN THE TRADITION OF HIS REGION.

- **POPULATION**
  64 MILLION
- **VISITORS PER YEAR**
  160,000
- **UNIT OF CURRENCY**
  BIRR
- **COST OF AN AVERAGE BOTTLE OF LOCAL WINE**
  BIRR10 TO BIRR50 = US$1.20 TO US$5.90
- **CAPITAL**
  ADDIS ABABA
- **LANGUAGES**
  AMHARIC, TIGRINYA, SOMALI, ARABIC, OROMIGA, GUARAGIGNA

'LIVE AID', BEFORE & BEYOND. Like it or not, it's probable that 'We are the world, we are the children' or 'Feed the wo-orld' will spring to your lips when you think of Ethiopia.

But long before the devastating wars and famine that had pop stars belting out charity chart-toppers in the mid-'80s, Ethiopia was the 'Cradle of Civilisation' – Abyssinia. Admittedly still dirt-poor of pocket, Ethiopia's riches are in its since-the-day-dot culture, history and landscape. If you want to check out Ethiopia's First Lady in the truest sense, at Addis Ababa's National Museum you'll find the remains of 'Lucy', possibly humankind's oldest ancestor dated at 3.5 million years old. Home to astonishingly well-kept ancient traditions, Ethiopia, aside from Libya, was the only African nation to escape colonisation. Here remains a uniquely Ethiopian Orthodox Christian heritage, devoutly maintained even when much of Africa embraced Islam around the 7th century.

HEY, IT'S THE SUN
Touted as having 13 months of sunshine (not just brochure speak; Ethiopia uses the Julian calendar), taking the rainy season from mid-June to the end of September into account, Ethiopia's climate is mostly agreeable. Temperatures in Addis Ababa average around 20°C (68°F) year-round; it's hotter in the east (towards the Dankalia region) and west (near Sudan). Although it still bears its battle scars from famine and war, Ethiopia is moving forward into a brave new world. Still, things move slowly: it takes at least two weeks to send a postcard home and, outside of Addis Ababa, Internet service is, at best, atrocious. Forget your laptop and get there before everyone else does.

DEFINING EXPERIENCE
- For devout Christians and the mildly inquisitive alike, head to Aksum for a hearty slab of the Old Testament, Abyssinia-style. According to Ethiopia's Orthodox church, the original Ark of the Covenant, the vessel of the Ten

HOT TOPIC OF THE DAY!

The new Eritrea/Ethiopia 'Border Official', Azouz Ennifar of Tunisia, recently appointed by UN Secretary-General Kofi Annan

»

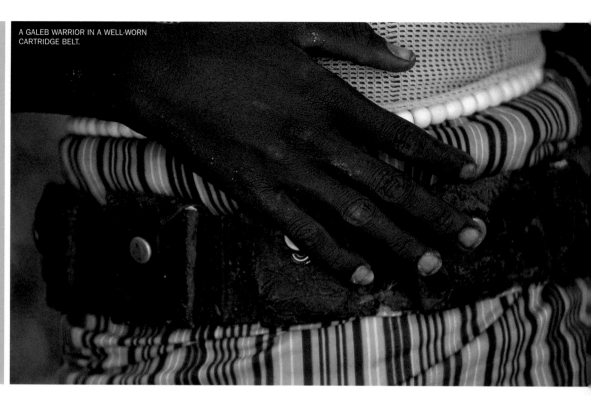

A GALEB WARRIOR IN A WELL-WORN CARTRIDGE BELT.

ETHIOPIA.

» Commandments, is somewhere on the grounds of the tiny 17th-century St Mary of Zion church. However, it's holiness by osmosis here: the Ark is strictly off limits; still, the small collection of ye olde bibles, crosses and crowns are well worth the trip.

RECENT FAD

○ Water sports in Ethiopia, who woulda thunk it? Dugout canoes or traditional papyrus boats can be hired anywhere there's water, and excellent swimming is available in the lakes of the Rift Valley. Lake Langano, in particular, offers a resort with good windsurfing and water-skiing facilities. Southeast, up in the Bale Mountains, trout abounds, making for a good day out fishing. White-water rafting

is also available on parts of the Blue Nile and Omo Rivers. Beware: before donning your flippers, be sure to check with local authorities about schistosomiasis (also known as bilharzia), a parasitic disease present in many waterways.

FESTIVALS & EVENTS

○ Ethiopia uses the Julian calendar, whereby the year is divided into 12 months of 30 days each. A 13th month has five or six days – for this reason internationally renowned dates (such as Christmas) seem a little awry. The following events are countrywide celebrations; the locations mentioned below are the best places to experience the festivities.

RECENT FAD! ⊛

Forget Pink Floyd, the Danakil Depression is truly the dark side of the moon: it's a dinner-plate abyss of sulphur fumaroles and lunarlike landscapes.

LANDSCAPE HIGHS & LOWS

Ranging from the high central plateau – with peaks from 2000m (6562ft) to 4000m (13,124ft) – to many river valleys, Ethiopia has a wide range of ecosystems, including deciduous forests, evergreen forests, desert scrublands, grasslands and wetlands. Considering a safari? Perhaps you might like to reconsider; with rampant deforestation not serving local wildlife well, the birds are where it's at – Ethiopia has at least 17 endemic species. For trekking, and a real taste of how things used to be, hop on a mule and ride in the Bale Mountains and Simien Mountains National Parks.

> "
> *In our opinion, the Timkat festival in Lalibela is excellent. There are many churches, and processions from all of them merge into one great parade, colourful and cheerful. Of course, as in other similar places in Ethiopia, you have to book accommodation well in advance.*
> "
>
> – Anna & Tomasz Galka, Poland

- Leddet (also known as *Genna* or Christmas); Lalibela; January. On Christmas Day, the traditional games of *genna* (a kind of hockey) and *gugs* (a kind of polo) are played.

- Timkat (Epiphany); Gonder; January. This three-day festival celebrating Christ's baptism is the most colourful of the year.

- Meskel (Finding of the True Cross); Addis Ababa; September. Bonfires are built, topped with crosses and blessed, and dancing and singing begins around them.

WHAT'S HOT...
- Bird-watching in the pristine Rift Valley
- Increasing numbers of tourists feeding the national economy

WHAT'S NOT...
- Rampant deforestation – in the name of 'progress' Ethiopia has lost more than 90% of its trees
- Reports of local residents being forcibly evicted, compensation free, by foreign tourism projects, particularly in southern Ethiopia's Nechisar National Park

DO MENTION
- Their fine brew of coffee. Ethiopians are very proud of their cuppa, and presently their primary importer is the USA.

DON'T MENTION
- Continuing unrest/friction with neighbours. Eritrea is still a very touchy subject.

RANDOM FACTS
- Merkato in Addis Ababa is one of Africa's biggest markets with enough spices to make your head spin.

- The 'hyena men' of Harar are an ages-old spectacle: watch as they feed the hyenas by nightfall outside the city walls of the old town.

- Health risks here are nasty and include schistosomiasis, HIV/AIDS, malaria, meningococcal meningitis, yellow fever, hepatitis and intestinal worms: prepare as best you can.

- Harar has more than 87 mosques – this is said to be the highest concentration of mosques anywhere in the world.

- For travel in Ethiopia budget on US$15 to US$20 a day.

- The Queen of Sheba's dynasty lasted until Haile Selassie, who reigned until 1974.

- Ethiopian pastry is really good! In Addis Ababa try out Le Notre on Tito St.

THINGS TO TAKE
- Your Sunday best – should you be invited to dine, show respect for your hosts by scrubbing up

- Heavy-duty sunscreens

- Spare change – in smaller towns locals may ask a small fee to be photographed; don't be surprised if you are asked to pay a nominal fee for photographing local landmarks, also

THREE WORDS TO DESCRIBE THIS COUNTRY
- Feed your mind

– *Samone Bos*

ETHIOPIA.

HOT TIP FOR TRAVELLERS!

Presently travellers are advised against visiting the Gambella region. Give the border areas of Tigray and Afar a very wide berth, and avoid the area east of the Harar to Gode line. Braving the Somalia border by road is also not recommended. The situation is changeable and at times very volatile, so check government sites for travel warnings before visiting.

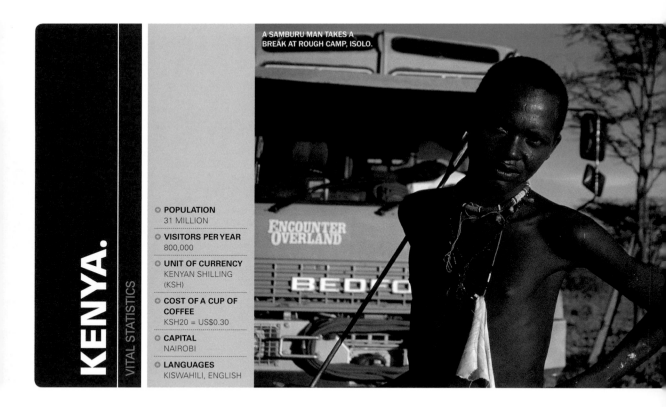

A SAMBURU MAN TAKES A BREAK AT ROUGH CAMP, ISOLO.

KENYA.

VITAL STATISTICS

- **POPULATION**
  31 MILLION
- **VISITORS PER YEAR**
  800,000
- **UNIT OF CURRENCY**
  KENYAN SHILLING
  (KSH)
- **COST OF A CUP OF COFFEE**
  KSH20 = US$0.30
- **CAPITAL**
  NAIROBI
- **LANGUAGES**
  KISWAHILI, ENGLISH

THE CHANGING FACE OF EAST AFRICA. Kenya has always been one of the more tourist-friendly countries in Africa, attracting large numbers of European package tourists to the popular, accessible coast region, the glaciated peaks of Mt Kenya and the famous Masai Mara National Reserve.

The last few years have seen many positive changes in the country, especially since the national elections in 2003, where long-standing President Daniel arap Moi finally resigned after 25 years in office and the opposition Rainbow Coalition won a surprising victory under their leader Mwai Kibaki. If you've been to Kenya previously you'll certainly notice some of the differences in the transport system, the security situation and the general attitude of the people towards their leaders, which seems that bit more open and opinionated than under Moi. Sadly corruption, the old bugbear of Kenyan politics, is still just as much an issue as ever, and virtually every day's newspapers contain some new scandal, allegation or rumour about the present government.

On the plus side, the country's commitment to tourism has been consolidated by the new leadership, and there's more investment in infrastructure in the high-density visitor areas. The minister of tourism recently expressed disappointment in the incoming traveller statistics, aiming for at least one million visitors a year to put Kenya on a par with some of the major destinations in northern and southern Africa. Outside capital, too, is exerting a lot of influence on the holiday industry, and the recent boom in privately owned guesthouses, hotels and conservation projects has created some of the best and most individual facilities in the country. With a busy summer season boosting the travel economy in 2005, Kenya should be at the peak of its game right now.

A HERD OF ELEPHANTS TRUDGES
THROUGH THE LONG GRASS OF MASAI
MARA NATIONAL PARK, RIFT VALLEY.

DEFINING EXPERIENCE

⊕ Talking to the locals and absorbing as much as you can of the diverse culture, from bustling tribal market towns to the barren northern desert, and from the lazy coastal heat to the nervous energy of Nairobi nightlife. Or just seeing a lion in the wild may be enough to fulfil all those African fantasies.

FESTIVALS & EVENTS

⊕ Maulid Festival; Lamu; May or June. The Muslim festival celebrating the birth of Mohammed is a major event on the island of Lamu, attracting huge numbers of locals and tourists for several days of music, ceremonies and events.

⊕ Safari Seven; Nairobi; June. A high-profile seven-a-side rugby tournament for teams from all over Africa, with a handful of British and international teams completing the line-up. It's always hotly contested and the Kenyan team has a strong record, though in 2005 Samoa took the main cup.

⊕ Maralal International Camel Derby; Maralal; July–October. This is a big event renowned for its wild afterparties. The man behind the race sadly died recently, but it's hoped the tradition will continue.

⊕ Mombassa Carnival; November. A lively street carnival in the coast's principal city, with parades, live music and a sailing regatta.

RECENT FAD

⊕ Ringtones! Around 80% of calls made in Kenya are from mobile lines, and with a massive 2.1 million subscribers compared to just 127,000 in 2000, the mobile phone accessories market is booming. You'll seldom get on a bus now without hearing a motley soundscape of tones based on the latest African and Western tunes, from Nameless to 50 Cent, peppered with occasional random choices such as 'Happy Birthday' or 'We Wish You a Merry Christmas'…

WHAT'S HOT…

⊕ Road safety: new regulations have been applied to the infamous matatu minibuses, which now operate under strict controls with speed governors, capacity restrictions, conductors' uniforms and even seatbelts. Of course »

MOST BIZARRE SIGHT! ⊛

Lake Magadi, a soda lake so saline that it has a pinkish salt crust, supporting large numbers of flamingos and other birds and giving the landscape a weirdly alien appearance completely removed from the customary African savanna stereotype.

KENYA.

> *One week stretched into a month in Watamu, Kenya – quite a change for travellers who had been spending just three or four nights in any one place for the previous six months. What we really loved about Watamu was the array of conservation-oriented groups and the chance to get involved with local projects.*

- David & Rayna Wigglesworth, USA

» operators have quickly found ways round half these rules, carefully noting the locations of every police checkpoint on the roads, but there's no denying the general improvement.

WHAT'S NOT…
⚙ Civil service strikes: 2005 saw widespread action across the country, with civil servants demanding better pay after years of low wages. Astonishingly, the government responded by denouncing the strikes, refusing to negotiate and firing more than 1000 of the workers involved, an extreme and somewhat ill-considered response that has done little to ease relations between the two groups.

HOT TOPIC OF THE DAY
⚙ The new Kenyan constitution – or rather the lack of it. After the 2002 elections the new government promised a full constitutional review within 90 days; the so-called Bomas Draft eventually materialised some time after the deadline, but discussions, committees and debates have been ongoing ever since. Unpopular ministers are suspected of trying to manipulate clauses to line their pockets

before the end of their term, and the process shows no signs of reaching a conclusion any time soon.

DO MENTION
⚙ Football. Kenyans love the beautiful game, particularly the English Premier League, and most will profess allegiance to either Arsenal, Manchester United or Liverpool (Chelsea is a distant fourth despite its recent success). In addition, the Kenyan national team has had its ban on competitive football lifted by FIFA and can now take part in the qualifying matches for the 2006 World Cup and African Cup of Nations.

RANDOM FACTS
⚙ Despite being the nation's capital and East Africa's largest city, Nairobi was actually only founded about 110 years ago.

⚙ There are very few real swear words in the Swahili language – English is usually used instead.

⚙ Men of the Luyha tribe are considered the best lovers in Kenya; Akamba women are supposedly the most libidinous, though the tribe as a whole is the butt of much the same sort of 'stupid' jokes that the Irish are subject to in Britain.

HOT TIP FOR TRAVELLERS
⚙ Try a *dawa*, fast becoming the Kenyan national cocktail: based on the Brazilian *caipirinha*, it's a rather seductive blend of vodka, fresh limes and honey. The name means 'medicine'…

THREE WORDS TO DESCRIBE THIS COUNTRY
⚙ Beautiful, wild, dramatic

- Tom Parkinson

THINGS TO TAKE! ★

Malaria precautions: the disease is endemic here, especially on the coast, and incidences among travellers are common.

A MAN STROLLS DOWN 'BAOBAB ALLEY' NEAR MORONDAVA.

○ **POPULATION**
18.5 MILLION

○ **VISITORS PER YEAR**
200,000

○ **UNIT OF CURRENCY**
MALAGASY FRANC
(FMG)

○ **COST OF A CUP OF COFFEE**
FMG1000 = US$0.11

○ **CAPITAL**
ANTANANARIVO

○ **LANGUAGES**
MALAGASY, FRENCH

★ **BEAUTY & THE BIZARRE.** The world's fourth-biggest island (fifth if you count Australia), Madagascar is famous principally for its sheer wilful uniqueness.

Its remote position off the East African coast means that virtually every aspect of its indigenous cultures and ecosystems has developed in isolation from the rest of the world, with some truly outlandish results. Like that kid at school who always had to be different, the island just can't help being a little out of line with the rest of the world; it amasses enough geographical, cultural and evolutionary anomalies to fill a whole parallel universe. You'll quickly lose track of the number of times you hear that this is the only place in the world where such-and-such is found, whether it's a singular lemur or a pluralist tribe, and if you manage to complete a single postcard without using the word 'spectacular' you must be either highly literate or deeply jaded. With tourists looking for alternative destinations away from Southeast Asia in the wake of SARS, bird flu and terrorism, Madagascar is in a good position to develop its modest standing as a travel destination over the next few years.

LAW & DISORDER

Politically, Madagascar has not always been as blessed. Originally settled by Malay-Polynesians in the 2nd century AD, the island was self-determined right up until 1896, when it officially became a French colony. Imperialism was the usual double-edged sword, abolishing slavery and creating infrastructure but imposing taxes, forced labour and land expropriation. Independence was granted in 1958, and since then governments have alternated wildly between pro- and anti-French stances, the most extreme being the military attempt at creating a socialist paradise in the 1970s. Civil unrest has been a recurring theme since 1971, and just about every decade has had its share of protests, constitutional crises and violent uprisings, »

MOST BIZARRE SIGHT! ★

The extraordinary 'stone forest' at the Parc National des Tsingy de Bemaraha, an entire landscape of huge eroded limestone pinnacles (the so-called *tsingy*, or needles) in *the* western part of the island. Virtually inaccessible in places, the vistas of jagged grey rocks are like little else you've seen, forming a striking contrast with the rainforest and gorges around them.

MADAGASCAR.

THREE YOUNG WOMEN FROM THE SMALL HIGHLAND
VILLAGE OF AMBALAVAO GO ABOUT THEIR DAY.

» with the most recent outbursts occurring in 2001. Yet despite all this, it remains a charming, unforgettable place for those visitors who do make it here – just one more paradox from the land of the unexpected.

DEFINING EXPERIENCE

✪ Arriving in Madagascar for the first time: the peculiar mixed ethnicity of the people baffles your every preconception; the tribal traditions leave you awestruck and freaked out in equal measures; the landscapes make you seriously question your geographical location; the flora and fauna resemble nothing else on earth; and the moment you think you've got the place figured out you discover a whole new corner of it

FESTIVALS & EVENTS

✪ Donia Festival; Nosy Be; May or June. This music and cultural festival draws participants and audiences from the Comoros, Mauritius and other Indian Ocean countries as well as Madagascar.

✪ *Famidihana* (turning of the bones); June–September. A tradition derived from Merina beliefs, where families disinter their dead for an ancestral 'visit' before washing the body, wrapping it in a fresh shroud and reburying it. These celebrations are generally private affairs but it's not unheard of for travellers to be invited to attend.

RANDOM FACTS

✪ Marc Ravalomanana, the current president, was previously mayor of Antananarivo, and started his career selling homemade yogurt off the back of a borrowed bicycle.

✪ Tortoise smuggling is a major problem here. Along with shells and skins, the livers are sold for use in traditional medicine.

✪ Madagascar's small wine industry was established in the 1960s, not by the French colonials (as you might expect) but by Swiss entrepreneurs.

✪ After the failure of a French settlement attempt in 1674, the island's first successful expat community consisted mainly of pirates from the USA and Europe, who established bases around Île Sainte Marie.

MADAGASCAR.

The village of Andavadoaka (42km – 26mi – south of Morombe) is not yet on the backpacker route, as it is difficult to reach. But once there, you will enjoy some of the best beaches on mainland Madagascar. There are Vezo with their large outrigger canoes, dozens of baobabs, seafood as much as you want (just tell the fishermen what you want the next day) and a small island (Nosy Hao) just off the coast with wonderful snorkelling. Scuba diving is said to be even better than in Ifaty, but bring your own equipment.

- Manfred Wolfensberger, Switzerland

traditional communities here and are at the centre of most common ceremonies and rituals, not to mention the many local *fady* (taboos). Foreigners aren't generally expected to abide by these customs, but showing some reverence for your own heritage as well as theirs should quickly endear you to your hosts.

DON'T MENTION
- The 2001 presidential election, which dragged on into 2002 amid accusations of corruption, international condemnation and outbreaks of violence, and finally ended with the incumbent fleeing to France to avoid prosecution for embezzling public funds. In fact, it's best not to mention politics at all.
- Lemurs – or at least not every five bloody minutes…

THREE WORDS TO DESCRIBE THIS COUNTRY
- Big, bizarre, unique

- Tom Parkinson

THINGS TO TAKE
- A mosquito net: malaria is endemic here, as it is in most of East Africa, and few hotels provide nets in good enough condition to keep the little buggers out
- Binoculars: essential for trying to spot the island's strange creatures in the thick of the rainforest

HOT TIPS FOR TRAVELLERS
- Plan your spending: you won't be able to change local currency outside Madagascar, and conversion rates back into hard currency are a blatant rip-off. Budget carefully and spend any excess before you leave.
- Take your time! Or if you don't have much, don't try to do everything. The island's so huge you'd need at least two months to cover the whole thing, so plan carefully, make judicious use of domestic flights, hire cars and start saving up for a return visit…

DO MENTION
- Your ancestors. The *razana* (ancestral spirits) are still highly respected in

A YOUNG MALI GIRL CAUGHT IN A MOMENT.

MALI.

VITAL STATISTICS

- **POPULATION**
  10.5 MILLION
- **VISITORS PER YEAR**
  95,000
- **UNIT OF CURRENCY**
  WEST AFRICAN CFA
  FRANC (CFA)
- **COST OF A CUP OF
  COFFEE**
  CFA100 = US$0.15
- **CAPITAL**
  BAMAKO
- **LANGUAGES**
  FRENCH, BAMBARA

MUD, MASKS & MOSQUES. Tourism is on the up in Mali, growing at a rate of 4% a year, and it's not hard to see how this often-overlooked part of the world is attracting visitors.

The largest country in West Africa and a former imperial power, its swathes of desert are watered by the mighty Niger River, interspersing the typical semiscrub of the Sahel region with areas of intense greenery, isolated fishing communities and bustling trade settlements. The country is best known for its amazing traditional mud architecture, typified by the jaw-droppingly huge Grande Mosquée in the town of Djenné; and the legendarily remote city of Timbuktu, long shrouded in mystery as a byword for the middle of nowhere and still a magnet for travellers captivated by the allure of the exotic. Vibrant and relaxed, and relatively stable compared with many of its warring neighbours, the Mali emerging today is unmistakably part of West Africa but has its own distinct character, with a culture full of charming eccentricities. Once you get over the initial bafflement it's impossible not to love everything new

you discover about this engagingly affable nation, where nothing should ever be taken *too* seriously.

DOGON IT

Alongside all these features, the area that makes Mali truly unique is Dogon Country. Physically, it's a spectacular region in its own right: the seemingly inhospitable 150km-long (93mi) Bandiagara Escarpment is speckled with mud villages and remarkable cliffside dwellings, providing some striking images. However, it's the inhabitants that really set the area apart, as the Dogon are one of the most unusual traditional peoples on the planet. The culture of this extraordinary tribe is based on an unprecedented knowledge of cosmology and astronomy, prompting even distinguished astronomers to speculate that they must have been given the information by aliens. In a country where 90% of the population is

A SPECTACULAR MUD-BRICK MOSQUE BUILT IN THE TRADITIONAL SAHEL STYLE NEAR THE TOWN OF MOPTI.

Muslim, they're an intriguing anomaly and a priceless piece of Mali's national heritage. However, their new status as a tourist attraction is seen by many as threatening the culture itself – the EU recently funded a new highway to the region which is drastically changing its traditional isolation, and the boom in unofficial guides, traders and hustlers that accompanies the tourist influx is seriously affecting local communities. Visitors should be very conscious of the risks of cultural erosion in this region, and insist on a degree of sensitivity.

DEFINING EXPERIENCE
☼ While few sights could compete with that first view of Timbuktu, the Bandiagara Escarpment or the Grande Mosquée in Djenné, the experience that brings you closest to the real heart of Mali will be dancing the night away to local music in one of Bamako's buzzing clubs, where you'll really start to understand what they call the 'rhythm of Africa'.

RECENT FAD
☼ Cinema: Mali has produced some of Africa's most acclaimed filmmakers. Director Souleymane Cissé, recently

honoured with a Lifetime Achievement award at the Zanzibar International Film Festival, is recognised worldwide for his work, particularly his 1987 classic *Yeleen*, considered one of the masterpieces of African cinema. More recently, up-and-coming auteur Assane Kouyaté has garnered attention and prizes galore for *Kabala*, a film following a village's fortunes after the loss of its well.

FESTIVALS & EVENTS
☼ Festival au Désert Timbuktu; near Timbuktu; January. A major Malian and international music festival.

☼ Fête des Masques; Dogon Country; April or May. This traditional Dogon ceremony celebrates the dead and the harvests, a typically offbeat combination.

☼ Sigui ceremony; Dogon Country. While imitation mask dances are performed all the time for tourists, don't hold your breath to catch the real thing – it's held just once every 60 years, when the orbits of Sirius B, Jupiter and Saturn come into line and the Dogon people appoint a new priest-astronomer. The next alignment is due in 2020.

»

THINGS TO TAKE! ☼

Cash: there's only one ATM in the whole country, and even that only accepts Visa cards.

MALI.

"

A gem in Mali is Teriya Bugu, an oasis/resort/ hotel/farm/development project on the Bani River between Bamako and Mopti. A must for people willing to witness what Mali can offer with dedication, kindness, hard work and the help of renewable energy.

"

- Herve Dhalluin, France

» WHAT'S HOT...
- Malian music, which has been 'discovered' in a big way by international musicians and audiences over the last few years. British popster Damon Albarn and US guitarist and composer Ry Cooder have both recorded albums with Malian artists, combining the traditional beats of the *griot* caste with the more modern aesthetic of the Western music scene.

WHAT'S NOT...
- Press freedom under threat – a recent wave of intimidation and attacks on Malian journalists, including one incident where a radio reporter was abducted in broad daylight, beaten and left for dead, has prompted the Mali Journalists' Union to appeal to the government for better measures to safeguard members of the press.

HOT TIPS FOR TRAVELLERS
- Take boats whenever you can: there are few better ways to experience the Malian landscape than by drifting at a suitably mellow pace to your destination. Timbuktu in particular is best approached by water, and catching your

first glimpse of the city from the Niger River is an unforgettable experience.
- The trade in traditional artefacts, particularly Dogon carvings, is strictly controlled in Mali, as so much of the national heritage has been sold illegally to foreigners. Be careful about what you buy, and choose modern imitations rather than authentic antiquities.

RANDOM FACTS
- At the height of its influence, the 13th-century Malian empire covered an area the size of Western Europe.
- Under colonialism, Mali was known as 'French Sudan', only taking the name Republic of Mali after independence.
- Timbuktu, properly known as Tombouctou in Mali, is supposedly named after a well belonging to a woman with a large navel.
- Djenné's iconic Grande Mosquée hasn't always been closed to non-Muslims; the ban was introduced in 1996 after French *Vogue* used the location for a rather inappropriate photo shoot.

THREE WORDS TO DESCRIBE THIS COUNTRY
- Affable, charming, eccentric
- *Tom Parkinson*

★ MOST BIZARRE SIGHT!

The Fetish Market in Bamako, perched between the main city mosque and the National Assembly, is where superstitious locals can come with a shopping list from their *marabout* (holy man) to pick up all those everyday essentials such as shrunken monkey heads, dried lizards, skulls, charms and animal skins. With all these strange objects laid out on the pavement, it's a bit like a macabre garage sale.

»

A PONTA DA BARRA LOCAL MOULDS A LIVING SELLING EXQUISITELY SIMPLE HAND-MADE EARTHENWARE.

VITAL STATISTICS

- **POPULATION**
  17 MILLION
- **VISITORS PER YEAR**
  450,000
- **UNIT OF CURRENCY**
  METICAL (MTC)
- **COST OF A MEAL**
  MTC123,000 = US$5
- **CAPITAL**
  MAPUTO
- **LANGUAGES**
  PORTUGUESE,
  BANTU, SWAHILI

MOZAMBIQUE.

★ **MOZAMBIQUE'S EXTREME MAKEOVER.** Based on its media image alone, the local tourism board's use of 'The Land of Smiles' to describe Mozambique seems quite the misnomer, especially when the face of Mozambique has for so long been any one of many anonymous starving children on our television sets.

However, after years of civil war, then nature's relentless wrath of famine, cyclones, droughts and floods, Mozambicans are picking up the pieces to rebuild and look optimistically towards the future. With a staggering one million unclaimed landmines still littering the landscape, going 'off the beaten track' is not really recommended to travellers in Mozambique. However, with a virtual 'nontourist' industry, the beaten track isn't all that beaten, anyway. Whether you're snorkelling with dolphins in the crystalline water and impeccable reefs of the Bazaruto Archipelago, or mixing it with friendly nondorsal-finned locals in the cute colonial cafés and salsa bars of Maputo, Mozambique's capital, you'll feel like you've stumbled across something very special and untouched, indeed. If you're after untouched, untouched is what you'll get: travelling Mozambique usually involves hair-raising rides in old jalopy-like buses with rowdy locals (often four-legged or with beaks).

SLOWLY DOES IT
Mozambique's infrastructure requires vast improvement, and there are five separate train lines running to Maputo, Quelimane, Beira, Nacala and Inhambane – none of these forms a 'network' and they are unreliable at best. In the rainy season from October to March, the dirt tracks and roads that traverse the interior become a boggy slush that even the beastliest off-road vehicles have trouble negotiating. If you want more to your holiday than basking on Mozambique's beautiful beaches, then it's best to visit when the weather's dry.

DEFINING EXPERIENCE
- Start by bobbing about with your snorkel and skins in the beautiful palm-lined »

HOT TIP FOR TRAVELLERS

Learn some Portuguese before you go – basic greetings will get you far, several stock phrases and the ability to ask directions will get you further.

SOFT-DRINK CANS, CARDBOARD BOXES AND A HEALTHY IMAGINATION MAKE FOR HIGH-OCTANE FUN ON BENGUELA ISLAND, BAZARUTO.

MOZAMBIQUE.

MOST BIZARRE SIGHT! ⭐

As a vestige of the brutal civil war and the need to show you were unarmed, when people regard one another in the street they continue to raise their hands above their head in an open-palmed surrender-like gesture. It may seem confrontational, but they're just saying hello.

»

beaches surrounding Mozambique Island, formerly Portugal's East African capital. Once you tire of the marine life, you can swap your goggles for sunglasses and head due north inland to the Unesco World Heritage–listed site dotted with 17th- and 18th-century Portuguese colonial buildings, centuries-old mosques, churches (including the Chapel of São Paulo) and a Hindu temple.

RECENT FAD
⊙ Making a livelihood from flowers. In 2001, the nation's first cut-flower company, Vilmar, was established in Messica, rural Mozambique, with the assistance of the nonprofit organisation TechnoServe. After Vilmar's first successful shipment of 10,000 roses to Europe in 2002, the company projects exporting a whopping 63 million rose stems per year by the end of the decade.

DO MENTION
⊙ Your birthday! Whether it really is your birthday or not, Mozambicans love to party and will use any excuse to kick up their heels, be it to a crackly old transistor radio or the biggest boom-box in town. Sunday is always a festive day; don't be surprised if a complete stranger hands you a bottle of home brew in the street.

TAKE HEED

Beneath the smiles, there's a grim reality. Mozambique is a country wracked with poverty, and, unfortunately, firearms are rife. There is petty pickpocketing (watch out in crowded markets and on buses), but things have a tendency to get violent, with armed robberies common. Bandits hit the open roads, so, to avoid carjacking, it's best to travel in convoys; and women should avoid walking anywhere alone, especially along beaches. Avoid flashing around money or jewellery and always carry your passport. Bribery and blackmail are also tools of the less confrontational thief, and such thieves are sometimes in uniform: if police stop you in the street and ask to see your passport, show it to them, but if they demand you hand it over, politely request that you do so at the police station.

MOZAMBIQUE.

"
We were in this little village in Mozambique when a local crazy guy began following us, talking gibberish. Another local guy came to our rescue and shooed him away. We asked him what was wrong with the guy and he said this guy had been perfectly normal up until a year ago when he stole from his work and the owner cast a spell on him and he has never been the same since.
"

- Deirdre Whelan, USA

FESTIVALS & EVENTS
- Mozambican Heroes' Day; February. Mozambicans remember their revolutionary heroes on this day.
- Independence Day; June. Celebrations take place to commemorate Mozambique's independence from the Portuguese colonial government in 1975.
- Revolution Day; Chai; September. Also known as Armed Forces Day, this public holiday commemorates Mozambique's independence struggle in Caso Delgado province.

RANDOM FACTS
- Mozambique is a seafood-lovers paradise; prawns as big as your head and crayfish like footballs are just a couple of tempters.
- The best time to visit is June to August, when the climate is at its most temperate.
- The population is 30% Christian, 20% Muslim and 50% indigenous beliefs.
- Get your jabs and be prepared for nasties: schistosomiasis (bilharzia), hepatitis, typhoid, diphtheria, tetanus, meningococcal meningitis and malaria are all present in Mozambique.

Remember to pack condoms and bring your own syringes if you need them, as the threat of HIV/AIDS is, as always, very very real.

- The best time for bird-watching is in the middle of the wet season – bring wipers for your binoculars and a umbrella for your head.
- From 1932 to 1968 Portuguese dictator António Salazar forced all Mozambican males aged 15 and above to slave on plantations, often in chains.

WHAT'S HOT...
- Photographing pristine beaches, vibrant locals (be polite – ask first) and tourist sites

WHAT'S NOT...
- Photographing soldiers, airports, bridges, and government and public buildings (it's illegal)

THINGS TO TAKE
Binoculars (for bird-watching)
- Flippers (for snorkelling)
- A hearty dose of sensibility (to avoid getting in difficult situations or wandering away into landmine-prone areas)

THREE WORDS TO DESCRIBE THIS COUNTRY
- Ravaged yet untouched

- Samone Bos

HOT TOPIC OF THE DAY!

Mozambique's big beautiful future – aside from the recent attempts to boost tourism, plans to export natural gas to South Africa are expected to boost the Mozambican economy with billions of much-needed dollars

SOUTH AFRICA.

VITAL STATISTICS

A ZULU WITCH DOCTOR OR HERBALIST SMILES BEWITCHINGLY FOR THE CAMERA.

- **POPULATION**
  44 MILLION
- **VISITORS PER YEAR**
  6.5 MILLION
- **UNIT OF CURRENCY**
  SOUTH AFRICAN RAND (R)
- **COST OF A CUP OF COFFEE**
  R3 = US$0.45
- **CAPITAL**
  PRETORIA
- **LANGUAGES**
  ZULU, XHOSA, AFRIKAANS, ENGLISH, TSWANA

★ REALITY'S BITE. It wasn't that long ago that South Africa finally jettisoned its shameful recent past and took its rightful place on the world stage.

Around the world, people cheered as an unjust and evil system was finally brought down, replaced by the hope of a prosperous, harmonious future – a future that South Africa could finally share with its fellow nations. Travellers were among the loudest cheerers, for they knew that this almost unimaginably beautiful land would now be open for them to explore and enjoy.

The optimism of those early years has been moderately tempered with reality. Apartheid may no longer be the first and only word that comes to mind when we think of South Africa, but its roots run deep and its bitter fruit will take decades, if not centuries, to disappear completely. The poverty that had almost exclusively afflicted black communities has now spread through all ethnic groups, some of whom resent the change and look back wistfully at the old days. Economic development has been patchy, and crime has skyrocketed in the cities. Carjackings are a daily event, as are sightings of men wandering the streets carrying heavy submachine guns. And HIV – often simply referred to as 'the virus' – has infected almost a fifth of the population, by some accounts.

For the traveller, this makes for a surreal world that may not reflect realities of modern South Africa. It's still all too easy to spend a couple of months as a backpacker in South Africa and interact solely with white South Africans who would prefer it if things were, well, the way they *were*. De facto segregation remains an ugly fact, and racism is not limited to any one community. The nation's past refuses to slink meekly away, seemingly putting up a fight at every turn.

KICKING THE HABIT

But let's get real here. It's an extraordinarily bad past, and South Africans have done a tremendous job in the short time they've

had. No other nation has ever undergone such a dramatic, almost pious process of moving forward as did South Africa during the days of Truth and Reconciliation. This monumental transition has refashioned and re-created South African identity in a way that no other event ever has. What used to be the law of the land is now seen as a minority view. Integration and the sharing of cultures are now seen as the path to enlightenment rather than aberrations. A government that could have sought vengeance instead sought rapprochement. Yes, democracy in South Africa is here to stay.

Lucky you. An open, free, democratic South Africa means an open, free, incredible wonderland for travellers. Initially overwhelmed by the surge of tourists who poured in as apartheid crumbled, the nation has had more than a decade to come to grips with the notion that everybody wants to visit. The infrastructure for travellers is now well developed and smooth. Nowhere else in Africa is it as painless to view wildlife, climb mountains or go surfing. No other African city is as staggeringly beautiful as Cape Town. Almost no destination in the Western world is as unlikely to be attacked by terrorists.

And there's nowhere else in the world where the sight of black kids and white kids playing soccer together is as likely to move you to tears.

DEFINING EXPERIENCE
- Being stalked by a pride of lions at Kruger National Park while hearing your machine gun–toting guide talk about the last group of tourists, who happened to get eaten

FESTIVALS & EVENTS
- National Arts Festival; Grahamstown; early July. This festival for lovers of high culture features mainstream and alternative art, opera and theatre.

- Pretoria Show; August. Carnival-style rides, animal demonstrations and free entertainment serve as a backdrop to the main event – a massive agricultural show that draws farmers from around the country.

- Arts Alive; Johannesburg; September. Musical acts, comedians and cultural workshops make up this festival.

- Reconciliation Day; December. This is something of a strange holiday. Originating as the Day of the Vow, which

RECENT FAD!

Using condoms! Well, hopefully this is more than just a fad, but the skyrocketing incidence of HIV has propelled the majority of South African teenagers into using prophylactics.

SOUTH AFRICA.

FROM THE ROAD

> " *I was having a shower in my lodge in South Africa. I cannot describe my distress as I cleared the soap from my eyes and found myself, almost literally, pink bottom to pink bottom (with the exception of a thankfully rather thick piece of glass) with 24 baboons!* "
>
> - Sophie Morris, Britain

» celebrated a Boer victory over the Zulus, today's holiday has seen everything from collective declarations of white sorrow over mistreatment of blacks to a reaffirmation of the principles of apartheid by right-wing whites. It's an odd – but very revealing – time to be in the country.

THINGS TO TAKE

⊛ The only thing you'll really desperately need is a clamp for your mouth – more often than not, you'll need to physically hold your tongue to refrain from commenting on how different ethnic groups interact. And the clamp may also be useful to help you gnaw on biltong, the incredibly tough South African answer to beef jerky. If you can chew it for an hour or two, it's worth the effort.

WHAT'S HOT...

⊛ The Springboks – South Africa's rugby team is back with a vengeance! Long playing the bridesmaid to Australia's Wallabies and New Zealand's All Blacks, the South Africans have begun to assemble a true powerhouse team that threatens to dominate the sport for years to come.

WHAT'S NOT...

⊛ South African cricket. Don't even ask. At least it still draws massive crowds, though how it's operating at such staggering financial losses is anyone's guess.

DO MENTION

⊛ Apart from sports (soccer, for example, transcends ethnic and linguistic bounds), talking about wine can be a real conversation-starter. For example: 'I hear Johannesburg rieslings are far better than anything you'd get in Paris.'

DON'T MENTION

⊛ Among traditional Zulu and Xhosa communities, open discussion of sex and sexuality is frowned upon.

RANDOM FACTS

⊛ The strange tradition of telephone booth–stuffing, which swept through the UK and USA in the late 1950s, originated in South Africa. South Africans still hold the record: 25 people in one phone booth.

⊛ The world's largest rough diamond – the over-3000-carat Cullinan – was found in South Africa. That's about the size of an adult man's fist.

⊛ More than half a million children (preteenage) are HIV positive. There is a 50-50 chance that any given South African 15-year-old will die of AIDS.

⊛ Before igniting India's independence movement, Mahatma Gandhi worked as a lawyer in South Africa. By most accounts, he wasn't very good at it.

⊛ South Africa completely surrounds the country of Lesotho.

MOST BIZARRE SIGHT

⊛ Seeing an ostrich stick its head in the sand. They really do this. One wonders why they're not extinct yet.

HOT TIP FOR TRAVELLERS

⊛ Sorry to harp on ostriches, but this really must be said: Never try to ride an ostrich, no matter who tells you to.

THREE WORDS TO DESCRIBE THIS COUNTRY

⊛ Confronting, confounding, moving

- Vivek Wagle

A FLOCK OF FLAMINGOS IN FLAMBOYANT REPOSE.

⊙ **POPULATION**
36 MILLION
(ZANZIBAR 990,000)

⊙ **VISITORS PER YEAR**
600,000

⊙ **UNIT OF CURRENCY**
TANZANIAN SHILLING
(TSH)

⊙ **COST OF A CUP OF
COFFEE**
TSH200 = US$0.20

⊙ **CAPITAL**
DODOMA

⊙ **LANGUAGES**
KISWAHILI, ENGLISH

EAST AFRICAN CLASSIC. Like its neighbour Kenya, Tanzania has long been one of Africa's prime destinations for package tourists and safari seekers, who are enticed by promises of stereotypically stunning landscapes, copious wildlife, low prices and relative political stability.

Even upheavals such as the embassy bombings in 1998 and the 2003 terrorist attacks in Kenya have done little to shake consumer confidence in Tanzania, maintaining respectable if unspectacular growth in the tourist industry. The capital, Dodoma, may only be relevant to travellers as the unexpected answer to a pub quiz question, but over the last few years principal city Dar es Salaam has cemented its reputation as a regional hub and an appealing alternative to Nairobi, with the added bonus of quick ferry access to one of the region's undisputed gems: Zanzibar.

SWEET SWAHILI DREAMS

It's hard not to discuss Tanzania and Zanzibar in the same breath, but it's equally tricky not to mention the huge differences between them – in fact most Zanzibaris would be very insistent that they are definitively not part of the mainland, and the archipelago is staunchly proud of its semi-autonomy, with its own president and 'Revolutionary Government'. Correctly known by its Swahili name Unguja, the main island gets the most attention from visitors for the string of lovely beaches all along its coastline and, above all, for the living Swahili culture of Stone Town, Unesco-listed as a repository of traditional architecture and design. This former slaving centre, once the fulcrum of an empire that put it alongside capitals such as London, Paris and Istanbul, has always been a popular honeymoon and backpacker destination and is now gaining increasing international prominence for its annual film festival – not bad for a city that barely covers 2.5 sq km (1 sq mi) and has just 150,000 inhabitants (roughly the size of Oxford, UK).

»

HOT TOPIC OF THE DAY!

The latest round of national elections in October 2005 is the main thing still on everyone's minds, especially given the protests and violence that flared up on Zanzibar and Pemba after the last ballot in 2000. Laura Bush's recent visit to the region also attracted a fair bit of humorous comment!

»»

A BOY CYCLES PAST, NOTORIOUS SLAVE TRADER, TIBBU TIB'S HOUSE ON ZANZIBAR.

TANZANIA + ZANZIBAR.

» DEFINING EXPERIENCE

☼ OK, so everyone does it, but cresting the lip of the Ngorongoro Crater to see a perfect microcosm of classic safari Africa neatly encapsulated in one massive volcanic caldera must still top the list of Tanzanian tourist attractions, and it's one sight you won't get anywhere else. For many unwary trekkers, however, it's a failed attempt to scale Kilimanjaro that sticks in the memory, for all the wrong reasons…

WHAT'S HOT…

☼ 'Bongo flava': local music blending hip-hop with traditional influences, rhythms and instruments. The genre's hugely popular with Tanzania's US-obsessed youth, and you won't have to go far to pick up a sample cassette; look out for angry urbanites Kikosi Cha Mazengi and Zanzibar slackers Wazenji Kijiwe. Of course the rap lyrics are mostly in Swahili, so don't expect to be singing along straight away.

WHAT'S NOT…

☼ Mass transit dolphin safaris: try not to pander to the boom industry in boat trips, which has led to a flooded market and some overhassled dolphins. It's not all the boatmen's fault either: surely the local World Wildlife Fund (WWF) really shouldn't need to spell out to visitors that 'shouting and waving your arms around will not encourage dolphins to approach your boat'!

RANDOM FACTS

☼ Ujiji, near Kigoma on the Congo border, was where Stanley finally caught up with Dr Livingstone to trot out his famous phrase.

☼ Zanzibar's Anglican Cathedral is built on the site of the former slave market.

☼ Under socialism Tanzania achieved one of the highest literacy rates in Africa, but life expectancy is still only 51 years.

FESTIVALS & EVENTS

☼ Kilimanjaro Marathon; February. If trekking Africa's highest mountain just isn't tough enough for you, you can now try and run up it, with potential prize money of TSh2 million on offer. Amateurs should stick to the fun run – regional competition is fierce, and the 2005 event

> *We are strolling along a beach in Zanzibar, the sun setting... Two Zanzibari guys motion us to go into the jungle with them; I politely refuse. Later I hear music coming from the jungle, and we follow the sound. In the middle of this tropical forest, we see huge speakers pumping music. There are the two guys from the beach, and some of their buddies. We sit around the fire, they whip out drums and we drum for an hour. Then more people appear at this makeshift club and we dance the night away to the tunes of Tanzanian hip-hop.*

- Joanne Corrigall, South Africa

the Zanzibar archipelago, was closed to foreigners entirely from 1964 up until the 1980s, and has been tipped as 'the new Zanzibar' for the last, ooh, 20 years or so. It remains an unchanged, unspoilt haven of hills and greenery in complete contrast to Unguja's flat landscape and tourist-focused resorts. It's also known as a centre of witchcraft, black magic and traditional healing.

☼ For a change from the standard Swahili diet, Zanzibar's Stone Town is one of the few places in Tanzania where you can get decent Thai food, should you crave such a thing!

THREE WORDS TO DESCRIBE THIS COUNTRY

☼ Captivating, unassuming, beautiful

- Tom Parkinson

was won by a Kenyan athlete who actually had malaria at the time!

☼ Zanzibar International Film Festival (ZIFF); July. In its eighth year, this ambitious cultural festival combines movies, music, dance, discussion, theatre, workshops and much more at venues across Zanzibar and Pemba islands.

THINGS TO TAKE

☼ Malaria precautions – an amazing number of travellers, short-term and long-term, come down with the disease, especially on Zanzibar

☼ A break from chocolate – most branded confectionery here is imported from the Middle East, which involves a long, hot trip with obvious consequences. So why not skip the Mars bar and try something local instead?

☼ Extra dollars – with a hefty US$33 departure tax and 'safety fee' payable at the airport it's easy to find yourself stuck without cash when you leave

HOT TIPS FOR TRAVELLERS

☼ Pemba island, the other major island in

MOST BIZARRE SIGHT! ★

It's debatable whether this actually counts as an attraction, but the UN International Criminal Tribunal on the Rwandan Genocide in Arusha is open to the public, allowing curious visitors the chance to sit in on proceedings aimed at prosecuting the perpetrators of the shocking mass killings in Rwanda in the 1990s. You could hardly imagine more of a contrast with the usual tourist pursuits.

ANGOLA

For most outsiders this sub-Saharan giant means war, diamonds and oil. More than a few label it an African basket case. But this land and its people are not to be underestimated. Angolans are unshockable, resilient and resourceful. They're fighters – but they're music-mad romantics too.

BENIN

The birthplace of voodoo and one of West Africa's most powerful kingdoms, Benin once had a historical renown extending far beyond its borders. Recently the country has abandoned Marxism for democracy and capitalism. You can find remnants of the vast palaces of the formidable Dahomey empire, take boat rides through villages built on stilts, stop off at deserted beaches where slave ships once sailed and see stunning indigenous architecture. There's even more to discover, but it takes time – Benin likes to keep its goodies hidden.

BURKINA FASO

Between Sahelian empires and coastal kingdoms, between Muslim and animist Africa, between Saharan desertscapes and southern waterfalls, Burkina Faso weaves many of Africa's diverging strands into a fascinating and thoroughly seductive fabric. The Burkinabé are descended from a long line of regal emperors who have suffered the plebeian indignities of colonialism and blackbirding, but this has only served to strengthen and preserve their cultural identity.

BURUNDI

Intertribal tensions have continued to plague Burundi since independence in 1962, culminating in the long civil war that engulfs the country today. Gunfire is not uncommon in the capital, Bujumbura, and the security situation is unstable throughout the country.

CAMEROON

Cameroon is rich in indigenous cultures, vibrant artistic and musical traditions, and wonderful Cameroonian hospitality. The country offers visitors the choice of rainforests and relaxing beaches in the south; rocky outcrops, terraced hillsides and hobbit-like villages in the north; and the wildlife of Parc National de Waza. There are lions – wild ones in the bush and indomitable ones on the football pitch.

CAPE VERDE

On the islands of Cape Verde you can find lush valleys and mountains, white sandy beaches, volcanoes, deserts and pretty towns with cobbled streets. There's diving and windsurfing, hiking and fishing. Islanders mix up African, Portuguese, Mediterranean and Latin influences and come out with a flavour that's distinctly 'Cabo'.

CENTRAL AFRICAN REPUBLIC

A country of rare natural beauty, with some of the world's most amazing wildlife, CAR nonetheless remains underdeveloped, fragmented and poverty-stricken, despite its mineral deposits and great natural resources. For centuries CAR has endured rapacity and the situation doesn't look like changing any time soon.

CHAD

With one of the most painful histories in Africa, Chad is a nation with its foundations built on conflict. The harsh climate, geographic remoteness, poor resource endowment and lack of infrastructure have created a weak economy susceptible to political turmoil. Despite a peace agreement between the government and rebels, rebellion occasionally flares up in the north.

COMOROS & MAYOTTE

The islands of Comoros and Mayotte offer an amazing diversity of people and cultures. Despite a succession of political coups and civilian riots, the islands boast cobblestoned medinas, ports bustling with dhows, active volcanoes, virgin rain forests, tropical moonrises over white-sand beaches and blazing ocean sunsets that set the sky on fire.

CONGO, DEMOCRATIC REPUBLIC OF

The Democratic Republic of Congo is a sprawling mass of rainforest, fast-running rivers, red clay and dust. Formerly called Zaïre, it remains intoxicatingly mysterious and largely cut off to visitors because of civil war, lamentable lack of development and naturally impenetrable terrain. The country clings to a fragile ceasefire after decades of brutal civil war and neglect.

CONGO, REPUBLIC OF

The Republic of Congo's countryside around Brazzaville is all rolling hills and lush green trees; further north there's bright orange earth and untamed tropical rainforest bristling with wildlife – the Congo boasts Africa's largest lowland gorilla population. Trawl street markets for an intoxicating exhibition of Congolese food, culture and music. After three devastating civil wars in less than a decade, the country is slowly regaining its stability.

CÔTE D'IVOIRE

Côte d'Ivoire's most powerful attraction is its people, with their art and music. There's also a lot of physical beauty, from towering mountains to fishing villages and beaches. For many years Côte d'Ivoire was the jewel of West Africa, but in recent times the country has been rocked by huge debts and a military coup. The situation remains very tense, with the risk of violence erupting at any time.

DJIBOUTI

Djibouti's blend of African, Arab, Indian and European influences is seasoned with a dose of khat, the mildly intoxicating herb. The capital may be little more than a minor port filled with peeling colonial buildings, but its streets are unforgettable, shared by traditionally robed tribesmen and French legionnaires, hennaed women and Somali refugees, and filled with the aromas of French cuisine and seedy bars. The hinterland is a bizarre treat of eerie volcanic landscapes and vast salt lakes.

EQUATORIAL GUINEA

Most of Equatorial Guinea remains densely covered with forest, but the discovery of underwater oil looks set to change the face of the country. Bioko Island has been taken over by oil money and an influx of foreign workers, but a trip to the mainland (Rio Muni) is still like taking a step back in time. This is real adventure travel, with amazing rewards – rainforest, beaches, traditional African villages and, with some hard hiking and luck, you might get to spend some time with gorillas in Monte Alen National Park.

ERITREA

Eritrea's richness and beauty did not escape the attention of the outside world and the country was made a colony of Italy for more than fifty years. Modern Eritrea is a lively country with an exuberant and optimistic population. The landscape is stark, arid, bleak and even bordering on the other-worldly in Dankalia – it will overwhelm you.

Relish Asmara, one of the most enchanting capitals in Africa, where evidence of Italy's imperial rule can still be seen in the magnificent architecture.

GABON

Outside Libreville, the capital, Gabon is a laid-back country of villages, rainforest, rivers and mountains. It's one of the richest and most stable countries in Africa, but people still know the value of relaxation. The jungle is full of wildlife and new national parks are opening the forests to ecotourism and closing them to loggers. Gabon is a place that rewards patience. The longer you stay, the more you'll find to explore and like.

GAMBIA

Beyond the European-flavoured resorts are African-style wildlife reserves and the ruins of long-abandoned slaving stations. The capital, Banjul, is nicely low-key for an African capital. The country's size, people, language and food make the Gambia the perfect gateway to West Africa.

GHANA

Ghana produces some of Africa's best highlife music and most famous sculpture, and is home to chilled-out and friendly people. If you want to sample West Africa's modern and ancient cultures, explore its historic slave forts, toast yourself on its beautiful beaches – and do it all speaking English – it's got to be Ghana.

GUINEA

Guinea exudes a marked energy and growing economic vitality. It is blessed with plenty of attractions: the hot coast with top-notch islands and beaches; the cool beauties of the Fouta Djalon plateau; the arid Sahelian landscape; and the teeming greenery of the dense southern forests. Also high on the country's list of attractions is the vibrancy of its music and dance traditions.

GUINEA-BISSAU

Guinea-Bissau is a gem, with some fantastic stuff waiting for those prepared to seek it out. Sleepy towns, quiet beaches and sacred rainforests dot the mainland, while the Arquipélago dos Bijagós has a unique culture and fantastic marine and animal life. Even by African standards it's a gut-wrenchingly poor country which has been badly served by its recent leaders, yet it remains peaceful.

« LESOTHO

Appropriately dubbed 'the kingdom in the sky', Lesotho is a mountainous country. It's a surprising combination of rapidly developing modernity and ancient culture, and offers a chance to escape the clamour of South Africa, enjoy some spectacular scenery and experience life in traditional villages along the way. It has managed to avoid recent wars and political instability.

LIBERIA

A regional peace initiative means one day travellers might again be able to explore this country. But for the moment it might be best to stay away.

MALAWI

Malawi's ever-changing landscape takes you from the top of lofty mountains, down steep escarpments, through woodland, farmland and empty grassland, to the shores of a magnificent lake. Nature lovers will adore the national parks and game reserves, mountain hiking and plateau trekking, lake diving and boating – plus the warm, welcoming Malawians.

MAURITANIA

Mauritania offers naked scenery, endless views, forgotten towns and a stunning coast. It is a deeply traditional Islamic republic, inhabited by warm, yet reserved, humorous people. There was a military coup in August 2005, and the situation remains uncertain. Consider if going to Mauritania is worth the risk and avoid the border area with Mali and Algeria altogether.

MAURITIUS

Mauritius boasts endless sugar-cane plantations, dramatic mountains, a vibrant cultural mix and some of the finest beaches and aquamarine lagoons in the Indian Ocean. The island has a distinct Indian flavour, seasoned with African, Chinese, French and British elements. Many people come to Mauritius to stay in the fabulous beach hotels, but there's no shortage of cheap-and-cheerful guesthouses, apartments and small, family-run hotels.

NAMIBIA

The only thing small about Namibia is its population. Everything else is larger than life: towering red dunes; bleak mist-shrouded coastlines of shipwreck lore; vast expanses of nothing; sky so big it swallows you up. It's a land of deserts, seascapes, wildlife reserves, ancient rock art, gentle bushwalking terrain and an exhilarating sense of sheer boundlessness. If you yearn to explore, get away from the crowds and lose yourself in a hauntingly beautiful place, then head to this friendly nation.

NIGER

Niger is a barren, windswept land ravaged by drought and colonial conquest, somehow surviving against the odds. It's a country of aristocratic desert nomads, skilled artisans, the Ténéré Desert and the ancient caravan town of Agadez. A hunger crisis has hit Niger, partly because many people are simply too poor to buy food.

NIGERIA

In Nigeria hundreds of different peoples, languages, histories and religions all sit shoulder to shoulder in a hectic, colourful and often volatile republic. A chronic crime problem, religious intolerance, large-scale unemployment and overcrowding in poor living conditions regularly push the rule of law to the brink. Lagos, its largest city, has an unrivalled reputation as every traveller's nightmare. Safety issues in Nigeria are still paramount, so take proper precautions.

RÉUNION

What Réunion lacks in beaches, it more than makes up for in its wildly dramatic mountain country. It is so sheer and lush, it looks as if it has risen dripping wet from the sea – which it effectively has, being the tip of a submerged volcano. The island is run as a département of France, and French culture dominates every facet of life but with a tropical twist and with subtle traces of Indian, African and Chinese cultures.

RWANDA

Rwanda is a scenically stunning little country with endless mountains. Hidden among the dense forest of the Virunga volcanoes' forbidding slopes are some of the world's last mountain gorillas. Rwanda is known for the horrific genocide that occurred here in 1994, but the country has taken giant strides towards recovery since. As long as security and stability persist, Rwanda is a refreshing country in which to travel, a top spot for the independent traveller.

SÃO TOMÉ & PRÍNCIPE

These sleepy islands are remote and rarely visited, but tourists are starting to discover their attractions: miles of deserted beaches, crystal-blue waters with excellent and uncharted diving and snorkelling, rolling hills and jagged rock formations and lush rainforests. All this, plus they are home to a unique Portuguese-Creole island culture.

SENEGAL

Surrounded by desert, Senegal offers a rich landscape, great beaches for soaking up the sun and some excellent scuba diving opportunities. Dakar, its capital city, is raw, crowded and exciting. Senegal is also noted for its music scene – many big names in world music hail from here. The country's seductiveness has made it West Africa's number one travel destination.

SEYCHELLES

Among the 115 coral islands that make up the Seychelles are some of the most idyllic island getaways in the world, such as the dazzling beaches and crystal-clear waters of Praslin and La Digue, or the cathedral-like palm forests of the Vallée de Mai. There's no denying, however, that the Seychelles is an expensive destination.

SIERRA LEONE

Throughout the 1990s Sierra Leone was gripped by a savage civil war between the government and Revolutionary United Front, and it will take time for things to get back to normal. Freetown has a happy-go-lucky and vibrant atmosphere and Freetown Peninsula has some of West Africa's most magical beaches. In the interior are lush landscapes, jungle and reserves abundant with wildlife.

SOMALIA

On the Horn of Africa, Somalia has had a long history of bloody internal conflict that continues to this day in most of the country. A transitional government has embarked on a plan to bring about stability and security, but success is unlikely to come soon.

SUDAN

Power and the promise of great hidden treasures made Sudan – the largest country in Africa – the object of invasion and exploration for much of its long and tumultuous history. Today much of the country remains unexplored – with access restricted to many regions and the security situation unstable.

SWAZILAND

The easygoing Swazis are more likely to celebrate for fun than demonstrate for reform. National parks and game reserves are alive with flora and fauna. In the rich and vigorous culture of the Swazi people, significant power is vested in the monarchy. While the kingdom is conservative and in many ways illiberal, it has popular support.

TOGO

Togo is relatively obscure, and tiny. Upcountry are beautiful hills and plateaus, while the region around Kpalimé, in the southwest, is particularly scenic. Political unrest and violence followed elections in 2005 and the situation remains volatile.

UGANDA

Uganda has been transformed from a tragic, war-torn nation into one of the fastest growing economies in Africa. It is home to superb scenery, half the world's majestic mountain gorillas and the continent's highest mountain range. Downtown Kampala has a contagious buzz and bustle. Rebel activity is frequent in the north and northeast, but there is plenty to experience beyond these areas.

ZAMBIA

Zambia's intrigue lies in its natural simplicity; here is the essence of remote, untamed wilderness areas, tranquil scenery and friendly, easy-going people. There are natural wonders such as the majestic Victoria Falls, hidden waterfalls, languid rivers, rich concentrations of wildlife and unending bush. Zambia's people still observe ancient traditional ceremonies. The areas bordering the Democratic Republic of the Congo and Angola are considered unsafe.

ZIMBABWE

A spectacular country, Zimbabwe boasts the grandeur of Victoria Falls, incredible wildlife, amazing ruins and the Zambezi River. Hippos, elephants and giraffes roam the grasslands. With a tense socio-political situation casting a cloud over the country at present, independent travel is not advised.

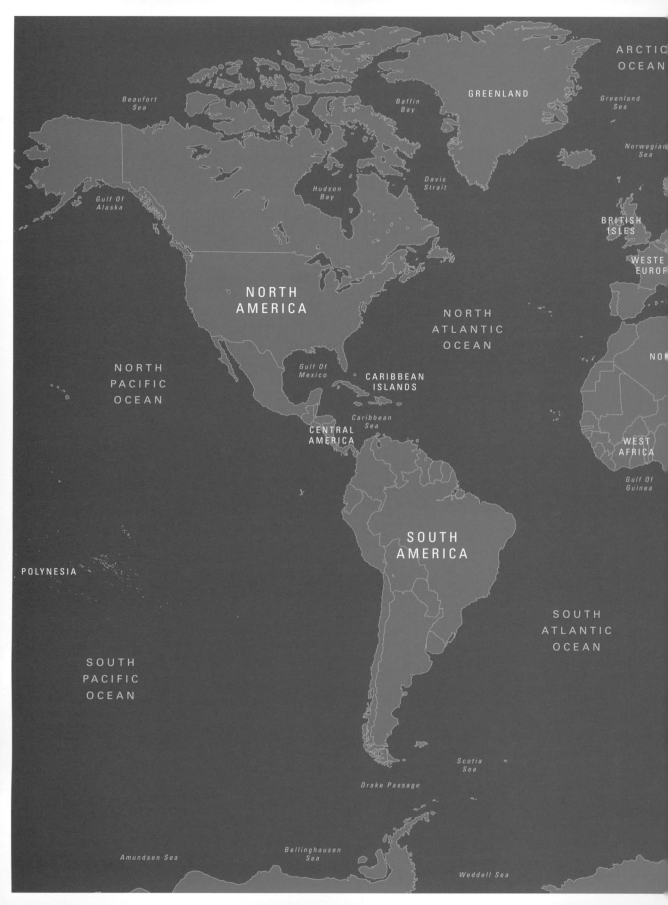

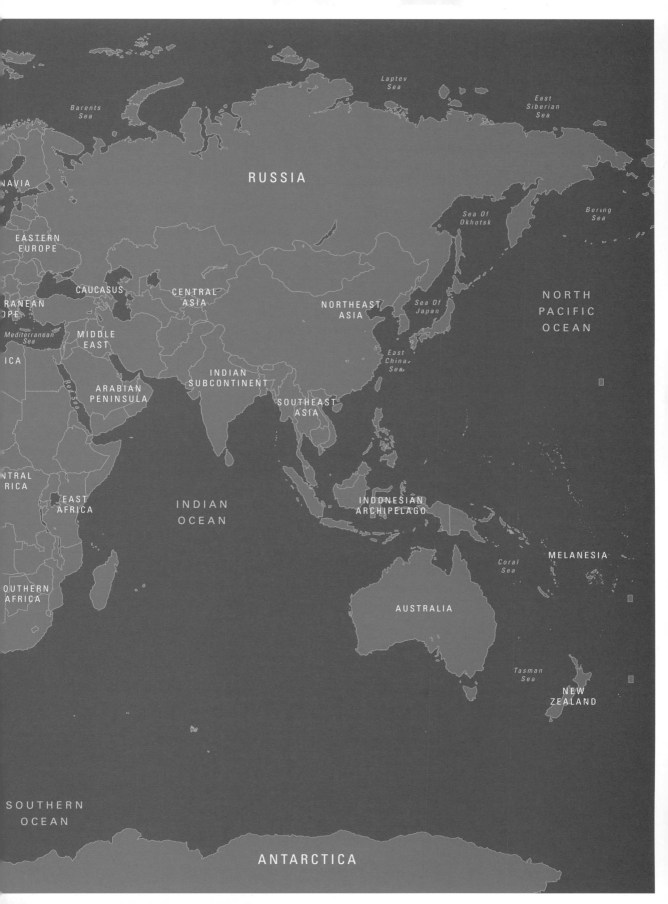

ACKNOWLEDGEMENTS.

PUBLISHER Roz Hopkins

PROJECT MANAGER Andrea Frost

COMMISSIONING EDITORS Ben Handicott, Bridget Blair

COORDINATING EDITOR Barbara Delissen

DESIGN Mark Adams

IMAGE RESEARCH Ellen Burrows, Nic Lehman, Marika Kozak, Daniel New, Valerie Tellini

IMAGE COORDINATORS Fiona Siseman, Lisa Tuckwell, Rebecca Dandens

CARTOGRAPHERS Paul Piaia, Wayne Murphy, David Connolly and Kusnandar

PRE-PRESS PRODUCTION: Ryan Evans

CREATIVE TEAM Jane Pennells, Nic Lehman, Daniel New, Mark Adams

PRODUCTION MANAGER Jo Vraca

PRINT PRODUCTION Graham Imeson

ASSISTING EDITORS Kate Evans, Yvonne Byron, Kim Noble

ASSISTING LAYOUT DESIGNERS Indra Kilfoyle, Steven Cann, Laura Jane, Jacqueline McLeod

TEXT PART ONE Simone Eggers and Simon Sellars

TEXT PART TWO Amanda Canning, Andres Vaccari, Andrew Nystrom, Anthony Ham, Brigitte Barta, Catherine Le Nevez, Errol Hunt, Etain O'Carroll, Fiona Buchan, Heather Dickson, Janine Eberle, Jay Cooke, Joe Bindloss, Judith Bamber, Julie Grundvig, Kalya Ryan, Kathleen Munnelly, Kerryn Burgess, Laura Jean McKay, Marg Toohey, Marika McAdam, Michael Kohn, Rebecca Chau, Richard Plunkett, Sam Trafford, Sam Trafford, Samone Bos, Sarah Wintle, Simon Sellars, Simone Eggers, Tim Brewer, Tom Parkinson, Vivek Wagle, Will Gourlay

WITH MANY THANKS TO Howard Ralley, Jason Shugg, Lonely Planet authors, staff and readers, Nick Wood, Roz Hopkins, Simon Westcott, Tony Wheeler and the team at the Lonely Planet Traveler Information Centre, in particular Trent Paton, Jessa Boanas-Dewes, Raphael Richards and Jennifer Mundy.

COVER IMAGES BLUELIST (LEFT TO RIGHT)
Dynamic Graphics | Photolibrary,
Index Stock Imagery | Photolibrary,
Tony Garcia | Getty Images,
John Foxx | Photolibrary,
It Stock | Photolibrary,
Brandx Pictures | Photolibrary,
Nonstock Inc. | Photolibrary

INDEX.

A Afghanistan 32, 185
Africa 36
Albania 255
Algeria 33, 291
Andorra 255
Angola 320
Anguilla 143
Antarctica 24, 26, 68, 143
Antigua & Barbuda 143
Argentina 29, 55, 104–106
Armenia 255
Aruba & the Netherlands Antilles 143
Australia 21, 25, 27, 30, 41, 43, 49, 51, 55, 57, 63, 65, 69, 72, 77, 81, 84, 87, 89, 93, 95, 192–194
Austria 70, 89, 255
Azerbaijan 255

B Bahamas 143
Bahrain 291
Bangladesh 185
Barbados 143
Belarus 255
Belgium 18, 61, 255
Belize 21, 107–109
Benin 320
Bermuda 143
Bhutan 69, 185
Bolivia 21, 25, 65, 69, 89, 144
Bombay 56
Bosnia & Hercegovina 255
Botswana 21, 296–298
Brazil 31, 39, 60, 63, 67, 87, 110–112
Brunei 185
Bulgaria 28, 34, 256
Burkina Faso 320
Burundi 320

C Cambodia 28, 35, 41, 59, 152–154
Cameroon 320
Canada 25, 34, 43, 52, 54, 65, 72, 144
Cape Verde 320
Cayman Islands 144
Central African Republic 320
Chad 320

Chile 25, 38, 42, 64, 81, 113–115
China 19, 23, 28, 35, 39, 45, 54, 56, 57, 58, 83, 155–157
Colombia 32, 116–118
Comoros & Mayotte 320
Congo, Democratic Republic of the 320
Congo, Republic of 320
Cook Islands 210
Costa Rica 21, 89, 144
Côte d'Ivoire 321
Croatia 38, 64, 216–218
Cuba 71, 144
Cyprus 256
Czech Republic 31, 47, 60, 256

D Dagestan 33
Denmark 256
Djibouti 321
Dominica 144
Dominican Republic 144

E East Timor 195–197
Ecuador 21, 43, 55, 72, 88, 119–121
Egypt 18, 53, 58, 82, 88, 264–266
El Salvador 38, 122–124
England 18, 27, 30, 36, 37, 56, 59, 63, 64, 70, 83, 84, 219–221
Equatorial Guinea 321
Eritrea 321
Estonia 93, 256
Ethiopia 42, 299–301

F Falkland Islands (Malvinas) 145
Fiji 68, 89, 210
Finland 27, 256
France 18, 22, 40, 47, 59, 60, 63, 74, 93, 222–224
French Guiana 125–127

G Gabon 321
Galápagos Islands 57, 119–121
Gambia 321

Georgia 256
Germany 27, 31, 47, 70, 80, 85, 257
Ghana 321
Greece 23, 57, 72, 225–227
Greenland 72, 75, 228–230
Grenada 145
Guadeloupe 145
Guam 198–200
Guatemala 66, 145
Guinea 321
Guinea-Bissau 321
Guyana 145

H Haiti 33, 145
Hawai'i 37, 62
Honduras 145
Hong Kong 56, 83, 158–160
Hungary 27, 257

I Iceland 38, 231–233
India 18, 22, 28, 36, 43, 48, 51, 52, 56, 57, 58, 66, 72, 76, 77, 87, 89, 93, 161–163
Indonesia 22, 44, 49, 201–203
Iran 45, 267–269
Iraq 291
Ireland 25, 27, 41, 61, 257
Israel 19, 44, 92, 270–272
Italy 18, 19, 22, 41, 53, 55, 67, 234–236

J Jamaica 146
Japan 22, 26, 37, 40, 47, 56, 61, 66, 76, 82, 87, 93, 164–166
Jordan 40, 41, 273–275

K Kazakhstan 185
Kenya 20, 302–304
Kiribati 210
Kuwait 291
Kyrgyzstan 185

L Laos 167–169
Latvia 257
Lebanon 291
Lesotho 322
Liberia 322

Libya 291
Liechtenstein 257
Lithuania 49, 257
Luxembourg 257

M Macau 185
Macedonia 257
Madagascar 20, 305–307
Malaysia 20, 49, 186
Malawi 322
Maldives 186
Mali 39, 42, 51, 308–310
Malta 57, 258
Marshall Islands 210
Martinique 146
Mauritania 322
Mauritius 322
Mexico 22, 28, 31, 37, 43, 48, 54, 60, 66, 76, 95, 128–130
Micronesia 210
Moldova 258
Monaco 63, 258
Mongolia 56, 186
Montenegro 237–239
Morocco 29, 56, 74, 276–278
Mozambique 34, 311–313
Myanmar (Burma) 45, 186

N Namibia 64, 68, 322
Nauru 210
Nepal 44, 50, 75, 170–172
Netherlands, The 31, 46, 258
New Caledonia 210
New Zealand 29, 41, 51, 52, 64, 69, 72, 81, 87, 95, 204–206
Nicaragua 131–133
Niger 322
Nigeria 33, 322
Northern Mariana Islands 198–200
North Korea 44, 185
Norway 25, 73, 258

O Oman 279–281

P Pakistan 32, 51, 186
Palau 211

Panama 146
Papua New Guinea 44, 211
Paraguay 146
Peru 50, 55, 59, 134–136
Phillipines 93, 186
Pitcairn Islands 211
Poland 35, 60, 81, 258
Portugal 258
Puerto Rico 146

Q Qatar 291

R Réunion 322
Romania 69, 258
Russia 24, 54, 56, 85, 88, 95, 259
Rwanda 69, 322

S Saint Kitts & Nevis 146
Saint Lucia 146
Saint Vincent & the Grenadines 147
Samoan Islands 207–209
San Marino 259
São Tomé & Príncipe 323
Saudi Arabia 291
Scotland 47, 52, 76, 259
Senegal 70, 323
Serbia & Montenegro 38, 237–239
Seychelles 323
Sierra Leone 33, 323
Singapore 37, 47, 187
Slovakia 259
Slovenia 34, 38, 80, 87, 240–242
Solomon Islands 211
Somalia 323
South Africa 34, 52, 55, 81, 94, 314–316
South America 57, 62, 73
South Korea 173–175
Spain 22, 46, 57, 62, 66, 71, 75, 80, 85, 94, 243–245
Sri Lanka 176–178
Sudan 323
Suez 56
Suriname 147
Swaziland 323
Sweden 86, 87, 259

Switzerland 51, 92, 246–248
Syria 33, 83, 282–284

T Tahiti & French Polynesia 57, 211
Taiwan 92, 187
Tajikistan 187
Tanzania 48, 89, 317–319
Thailand 23, 28, 31, 49, 63, 82, 83, 95, 187
Tibet 179–181
Togo 323
Tonga 211
Trinidad & Tobago 147
Tunisia 18, 285–287
Turkey 46, 52, 57, 83, 86, 249–251
Turkmenistan 187
Turks & Caicos 147
Tuvalu 211

U Uganda 69, 323
Ukraine 38, 252–254
Uruguay 137–139
United Arab Emirates 291
United States of America 21, 24, 25, 27, 30, 31, 34, 37, 41, 43, 44, 47, 49, 51, 52, 55, 56, 59, 60, 63, 64, 66, 67, 69, 70, 71, 75, 76, 77, 81, 83, 84, 86, 93, 95, 140–142
Uzbekistan 187

V Vanuatu 211
Vatican City 259
Venezuela 64, 147
Vietnam 28, 34, 73, 182–184
Virgin Islands 147

W Wales 74, 259
West Bank & Gaza Strip 270–272

Y Yemen 33, 288–290

Z Zambia 94, 323
Zanzibar 317–319
Zimbabwe 44, 94, 323

LONELY PLANET BLUELIST.
618 Things to Do and Places to Go. 06-07.
January 2006

PUBLISHED BY
Lonely Planet Publications Pty Ltd
ABN 36 005 607 983
90 Maribyrnong St, Footscray,
Victoria, 3011, Australia

www.lonelyplanet.com

Printed by SNP Security Printing Pte Ltd, Singapore

PHOTOGRAPHS
Many of the images in this book are available for licensing
from Lonely Planet Images.
www.lonelyplanetimages.com

ISBN 174104734X

LONELY PLANET OFFICES

AUSTRALIA
Locked Bag 1, Footscray, Victoria, 3011
Phone 03 8379 8000 **Fax** 03 8379 8111
Email talk2us@lonelyplanet.com.au

USA
150 Linden St, Oakland, CA 94607
Phone 510 893 8555 **Toll free** 800 275 8555 **Fax** 510 893 8572
Email info@lonelyplanet.com

UK
72-82 Rosebery Ave London EC1R 4RW
Phone 020 7841 9000 **Fax** 020 7841 9001
Email go@lonelyplanet.co.uk